The Georgia Conservancy's Guide To The North Georgia Mountains

Edited by Fred Brown and Nell Jones

Second Edition

Revised by Nell Jones and Thomas Perrie

Preface by Jimmy Carter

Charles H. Wharton, Ph.D., Science Advisor
Mozelle Funderburk, Art Director

LONGSTREET PRESS
Atlanta, Georgia

Published by
LONGSTREET PRESS, INC.
2150 Newmarket Parkway
Suite 102
Marietta, Georgia 30067

Printed in the United States of America

3rd printing 1992

First Edition, Library of Congress Catalog Number 90-082706
Second Edition, Library of Congress Catalog Number 91-070085

First Edition, ISBN 0-929264-81-9
Second Edition, ISBN 0-929264-46-0

This book was printed by Courier Printers, Kendallville, Indiana
The text type was set in Times Roman by The Georgia Conservancy, Atlanta, Georgia
Design by Robert H. Clark, Jr.
Cover photo by Bob Busby
Art direction by Mozelle Funderburk
Computer graphics and format by Thomas D. Perrie
Illustrations by Mozelle Funderburk, Sheila Ward, Alyce Graham, Mary Jane Warren Stone
and James deSana
Maps by Frank Drago, Inc.

Dedication

This book is dedicated to the bioregion of the Southern Appalachian Mountains, and to those human members of this great community who will ensure that its life-giving qualities will continue to sustain not only themselves, but generations to come.

The Georgia Conservancy

Sponsors

The Georgia Conservancy gratefully acknowledges the following sponsors who made the publication of this guidebook possible:

Georgia Department of Natural Resources

Georgia Power Company

Nell H. Jones

The Lyndhurst Foundation

Thomas D. Perrie

Charles and Deen Day Smith

Charles A. Smithgall

Charles H. Wharton

Common blue violet
Viola papilionacea

This is a large species, often standing 10 inches high. It has large, heart-shaped leaves which have a slightly oily but tasty flavor and make a delicious vitamin-rich addition to salads and sandwiches.

Some Things Never Change

In Memory of Byron Herbert **Reece**, Georgia Mountain Poet
September 14, 1917 — June 3, 1958

Some things never change—
Madrigals still wake soft under rains;
The green of the mountains far fades into blue
As a bird flying close gives its music to you.

The creeks in their shallows still ripple along
Making from every stone a song,
While the dapple of light on a single tree
Is more splendor than needed for any who see.

Deer gaze out in mild surprise
Then turn to shadow before your eyes;
In Elder's Wood and Hughly's Glen
They call us now, as they called you then.

The flowers in bloom on the valley floor
Were surely the same by your mother's door.

The breezes that drift down Dooley's glades
Still whisper to lovers in Pindar's shades;
The message they breathe is as old as new
(I'm so glad I can tell these things to you) —
Some things never change.

Oh, it's true some have come to change what they can
But the mountains, in time, will say "No!" to man;
In vain they move boulders, in vain alter streams—
They never will ever learn how to pave dreams.
For your words bear them witness as time passes by
And the mountaintops still define the whole sky.

The mountaintops still define the whole sky.

Mildred Greear
© 1988

Table of Contents

PREFACE i

FOREWORD iii

ACKNOWLEDGMENTS v

INTRODUCTION TO THE NATURAL HISTORY
OF THE NORTH GEORGIA MOUNTAINS viii

GUIDE TO ILLUSTRATIONS xvi

GUIDE TO MAPS AND DRAWINGS xix

**THE CUMBERLAND PLATEAU AND
THE VALLEY AND RIDGE** 1

THE CUMBERLAND PLATEAU 3
    Lookout Mountain 5
    Pigeon Mountain 15
    Little River, Alabama 19

THE CHICKAMAUGA VALLEY 25

THE ARMUCHEE RIDGES 29

THE GREAT VALLEY 35

THE BLUE RIDGE 43

THE WESTERN BLUE RIDGE 45
    The Cohutta Wilderness 47
    Lake Conasauga 55
    The Big Frog Wilderness 59
    Carters Lake 61
    Fort Mountain State Park 65
    The Copper Basin 71
    The Rich Mountains 73
    The Etowah River and Toccoa River Watersheds 79

THE EASTERN BLUE RIDGE 89
    Cooper Creek and Duncan Ridge 91
    Blood Mountain 97

Table of Contents

Raven Cliffs 105
Helen and The Upper Chattahoochee 113
Tray Mountain 119
Brasstown Bald and the Brasstown Wilderness 129
The Hightower Area of the Southern Nantahala Wilderness 133
White Oak Stamp 139
Buck Creek and Chunky Gal Mountain 143
The Nantahala Basin 145
The Tallulah Basin 153
Coweeta Creek and Betty Creek Valleys 175
Black Rock Mountain State Park 179
Rabun Bald 185
The Chattooga River 191
The Ellicott Rock Wilderness 211
Highlands, North Carolina 215
The Escarpment Gorges 225
The Cowee Gem Region 229

LONG TRAILS 233

The Appalachian Trail 235
The Benton MacKaye Trail 245
The Bartram Trail 249
Other Long Trails and Cross-Georgia Hike 251

APPENDICES

A. Map Sources A-1
B. State Parks in the Mountains B-1
C. Outfitters, Guides and Suppliers C-1
D. Books and References D-1
E. Special Events, Fairs and Festival E-1
F. Conservation and Outdoor Organizations F-1
G. Safety in the Mountains G-1
H. Southeastern Wilderness Areas H-1
I. Forest Planning I-1
J. Glossary of Plants J-1

INDEX

THE GEORGIA CONSERVANCY

MEMBERSHIP APPLICATION

Preface

Looking out from our little log cabin on Turniptown Creek, which flows out of the Rich Mountain Wilderness, Rosalynn and I behold the breathtaking beauty of another Georgia mountain spring. The mountain laurel—which locals call "ivy"—is bursting forth with its delicate, pale pink blossoms. The waterfalls outside my window are brimming with spring's fresh rains, rapidly rushing downstream to their rendezvous with the Ellijay River. The hardwood forest surrounding us is clothed in nature's fresh green habit, and the cool spring air is sweet and clean. Phoebes are building a nest nearby in anticipation of the new life soon to appear. In the stream, rainbow trout chase stoneflies emerging to begin their brief mating flights. Everywhere there is evidence of the renewal of life.

Here in this natural setting Rosalynn and I have found peace and serenity we seldom enjoyed in our earlier years. For us, Washington, D.C. was an extraordinary center of temporal power, international politics and human sophistication. These mountains are the antithesis of the political and military power embodied in the statehouses of man's government. Here in the Georgia mountains we enter an earth-centered consciousness where nature's laws are in charge. Here, we return to the physical source of our nurturing—nature's management of our air, water and soil, without which our civilization could not survive. We return also to a great spiritual resource, amidst God's handiwork.

Our cabin in the Rich Mountains has been a refuge from the press of civic duties. Here, the rumble of thunder over our mountain hideaway has replaced the 21-gun salute in some foreign port of call, and the water music of a trout stream, the sound of public ovation.

Both Hernando DeSoto, in the sixteenth century, and William Bartram, in the late eighteenth century, found these Georgia mountains clothed with verdant forests and crystal streams and peopled with the proud Cherokee. Later, Americans of European origin settled far back in the mountain coves, treasuring the solitude and the ability to sustain themselves on the rich mountain soils and forests. Today, our citizens crave these qualities that gave the early Americans spiritual strength and fierce independence. We steal back to the mountains at every opportunity to revel in the pure air and water and untrammelled wildness. This closeness to nature restores us in body and soul. We sit once again by an eternal pool and stare in wonder at the diversity of a forest that has endured the great ice ages—a forest that remembers the howl of the wolf, the bugle of the elk, the thunder of the bison and perhaps even the cautious footfall of the first humans many years ago.

The Carter cabin

For over two centuries we have wrested from our mountains the wealth that made our nation strong—mica, corundum, coal, iron, gold and timber. Our cities have flourished on the water from mountain rivers, filtered and purified by mountain soils. Now is the time for us to acknowledge that we can no longer live without respecting and understanding our mountain forests and the other great ecosystems of the earth which have for millennia supported the habitat of man.

This guide, painstakingly produced by many volunteers of The Georgia Conservancy, opens the door to adventure in a cherished part of our natural heritage. In addition, it introduces the remarkable diversity of mountain environments whose vital functions are powered only by the sun. Here, we stand in awe of divine forces that have shaped our planet. In a remote cove or on a high wind-swept ridge, thoughts and cares of the modern world drop away, letting us for a little while become children of the earth.

Having known the fine work of The Georgia Conservancy for over twenty years, Rosalynn and I are not surprised that this strong conservation organization has produced another excellent publication for those who enjoy nature's wonders. As one of the Conservancy's founding members in 1967, I recall very favorably participating in its annual conferences in the early seventies. Rosalynn joins me in recommending this valuable guide to all those who seek to discover the natural treasures awaiting them in the Georgia mountains.

Jimmy Carter

Foreword

What you have in your hands is the best single guide ever assembled for anyone who wants to explore, really explore, and understand the Georgia mountains.

I say that after living in Georgia for 48 years and spending a good part of that time involved somehow with the northern part of the state—driving it or walking it, or writing about it, or editing the material that others had written about it.

The year-long process of helping compile and edit this book has shown me plenty I didn't know about the mountains, and I promise that reading and using it will do the same for you.

The book looks at the mountains the way everyone should, but few people do: as two separate and distinct mountain ranges—the Cumberlands in the west and the Blue Ridge in the east—separated by three regions of valleys and ridges. This geology is what accounts for the tremendous diversity of terrain from one side of the state to the other and for the intense interest in the area by botanists and geologists. Those readers who come to terms with the mountains' geology, botany and wildlife as described and illustrated throughout the book will know more about the basic structure and the natural environments of the Georgia mountains than most people ever do.

In addition, the exploration of the Georgia mountains in this book follows "nature's organization" rather than political boundaries; it doesn't stop at the state line, but follows the natural terrain where it leads, be that into Alabama, Tennessee, North Carolina or South Carolina. As a result, readers who drive the Lookout Mountain Parkway from Gadsden, Alabama, across the northwestern tip of Georgia to Chattanooga will gain a clearer perspective of the dramatic 100-mile sweep of this flat-topped mountain. Likewise, visitors who discover the corundum deposits of Rabun County can trace them to Franklin, North Carolina, and see the mines that have produced some of the world's finest rubies and sapphires. This guidebook contains much "new" information never before assembled in one place. This happened because a large number of very knowledgeable and dedicated people contributed research, articles, maps and notes about trails, rivers, vistas or waterfalls that they have collected personally over the years or, in some cases, specifically for this book. Al Tate, for example, is a professional ecologist who, in these pages, leads readers on several hikes in the Raven Cliffs area. Mildred and Philip Greear, both recognized experts on the geology, botany, history and wildlife of the area, tell readers where to find fossils in northwest Georgia. Botanist Chick Gaddy, and Hugh and Carole Nourse share wonderfully detailed information about exploring the escarpment gorges, an area Chick has hiked for many years. Few people know more about Georgia's rivers or write about them with more feeling than Reece Turrentine, long-time canoeing editor of Brown's Guide to Georgia. In this book, Reece's guide to Lakes Rabun, Seed, Burton and Tallulah is a gem of guidebook journalism.

Chief among those contributing to this book is Charles Wharton, Research Associate at the University of Georgia's Institute of Ecology, for 20 years professor of biology at Georgia State University and author of *The Natural Environments of Georgia*. I believe Charlie knows more about Georgia's mountains, their geology, trails, trees, flowers, wildlife, rivers and vistas than any single person alive. Much of the new information in this volume was until now in his files, library and brain—it was Charlie's private stash—and he has now generously and lovingly shared it with all of us. Many of the others who contributed bits and pieces of hard-earned information from their personal data bank or did original research specifically for this book are listed in the acknowledgments.

The most gratifying thing for an editor is to witness the pooling of information from a variety of sources into something that is bigger than any one of the contributors could have done on his or her own. I have never been associated with a project that did that more successfully than this one. This book has been compiled and designed for both the casual reader and for those committed to more serious explorations. It is not a guide to the more obvious tourist attractions of the mountains, although some of those attractions are included when they add to our understanding of the natural development, history or culture of the region. It is a book filled with detail, directions and maps. There are no color pictures. To some readers it may appear at first somewhat intimidating. But I promise you that no matter how well or how little you know the mountains, whether you are taking a Sunday drive, introducing young children to their first hiking trail or setting off on a week-long backpacking trek, if you read and use this guide, it will open up a world of mountain experience that will surprise and amaze you.

Fred Brown
Editor

Acknowledgments

The idea for this guidebook grew out of The Georgia Conservancy's very successful publication of *A Guide to the Georgia Coast*. Produced in 1984 by the Conservancy's Savannah office under the direction of Hans Neuhauser and Becky Shortland, with guidebook chairman Dale Thorpe, editor Gwen McKee and numerous volunteers, it is now in its Second Edition and has introduced many lovers of nature to the beauties of the Georgia coast. Inspired by the coastal guide and wishing to emulate its success, a mere handful of north Georgia volunteers set out in 1988 to produce a comparable guide to the mountains.

Any project attempting to cover an area as expansive and complex as the Georgia mountains naturally requires a great deal of effort and cooperation from many sources. This mountain guidebook is certainly no exception. Over a period of two and one-half years, so many individuals gave of their time and talents to make the guidebook a reality that it would be impossible to recount every contribution. Without certain dedicated Georgia Conservancy volunteers, however, this mountain guide could not have been published.

Foremost among these was Dr. Charles Wharton, Research Associate at the University of Georgia's Institute of Ecology and acknowledged expert in the field of natural environments in the Southeast. We are most grateful for his unflagging dedication and support, which were an inspiration to all who worked with him.

Other steering committee members worked to shepherd the guide on its perilous passage from planning to publication. Committee members Donna Wear Veal, Frank McCamey and Jack Byrne served tirelessly as team leaders of more than 150 volunteers who went enthusiastically into the field to obtain much of the basic data used in the book. Priscilla Golley spent months organizing, further researching, consolidating and writing text from reports as they were received. Tom Perrie displayed infinite patience in setting up computer forms and formatting graphs, memos and agendas. Other invaluable committee members included Steve Bowling and Fred Brown, as well as Bob Kerr, who participated in every phase of the book's development and production.

The Georgia Conservancy is especially grateful to Mildred and Philip Greear, who diligently reviewed site selections and data and wrote and rewrote several portions of the text. Other volunteers contributed reports and graphics, wrote and proofread text and carried out numerous special assignments. These included Miriam Talmadge, Chick Gaddy, Judy Alderman, Edwin Dale, Anthony Lampros, Jim Renner of Wapora, Inc., Tracy Battle of Gainesville Whiteprint, Jim Mackay, Kathy Mackay, George McGee, Pat Marcellino, Bill Mitchell, Michael Terry, Sherri Smith and Bob Humphries.

Acknowledgments

Trailing arbutus
Epigaea repens

This evergreen plant is a heath, along with blueberries and rhododendron. It grows in sandy, rocky, dry, acid soils. Its pinkish flowers are among the first wildflowers of spring, blooming from late February to early May.

Mozelle Funderburk, Sheila Ward, Alyce Graham, Mary Jane Warren Stone and Jim deSana provided the outstanding illustrations for the guidebook, and Bob Clark created its beautiful cover and design with production assistance by Endra Widjanarko of Osgood and Associates and Martha O'Kelley. Bob Busby searched out and photographed the scene on our cover. The intricate maps were created by Frank Drago.

Acknowledgments are also made to the Georgia Department of Industry, Trade and Tourism; the Northwest Georgia Travel Association; the Georgia Department of Natural Resources; and Georgia Power Company and the U.S. Forest Service, Chattahoochee-Oconee National Forests, for providing and testing key information. The law firm of English, Tunkle and Smith in Clayton kindly permitted the use of its fax machine to receive and transmit documents. Special thanks are extended to the law firm of Perrie, Buker, Stagg & McCord for administrative assistance.

We particularly appreciate those who participated in the creation of this Second Edition, to which are added 14 drawings and maps (including wilderness boundaries), 52 cross-referenced map keys, 67 illustrations and an introduction by Dr. Charles Wharton describing typical natural environments of the mountains. Several sections have been re-organized to better reflect the order in which a visitor would most likely travel through those areas. Volunteers have expended substantial time and effort returning to the field to check the accuracy of descriptions, directions and facilities. We especially note the contributions of Anthony Lampros for additions to the sections on Black Rock Mountain State Park, Rabun Bald and the physiography of north Georgia; Brian Boyd for extensive revisions to the Chattooga River section; Jack Byrne for comprehensive rewriting of the Tallulah Gorge section; Jim and Kathy Mackay for reorganization of the Lookout Mountain section; Peter Kirby for information on wilderness and forest planning; our five artists for many beautiful new illustrations; Tom Perrie for map keys, layout, computer graphics and a greatly-expanded Index; and Charles Wharton for numerous hours of painstaking revision.

Without the generosity and commitment of so many others to the recognition, protection and enjoyment of Georgia's natural environment, this mountain guidebook would have remained a great idea waiting to be realized. To all the volunteers listed on the following page who helped take our mountain guidebook project from concept to culmination, The Georgia Conservancy and I offer sincere thanks for countless jobs well done!

Nell Jones
Editor
Guidebook Chairman

Mountain Guidebook Volunteers

Cary Aiken
Judy Alderman
Walter Allen
John Ambrose
Pat Axsiom
Crawford Barnett
Tracy Battle
Peter Beney
Joseph Biesbrock
Toby Blalock
Polly Boggess
Steve Bowling
Brian Boyd
Gary Breece
Fred Brown
John M. Brown
J. Marion Brown, Jr.
Barbara Burch
Elmer Butler
* Jack Byrne
Larry Caldwell
Darcy Camp
Chris Canalos
Terry Centner
Linda Chafin
Henry Chambers
Bob Clark
Linda Cobb
Nancy Coile
Taylor Crockett
Edwin Dale
Lisa Davis
Tony Darnell
Chris deForest
Jim deSana
Jeanne deSana
Huck DeVenzio
Harriett DiGioia
Mary Lou Dixon
Marty Dominy
Frank Drago
Diana Durden
Lisha Duvaritanea
Bo Edwards

Lamar Edwards
Bud Elsea
Betty Fairley
Willard Fairley
Larry Farist
Elaine Fatora
Pat Fincher
Henry Finkbeiner
Louise Franklin
Dave Funderburk
Mozelle Funderburk
Chick Gaddy
Jerry German
Frank Golley
Priscilla Golley
David Gomez
Norma Gordon
Vernon Gordon
Tom Govus
Alyce Graham
Delbert Greear
Mildred Greear
Philip Greear
Wilson Hall
Fran Hallahan
Jane Harrell
Baker Harrison
Mahala Harrison
Anne Heath
Maryann Herbermann
Linda Hinton
Jan Holland
Amy Horne
Carol Howel-Gomez
Bob Humphries
Dick Hurd
Janet Hurlburt
Mary Ann Johnson
Nell Jones
Bill Kaliher
Lorraine Kaliher
Eleanor Kelly
Bob Kerr
Carolyn Kidd

Jim Kidd
Reggie Kimsey
Mark Kinzer
Peter Kirby
Tom Knight
Christy Lambert
Anthony Lampros
Bobby Ledford
Debra Lee
Jim Mackay
Kathy Mackay
Pat Marcellino
Brian Markwalter
Holly Markwalter
Frances Mason
Barbara Massey
Terry McCallum
* Frank McCamey
Jerry McFalls
George McGee
Ed McGowin
Lucia McGowin
Gwyn McKee
Marie Mellinger
Bill Mitchell
Michelle Moran
Ed Morgan
Marilou Morgan
Mark Morrison
Paul Nelson
Sharon Nelson
Hans Neuhauser
Steve Nix
Hugh Nourse
Carolyn Nourse
Martha O'Kelley
Mark Ogilvie
Steven Pagano
Dan Patillo
Tom Perrie
Ray Pierotti
Scott Ranger
Annette Ranger
Ted Reissing
Jim Renner

Ann Rhea
Rope Roberts
Carol Schneier
Damaris Schotsmans
Diana Shadday
Ed Shanahan
Sandy Shobe
Nancy Shofner
Becky Shortland
Judy Silverman
Bob Slack
Andy Smith
Cina Smith
Sherri Smith
Betty Smithgall
Brian Smithgall
Lloyd Snyder
Annice Snyder
Marvin Sowder
Rosalie Splitter
Mary Jane Warren Stone
Kathryn Stout
Allen Stovall
Miriam Talmadge
Al Tate
Alice Taylor
Claude Terry
Michael Terry
Dale Thorpe
Bill Timpone
Dawn Townsend
Richard Tunkle
Ann Vanderbeek
Glen Vanderbeek
* Donna Wear Veal
Sheila Ward
Richard Ware
Burt Weerts
Charles Wharton
Endra Widjanarko
Kristin Williams
Sue Worley
Janie Yearwood
Bob Zahner
Glenda Zahner

* *Team Leaders*

Introduction to the Natural History of the North Georgia Mountains

Charles Wharton, Ph.D.
Research Associate
Institute of Ecology, The University of Georgia

Our north Georgia mountains are masses of ancient rock on which life has but a tenuous foothold. A short history of the area's geology helps us appreciate nature's management of such finite entities as water, air and soil in such remarkably beautiful surroundings. Moreover, greater knowledge of the function of ecological systems like the southern Appalachian bioregion is essential for the survival of man as a part of—not apart from—the natural world. This understanding, transcending economic and political considerations, now becomes the major bridge uniting peoples of the earth.

Compared with the youthful Rockies or Himalayas, Georgia's mountains are hoary with age. Some of the basement rocks, or roots, of the early Blue Ridge formed over a billion years ago. The bulk of our mountains, however, was derived from ancient marine sediments between 200 and 450 million years ago. These sediments, such as sands and silts, were transformed or metamorphosed into the hard rock that forms the backbone of the Blue Ridge. This was accomplished by uplift, heat and pressure resulting from enormous forces generated by the collision of North America with other drifting continents.

Look at any rock face exposed in highway cuts such as at Hogpen Gap on the Richard Russell Scenic Highway or at Woodall Shoals on the Chattooga River. Here it can be seen how heat and pressure deep within the earth caused near-molten rock to flow and fold into visible contortions. In the western part of the Blue Ridge the rocks were less metamorphosed by these processes.

Least changed of all were the thick beds of sediments in northwest Georgia. Here, sands hardened into sandstone, and mud or silt into shale, while the shells of minute marine life became limestone. These rocks show little of the folding and distortion east of the great fault line between Chatsworth and Cartersville which divides the Valley and Ridge from the Western Blue Ridge.

Regardless of bedrock type, however, most forest communities form soils that are remarkably similar. Normally, about 22 minerals occur in most rock types; two or three others are supplied by atmospheric fallout. These minerals are carefully concentrated and recycled by the forest. Occasionally, where carbonate rocks, such as limestone, outcrop near the surface, unique plants grow and require

Canadian hemlock
Tsuga canadensis

This hemlock is a mountain species and our most attractive evergreen. Along with rosebay rhododendron, it forms the hemlock/heath environment that protects and cools the streamside zone of our mountain trout streams. Huge, old Canadian hemlocks were once cut solely for the tannic acid in their bark.

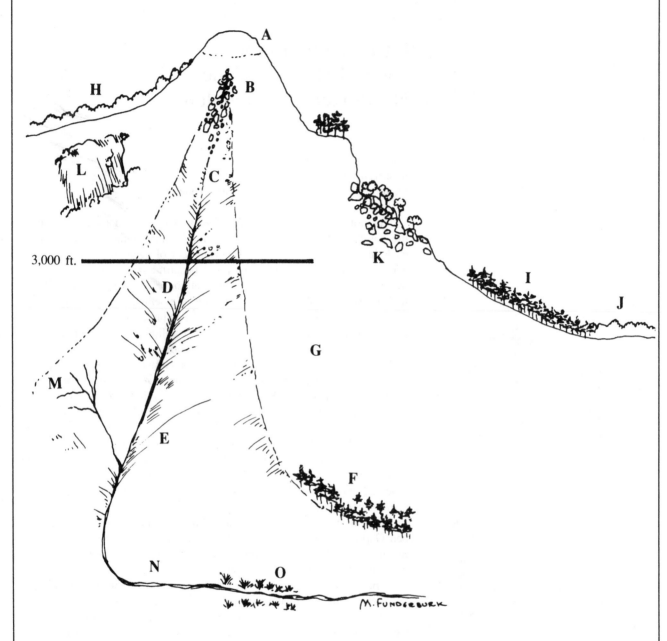

(page references in parentheses)

A Shrub bald/rock bald (xi)
B Boulderfield (xi)
C Northern hardwoods (xi)
D Cove forest (xii)
E Hemlock/heath forest (xii)
F White pine forest (xii)
G Slope forest (xiii)
H High elevation oak ridge forest (xiii)

I Pine ridge forest (xiii)
J Low elevation oak ridge forest (xiv)
K Rocky ridge and slope forest (xiv)
L Cliff and rock outcrop (xiv)
M Spring seep (xv)
N Streamside forest (xiv)
O Bog (xiv)

Figure 1 — **TYPICAL NATURAL ENVIRONMENTS**

lots of calcium, as at Pigeon Mountain or Panther Creek. Sometimes, when rocks are low in some essential minerals, as at Buck Creek, a peculiar pine barren community develops.

Stripped of their forest cover, our Blue Ridge Mountains would resemble Stone Mountain. The thin skin of soil that hides their nakedness is made possible only by plant life, aided by abundant rainfall. Unless one has seen the bare rock where the entire side of a mountain has slid off, or has gazed into Toxaway Gorge, it is hard to understand how important is the vegetation cover and how powerful the force of water.

While collisions with other continents slowly raised the Appalachians, rains kept eroding them almost as fast as they were uplifted. Incredibly, geologists claim that a thickness of from five to ten miles of Appalachian mountain rock has disintegrated and washed downhill in the last 300 million years. These sediments formed south Georgia, the coastal landforms and much of the continental shelf. Rains from the sun-powered water cycle are still trying to wash our mountains away, but nature has developed a remarkably tough and protective forest cover that slows down this process.

Ironically, the mountain forest cannot exist without this five to eight feet of water that pours down in a single year. The mountain forests are expert in conserving and managing this precious substance through many millennia of trial and error. The forest operates as a soil-building and water-holding device, powered by solar energy. The excess water not used by the system runs off as streams and rivers which we can, with wisdom, use ourselves. While there are mountain "products" other than water, we must never lose sight of the primary value of the mountains—the cost-free (to us) management of rock, soil, water, air, life and sun energy. Anything that man does there must be prefaced with the question, "Are we compromising or damaging these vital life-support functions?"

Our mountains have been forested for at least two million years. Unglaciated during this time, they have stood as temperate-zone refuges for a diverse assemblage of terrestrial plants and animals, perhaps unequalled outside of the tropical rainforest. Biologically speaking, a trip up a 6,000-foot mountain is equivalent to driving 1,000 miles north. Because of this, many species of plants and animals can live in our mountains, especially in north-facing coves where it is always moist and cool. Once, boreal spruce/fir forests, such as now clothe much of Canada, covered our Georgia mountains, with alpine tundra on the highest peaks. When the climate warmed, these cold-adapted environments disappeared. Along the highest elevations of the Georgia Blue Ridge, they left behind some ice-age animal life—relics such as the red-back vole and perhaps the red squirrel.

From the top of our highest peaks, as far as the eye can see, mountain slopes appear to be clothed in a uniform sea of green. Actually, this vista is not at all uniform, for what one sees is a remarkable mosaic of various combinations of rock, soil, plants and animals organized into specific environments. Some of these combinations are considered by ecologists as communities, associations or forest types. Each is adapted to certain slopes, temperatures, soil depths, compass exposures and rainfall.

Described below are the major natural environments that occur in the Georgia mountains and are often encountered in the text. A simple diagram [Fig. 1] enables the reader to see where these special environments are most likely to occur.

The first five environments are presented as a visitor might encounter them, beginning on top of a high peak, such as Brasstown Bald, travelling down a north-facing cove and terminating in the hemlock/heath zone along the stream at the bottom of the cove.

~**SHRUB BALDS AND/OR ROCK BALDS.** [Fig. 1(A)] Examples are Brasstown Bald [Fig. 27(2))], parts of Standing Indian [Fig. 31(13)], Pickens Nose [Fig. 37(29)], Tray [Fig. 26(50)] and Blood [Fig. 21(1)]. At the highest elevations, which were once alpine tundra, we now find catawba rhododendron, mountain ash and dwarf willow as plants characteristic of the shrub bald. Some mountains are called "balds" but have forested tops. Hightower Bald and Dick's Knob have, for example, dwarfed oak forests covering their summits. There may be a thick understory of beaked hazelnut or another shrub.

~**BOULDERFIELDS.** [Fig. 1(B)] Lying just down slope from the summit of most of our peaks are boulderfields, which fill the top part of north and northwest-facing coves, particularly if there is seeping or running water. The jumbled mass of boulders has resulted from ice-wedging during the Pleistocene period, perhaps 20,000 years ago. Boulderfields seldom extend below 3,200 feet. Although the moss-covered boulders are difficult to walk across, they are a photographer's delight and are most photogenic after leaf fall. In spite of the rocky nature of this environment, spring wildflowers are abundant. Trees such as yellow birch and basswood may occur. Perhaps the "best" boulderfield is on the north face of Tray Mountain [Fig. 26(62)] between the summit and Corbin Creek Road. The one most accessible by car lies just above the parking area at Sosebee Cove [Fig. 21(6)] where, with diligent search, a few rare yellowwood trees may be found.

~**NORTHERN HARDWOODS** [Fig. 1(C)]. This forest type usually lies between the boulderfields and the cove hardwoods (below), generally above 3,000 feet. Buckeye, basswood and yellow birch are diagnostic. Sometimes beech and sugar maple may be present. This environment has exceptional wildflower displays. The dense, often knee-deep herb layer helps create a deep, black, loamy soil. Expect to find the mountain garlic or ramp (*Allium tricoccum*), spring beauty, ginseng, squirrel corn, Dutchman's breeches, waterleaf and

Red-back vole
Clethrionomys gapperi

A creature of the alpine tundra and the deep spruce-fir forests, this animal can survive only on our higher peaks and ridges and in a few deep gorges such as that of Beech Creek (Tallulah River section). It has been taken as far south as Brasstown Bald but is rare in any trapline.

umbrella leaf. The giant hellebore (*Veratrum viride*) may be present. Three wood ferns are characteristic: Goldie's, marginal and intermediate. The higher the elevation, the rarer the herbaceous plants. To see the upper limit of the hardwood forest and a boulder-field, take the old Wagon Road Trail [Fig. 27(3)] crossed by the trail from the parking lot to the top of Brasstown Bald. Around on the north face just below the tower are giant yellow birch festooned with "old man's beard" lichen and dripping with moisture from cloud condensation. This environment is Georgia's only cloud forest. This relict community is extremely vulnerable to fire or logging.

~COVE FORESTS. [Fig. 1(D)] Below the northern hardwoods is the more extensive cove hardwood forest. There is a greater diversity of trees here, including various oaks, tulip poplar, ash, silverbell and magnolia. Before the chestnut blight of the 1930's, many cove forests were full of chestnut trees. Since tulip poplars are present in most cove forests, and they have wind-borne seeds, they were able to seed in on the death of the chestnut. Poplar also follows over-intensive logging, as below the parking area in Sosebee's Cove. The whitish stumps of dead chestnut can still be seen in many coves. Old mountain pastures often reverted to almost pure stands of poplar. Near-original old-growth cove forest can be seen in the northeast sector of the Cooper Creek Scenic Area [Fig. 19(1)]. There, the dead chestnut logs were removed and sawed up on the spot. Some of the old poplars, some 17 feet in circumference, still remain, standing among huge white and red oaks. While shrubs are limited in cove forests, a variety of herbs is present, depending on soil depth and moisture.

~HEMLOCK/HEATH FORESTS. [Fig. 1(E)] Below the cove hardwoods and often extending up the streams through it, grows the moisture-loving Canadian hemlock, with its delicate, evergreen foliage. It generally always has an understory of the common, evergreen rosebay rhododendron, which is a member of the heath family. Rhododendron may create nearly impenetrable thickets. This is one of the challenges facing trout fishermen where there are no trails. Few herbs are present. This environment may be seen along the lower reaches of Mulky Creek [Fig. 19(12)] near the Cooper Creek Scenic Area. A few large hemlocks remain on Soapstone Creek along the drive to Jacks Gap [Fig. 27(4)].

~WHITE PINE FORESTS. [Fig. 1(F)] There is some question as to the existence of stands of white pine prior to human clearing, logging and fire prevention (white pine is very sensitive to fire). Some very beautiful open stands of white pine occur along the Chattooga River, especially above Burrell's Ford Bridge [Fig. 46(45)] and along the Reed Creek bottoms [Fig. 41(29), Fig. 42(29)] north of the Russell Bridge. Much white pine can also be seen from the Richard

Russell Scenic Highway and near the Cooper Creek Scenic Area. It is believed that originally the white pine grew as scattered trees in fire-protected areas in places like the extensive bluffs along the Chattooga River. White pines are less prone to beetle attack than are the successional stands of Virginia pine which follow disturbance at low elevations throughout much of the Blue Ridge.

~**SLOPE FORESTS.** [Fig. 1(G)] These are mostly oak/hickory/chestnut and cover the most terrain of any environment. The chestnut—unfortunately for the wildlife which fattened for the winter on its nuts—is gone, except as sprouts and small trees at high elevations. Slope forests vary tremendously in species composition that in turn, depends on soil depth, percent slope, compass exposure and so on. Given sufficient soil moisture, white oak will dominate. Sourwood and black gum thrive on drier sites. Hickories are adaptable and widespread. While the herbaceous plants are not as rare and interesting as those in mountain coves, they are numerous. As distinguished from the cove forests, the slope forests have an abundance of shrubs. Blueberries are widespread under more open canopies here, as well as on ridges. Sweetshrub and buffalo nut (a favorite deer food) are common, as are azaleas. On drier sites horsesugar is outstanding.

~**RIDGE FORESTS.** Among the types of ridge forests, the high elevation oak ridge forest [Fig. 1(H)] is outstanding. This forest covers the higher ridges of the Blue Ridge, such as those traversed by the Appalachian Trail. This forest, mostly virgin red oak, has trees that are dwarfed and limby. A 12-inch diameter tree may be 100 years old. These old-growth ridge forests were rarely logged, since the trunks were too short. Sometimes, as in the Cohuttas, white oaks may dominate. High altitude ridge forests have a variety of attractive understory plants. From Standing Indian one descends through tunnels of Catawba or purple rhododendron. Elsewhere, flame azalea dominates or ferns (New York, hayscented), or beautiful little wiry sedges or grasses may carpet the ridgeline. In summer, dense herb growth may encroach, particularly white snakeroot (*Eupatorium rugosum*), one of the plants suspected of causing the "milk sick" that killed numerous settlers who grazed cattle in the mountains.

A variety of blueberries occupies mountain ridges, which are more open than cove forests. The highbush blueberry (*Vaccinium constablei*) is associated with high elevation red oak forests. On rocky white oak ridge forests, both deerberry (*V. stamineum*) and buckberry (*Gaylussacia ursina*) occur, while on lower, drier ridges the low blueberry (*V. vacillans*) forms thick ground cover. Grouse and bear feast on blueberries in summer and fall.

Another type of ridge forest is a pine ridge forest [Fig. 1(I)]. At higher elevations, the pines are chiefly table mountain pine, which

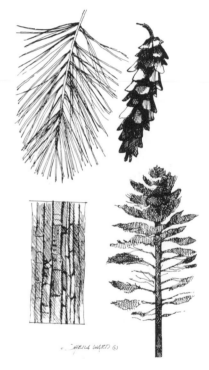

White pine
Pinus strobus

In the eastern Blue Ridge, this stately tree is confined to ravines and narrow floodplains, where it comes in after heavy logging. Beautiful stands occur along the Chattooga River above Burrell's Ford Bridge and up Reed Creek, a tributary above the GA 28 bridge. It occupies moist, lower slopes north and west of the Russell Scenic Highway and is found in the lower Cooper Creek basin.

seems to prefer rocks and cliff edges. It is common on ridges off the south face of Rabun Bald [Fig. 39(11)] and along the edge of the Cedar Cliffs along Big Creek [Fig. 42(19)] and occurs along the rim of Tallulah Gorge. At lower elevations pitch pine is dominant, as on the scenic road across Patterson Gap [Fig. 37(9)], where the rare sweetfern grows in the herb layer. The soils of these pine communities appear drier and more acid. Various acid-loving heaths occur in the understory.

There is a low elevation hardwood ridge forest [Fig. 1(J)], a "dry" forest which is widespread. Three oaks tend to predominate: scarlet, post and southern red.

~ROCKY RIDGES AND SLOPE FORESTS. [Fig. 1(K)] Chestnut oaks tend to dominate on rocky ridges in the Blue Ridge and on slopes where the soil is thin and rocky. The upper west-facing slopes of Lookout Mountain are often largely chestnut oak. On the western flank of Pigeon Mountain near The Pocket, in what can be called a limestone terrace environment, is a curious forest of chinquapin oak, red cedar and the rather rare smoketree.

~CLIFFS AND ROCK OUTCROPS. [Fig. 1(L)] Our Blue Ridge is really solid rock with only a thin veneer of soil held by plant roots. When it is too steep for plants to stabilize, a naked cliff emerges. If the rock is perennially wet, very rare northern or tropical ferns and mosses may occur (Cullasaja Gorge [Fig. 47(5)], Escarpment Gorges [Fig. 49(1,3,4,5)]). Around drier cliffs (Tallulah Gorge [Fig. 36(64)], Satulah Mountain [Fig. 47(21)], Cedar Cliffs [Fig. 42(19)], you may see two rare conifers, Carolina hemlock and table mountain pine. Around and above cliffs on the north side of high ridges, rosebay rhododendron prevails; on the drier south side, mountain laurel. The highest rocky tops almost always bear the gorgeous purple rhododendron. In some moist, rocky areas at lower elevations (Tallulah Falls) Carolina rhododendron predominates. Big dense patches of evergreen heaths are known by the mountaineers as "slicks" or "hells." Mountaineers also call rhododendron "laurel" and mountain laurel "ivy." One of the most remarkable environments on an outcrop is called a cedar glade. In Georgia, it is found in the Chickamauga and Chattanooga National Military Park. It occurs on shallow-soiled limestone slopes and low ridges. It is a shrub-free area thick with red cedars, along with old, dwarfed chinquapin oaks and with rare grasses and herbs allied to those of mid-western prairies. This is the only Georgia outlier of vast glades that cover central Tennessee.

Red cedars are also common along the rocky bluffs in the Valley and Ridge and sometimes occur on rock outcrops in the Blue Ridge, as on top of Chimney Mountain [Fig. 26(66)].

~**STREAMSIDE FORESTS.** [Fig. 1(N)] Along most of our rivers and larger streams, a streamside forest grows. This is distinguished by colorful and often rare trees and shrubs. Hemlocks and rosebay rhododendron are generally present. The rocky, more open bluffs support small trees such as the rare mountain camellia (*Stewartia*), serviceberry and witch hazel. If moist enough, the environment supports mountain pepperbush, viburnums and alders, either as shrubs or as small trees. Dense evergreen thickets of dog hobble, also known as leucothoe, are common. Characteristic herbs, such as yellowroot, may be present.

~**BOGS AND SPRING SEEPS.** [Fig. 1(M), Fig. 1(O)] Bogs and spring seeps are wetlands. Bogs were formerly widespread on floodplains and on colluvial, or unflooded, flats. As in the "flats" near Rabun Bald [Fig. 39(8)] and in Horse Cove near Highlands, landowners have unwittingly or intentionally destroyed their irreplaceable bogs. Bogs are often replete with rare boreal or arctic plant species and are the only known haunts of rare northern turtles. They are a habitat for several orchids and lilies such as the swamp pink (*Helonias*). The second largest bog complex south of the Pink Beds near Brevard is that along the Nantahala River south of White Oak Bottoms campground [Fig. 31(5)]. These areas are under strict protection because man has eliminated most of them. They must not be disturbed.

~**SAGPONDS AND LIMESINKS.** Sagponds are northwest Georgia's equivalent of south Georgia's limesinks. Several sagponds occur on top of Pigeon Mountain. Scientists consider them valuable. They have drilled down through deep peat layers and identified ancient pollen that helped determine the vegetation of the area during the Ice Age. A large sagpond on the Chickamauga and Chattanooga National Military Park [Fig. 4(26)] has a stand of large (thirty-six inch diameter) buttressed willow oaks growing on it. A more famous sagpond on the park is called Bloody Pond, after a Civil War battle.

Giant dry sinks found near Pigeon Mountain [Fig. 7(4)] may have interesting plants, such as the glade fern, growing in them. Since there is no standing water, they contain a moist oak/hickory forest rather than the swamp black gum and marsh vegetation of wet sagponds. They are so large that going down inside one is like descending the slope of a mountain.

New York fern
Thelypteris noveboracensis

This delicate, non-clumping fern, with leaflets tapering at both ends of the frond, forms extensive beds, sometimes on mountain ridges beneath red oak ridge forest. It grows also in coves and on moist, rich slopes. Deciduous, it is very beautiful where it forms extensive ground cover.

Guide to Illustrations

Alum root, *Mozelle Funderburk*	138
American chestnut, *Mary Jane Warren Stone*	I-1
American toad, *Mozelle Funderburk*	13
Ballooning at Helen, *Sheila Ward*	113
Beaked hazelnut, *Mary Jane Warren Stone*	136
Beech, *Alyce Graham*	32
Berry College waterwheel, *James deSana*	39
Big brown bat, *Sheila Ward*	8
Bird-foot violet, *Mary Jane Warren Stone*	E-1
Black locust, *Mary Jane Warren Stone*	22
Black-capped chickadee, *Alyce Graham*	64
Bloodroot, *Sheila Ward*	103
Blue cohosh, *Mozelle Funderburk*	249
Bobcat, *Sheila Ward*	50
Bog turtle, *Mozelle Funderburk*	139
Brook trout, *Alyce Graham*	145
Brown trout, *Sheila Ward*	191
Buckeye, *Alyce Graham*	119
Canadian hemlock, *Sheila Ward*	viii
Cannon and cannonballs, *James deSana*	28
Carolina hemlock, *Alyce Graham*	223
Carolina rhododendron, *Mozelle Funderburk*	161
Carter cabin, *James deSana*	ii
Chestnut oak, *Mary Jane Warren Stone*	H-1
Chestnut-sided warbler, *Mary Jane Warren Stone*	229
Chipmunk, *Mary Jane Warren Stone*	B-1
Christmas fern, *Alyce Graham*	109
Cloud forest, *Mary Jane Warren Stone*	131
Common blue violet, *Sheila Ward*	-iv
Confederate cap, belt and sword, *Sheila Ward*	25
Cucumber magnolia, *Mary Jane Warren Stone*	89
Dogwood, *Mary Jane Warren Stone*	26
Dutchman's breeches, *Mozelle Funderburk*	97
Entrance to Cave Spring, *James deSana*	38
Etowah Mounds, *Mozelle Funderburk*	42
Flame azalea, *Mary Jane Warren Stone*	181
Fort Mountain stone wall, *Mary Jane Warren Stone*	65
Fossils: crinoid, brachiopod and bryozoan, *Alyce Graham*	34
Fraser's magnolia, *Mary Jane Warren Stone*	A-1
Freshwater drum, *Mozelle Funderburk*	35
Galax, *Mary Jane Warren Stone*	87
Garter snake, *Alyce Graham*	247
Gay-wings, *Mozelle Funderburk*	173

Guide to Illustrations

Golden eagle, *Mary Jane Warren Stone*	194
Gray treefrog, *Mozelle Funderburk*	118
Green salamander, *Mozelle Funderburk*	16
Hang gliding at McCarty Bluff, *Mary Jane Warren Stone*	9
Hellbender, *Mozelle Funderburk*	53
Hellebore, *Mozelle Funderburk*	71
Hop hornbeam, *Sheila Ward*	154
Horsetail, *Sheila Ward*	148
Jack-in-the-pulpit, *Sheila Ward*	54
Land snail, *Mozelle Funderburk*	F-1
Large-flowered trillium, *Sheila Ward*	43
Lily of the valley, *Alyce Graham*	241
Mayapple, *Mary Jane Warren Stone*	C-1
Mountain camellia, *Mozelle Funderburk*	201
Mountain laurel, *Sheila Ward*	79
Mountain pepperbush, *Sheila Ward*	217
Muskellunge, *Alyce Graham*	76
New Echota print shop, *James deSana*	41
New England cottontail, *Mozelle Funderburk*	233
New York fern, *Mozelle Funderburk*	xvi
Northern copperhead, *Mary Jane Warren Stone*	2
Northern dusky salamander, *Mozelle Funderburk*	213
Northern red oak, *Mozelle Funderburk*	235
Northern red salamander, *Mozelle Funderburk*	62
Northern water snake, *Mary Jane Warren Stone*	209
Oconee bells, *Mozelle Funderburk*	227
Painted trillium, *Sheila Ward*	151
Peregrine falcon, *Sheila Ward*	78
Persistent trillium, *Mary Jane Warren Stone*	158
Pignut hickory, *Mary Jane Warren Stone*	D-1
Pileated woodpecker, *Alyce Graham*	236
Pilot black snake, *Alyce Graham*	163
Pink lady slipper, *Alyce Graham*	167
Pitch pine, *Sheila Ward*	144
Pygmy shrew, *Sheila Ward*	155
Rainbow trout, *Alyce Graham*	83
Ramp, *Alyce Graham*	122
Raven, *Alyce Graham*	105
Red-back vole, *Sheila Ward*	xi
Red elderberry, *Alyce Graham*	127
Red squirrel, *Sheila Ward*	162
Red-tail hawk, *Sheila Ward*	54
Ringneck snake, *Alyce Graham*	G-1
Rose-breasted grosbeak, *Mary Jane Warren Stone*	51
Rosy twisted stalk, *Alyce Graham*	124
Ruffed grouse, *Alyce Graham*	86
Scarlet tanager, *Mary Jane Warren Stone*	44

Showy orchis, *Mary Jane Warren Stone*	228
Silverbell, *Mozelle Funderburk*	73
Slimy salamander, *Mozelle Funderburk*	19
Solomon's seal, *Mary Jane Warren Stone*	132
Strawberry bush, *Mary Jane Warren Stone*	177
Striped maple, *Sheila Ward*	61
Three-leaved cinquefoil, *Alyce Graham*	149
Timber rattlesnake, *Mary Jane Warren Stone*	29
Trailing arbutus, *Sheila Ward*	vi
Tufted titmouse, *Alyce Graham*	56
Tulip poplar, *Sheila Ward*	94
Turkey vulture, *Mary Jane Warren Stone*	C-3
Twisted hair spike moss, *Mary Jane Warren Stone*	220
Two-lined salamander, *Mozelle Funderburk*	95
Umbrella leaf, *Mozelle Funderburk*	J-1
Vasey's trillium, *Sheila Ward*	3
Walking fern, *Sheila Ward*	189
White pine, *Sheila Ward*	xiii
White tail deer, *Sheila Ward*	104
Wild boar, *Mozelle Funderburk*	185
Wild turkey, *Mary Jane Warren Stone*	250
Witch hazel, *Mary Jane Warren Stone*	176
Wood frog, *Mozelle Funderburk*	60
Wood rat, *Mozelle Funderburk*	199
Yellowwood, *Mozelle Funderburk*	133

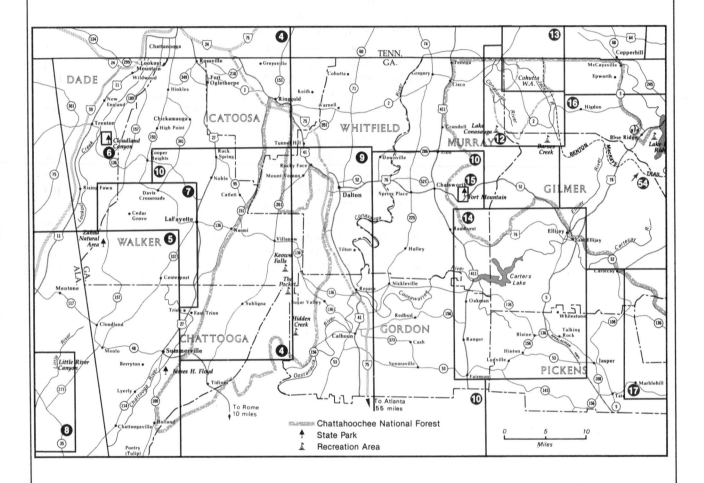

Figure 2 — **FIGURE NUMBERS AND AREAS COVERED BY MAPS IN THIS GUIDEBOOK**

Guide to Maps and Drawings

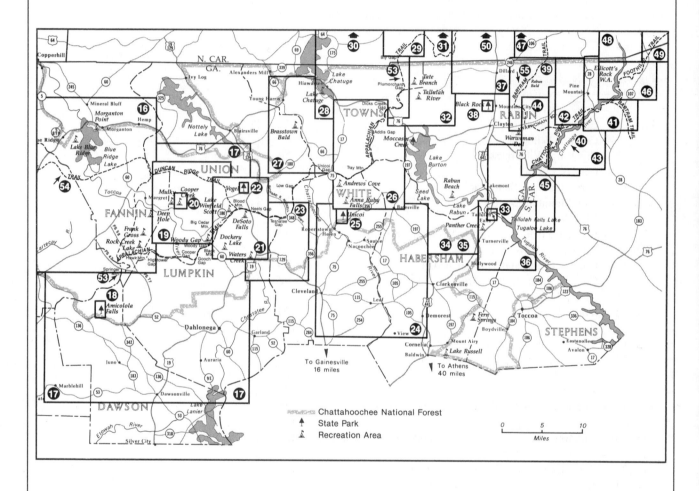

Chattahoochee National Forest
▲ State Park
⚕ Recreation Area

0   5   10
Miles

Guide to Maps and Drawings

Fig. 1 — Typical Natural Environments   ix
Fig. 2 — Reference Map   xix
Fig. 3 — Cumberland Plateau and Valley and Ridge   xxiii
Fig. 4 — Cumberland Plateau and Chickamauga Valley, North   4
Fig. 5 — Cumberland Plateau and Chickamauga Valley, South   6
Fig. 6 — Cloudland Canyon State Park   10
Fig. 7 — Pigeon Mountain   14
Fig. 8 — Little River, Alabama   20
Fig. 9 — Armuchee Ridges   30
Fig. 10— Great Valley   36
Fig. 11— Cohuttas Access   46
Fig. 12— Cohutta Wilderness   48
Fig. 13— Big Frog Wilderness   58
Fig. 14— Carters Lake   62
Fig. 15— Fort Mountain State Park   66
Vistas — Fort Mountain State Park   68-70
Fig. 16— Rich Mountains   74
Fig. 17— Etowah River and Toccoa River Watersheds   80
Fig. 18— Amicalola Falls State Park   84
Fig. 19— Cooper Creek and Duncan Ridge   90
Fig. 20— Cooper Creek Scenic Area   92
Fig. 21— Blood Mountain   98
Fig. 22— Vogel State Park   100
Fig. 23— Raven Cliffs   106
Vistas — Richard Russell Scenic Highway   110, 111
Fig. 24— Helen and the Upper Chattahoochee   114
Fig. 25— Unicoi State Park   116
Fig. 26— Tray Mountain   120
Fig. 27— Brasstown Bald and Brasstown Wilderness   128
Vistas — Brasstown Bald   130
Fig. 28— Hightower Area of Southern Nantahala Wilderness   134
Fig. 29— White Oak Stamp   140
Fig. 30— Buck Creek and Chunky Gal Mountain   142
Fig. 31— Nantahala Basin and Standing Indian   146
Fig. 32— Upper Tallulah Basin   152
Fig. 33— Tallulah Gorge   156
Fig. 34— Tallulah Basin Canoeing Guide   164
Fig. 35— Tallulah Basin Recreation Areas   168
Fig. 36— Lower Tallulah Basin and Panther Creek   170
Fig. 37— Coweeta Creek and Betty Creek Valleys   174
Fig. 38— Black Rock Mountain State Park   178
Vistas — Black Rock Mountain State Park   182-184
Fig. 39— Rabun Bald   186

Fig. 40— Chattooga River Rapids   190
Fig. 41— Chattooga River/Section 0—The Headwaters   192
Fig. 42— Chattooga River/Section I—The West Fork   196
Fig. 43— Chattooga River/Section II   202
Fig. 44— Chattooga River/Section III   204
Fig. 45— Chattooga River/Section IV   206
Fig. 46— Ellicott Rock Wilderness   210
Fig. 47— Scaly Mountain and Highlands   214
Vistas — Satulah Mountain   216
Fig. 48— Highlands and Whiteside Mountain   218
Fig. 49— Escarpment Gorges   224
Fig. 50— Cowee Gem Region   230
Fig. 51— Long Trails   232
Fig. 52— Appalachian Trail   234
Fig. 53— Appalachian Trail in Georgia   242, 243
Fig. 54— Benton MacKaye Trail   244
Fig. 55— Bartram Trail   248

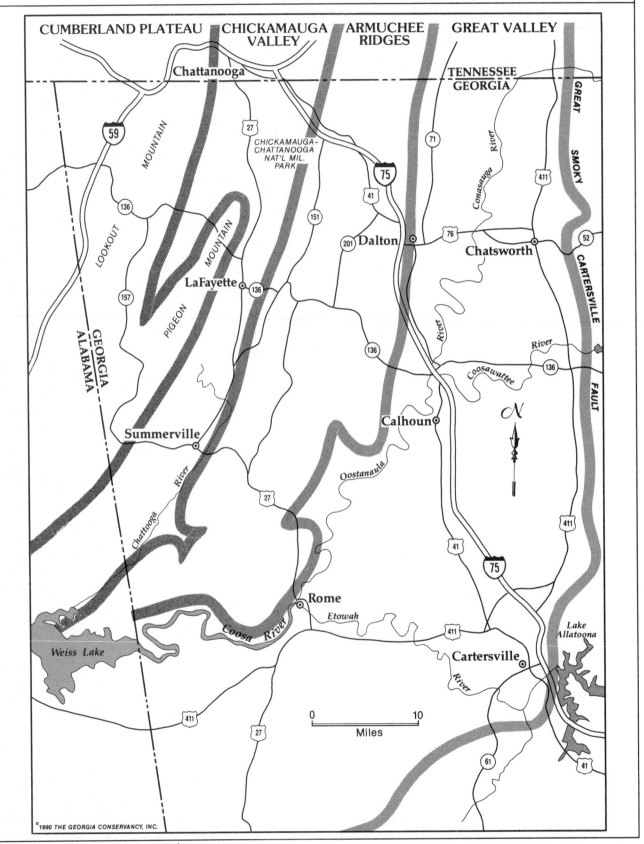

The Cumberland Plateau and The Valley and Ridge

Figure 3 — **CUMBERLAND PLATEAU AND VALLEY AND RIDGE**

THE CUMBERLAND PLATEAU AND THE VALLEY AND RIDGE

Northwest Georgia is here divided into four parts—the Cumberland Plateau, the Chickamauga Valley, the Armuchee Ridges and the Great Valley. The Chickamauga Valley, Armuchee Ridges and Great Valley are collectively known as the Valley and Ridge. Physiographers consider the Cumberland Plateau to be part of a larger area to the west, the Appalachian Plateau Province, which extends from Alabama northeastward through Tennessee and Kentucky.

Northwest Georgia is distinctly divided from the remainder of the Georgia mountains to the east by a great break in the earth's surface called the Cartersville-Great Smoky fault. Strange-looking rocks, arranged in layers and often embellished with fossil sea life, tell the visitor that he is in a quite different world from the more familiar Blue Ridge Mountains. Here in the northwest one finds long, linear ridges alternating with equally long valleys and straight streams—unlike the irregular mix of peaks and valleys in the Blue Ridge, where the drainage is dendritic like the branches of a tree.

This area is also called the "sedimentary region" because its rocky beds of sandstone, shale, coal and limestone are clearly recognizable as having once been, respectively, sand, mud, plants and marine life deposited in shallow seas that covered this area in Paleozoic times. The mountains may be flat-topped—especially in the Cumberland Plateau, where the more-nearly horizontal beds occur in "layer-cake" fashion, the younger ones lying on top.

This was an era of ancient life—largely marine invertebrates and primitive fishes. Between 300 and 425 million years ago (Mississippian and Silurian periods), these animals were entombed as fossils in various types of ocean floor materials—some in the limy shells of tiny organisms which formed limestone, and others in mud which became shale. These older animal fossils are most easily found in the Armuchee Ridges. During the Carboniferous or "coal measures" some 300 million years ago, the top of the Cumberland Plateau was the scene of swamps and fertile deltas. These deposits now yield plant fossils as well as coal deposits. Fossils are found in northwest Georgia because heat and pressure were not great enough to destroy them, as happened in the Blue Ridge.

The long, southwest-northeast-trending, limestone-floored valleys have been natural corridors for the passage of Coastal Plain life into the interior of Appalachia. Man, too, has used these fertile corridors

PLATEAU, VALLEY AND RIDGE

in agriculture and in war. Because these plateaus, ridges and natural passageways are coupled with extensive beds of mineral-rich carbonate rocks, one finds many plants and animals here which occur nowhere else in the Georgia mountains. The caves, springs, sinkholes and animals (such as the cottonmouth water moccasin) of the Cumberland Plateau and Valley and Ridge are not what one would expect to find in the northern part of our state; hence, this area seems more closely allied with southwest Georgia than with the Blue Ridge. Also, a number of plants and animals that seem rare to us range into Georgia only here, representing species more commonly found to the west in areas such as the Cumberland Mountains of Tennessee and Kentucky.

Rugged and isolated, this is a region with its own geography, color and personality. The landscape is dominated not only by the 100-mile-long Lookout Mountain, but also by the dramatic interplay of clouds and sunlight across the mountain and its valleys. Little wonder former residents chose place names like Cloudland, Craigsmere, Rocktown and Lookout.

This is a land relatively unknown until recently to tourists, casual visitors or even outdoor recreational enthusiasts, who have long been attracted to the mountains in the eastern part of the state. It has remained the province of local inhabitants; summer residents around Mentone, Alabama; adventurous cavers; and hang gliders seeking the best take-off point on the East Coast. Those who discover this region are soon under its spell and find themselves returning again and again.

Northern copperhead
Agkistrodon contortrix mokasen

The copperhead is one of the two poisonous snakes that are likely to be encountered in the mountains. Copperheads are not aggressive, but are difficult to see when coiled in the leaves. Like rattlesnakes, they den in rock cliffs. Young copperheads have a yellow tail tip, which they wiggle as a lure to attract lizards.

Vasey's trillium
Trillium vaseyi

In rich, moist areas this trillium has huge leaves and stands nearly two feet tall. Lift the wide leaves to see the remarkable maroon-colored flower nodding below.

The Cumberland Plateau

The Cumberland Plateau begins near Birmingham, Alabama and crosses the extreme northwest corner of Georgia before entering Tennessee just to the west of Chattanooga. Northwest of Knoxville, the plateau becomes highly dissected due to erosion, and the region—although geologically still a plateau—is called the Cumberland Mountains.

The two principal features of the Cumberland Plateau in Georgia are Sand Mountain and Lookout Mountain, which are separated by two-mile-wide Lookout Valley, in which the towns of Trenton and Rising Fawn are located.

From a physiographic standpoint, the flat-topped mountains of the Cumberland Plateau are quite different from the narrow Armuchee Ridges beyond the Chickamauga Valley to the east. Geologically, the Cumberland Plateau is transitional between the flat-lying sedimentary beds of central Tennessee and the ridges and valleys to the east in Georgia, which show more intensive folding and faulting.

The flat top of the Cumberland Plateau is sandstone which, while harder than limestone or shale, has nevertheless been carved and sculpted for millions of years by wind and water. Because of a tendency to fracture into squarish blocks, the sandstone has weathered into fantastic boulder formations in places like Rocktown and the Zahnd Tract, commercially called "rock cities". In addition, thick layers of soft, water-soluble limestone undergird the Cumberland Plateau. Because the top is actually slightly concave, surface water accumulates and seeps downward through cracks and crevices, where it dissolves the limestone and creates miles of underground passages or caves, issuing forth at numerous springs around the base of the mountain.

The great gulfs, or canyons, eroded in the sides of the Cumberland Plateau are spectacular in a geologic, biotic and scenic sense. Two on Lookout Mountain are notable — a wide canyon known as Johnson's Crook, and a narrow one called Sitton's Gulch and renamed Cloudland Canyon.

Pigeon Mountain, a thumb-like protrusion of Lookout Mountain, deserves special mention. It is a geological, botanical and zoological treasure house. Happily, most of it was purchased by Heritage Trust funds under the far-sighted Carter administration.

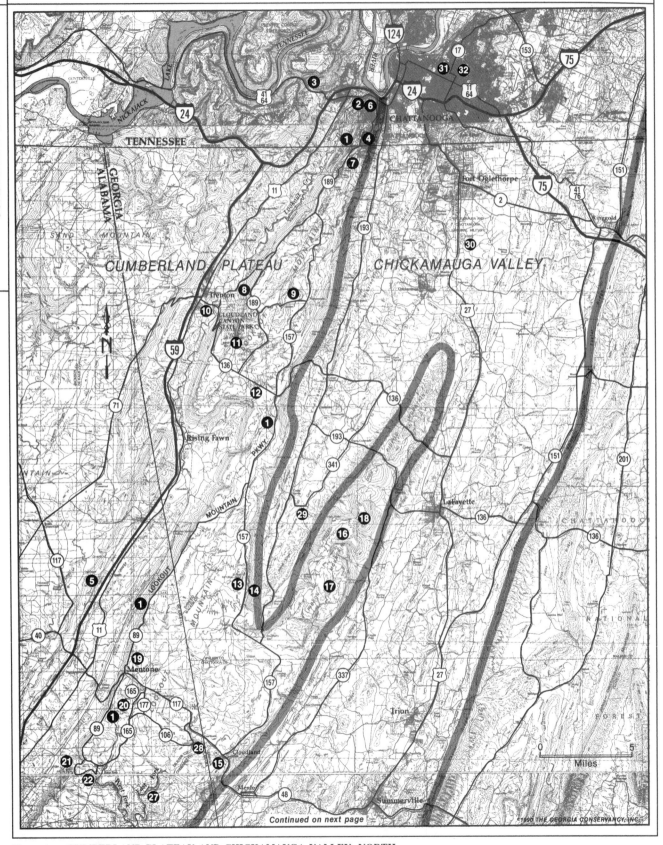

Figure 4 — **CUMBERLAND PLATEAU AND CHICKAMAUGA VALLEY, NORTH**

Continued on next page

4

Fig. 4 - Cumberland Plateau North
(page references in parentheses)

1   Lookout Mountain Parkway (5)
2   Reflection Riding & Chattanooga Nature Center (5)
3   Raccoon Mountain Caverns (8)
4   Ruby Falls (8)
5   Sequoyah Caverns (8)
6   Point Park (9, 27)
7   Covenant College (9)
8   McCarty Bluff (9)
9   Fossil Site (9)
10 Lookout Creek (11)
11 Cloudland Canyon State Park (11)
12 Johnson's Crook (13)
13 Zahnd Tract (13)
14 Scenic Overlook (13)
15 Exposed Coal Seam (13)
16 Pigeon Mountain (15)
17 Rocktown Trail (16)
18 The Pocket Trail (17)
19 Brow Park (19)
20 DeSoto Falls (19)
21 DeSoto State Park (19)
22 DeSoto Scout Trail (19)
27 East Fork of Little River canoe trip (23)
28 Put-in for East Fork Of Little River canoe trip (23)
29 McLemore Cove (13, 15, 25)
30 Chickamauga (26)
31 Orchard Knob (27)
32 Missionary Ridge (28)

Lookout Mountain

Lookout Mountain is the southernmost extension of the Cumberland Plateau, which is parallel to but inland from the Appalachian Mountains. Long and relatively flat on top, it extends for 100 miles in a diagonal that cuts across Alabama, Georgia and Tennessee. There are 3 miles of Lookout Mountain in Tennessee, 21 in Georgia and 76 in Alabama. The mountain is in one of the world's richest cave regions.

~LOOKOUT MOUNTAIN PARKWAY. [Fig. 4(1)] The designation is sometimes confusing because the "parkway" includes several roads, not just one. Nevertheless, this multi-highway driving route provides visitors to the region with an overview of the dramatic piece of geography between Gadsden, Alabama, and Chattanooga, Tennessee, that is Lookout Mountain. The route begins in Gadsden as AL 176 and runs in a northeasterly direction to Chattanooga. The mountain can be traversed not only in a north-south direction, but east-west as well. Visitors who explore county roads across the width of the mountain will have a better understanding of how this long flat mountain of the Cumberland Plateau differs from the peaks and ridges of the Blue Ridge Mountains.

~REFLECTION RIDING AND CHATTANOOGA NATURE CENTER. [(Fig. 4(2)] Reflection Riding is a 300-acre nature preserve along Lookout Creek at the base of Lookout Mountain. It adjoins 2,000-acre Point Park and Lookout Mountain Battlefield National Military Park. The area is maintained in the style of an English natural landscape and is crisscrossed by winding paths and graveled roads. It gains its name from Reflection Pond, a landmark on the property, and the English word *riding*, meaning an inviting pleasure path. The Great Indian War Path and the St. Augustine and Cisca Trail crossed Reflection Riding. Hernando de Soto's troop followed the Great Indian War Path over this area looking for gold. A grist mill operated by two Cherokees was on this site. Only the millstones remain today. In 1863 Union forces under General Hooker crossed Lookout Creek to engage the Confederate Army in the Battle of Lookout Mountain. Markers describing the battle are placed at many points along the drive.

Deep gorges, rock fields and moss-covered boulders provide interesting topography as well as shelter for many species of birds and other wildlife. The edges of Lookout Creek furnish habitat for bog plants, frogs and other small water creatures. Wild flowers and grasses cover the open meadows. Native rhododendron and azaleas have been planted on the mountain slope. The forest is predominantly oak with scattered groves of pine.

CUMBERLAND PLATEAU

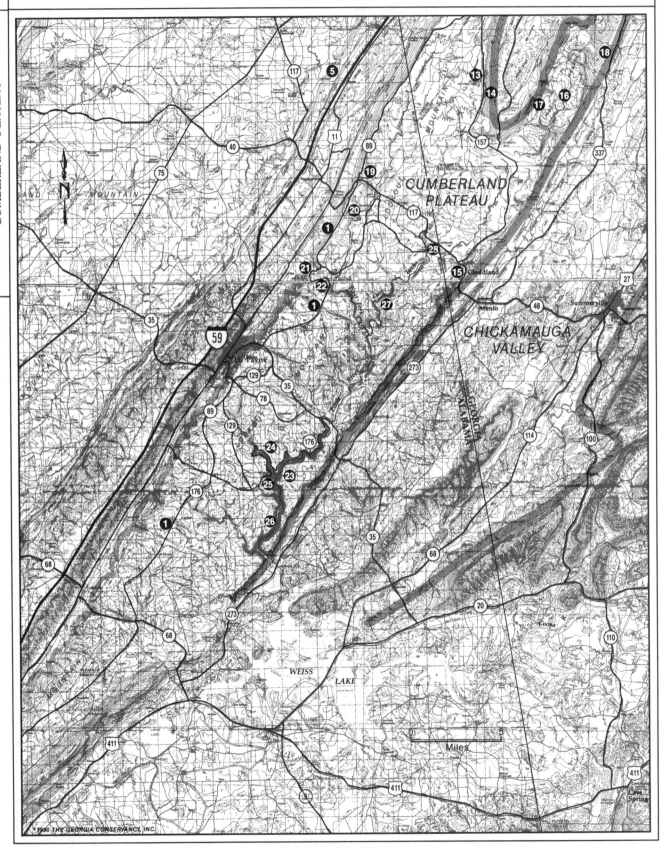

Figure 5 — **CUMBERLAND PLATEAU AND CHICKAMAUGA VALLEY, SOUTH**

CUMBERLAND PLATEAU

6

Fig. 5 - Cumberland Plateau South
(page references in parentheses)

13 Zahnd Tract (13)
14 Scenic Overlook (13)
15 Exposed Coal Seam (13)
16 Pigeon Mountain (15)
17 Rocktown Trail (16)
18 The Pocket Trail (17)
19 Brow Park (19)
20 DeSoto Falls (19)
21 DeSoto State Park (19)
22 DeSoto Scout Trail (19)
23 Little River Canyon (21)
24 Grace High Falls (21)
25 Little River Canyon Hiking Trail (21)
26 Little River Canoe Trip (22)
27 East Fork Of Little River canoe trip (23)
28 Put-in for East Fork Of Little River canoe trip (23)

The 12 miles of trails are well marked and make for relatively easy walking. All of the trails are interconnected, so a hike can be as long or short as desired and flexible in destination. From the park border trail and the driving loop there are connections to the National Park Service trails. Maps are available at the nature center. The wetland walkway, accessible to handicapped visitors with wheelchairs, leads from the road in front of the nature center through the animal habitats to a lovely overlook beside the creek.

Along the three miles of driving loop, most of the trees and shrubs are identified, as are points of historical interest. During the blooming seasons of spring, summer and fall a variety of wild-flowers can be seen. Plant identification guides corresponding to the numbered plant labels are available at the nature center. There are frequent stopping places along the way. Surrounded by ferns, the secluded gazebo overlooking Siren Pool has benches and shade where visitors can sit quietly and relax. The screened pavilion at the fragrance garden has benches and outside picnic tables.

Located at the gateway to Reflection Riding, the nature center features passive solar designed buildings containing a wildlife diorama, exhibits, a library, resource collections and a gift shop. An auditorium and solar greenhouse are next to the wildlife rehabilitation laboratory, where visitors can visit injured and orphaned wild animals, including hawks and owls. On weekends, programs including workshops, films, classes and interpretive walks are offered. Special programs are available upon request. Hand-fed Canada geese, mallards and wood ducks are year-round residents of Reflection Pond. Visitors are allowed to feed them.

DATES/HOURS: *Mon.-Sat. 9-5, Sun. 1-5; closed holidays.*
FEES: *Adults $1.50; children $1.*
SPECIAL EVENTS: *Weekend programs, summer day camp, annual wild-flower walk (mid Apr.).*
DIRECTIONS: *From I-24 take exit I-75 (Brown's Ferry Road) south to US 41; go east to Garden Road; turn right (south) to Reflection Riding and Nature Center. Garden Road is also reached from Scenic Hwy. 148.*
ADDITIONAL INFORMATION: *Reflection Riding and Chattanooga Nature Center, Rt. 4, Garden Road, Chattanooga, TN 37409. (615) 821-1160.*

~CAVES OF LOOKOUT MOUNTAIN. Here in the northwest corner of Georgia, the northeast corner of Alabama and the southern part of Tennessee, cavers have discovered a region linked by the Cumberland Plateau and characterized by a vast network of caves cut through limestone rock. To cavers this region is not Tennessee, Alabama and Georgia, but "TAG." They come from all over the world to explore its labyrinthine underground passages. Tennessee alone has more than 5,500 caves—more than any other state. Ellison's Cave on Georgia's Pigeon Mountain is the deepest cave east of

CUMBERLAND PLATEAU

the Mississippi River.

A few caves in the region are commercial, open to the public for a fee. These include famous caves such as Ruby Falls in Lookout Mountain and lesser-known sites such as Sequoyah Caverns near Valley Head, Alabama. Business volume varies greatly at different caves. Raccoon Mountain Caverns estimates some 10,000 visitors a year, while perhaps 350,000 see Ruby Falls.

RACCOON MOUNTAIN CAVERNS. [Fig. 4(3)] The absence of props such as dramatic music and sophisticated lighting allows the visitor to experience more directly the actual natural environment of the cave. Visitors may receive a personal tour by a knowledgeable caver. Wild tours—explorations of parts of the cave not normally seen by those taking commercial tours—last about four hours and are available by appointment only. Hardhats, lights and other necessary caving equipment are furnished.

DIRECTIONS: *From I-24 at Tiftonia/Lookout Mountain Exit, go north on US 41 and follow signs. From Lookout Mountain, follow 41 north.*
ADDITIONAL INFORMATION: *Raccoon Mountain Caverns, Rt. 4, Cummings Hwy., Chattanooga, TN 37409. (615) 821-9403.*

RUBY FALLS. [Fig. 4(4)] This is the most heavily promoted and commercially successful cave in the Southeast. Visitors ride an elevator 260 feet down into the cavern. They then walk 0.4 mile one way, past a variety of rock formations to Ruby Falls, with its 145-foot cascade lighted from below with multicolored spots and accompanied by the theme from the movie *2001*. Tour guides are cheerful and enthusiastic college students.

FACILITIES: *Gift shop & lookout platform with good views of Chattanooga.*
DATES/HOURS: *8-9 daily.*
FEES: *Adults $6.*
DIRECTIONS: *Main entrance is on TN 148, 0.5 mile off US 41, 11, 64 and 72. From I-24 follow signs to Lookout Mountain.*
ADDITIONAL INFORMATION: *Ruby Falls, Scenic Highway, Chattanooga, TN 37409. (615) 821-2544.*

SEQUOYAH CAVERNS. [Fig. 4(5)] Also called Looking Glass Caverns because of the mirror-like reflection of cave formations in cave pools. A commercial tour lasts about 30 minutes. The path behind the log cabin labeled Sequoyah's Cabin leads to the entrance to a wild cave. The Dogwood City Grotto, Atlanta chapter of the National Speleological Society, uses the pretty campground here for its annual fall gathering in October, when approximately 800 cavers gather for a weekend of cave exploring, camping and partying.

FACILITIES: *Campground, fishing pond, hay rides. Animals on the grounds include buffalo, Rocky Mountain sheep, goats, llama, black antelope and white fallow, spotted fallow and wild deer.*

Big brown bat
Eptesicus fuscus

One of our largest bats (wingspread one foot), this species does not hibernate for long periods and may remain active throughout the winter, according to Frank Golley. Many species of bats inhabit mountain forests where hollow trees and rock crevices afford them daytime protection, and where insects are abundant.

Hang Gliding at McCarty Bluff

DATES/HOURS: *Mar.-Dec., open daily 8:30-5:30 (6 during summer months); Jan. and Feb., Sat. and Sun. only 8:30-5.*
FEES: *Adults $5, children $3, under 6 free.*
DIRECTIONS: *Take the Hammondville/Valley Head exit or the Sulphur Springs/Ider exit off I-59 and follow signs.*
ADDITIONAL INFORMATION: *Sequoyah Caverns, Rt. 1, Valley Head, AL 30359. (205) 635-6423.*

~POINT PARK. [Fig. 4(6)]. See Chickamauga National Military Park—Point Park in the Chickamauga Valley section, page 27.

~COVENANT COLLEGE. [Fig. 4(7)] Called the "Castle in the Clouds," a name first applied to the luxury hotel and gambling casino that first occupied this site in the late 1920's, Covenant is a four-year Presbyterian-affiliated college. A visit to the campus affords the visitor with the only unobstructed 360-degree panorama of the country beyond the mountain.
DIRECTIONS: *Covenant College is on the Lookout Mountain Parkway, just south of the Tennessee/Georgia border. If approaching from Chattanooga, follow the "See Rock City" signs until the Lookout Mountain Parkway signs and Covenant College signs are apparent. Approaching from the south on either SR 157 or SR 189, continue north and follow the Covenant College direction signs.*

~McCARTY BLUFF. [Fig. 4(8)] (Lookout Mountain Flight Park and Training Center). Sixty miles of ridgeline and the unique thermal-producing qualities of the valley floor make this the premier hang gliding site on the East Coast. Pilots from all over the world sail high above the Lookout Mountain Ridge and fly for hours up and down the valley. There is usually activity every day, and spectators get a close-up, breathtaking view of winged participants jumping off the sheer cliffside. The East Coast hang gliding distance record was set here, a flight of 130 miles ending in Social Circle, Georgia. National and regional competitions are held here on a regular basis.
DIRECTIONS: *On GA 189, seven miles north of 136.*
ADDITIONAL INFORMATION: *For information on flight training and equipment contact Lookout Mountain Flight Park and Training Center. (404) 398-3541.*

~FOSSIL SITE. [(Fig. 4(9)] Pennsylvanian plant fossils. Fossils to be found include tree-fern-like plants called *Sigillaria*, small ferns such as *Pecopteris, Alethopteris, Neuropteris, Archeopteris* and others.
DIRECTIONS: *From the intersection of GA 136 and GA 157 west of LaFayette, go north on GA 157, 5.7 miles. Turn left on Durham Road*

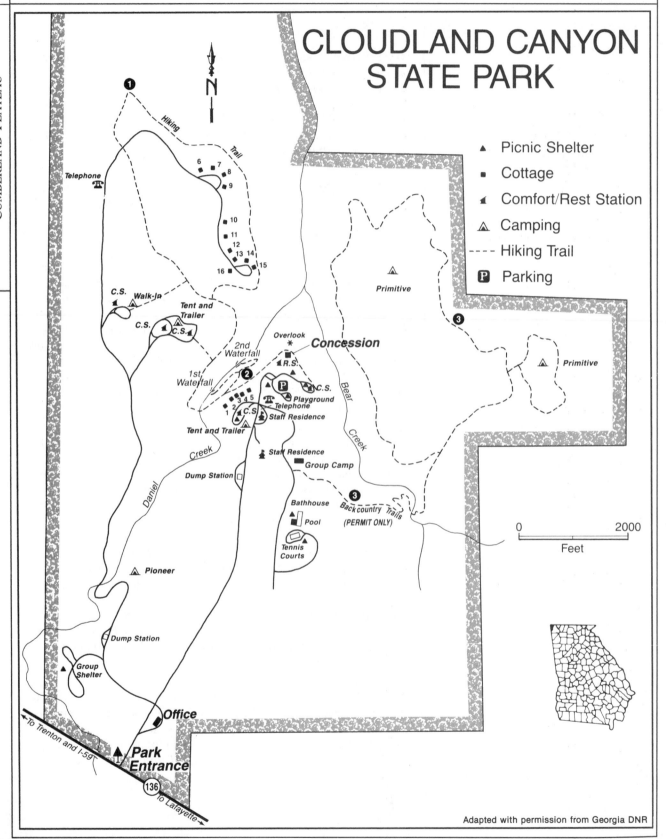

CLOUDLAND CANYON STATE PARK

Legend:
- ▲ Picnic Shelter
- ▪ Cottage
- ◀ Comfort/Rest Station
- ⌂ Camping
- --- Hiking Trail
- P Parking

CUMBERLAND PLATEAU

Adapted with permission from Georgia DNR

Figure 6 — **CLOUDLAND CANYON STATE PARK**

Fig. 6 - Cloudland Canyon State Park

(page references in parentheses)

1 West Rim Loop Trail (12)
2 Waterfall Trail (12)
3 Cloudland Backcountry Trail (12)

and go 0.6 mile. There are large spoil banks on the right made up of minerals taken from coal mines nearby.

~LOOKOUT CREEK. [Fig. 4(10)] Lookout Creek runs through Lookout Valley, along the base of Lookout Mountain. It begins just across the state line near the little town of Valley Head, Alabama. It then flows northeastward, slicing across the extreme northwestern corner of Georgia, then into Tennessee, where it empties into the mighty Tennessee River at the base of Lookout Mountain in Chattanooga. It weaves its way through Georgia for 30 miles, in and out of wilderness areas and pasture land, offering the canoeist briskly flowing flat waters and a moderate number of Class I shoals. Scenery varies dramatically during the nine-mile run between the put-in and take-out points described here. At one moment canoeists pass through heavy forests, the next through open pastureland that offers impressive views of Lookout Mountain, a constant companion to the east. Although the headwaters of Lookout Creek are scarcely a mile from the headwaters of Little River, these two neighboring rivers flow in opposite directions. The former flows north, placidly winding through Lookout Valley. The latter flows south, roaring violently down the spine of the mountain. The explanation is that although born in the same neighborhood, the streams belong to different watersheds. Lookout Creek belongs to the Tennessee Valley watershed; the Little River, to the Coosa Valley watershed. This fact also explains why Lookout Creek can maintain its water level, since it is filled by water running off the western slopes of the entire Lookout Mountain Plateau, while its rocky-bottomed neighbor up on the mountain, fed by a smaller watershed, can quickly run dry.

DIRECTIONS: *The take-out bridge is on GA 136, 0.7 mile east of where 136 meets US 11 in Trenton [Fig. 4(10)]. The best take-out spot, however, is not at the bridge but down a dirt road that runs south along the west side of the creek for 0.2 mile to a good access point above an old mill dam. To reach the put-in, return to Trenton on GA 136, turn left (south) on US 11 and drive 7.5 miles to Rising Fawn. Turn left (east) on Newsome Gap Road (County Road 197) and drive 0.3 mile to the put-in bridge.*

~CLOUDLAND CANYON STATE PARK. [Fig. 4(11), Fig. 6] Located on the western edge of Lookout Mountain, Cloudland Canyon is one of the largest and most scenic state parks in Georgia. The park provides visitors with beautiful vistas of the rugged geology of this area and an excellent outdoor setting for the camper or hiker wanting to experience the beauty of the natural world. Cloudland was established in 1939 when the state of Georgia began the acquisition of land from several private landowners. Today it encompasses some 2,200 acres of beautiful mountain land. Until 1939, when construction of a Georgia highway through this area was finally completed, the only access was through Alabama or Tennessee. The park is perhaps one of the best places to view and understand the geology of northwest Georgia. An excellent guidebook, the *Geologic Guide to Cloudland Canyon State Park* by Martha Griffin and Robert Atkins, is available at the park office. It discusses the fascinating geology of this area at ten stations around the rim trails and along the trails to waterfalls on Daniel's Creek.

The park straddles a deep gorge cut into the west side of Lookout Mountain by Sitton Gulch Creek. The elevation here drops from 1,800 to 800 feet above sea level at the bottom of the gorge. The rimrock and steeper cliffs are resistant sandstone formed over 200 million years ago from beach and dune sands of an ancient shoreline. Shale layers below the sandstone are marked by a growth of pines. At the canyon bottom is a slope of rock fragments called "talus" and now heavily forested. The valley floor and gentle slopes seen in the distance are formed of fossil-bearing limestone.

FACILITIES: *75 tent and trailer sites, 16 rental cottages, 40-bed group camp, winterized group shelter, tennis courts, swimming pool, 30 walk-in campsites.*

DATES/HOURS: *Daily 7am-10pm year round; office open 8am-5pm*

SPECIAL EVENTS: *Crafts in the Clouds, third weekend in May; Wildflower Program, May; Backpacking Trip, Oct.*

DIRECTIONS: *Located on GA 136, eight miles east of Trenton and I-59, 18 miles northwest of LaFayette.*

ADDITIONAL INFORMATION: *Cloudland Canyon State Park, GA Department of Natural Resources, Rt. 2, Box 150, Rising Fawn, GA 30738. (404) 657-4050.*

~HIKING TRAILS OF CLOUDLAND CANYON STATE PARK.

The canyon's rugged beauty is a joy year round, each season offering special sights and sounds for visitors. A hike down Cloudland's trails to the canyon floor is a walk through millions of geologic years. Trails are well marked and easy to follow. The park provides good interpretive information about the history and geology of the area. Maps and directions to the trailheads are available in the park office.

WEST RIM LOOP TRAIL. [Fig. 6(1)] 4.9 miles. Part of the trail follows the canyon rim close to its edge. An overlook provides views into the three park gorges.

WATERFALL TRAIL. [Fig. 6(2)] 0.3 mile. Walk to two waterfalls on Daniel Creek.

CLOUDLAND BACKCOUNTRY TRAILS. [Fig. 6(3)] 5.4-mile loop. Backpacking and camping are permitted on this trail. Stop by the park office to obtain a permit and pay the $3-per-person fee.

American toad
  Bufo americanus

Of the two large toad species in the mountains, this one is the more northern and is confined more or less to mountain and Piedmont forests. It is the first to emerge from hibernation and may breed in temporary water in March or April.

~JOHNSON'S CROOK. [Fig. 4(12)] Johnson's Crook is a deep indentation or cove on the west side of Lookout Mountain, located entirely in Dade County, Georgia. The valley of the crook is about 1,100 feet above sea level, and the brow around it ranges from 1,900 to 2,100 feet. The village of Rising Fawn and impressive Fox Mountain are immediately to the west of the crook.

In September, 1863, shortly before the Battle of Chickamauga, an epic event occurred when 40,000 Union Troops marched from Rising Fawn east into the crook and up, over and down Lookout Mountain, building a road as they advanced and carrying with them all of the equipment of war.

~ZAHND TRACT. [Fig. 4(13), Fig. 5(13)] This is an area of large, unusual rock formations characteristic of this region. Also present is a mixture of mesic (liking moist conditions), xeric (liking dry conditions) and Coastal Plain plants. Most visible from the road is the mountain laurel, which is especially abundant and blooms in May. The plot is owned by the state of Georgia. The rocks are about 200 feet off the road, east of GA 157.
DIRECTIONS: *From the intersection of GA 48 go north 12.9 miles on GA 157, or from GA 136 go 9.7 miles south on GA 157.*

~SCENIC OVERLOOK. [Fig. 4(14), Fig. 5(14)] On GA 157, look for a metal highway rail about 11.9 miles north of GA 48 (or 10 miles south of the intersection of GA 136 and GA 157 south.) which views McLemore Cove [Fig. 4(29)], a breached eroded anticlinal valley between Pigeon and Lookout Mountains.

~EXPOSED COAL SEAM. [Fig. 4(15), Fig. 5(15), Fig. 6] Just before the brow of the mountain, a thinly beaded seam of coal is visible under massive sandstone and over shale. One must climb the bank to see it. During the millions of years of the Carboniferous era, huge tree ferns and giant horsetails which were one to two feet in diameter and sixty or more feet high lived in the great swamps and river deltas that circled the northern hemisphere. As these plants died and fell to the earth the swamp water prevented them from losing their carbon by oxidation. After eons of peat formation these carbonized remains were compressed into layers of coal, which has powered mankind ever since. To split a piece of coal and find the imprint of the leaves of these ancient forests is one of the most significant experiences in the study of natural history. Birmingham, Alabama, became a great metallurgical center because of its combination of coal and iron deposits somewhat similar to those around Lookout Mountain.
DIRECTIONS: *Two miles east of Menlo on the south side of GA 48.*

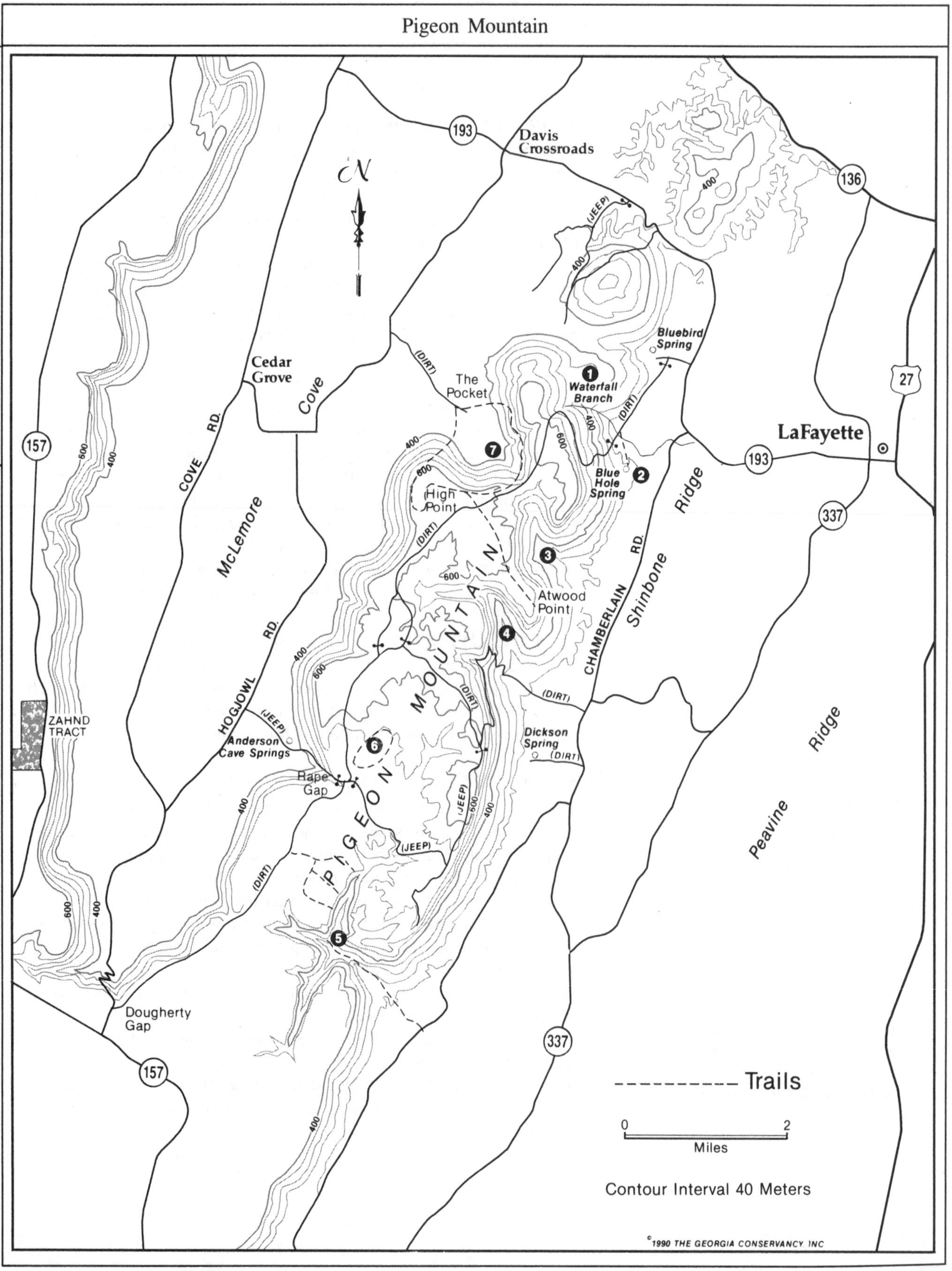

Figure 7 — **PIGEON MOUNTAIN**

Fig. 7 - Pigeon Mountain
(page references in parentheses)

1 Waterfall Branch (16)
2 Blue Hole Spring (16)
3 McWhorter Gulf (16)
4 Dickson Gulf (16)
5 Harrisburg Gulf (16)
6 Rocktown Trail (16)
7 The Pocket Trail (17)

Pigeon Mountain

Pigeon Mountain [Fig. 4(16), Fig. 5(16), Fig. 7] and Lookout Mountain form a "V" like the thumb and index finger of a person's left hand held palm down, with Lookout being the index finger and Pigeon being the thumb. Nestled in the "V" shape is the Chickamauga Valley's lovely McLemore Cove [Fig. 4(29)]. The northern tip of Pigeon Mountain lies about three miles west of LaFayette and stretches southwest for ten miles, where it joins with Lookout Mountain. The mountain was named for the passenger pigeon, now extinct, which in the 1800's roosted there by the thousands. In the twenties and thirties some 30 families lived on Pigeon Mountain, working small farms and perhaps making moonshine liquor. Their names have stayed behind as part of the landscape, as in Rape Gap, Ellison's Cave and Pettijohn's Cave. The thirties, however, saw a lowering of the water table on the mountain, causing all the wells to dry up and the families to abandon their homes. To date, the water table has yet to return to its former level.

This is an area with many natural features of exceptional value for wildlife, recreation, historical, archeological and educational purposes. For 10 years it has been studied by scientists, who are still finding new and exciting plants, animals and natural environments. Some 21 rare plants and several rare salamanders are found here. The area was leased by the Georgia Department of Natural Resources in 1969. Since that time, the state has purchased more than 13,000 acres of the mountain. The land is managed as the Crockford-Pigeon Mountain Wildlife Management Area, primarily for wildlife and the protection and enhancement of the mountain's many natural features.

ADDITIONAL INFORMATION: *The Georgia Department of Natural Resources, Route 1, Floyd Springs Road, Armuchee, GA 30105. (404) 638-3944 or 295-6041.*

~CAVES OF PIGEON MOUNTAIN. Like Lookout Mountain, Pigeon Mountain is laced with caves that wind all through the limestone rock. There are many cave entrances on the mountain, and it is an important location for cavers from all over the Southeast. One of these, Ellison's Cave, contains two exceptionally deep pits—Fantastic Pit at 510 feet and Incredible Dome Pit at 440 feet. About 13 miles of Ellison's Cave have been explored and mapped, but all indications are that it is much more extensive. In fact, it is likely that Pigeon Mountain is a vast system of underground caverns and stream channels. Pettijohn's Cave was first described in 1837. Approximately five miles of passageways in this cave have been mapped, and new passages are still being discovered. This cave has seen much more use than Ellison's and has sustained more damage to its mineral formations.

CUMBERLAND PLATEAU

It should be emphasized that the underground can be an extremely dangerous area to explore for individuals unfamiliar with the skills required in caving. Caves should be explored only in the company of well-equipped, experienced cavers.

ADDITIONAL INFORMATION: *Because of the danger of caving, directions are not provided. For information on the sport of caving, contact the National Speleogical Society, Cave Ave., Huntsville, AL 35810.*

~PIGEON MOUNTAIN SITES.

WATERFALL BRANCH. [Fig. 7(1)] A small stream containing a scenic waterfall. Several rare plants have been recorded on the east- and northeast-facing slopes in the vicinity of this stream, including the hairy mock-orange, the hedge nettle, the Alabama snow-wreath, the wild hyacinth, the nodding spurge, celandine poppy and the state-protected twinleaf.

BLUE HOLE. [Fig. 7(2)] This is a large spring located at the base of the eastern slope of Pigeon Mountain. The unusual bluish color of its waters, along with the fact that it represents a hydrological discharge of the extensive Ellison's Cave system, makes this a significant feature. It is accessible by vehicle during the summer months. If gated, access is available by foot or bicycle only.

MCWHORTER GULF [FIG. 7(3)], DICKSON GULF [FIG. 7(4)] AND HARRISBURG GULF [FIG. 7(5)]. These "gulfs" contain the important and rare Pigeon Mountain salamander, a species known from only four sites, all located along the eastern slope of Pigeon Mountain. The green salamander has also been collected from this area.

SAGPONDS. These are water-filled depressions formed when underlying limestone strata are dissolved by groundwater and "slumping" occurs. Many of these sagponds serve as important groundwater recharge areas, slowly adding water to underground reserves. Several natural sagponds are found atop Pigeon Mountain. Some of these have been valuable to scientists who drilled them through deep layers of peat and found ancient pollen samples which enabled documentation of the vegetation that covered the area during the Ice Age.

~HIKING ON PIGEON MOUNTAIN.

ROCKTOWN TRAIL. [Fig. 4(17), Fig. 5(17), Fig. 7(6)] About 1.0 mile one way. The exploration of the massive boulders within the 150 acres of Rocktown can easily consume the better part of a day. The biggest mistake visitors can make is not to allow enough time to

Green salamander
Aneides aeneus

This cliff-dwelling salamander lives in damp crevices. It has a flattened body and green lichen-like markings on a dark background color. It is found in the cliffs of Pigeon Mountain and in Tallulah Gorge. A flashlight and a coat hanger are often required to capture it.

inspect this unusual site. Some of the boulders are as large as three story office buildings; a narrow pedestal supporting a caprock resembles a 25-foot tall champagne glass; deep inside a narrow, dark crevice it is cool enough for hikers to see their breaths even though outside temperature may be close to 80 degrees.

The reddish rocks that hikers see along the trail or imbedded in the sandstone formations of Rocktown are iron ore deposits. At one time there were 10 iron mines on the mountain. These deposits add a special visual interest to the Rocktown environment, because the softer sandstone erodes around them. Rocktown is easy to reach and would be a suitable hike for those of almost any age or physical condition. The trail is marked with white blazes.

DIRECTIONS: *From US 27 in LaFayette, go west 2.8 miles on GA 193 to Chamberlain Road; turn left and go 3.4 miles; turn right (marked by a wooden sign for Crockford-Pigeon Mountain Wildlife Management Area). Pass the Department of Natural Resources' check station and continue straight on the gravel road. Where the road forks, 4.2 miles from the check station, continue on the right fork. Past some cleared fields on the left, there is a road to the left 1.3 miles after the fork. Turn left there and go 0.7 mile to a clearing near the trailhead.*

THE POCKET TRAIL. [Fig. 4(18), Fig. 5(18), Fig. 7(7)] This is a loop trail about six miles long. This steep trail climbs Pigeon Mountain and follows the ridgeline for 2.3 miles. The view to the northwest looks down on McLemore Cove, a valley of farmland between Pigeon and Lookout Mountains, and across to Lookout Mountain itself. Here the hiker has an excellent opportunity to observe and carefully climb on the unusual rock formations typical of this portion of the Cumberland Plateau. The fractured sandstone has been weathered and eroded over thousands and thousands of years into spires and teetering boulders that are most dramatic, particularly when perched—as many of them are—on the very edge of the mountain.

Several rare or uncommon plant species have been recorded here, making it one of the most remarkable botanical areas in northwest Georgia. There are at least eleven significant species found almost nowhere else in Georgia which are present in the small patch of mesic hardwood forest below the wet-weather falls. These include celandine poppy, Ohio buckeye, bent trillium, nodding spurge, lance-leaf trillium, wild hyacinth, log fern, harbinger of spring, Virginia bluebells, hairy mock-orange and blue ash. When the plants are in bloom the forest below the waterfall near the start of the trail is truly remarkable, with some species occurring in quite thick beds. The rocky slopes above the Pocket contain an unusual open forest community dominated by red cedar and chinquapin oak. It also includes the smoketree, a rarity in Georgia. Hedge nettle, another new occurrence for the state, was first observed on slopes above the open meadow.

DIRECTIONS: *From LaFayette, take GA 193 west eight miles to Davis Crossroads. Turn left on Hog Jowl Road and go about 2.7 miles. When the road forks, take the left fork and pass Mt. Hermon Baptist Church on the left. At the top of the hill, just past the church, a paved road turns left. Turn there and follow the road (it is paved only for about 0.5 mile) into the Pocket. The road winds 1.6 miles past several fields and up a narrow mountain track that may require four-wheel drive in severe weather. Notice the falls to the right as the open area is reached. A cable across the road at the end of a small field prevents further auto travel. Park in the field. The hiking trail begins near a wooden sign beside Pocket Branch. Look for a small sign designating the trailhead and for blue blazes that mark the trail.*

~MCLEMORE COVE. [Fig. 4(29)] Before leaving this area, the reader may wish to visit nearby McLemore Cove, located in the Chickamauga Valley and discussed on page 25.

Little River, Alabama

~BROW PARK. [Fig. 4(19), Fig. 5(19)] Here visitors can get a representative sample of what the views are like along the entire length of Lookout Mountain. Picnic tables, good sunset views.
DIRECTIONS: *0.2 mile north of Mentone, AL on County Road 89.*

~DESOTO FALLS. [Fig. 4(20), Fig. 5(20)] In addition to a beautiful 100-foot waterfall, there is a dam creating a lovely mountain lake which provides swimming, fishing and boating.

~DESOTO STATE PARK. [Fig. 4(21), Fig. 5(21)] This fine Alabama state park has approximately 20 miles of easy-to-follow, well marked hiking trails. Rustic foot bridges span many of the streams; unusual rock formations and rare forms of plant life are found along these trails.
FACILITIES: *A variety of lodging, including rustic log cabins, mountain chalets, a lodge, and a 25-unit motel, as well as campgrounds. The information center has a coin-operated laundry, restrooms, country store and a local craft and gift shop. The store is stocked with all items necessary for camping, picnicking and housekeeping in the cottages. Additional facilities include a picnic area with rustic stone shelter, picnic tables and grills, volleyball court and ball field (equipment may be checked out at the country store), Olympic-size pool and two unlighted tennis courts.*
DIRECTIONS: *On Alabama county road 89. Follow signs from Mentone, AL.*
ADDITIONAL INFORMATION: *For general information on DeSoto State Park camping, hiking and picnicking contact DeSoto State Park, Rt. 1, Box 210, Fort Payne, AL 35967. (205) 845-0051. For information on the lodge, reservations for cottages or rooms contact DeSoto State Park, Rt. 1, Box 205, Fort Payne, AL 35967. (205) 845-5380.*

~DESOTO SCOUT TRAIL. [Fig. 4(22), Fig. 5(22)] This is a 12-mile trail that begins at Comer Scout Camp and follows the West Fork of Little River to a spot north of AL 35. Inquire at the DeSoto State Park information center for detailed directions to the trailhead. (205) 845-0051. The trail is closed during November, December and January.

Slimy salamander
Plethodon glutinosus

This is the most common terrestrial salamander, occurring under nearly every log in the forest. It is replaced by a different species at higher elevations. It is distasteful to predators and has a copious, sticky discharge that is difficult to remove from hands and fingers.

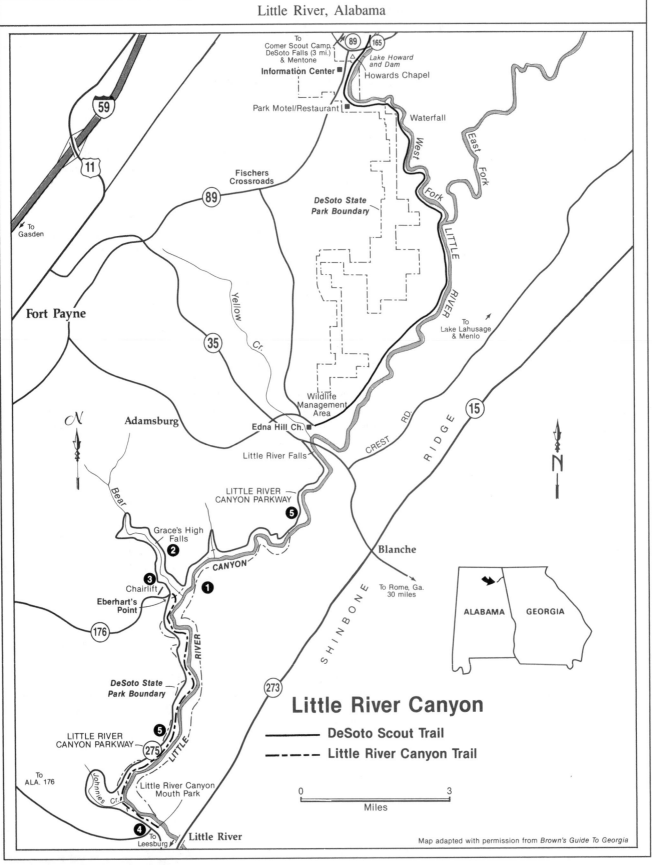

Figure 8 — **LITTLE RIVER, ALABAMA**

Fig. 8 - Little River
(page references in parentheses)

1 Little River Canyon (21)
2 Grace High Falls (21)
3 Little River Canyon Hiking Trail - Chairlift (21)
4 Little River Canyon Hiking Trail - Canyon Mouth Park (21)
5 Little River Canyon Parkway - Rim Drive (21)

~**LITTLE RIVER CANYON.** [Fig. 5(23), Fig. 8(1)] Little River Canyon on long, flat Lookout Mountain is one of the deepest gorges in the eastern United States. With an average depth of 400 feet, it is 600 feet at its deepest point and three-quarters of a mile across. Little River flows right down the middle of the canyon and, therefore, down the spine of Lookout Mountain, making it the only river in North America to flow its entire length along a mountaintop.

Geologists have devised two theories to explain the canyon's formation, neither of which has been proved or disproved. One is that the river may have once flowed underground until its roof overhead caved in and exposed it. Or perhaps an upheaval within the earth opened up a crevice which was enlarged over time by the erosive action of the river formed within it.

GRACE HIGH FALLS. [Fig. 5(24), Fig. 8(2)] The highest waterfall in Alabama, it is located on the south side of Bear Creek Canyon but can be seen only from the north side of the canyon.

LITTLE RIVER CANYON HIKING TRAIL. [Fig. 5(25), Fig. 8(3), Fig. 8(4)] This six-mile hiking trail follows the north bank of Little River. (Note: A flood in 1985 brought 15 inches of rain in three hours to the canyon and resulted in road washouts, rock slides and tree falls. When this trail was last hiked by our reviewer, those obstructions had still not been cleared, making the trail difficult to follow, particularly on the north end.)

DIRECTIONS: *To begin the trail at its northern end, follow the Little River Canyon Rim Road (AL 275) to its intersection with 176. There on the Rim Road see an abandoned chairlift that at various times has transported tourists to and from the canyon floor. The trail down to the river is just a few yards north of the chairlift [Fig. 8(3)]. It is extremely steep. The trail leads south along the river. The easiest access is from the southern end of the trail at Canyon Mouth Park [Fig. 8(4)] operated by Cherokee County. The trail, at this point designated the John F. Kennedy Trail and marked with yellow blazes, begins at a dirt-and gravel parking area on the back side of the park.*

ADDITIONAL INFORMATION: *The park manager at Cherokee County Park will discuss setting up a shuttle to the northern trailhead—a good idea since cars have been vandalized along Rim Road. Contact Little River Canyon Mouth Park, Rt. 2, Box 150, Cedar Bluff, AL 35959. (205) 779-6814.*

LITTLE RIVER CANYON PARKWAY - RIM DRIVE. [Fig. 8(5)] This is a spectacular 22-mile drive along the western rim of Little River Canyon. The road passes a dozen lookout points and is a rewarding route to experience one of the most outstanding natural landscapes in the Southeast.

~CANOEING ON LITTLE RIVER.

LITTLE RIVER. [Fig. 5(26)] Little River is classified as an Alabama Wild and Scenic River. It would have qualified as a National Wild and Scenic River had it not been for the now-abandoned chairlift near the intersection of AL 176 and Rim Road. It is the only river in North America that flows its entire length on top of a mountain. Etched deep in the spine of the long Alabama portion of Lookout Mountain, it flows through one of the deepest canyons east of the Rockies.

Born in the uplands around Mentone, Little River grows until it reaches the dramatic 100-foot DeSoto Falls at DeSoto State Park. It is a pretty Class II run until it is joined by its east fork just above the AL 35 Bridge. Just below the bridge it takes a lethal, 60-foot plunge downward and the Little River Canyon is born dramatically.

When the water level is right, the river is a fast and heavy whitewater run of repeated Class II, III and IV rapids. Only experienced canoeists should attempt it. Even then, it should be run only after careful preparation and on-the-spot information checks with the DeSoto State Park information office. There are no water gauges in Little River, and levels can change from unrunably bumpy in low water to suicidally heavy in high water. This river requires a support team of at least three canoes equipped with heavy throw ropes, life vests and helmets. The canyon section of the river runs 16 miles from the AL 35 Bridge to Canyon Mouth Park, but only half of this is suitable for canoeing.

The run from Eberhart's Point to Canyon Mouth Park is approximately eight miles, but the distance is deceptive. Canoeists will need all the daylight hours available for unpredictable portages and unavoidable delays. Once in the canyon, one has no way out but downriver. In moderate water some of the rapids must be portaged. Do not try to run the section of the river from AL 35 to Eberhart's Point. According to park officials, most who try this end up having to rope themselves and their damaged canoes up the 500-foot cliffs to get out. Consider coordinating a canoe trip with an accompanying hiking party (see Little River Canyon Hiking Trail, above). This will provide additional support for the put-in portage and other necessary portages around unrunable rapids.

DIRECTIONS: *To put in and take out, from Rome go west on GA 20 into Alabama. About 10 miles into Alabama, turn north on AL 35 continuing to the Little River Canyon Bridge. At the northwest corner of the bridge begins the Canyon Rim Parkway. Follow this for approximately 15 scenic miles to Eberhart's Point, the site of a now-defunct chairlift. Several trails lead down the canyon wall to the put-in. Each is tortuous and long, a portage of almost 600 feet virtually straight down. Only the most determined of paddlers will attempt it. Vehicles can be shuttled to the take-out at Canyon Mouth Park or, alternately, at AL 273 if the park is closed.*

Black locust
Robinia pseudo-acacia

While not confined to the mountains, the black locust commonly seeds into mountain coves following heavy logging or other disturbance. Its wood is much in demand for fence posts, since it contains a chemical that prevents fungal growth.

EAST FORK OF THE LITTLE RIVER. [Fig. 4(27), Fig. 5(27)] The East Fork of Little River provides the average canoeist with a safe yet exciting way to experience this canyon area without having to face the dangers and difficulties of Little River Canyon farther downstream. Located north of the actual canyon area, the East Fork is a canoeable Class I - III tributary for paddlers of beginner and intermediate skills. It begins in the southwest corner of Georgia's Walker County and flows into Alabama for a distance of 16 miles before it joins with the west fork to form Little River. The information here covers the last six miles of the East Fork (from Lake Lahusage to the confluence with the west fork) and the first five miles of the Little River (down to the AL 35 bridge). It is just beyond this bridge that the Little River takes its dramatic plunge into the canyon. The total canoeing distance from this run is 11.2 miles, a distance that can be covered in one full day of paddling.

DIRECTIONS: *For the shortest and fastest shuttle, leave the take-out bridge on AL 35 and go south on this road for 3 miles until it meets County Road 15 at Blanche, AL. Turn left (northwest) on County Road 15 and go 11 miles (crossing back into Georgia) to Menlo. There, turn left onto GA 48 and go four miles to the Alabama state line. Two hundred yards past the state line sign is a paved road to the left, the Old Dam Road. Turn left here and go 1.4 miles to the dead end at the put-in [Fig. 4(28), Fig. 5(28)].*

For a more scenic shuttle, only 4.8 miles longer than the one above, go north from the take-out bridge on AL 35 for 5.4 miles, then turn right on AL 89 (the DeSoto State Park Road) and follow this road through the state park, past DeSoto Falls for 11.4 miles to Mentone. In Mentone, turn right on AL 117 and go six miles, arriving at the Old Dam Road leading off to the right, about 200 yards before the Georgia state line. Follow the Old Dam Road 1.4 miles to the put-in.

~NOCCALULA FALLS PARK AND CAMPGROUND.

A rushing waterfall on Black Creek is the centerpiece of Noccalula Falls Park and Campground, located at the southwestern end of the Lookout Mountain Parkway. A re-created pioneer community depicts life of early settlers in this area of the Appalachian foothills. Some of the buildings were moved from their original sites to be preserved here. Among these are a house built in 1877 and a large cotton warehouse built in 1888. From March until September a train circles the edge of the park, which includes a botanical garden. A stairway leads to the gorge below the falls and the Gorge Trail. Interesting rock formations are found in the center of the park.

FACILITIES: *Restrooms, concessions, swimming, camping, picnicking, tennis, restaurant, playground, dump station, store, laundry facilities.*
DATES/HOURS: *Park—8 until sundown year round; campground— summer 7-7, fall 8-5, winter 8-4.*

Confederate Cap, Belt and Sword

The Chickamauga Valley

The Chickamauga Valley lies between the Cumberland Plateau's Lookout Mountain to the west and the Armuchee Ridges to the east. Where it divides the "thumb" of Pigeon Mountain from Lookout Mountain is the famed McLemore Cove. The Chickamauga Valley forms a natural passageway between the high ridges on either side. Since it gives access to both Chattanooga and the Tennessee River and contains a few low ridges, it was naturally the site of much movement and conflict during the Civil War. The Chickamauga Valley is not just one valley but a series of northeast-southwest trending valleys with limestone floors and ridges some 200 to 300 feet high, capped with more weather-resistant rock. Down through these valleys and across the ridges between Chattanooga and Atlanta, Union Army forces under General William Sherman pursued Confederate troops during the fighting which led to the Battle of Atlanta, near the end of the Civil War. Visitors to the military parks at Chickamauga, Missionary Ridge and Orchard Knob, as well as other areas such as the lovely and serene McLemore Cove, will come away with a clearer understanding of how the natural geology of the region has helped shape recent human history. From the Chickamauga Valley, especially GA 337, one can reach a variety of natural features lying at the base of the Pigeon Mountain escarpment. These include giant, dry, forest sinkholes; Blue Hole; and the entrances to the enchanting Dickson and McWhorter Gulfs, deeply eroded into Pigeon Mountain's east wall.

~McLEMORE COVE. [Fig. 4(29)] A post-card-pretty valley nestled in the "V" formed by Lookout Mountain and Pigeon Mountain. The steep limestone and sandstone walls of the mountains form a dramatic backdrop for a scenic drive through the cove. The area is almost exclusively agricultural, with small dairy farms taking up most of the land. At the southwest end of the cove is a portion of the picturesque 11,500-acre Mountain Cove Farm. Red cedars which thrive on the limestone soil here are profuse throughout the cove, particularly along West Cove Road, as indicated by the names of the natural features and landmarks: Cedar Grove Creek, Cedar Grove community and Cedar Grove Church and Cemetery. Perhaps nowhere else in Georgia are so many cedars concentrated in such a small area.

The cove, which was named for Robert and John McLemore, sons of a white trader and a Cherokee mother, is just south of Chickamauga Battlefield. One of the Civil War battles took place at Davis Crossroads.

Near Cedar Grove Methodist Church, a large number of Union soldiers spent the night of September 17, 1863, immediately prior to the historic battle of Chickamauga. Another antebellum structure is the 130-year-old plantation-plain style farmhouse where the Hise family has lived for generations. It is located a half mile south of Mt. Hermon Church on Hog Jowl Road. Most of the other old houses and buildings in the cove are not antebellum but date from the 1890's, when the railroad was built through the northern part of the cove.

DIRECTIONS: *Take GA 193 west from LaFayette 8 miles to Davis Crossroads. Note that the best view of McLemore Cove is from GA 157 atop Lookout Mountain.*

~CHICKAMAUGA AND CHATTANOOGA NATIONAL MILITARY PARK.

This park is comprised of four separate battlefield sites—Chickamauga, Point Park, Orchard Knob and Missionary Ridge. The park became the first of four military parks established by Congress between 1890 and 1899, the others being Shiloh, Gettysburg and Vicksburg.

CHICKAMAUGA. [Fig. 4(30)] The Civil War battle of Chickamauga, in the northwest corner of Georgia, was the first of a series of decisive battles that culminated in the fall of Atlanta and brought the Civil War to a close. A Union force of about 58,000 men and a Confederate force of about 66,000 men clashed on the battlefield at Chickamauga on September 19-20, 1863. The result, after 34,000 casualties (3,969 dead), was that the Union Army retreated north to Chattanooga, then a town of about 2,500 people, and the Southern forces occupied Missionary Ridge and Lookout Mountain, which bordered the town. Troops from 29 of the 33 states east of the Rockies engaged in the campaign; four states had troops on both sides.

The Chickamauga Battlefield visitor center has an excellent museum containing artifacts related to the Civil War. It also houses the Fuller Gun Collection, which consists of 355 weapons dating from the Revolutionary War period through World War II. A 26-minute multi-media show is presented daily. Books on Civil War history and four rental audio cassettes are available.

The major points of interest on the Chickamauga Battlefield, which when the battle was fought were small fields, dense woods and thick underbrush, can be reached by following a seven-mile driving tour. Monuments and markers along the road indicate the locations of units and batteries engaged in the battle.

Chickamauga contains remarkable natural environments. In the eastern portion is Georgia's best example of the remarkable "cedar glades," where red cedars dominate an open forest community. The thin soil over a limestone outcrop supports rare and unique prairie plants, some found nowhere else in the state. There are late-summer displays of showy coneflowers and black-eyed susans. The only year-round stream, Cave Springs Creek, has rich aquatic fauna; large

Dogwood
Cornus florida

While common in the Piedmont, dogwood is also a sub-canopy tree in several deciduous forest communities in the mountains. Its wood is very shock-resistant and used in tools and as shuttles in cotton mills. The energy-rich berries fuel migratory birds and feed squirrels.

shell-bark hickories grow along it. Two quarry ponds lie just east of U.S. 27 near its junction with Viniard Road. Several limesinks, or sagponds, occur. The most historic is Bloody Pond, near the southwestern corner of the park. The largest and most interesting limesink is just north of Alexander's Bridge over Chickamauga Creek in the southeast corner of the park. It contains huge 36-inch-diameter willow oaks buttressed at the base. Staff is not available to assist in nature tours.

FACILITIES: *Museum, orientation program, bookshop, guided tours, maps, brochures, driving tour.*

DATES/HOURS: *9 to 5 daily, year round.*

DIRECTIONS: *Exit I-75 at GA 2 and go west about six miles to US 27; go south to the park 1.0 mile from the town of Fort Oglethorpe.*

POINT PARK. [Fig. 4(6)] Point Park, although located in the Cumberland Plateau, is more conveniently treated here. After the Battle of Chickamauga, the Union Army retreated to Chattanooga and the Confederate Army re-formed siege lines around the city with the intention of starving and freezing the Union troops into submission. Point Park, strategically positioned on top of Lookout Mountain, was the location of one of those siege lines. The dominance of the location over the city below cannot be fully grasped until one stands on the edge of Point Park and looks down on Chattanooga. A visit to this park is an opportunity, possible nowhere else in America, to visualize the grand strategy of a major Civil War battle. During the Battle of Lookout Mountain, termed the "Battle Above the Clouds" because during the fighting a band of mist and fog hung around the middle of the mountain, the Union Army drove the Confederates from their position and effectively gained control of the city.

Point Park is on the northeastern tip of Lookout Mountain. The welcome center contains a fine 13' x 30' mural painted by James Walker, an eyewitness to the battle. A tape recording provides a narrative that describes the scene and effectively draws the visitor into the action. The small Ochs Museum in the park displays clothing, equipment and photography pertinent to the battle and has an observation deck which affords a commanding view of the area.

DIRECTIONS: *From I-24 in Chattanooga take the Lookout Mountain exit and follow the signs for Lookout Mountain Parkway (which is Broad Street and also Hwys. 11, 41, 64 and 72). Follow the signs for Ruby Falls (Point Park is past that) and, when past the Falls, pick up the signs for the Cravens House and Point Park. The route goes up the mountain on TN 148 (Scenic Highway).*

ORCHARD KNOB. [Fig. 4(31)] This hill in front of Missionary Ridge was initially the forward position of the Confederate defense line. It was taken by Union forces, and from here General Ulysses Grant commanded the assault on Missionary Ridge. On November 25, 1863, a prearranged signal of six cannon shot from this hill signaled the beginning of the battle for the ridge. Visitors will find a half dozen state monuments and a number of cannon, but the real reason to visit Orchard Knob is the geographical perspective it gives to the fighting between Lookout Mountain and Missionary Ridge.

DIRECTIONS: *Follow Broad Street in Chattanooga to Fourth St. Turn right and pass the Erlanger Medical Center. Turn right onto Orchard Knob Ave. Note that just before Orchard Knob Ave. is Holtzclaw; turn right there to see the National Cemetery.*

MISSIONARY RIDGE. [Fig. 4(32)] Missionary Ridge was occupied by the Confederate forces after the Battle of Chickamauga and was part of the siege line around Chattanooga. During the battle for the city, Union troops attacked and captured the ridge. Along the ridge are remarkable views of Orchard Knob, Chattanooga and Lookout Mountain. Markers, plaques and gun positions give details of troop positions and describe the action in which various units participated. The historical markers are dispersed among elegant houses.

DIRECTIONS: *From Orchard Knob continue on Third St. Turn right on Glenwood and left on Oak, which merges with Shallowford and then intersects with Crest Road to run along Missionary Ridge.*

ADDITIONAL INFORMATION: *Chickamauga and Chattanooga National Military Park, Point Park and Lookout Mountain, National Park Service, P.O. Box 2128, Fort Oglethorpe, GA 30742.*

Cannon and Cannonballs

Timber rattlesnake
Crotalus horridus

One can hike for years in the mountains without seeing a rattlesnake. It is patchy in distribution and lives in isolated areas near rock cliffs where it dens in the winter. This snake is not aggressive and seldom rattles, preferring to be passed by unnoticed. Take care before putting hands and feet in thick, brushy places.

The Armuchee Ridges

Unlike the Cumberland Plateau's broad flat-topped mountains complete with streams, the Armuchee Ridges are true ridges, relatively narrow and linear. The principal ridges are Taylor Ridge, John's Ridge, Horn Mountain and Rocky Face. Roadside ditches along Taylor Ridge are filled with multimillion-year-old fossils from former sea floors. There are also "pockets" or coves, outcrops of iron ore and attractive waterfalls to provide visitors with pleasant travel destinations.

Instead of both sides of these ridges being similar, as in the Cumberland Plateau, here opposite sides are different. For example, on Taylor Ridge the western summit face is sandstone, while the east-face cliffs are hard chert, a non-crystalline quartz. Rocky Face is similar, except that siltstone instead of limestone underlies its western flanks. These differences lead to changes in both topography and plant communities.

Interstate 75 crosses Rocky Face in a deep notch just west of Dalton and continues, crossing Taylor Ridge at the famous Ringgold Cut, where the subsurface rocks are highly visible and fossils are found in the wall of the highway cut adjacent to the southbound lane.

~**TAYLOR RIDGE.** [Fig. 9(1)] Taylor Ridge extends as one geological unit from the village of Holland on GA 100 in Chattooga County northwestward beyond the Tennessee line. Remnant of an ancient, larger ridge which once reached all the way to Lookout Mountain, it eroded over a period of some 200 million years. In the valley between Taylor Ridge and Lookout Mountain are located the towns of Summerville, LaFayette and Ringgold. The ridge is broken by a gap at Ringgold, the Ringgold Cut, where its name is changed to Whiteoak Mountain, although it is the same structure geologically. GA 100 passes the southwest tip of the ridge. It is crossed by US 27 between Gore and Summerville, by GA 136 between Villanow and LaFayette, by I-75 at Ringgold and by several U.S. Forest Service roads. Because of federal ownership both John's and Horn Mountains are in a wildlife management area. Gate closure is seasonal; some gates are open only for hunting.

Geological time periods which can be observed in road cuts are Silurian (the age of fishes) and Mississippian (the carboniferous "coal age" and the age of amphibians).

TAYLOR RIDGE TRAIL. [Fig. 9(2)] 2.4 miles. The trail, for foot traffic only, runs along the ridge to FS 635-A.

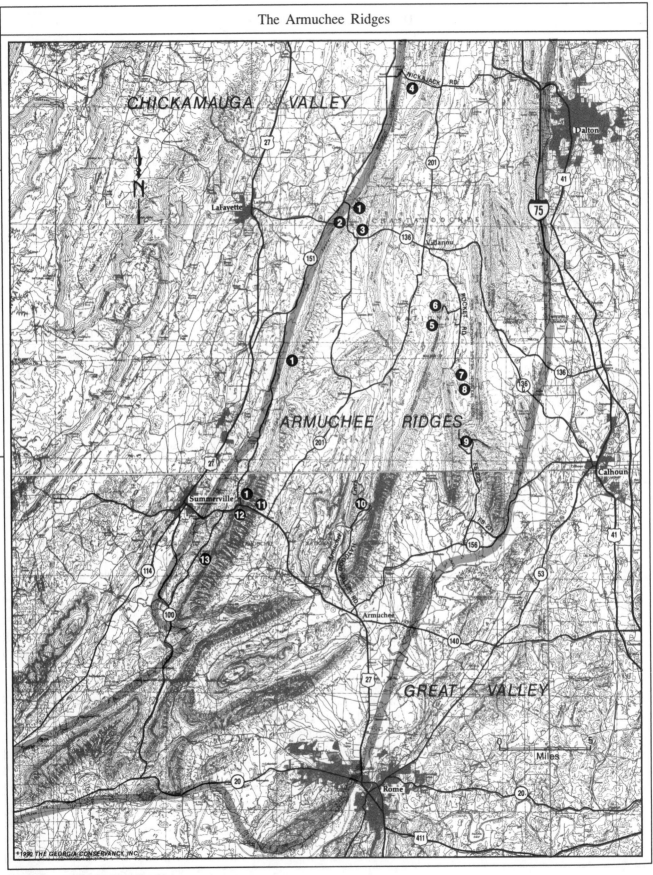

Figure 9 — **ARMUCHEE RIDGES**

Fig. 9 - Armuchee Ridges
(page references in parentheses)

1   Taylor Ridge (29)
2   Taylor Ridge Trail (29)
3   Chickamauga Creek Trail (31)
4   Houston Valley ORV Area (31)
5   Keown Falls Scenic Area & Hike (31)
6   John's Mountain Trail (32)
7   The Pocket Recreation Area (32)
8   The Pocket Trail (32)
9   Hidden Creek Recreation Area (33)
10 Armuchee Creek Canoe Trip (33)
11 Mississippian Fossil Site (34)
12 Silurian Fossil Site (34)
13 James H. "Sloppy" Floyd State Park
    (34)

DIRECTIONS: *Take GA 136 east from LaFayette for about seven miles to the top of Taylor Ridge. Turn right (south) onto FS 217 (at gate). The trail begins at this point in the left fork of the road.*

CHICKAMAUGA CREEK TRAIL. [Fig. 9(3)] 6.2 miles. A loop trail which begins and ends at the end of Ponder Creek Road. Foot travel only.

DIRECTIONS: *Take GA 136 east from LaFayette for nine miles. Turn left onto Ponder Creek Road and go about 0.6 mile. Take the right fork onto FS 219 to the end of the road. The trail can also be reached along FS 250, located at the intersection of GA 136 and Taylor Ridge.*

~**HOUSTON VALLEY ORV AREA.** [Fig. 9(4)] This 2,600-acre off-road-vehicle area has a network of trails for motorbikes and all-terrain vehicles. Timbering is conducted in this area, so visitors are asked to stay on the trails.

DIRECTIONS: *From I-75 take the LaFayette exit 133 west onto GA 136 connector and go seven miles. Turn right at GA 136 and go 11 miles. Turn right onto GA 151 and go six miles to Nickajack Road, located beside Wood Station Volunteer Fire Department. Follow Nickajack Road for two miles, crossing Taylor Ridge. At the base of Taylor Ridge, turn right onto Capehart Road and go one mile until the pavement ends. A parking area for Houston Valley is on the left at the beginning of a USFS gravel road.*

~**KEOWN FALLS SCENIC AREA AND HIKE.** [Fig. 9(5)] This scenic area was set aside because of the unique rock bluffs and high elevation swampy areas formed from springs. Keown Falls, named for land surveyor Gordon Keown, are twin falls located along two spring-fed streams within the 218-acre scenic area. The larger tumbles 60 feet and the smaller about 40 feet. During summer the streams may become dry. A sign posted at the trailhead informs visitors whether the falls are flowing. The area is scenic even when the falls are dry. The 1.8-mile Keown Falls Loop Trail begins and ends at the picnic area parking lot. It is unmarked but easily followed. The northern part of the loop provides views of moisture-loving cove hardwood tree species, and the southern portion gives views of tree species indicative of dry ridges. This trail may be used to access the 3.5-mile John's Mountain Loop Trail, which is marked with white blazes. An overlook at the top of John's Mountain offers a scenic vista of Taylor Ridge, Lookout Mountain and the surrounding valley.

Keown Falls Recreation Area, located adjacent to the scenic area, offers an abundant variety of colorful wildflowers and shrubs. Mountain laurel blooms throughout the late spring and early summer months; both the pink and white varieties bloom in June. Azaleas and dogwood add to the springtime color. The mixture of hickory, sourwood, oak, beech and yellow poplar presents a brilliant spectrum for autumn leaf watchers. The picnic area located in a forest at the foot of John's Mountain has a flowing creek where children can wade and tired hikers can cool their feet.

FACILITIES: *Parking, picnic area with tables and pedestal grills, restrooms, hand pump for water, hiking trail. Maps and brochures available at the U.S. Forest Service office (see below).*

DATES/HOURS: *Dawn to dusk every day, Apr.-Oct. 31 (opening date subject to change).*

DIRECTIONS: *Take GA 136 east from LaFayette 13.5 miles; turn right (south) at Villanow onto Pocket Road; go approximately five miles to the Keown Falls entrance road, FS 202.*

ADDITIONAL INFORMATION: *Keown Falls Recreation Area, U.S. Forest Service, P.O. Box 465, Lafayette, GA 30728. (404) 638-1085.*

JOHN'S MOUNTAIN TRAIL. [Fig. 9(6)] 3.5 miles. This loop trail begins and ends at the John's Mountain Overlook located at the end of FS 208. The trail connects with the Keown Falls Trail above the falls.

DIRECTIONS: *Take GA 136 east from LaFayette for 13.5 miles. Turn right (south) past Vilanow onto a county road (Pocket Road) and go about four miles. Turn right onto FS 208 to the observation deck.*

~**THE POCKET RECREATION AREA.** [Fig. 9(7)] Not to be confused with the Pocket on Pigeon Mountain, it got its name because it lies in a low pocket created by the steep ridges of Horn Mountain, which surrounds it on three sides. From 1938 through 1942 it was the site of a Civilian Conservation Corps camp. The foundations of the old structure are still visible. A large, clear, ice-cold spring bubbles up in the middle of the picnic area and flows through the recreation area as a refreshing creek for wading. Watercress grows abundantly in this spring.

FACILITIES: *Camping, picnicking, hiking, restrooms (handicapped facilities), drinking water.*

DATES/HOURS: *6-1, Apr.-mid Nov.*

SPECIAL EVENTS: *Campfire program on weekends.*

FEES: *Campsites $5.*

DIRECTIONS: *Exit I-75 onto GA 136; go approximately 14 miles west toward Villanow; 0.5 mile east of Villanow, turn left (south) on Pocket Road, county road 230, and go approximately 7 miles past Keown Falls.*

THE POCKET TRAIL. [Fig. 9(8)] A well-maintained and clearly marked hiking trail makes an east 2.5-mile loop from the picnic area along low-lying streambeds and back to the campgrounds. When spring arrives, azaleas, dogwood, sourwood and mountain laurel enliven the area with color. In the fall it is brilliant with the leaves

Beech
Fagus grandifolia

Beech prefers rich, moist soils and is most often found in ravines and along streams. Three altitudinal varieties have been identified. Beech often grows with yellow birch at high elevations and may form stands as on the head of Buck Creek at White Oak Stamp [Fig. 26(57)]. Its nuts feed a variety of wildlife. It was said to be one of the major foods of the extinct passenger pigeon.

of hickory, maple, oak, beech and yellow poplar. The soil's subsurface in this area, made up of white limestone, erodes more easily than the harder rocks which make up the higher elevations in northwestern Georgia. This erosion has resulted in the area's unusual topography.

~HIDDEN CREEK RECREATION AREA. [Fig. 9(9)] The recreation area is located on a creek which appears and runs clear and cool for a day or so, then disappears. The area is a prime example of an oak/hickory forest, with a few beech trees in low-lying areas. There is a wide variety of flowering shrubs and plants. Dogwood, sourwood, hickory, maple, yellow poplar and red oak abound. The varied forest conditions offer excellent opportunities for the birder. There are no hiking trails but many dirt roads to walk.

FACILITIES: *16 campsites with tent pads, picnic tables and fire rings are seldom full, even on weekends; water pump near the entrance; sanitary facilities.*

DATES/HOURS: *Memorial Day - Oct. 31.*

DIRECTIONS: *Exit I-75 onto GA 156 at Calhoun; go southwest for 7.5 miles; turn right (northwest) on FS 231 and go two miles; turn right (north) on FS 228 and go four miles.*

ADDITIONAL INFORMATION: *Hidden Creek Recreation Area, U.S. Forest Service, Armuchee Ranger District, 706 Foster Blvd., LaFayette, GA 30726. (404) 638-1085.*

~ARMUCHEE CREEK CANOE TRIP. [Fig. 9(10)] This is a canoe float through peaceful rural surroundings with excellent fishing for redeye and largemouth bass, red breast bream and catfish. The trip lasts from four to five hours for those who do not fish, and a day or more for those who do. Twenty minutes is required to float from the put-in to the bridge at Ebenezer Church, three hours from the church to US 27 bridge north of Armuchee (an alternate take-out) and an additional hour from there to the take-out in Armuchee. Livestock may be present where the creek winds through a cattle pasture and a pig farm; these are quickly passed, however.

DIRECTIONS: *From Rome take US 27 north to Armuchee; then take the Haywood Valley Road north to Ebenezer Baptist Church; cross the bridge just beyond the church and turn right. Follow this unnamed road to the next bridge, which is the location of the put-in. The take-out is in the Armuchee community. Following US 27 north from Rome, turn left on the first road after crossing the creek. The Armuchee post office is on the right after the turn. Go 0.25 mile to the creek.*

~FOSSIL SITES. This region of Georgia contains numerous fossil deposits. Many are exposed in road cuts which are accessible to the public.

MISSISSIPPIAN SITE. [Fig. 9(11)] From Rome take US 27 north 18.8 miles to the Gore intersection. Go 0.3 mile from Gore, turn right (north) onto a Forest Service road and park almost immediately by a gate. Walk up an old woods road to the left. There are many crinoid stems, some brachiopods, some bryozoa and rare small geodes. At this site the best picking is after a hard rainfall, which tends to expose the fossils.

SILURIAN SITE. [Fig. 9(12)] From the Gore intersection, above, go an additional 1.5 miles; turn left at the top of Taylor Ridge on a Forest Service road; go 0.2 mile. In the road bank on the right find chunks of iron ore containing Silurian cephalopods such as Homotoma. Usually one must break open the ore to find the fossils. They are very small—5 to 15 mm long and 2 to 3 mm in diameter.

~JAMES H. "SLOPPY" FLOYD STATE PARK. [Fig. 9(13)]

The park covers 269 acres at the base of Taylor Ridge. It was named for a Georgia state representative who served in the legislature from 1953 until his death in 1974.

Two fishing lakes have wooden porch swings along their shorelines where visitors can sit and relax. Trails circle each lake. Rental boats are available and private boats are welcome. Only rowing, paddling or trolling motors are permitted. The lakes are stocked with channel catfish, bream and bass and are open for fishing all year round. The park has a program of wildflower planting and an ongoing program for restoring the bluebird population.

FACILITIES: *25 shaded tent and trailer campsites with water and electrical hookups, within walking distance of the lake; a primitive camping area with only water and pit toilets, available for organized groups; two picnic shelters; fishing; boat ramps and docks; boat rental; hiking; playground; trailer dump station.*

DATES/HOURS: *7am-10pm year round; office open 8am-5pm.*

DIRECTIONS: *Two miles south of Summerville on US 27, turn south onto well-marked road to the park.*

ADDITIONAL INFORMATION: *James H. "Sloppy" Floyd State Park, Georgia Department of Natural Resources, Rt. 1, Box 291, Summerville, GA 30747. (404) 857-5211.*

MAP REFERENCES: *USGS 1:100,000 series: Chattanooga - Chickamauga - Rome - Cleveland - Dalton - Cartersville.*

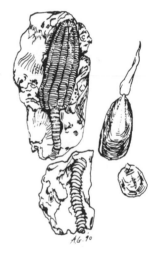

Fossils: Crinoid, Brachiopod and Bryozoan

These ancient life forms lived on ocean bottoms between 300 and 600 million years ago. The crinoid (left) resembles a lily. Pieces of its jointed stalk are common in road cuts on Taylor Ridge [Fig. 9(11)]. Of the other two fossils shown, the clam-like brachiopod is rare in today's seas, but bryozoans (some are called "sea fans") are relatively common around coral reefs.

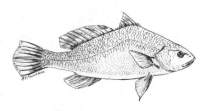

Freshwater drum
Aplodinotus grunniens

This fish, which feeds on crustaceans and shellfish, was captured in great numbers by the Indians in the Coosa River headwaters. It reached a weight of 50 pounds and a length of four feet.

The Great Valley

The Great Valley, situated between the Armuchee Ridges and the Cohutta Mountains, has long presented to all types of life an easy route from the coastal lowlands of Alabama to the north Georgia mountains and farther north into Tennessee and possibly North Carolina. This was true even in prehistoric times, when such animals as barking tree frogs and cottonmouth moccasins moved northward along the sluggish streams, swamps and oxbow lakes of the Coosa River. These watery roads were probably main trading routes between Creek and Cherokee nations. The names of great rivers like Conasauga, Oostanaula, Coosawattee and Etowah attest to their Indian heritage. Etowah Mounds, Georgia's best known Indian village, is near the junction of the Etowah River and Pumpkinvine Creek. The wide bottomlands of the valley, their timbers already killed in many areas by beaver, presented fertile settings for the corn-bean-squash agriculture of the Mississippian period of Indian culture (1000 A.D. - 1500 A.D.). Here in this region Indians trapped great spawning runs of fish such as the small-mouth buffalo and the freshwater drum. Tons of these fish were captured, smoked and dried. The unpolluted rivers were also full of large freshwater clams. Chestnuts, black walnuts and acorns of the lush valley forest, together with abundant game, supplemented the Indian diet.

The first white settlers must have eyed the Great Valley as a land of Eden when they arrived. As settlement of the territory continued, the Coosa River system opened up a large market for the goods grown here.

~**THE CHIEFTAIN'S MUSEUM.** [Fig. 10(1)] Located on the banks of the Oostanaula River, this was the nineteenth-century home of Major Ridge, a prominent Cherokee Indian who, along with his family, operated a ferry boat, owned a store and lived as slave-owner planters. The museum in the white clapboard plantation house contains exhibits describing Ridge's life and the history of Rome and northwest Georgia. Visitors can walk on a paved trail along the river. There is also an archeological dig at the site.
DATES/HOURS: *11-4 Tue.-Sat., 2-5 Sun.; closed Mon.*
FEES: *Adults $1, children free, groups $.75 per person.*
DIRECTIONS: *Located in Rome on Riverside parkway between GA 53 spur and US 27.*
ADDITIONAL INFORMATION: *The Chieftain's Museum, 501 Riverside* Parkway, P.O. Box 373, Rome, GA 30162. (404) 291-9494.

~**MARSHALL FOREST NATURE PRESERVE.** [Fig. 10(2)] Marshall Forest, an old-growth forest with remnants of virgin forest,

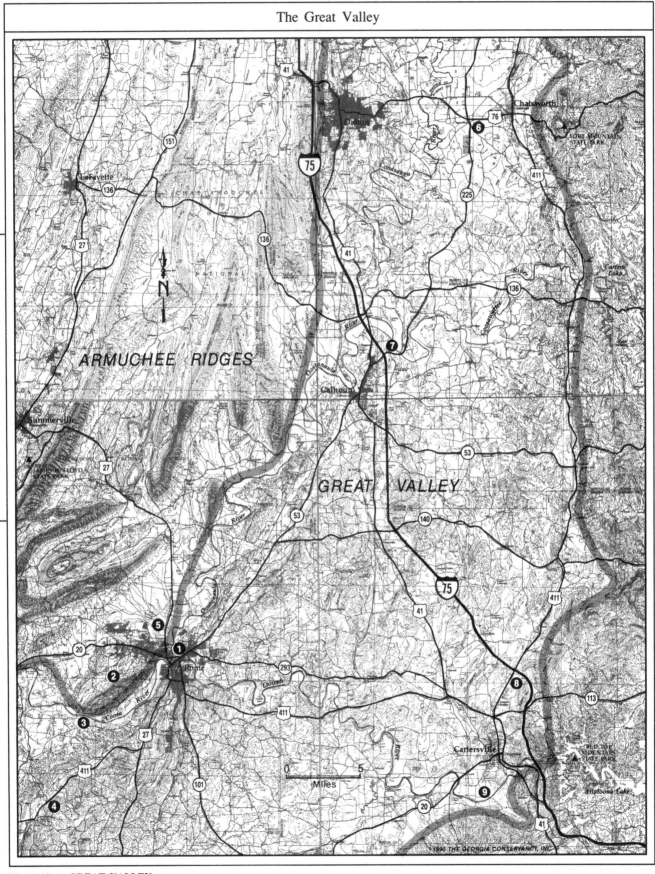

Figure 10 — **GREAT VALLEY**

Fig. 10 - Great Valley
(page references in parentheses)

1 The Chieftain's Museum (35)
2 Marshall Forest Nature Preserve (35)
3 Lock and Dam Park (37)
4 Cave Spring (38)
5 Berry College (driving tour) (39)
6 Vann House (39)
7 New Echota (40)
8 William Weinman Mineral Museum (41)
9 Etowah Mounds (42)

was designated Georgia's first National Natural Landmark in 1966. The 104-acre forest was donated to The Nature Conservancy in 1976 by the Marshall family, who had owned and protected it for nearly a century. About 300 plant species, including 46 tree species, grow here. The trees are a mixture of northern and southern species. Northern red oak and chestnut oak are near the southern limits of their ranges, while longleaf pine is near its northern limit. The forest is home to several rare or unusual species. Access to the area is by special permission or guided tour only. Tours are provided by the Marshall Forest Stewardship Committee and may be arranged by calling the office. Students from several colleges and universities in the state have used the forest as a research site.

There are five trails, but most tours are conducted on the braille trail, which was designed for the visually impaired. Unfortunately, all of the trails are unkept. Lists of plants, birds and trees are available.

FACILITIES: *Tours, braille trail, other trails. Note: Access to the forest is by reservation only.*

DIRECTIONS: *In Rome go west on Shorter Ave. (GA 20); turn south (left) on Horseleg Creek Road. Forest begins approximately 0.5 mile from Rome city limits.*

ADDITIONAL INFORMATION: *Marshall Forest Nature Preserve, The Nature Conservancy, Chamber of Commerce, Rome, GA 30161. (404) 291-0766.*

~LOCK AND DAM PARK. [Fig. 10(3)] Mayo's Bar Lock and Dam were built on the Coosa River at Horseleg Shoals to facilitate the movement of steamboats and barges upstream from Alabama to Rome. As many as 50 steamboats operated on the Coosa River between Rome and Greensport, Alabama, during the mid-to-late 1800's. These had difficulties navigating through shoals located throughout the river. The worst of these was Horseleg Shoals, and local citizens built temporary dams to create a deeper pool of water. Congress ordered a survey of the Coosa River in 1870, but it was not until 1913 that the lock and dam near Rome was completed. By the time of its completion, only three commercial boats remained on the river, and one of these was the Corps of Engineers' dredge. The steamboats turned to transporting passengers for picnics, parties and hunting and fishing trips. River traffic dwindled until the lock was finally closed in 1941.

FACILITIES: *25 campsites equipped for recreational vehicles, fishing, hunting, picnicking, boat launch ramp, boat dock, fuel and supplies, restrooms, canoe rental, trail, handicapped facilities, brochures, maps, restaurant, dump station.*

DATES/HOURS: *8-6 Mon.-Fri., 7-7 Sat.-Sun.; closed Christmas and New Year's Day.*

FEES: *Individual camping $8-$10, groups $1.50 per person ($15 minimum).*

DIRECTIONS: *On the Coosa River 7.5 miles south of Rome. Take US 27 to Walker Mountain Road; turn west; go 3.4 miles to park.*
ADDITIONAL INFORMATION: *Lock and Dam Park, Rome-Floyd County Parks and Recreation Authority, 181 Lock and Dam Road, Rome, GA 30161. (404) 234-5001.*

Entrance to Cave Spring

~CAVE SPRING. [Fig. 10(4)] Cave Spring, settled in 1829, is a picturesque village in beautiful Vann's Valley. Definitely off the beaten track (about eight miles east of the Alabama border, fifteen miles south of Rome), the small community has been able to preserve its charm and integrity from modern development. Over 90 structures in Cave Spring are listed on the National Register of Historic Places.

Cave Spring's original claim to fame is its namesake mineral spring, flowing from a cave in Rolater Park, which covers 29 acres of natural landscape inside the village. Little Cedar Creek flows through the park and village. The park has covered pavilions and picnic tables under beautiful trees. The large limestone cave is a popular attraction. It is open to the public during the summer and boasts a cool temperature of 56 degrees. The mineral spring has a capacity of about four million gallons a day of the "purest water in Georgia, " which is now being bottled and sold in stores. There is a 1.5-acre swimming pool, the second largest in Georgia, which is fed by spring waters. The Hearn Academy Inn is also on park grounds. Begun in 1839 as a dormitory for the Hearn Manual Labor School, it has been restored by the Cave Spring Historical Society, which offers tours of the building during Country Festival Week. Bed and breakfast are available here, as well as catered parties and weddings by reservation.

Also in Cave Spring is the Georgia School for the Deaf. Its first five students were admitted in 1846. The school is still in its original location.

FACILITIES: *Historic village with many old buildings; 29-acre Rolater Park with limestone cave, mineral spring, swimming pool and picnic tables. Hearn Academy Inn features bed and breakfast (404) 777-8439; antique shops in village, including Country Roads Antique Mall, 14,000 square feet; 2 village restaurants feature home cooking.*
SPECIAL EVENTS: *Annual Country Festival and Road Race, second weekend in June, incudes tours of Hearn Academy and arts festival.*
DATES/HOURS: *Rolater Park 7am-9pm year round, staff on duty Memorial Day to Labor Day. Swimming pool 10-5; cave 11-4 and by request.*
FEES: *Pool $1.50, cave $1.*
DIRECTIONS: *On US 411 about 15 miles south of Rome.*
ADDITIONAL INFORMATION: *Hearn Academy and Rolater Park (404) 777-8439.*

~BERRY COLLEGE DRIVING TOUR. [Fig. 10(5)] Berry College was founded around the turn of the century by the remarkable Martha Berry. She lured industrialists such as Henry Ford and politicians such as Teddy Roosevelt here and convinced them to support her efforts to educate rural mountain children getting their first chance at formal schooling. It has one of the largest campuses in the world (28,000 acres). In the early years studies were conducted in log cabins which still stand, well preserved, but now Berry students use 40 more-modern buildings. Most of the property owned by the college is farmland which is worked by students in accordance with the founder's idea that every student should work part time on campus to help defray tuition costs. The campus is testimony to one woman's determination to bring education to children of the mountains. A tour of its grounds and buildings provides the visitor with insight into the isolated, hard, determined and proud nature of life in these hills during the first half of the century. The guard at the main entrance has maps for a self-guided tour. Highlights of this include the Gothic architecture of the Ford Quadrangle; the old mill wheel, one of the largest overshot waterwheels in the world; and picturesque agricultural buildings.
DIRECTIONS: *From Rome, follow US 27 north to the Berry College campus on the left.*
ADDITIONAL INFORMATION: *(404) 232-5374.*

~VANN HOUSE. [Fig. 10(6)] The house built by the Cherokee chief, James Vann, in 1804 and called "Showplace of the Cherokee Nation" is preserved as the Vann House Historic Site. James Vann, son of a Scottish trader and a Cherokee woman, helped establish the Moravian mission at Spring Place in 1801. In sponsoring the mission school, he contributed to the education of the Cherokee young, including several of the nation's future leaders. He was reputed to be generous when sober and pugnacious when drinking—which was often. He was shot at Buffington's Tavern on February 21, 1809, at age 41. He had expected to leave his vast holdings to his young son, Joseph, but the Council of Chiefs intervened to divide the property between his widow and all of his children.

Joseph Vann managed nevertheless to acquire the house and much of his father's other property. An even better businessman than his father, he became known as "Rich Joe Vann" by the Indians and whites alike. During the 1830's push for Indian removal in Georgia, Vann made the mistake of hiring a white man as overseer of his plantation. Thus he unwittingly violated a new Georgia law declaring illegal a white man's working for an Indian. Because of this, his house and land were claimed by the state. During a dispute over ownership between a white boarder in the house and the Georgia Guard, the stairway was set on fire. The charred flooring is still visible.

Berry College Waterwheel

When turned out of their home in Georgia, the Joseph Vann family moved first to a farm he owned in Tennessee and then traveled by steamboat to Webbers Falls, Oklahoma, where he built a duplicate of the Georgia Vann House. That house was also destroyed by Union forces during the Civil War. In the 1840's the federal government, after much litigation, paid Joseph Vann $19,605 for his property in Georgia: a fine brick house, 800 acres of cultivated land, 42 cabins, 6 barns, 5 smokehouses, a grist mill, a sawmill, a blacksmith shop, 8 corn cribs, a shop and foundry, a trading post, a peach kiln, a still, 1,133 peach trees, 147 apple trees and more.

Joseph Vann operated a steamboat line after he moved to Oklahoma. He met his death in October, 1844, when an overheated boiler on his steamboat exploded during a race with another vessel on the Ohio River.

After deteriorating for 150 years, the house and three acres were purchased by the community and presented to the Georgia Historical Commission in 1952. The house was restored and dedicated in July, 1958. Many priceless relics of the family were returned to the house as exhibits.

FACILITIES: *Restrooms and picnic area; brochures and tours available.*

DATES/HOURS: *House open Tue.-Sat. 9-5, Sun. 2-5:30; closed Mon. (except legal holidays), Thanksgiving and Christmas.*

FEES: *Admission $1.50 per adult, children 12 and under $.75, under 6 free. Groups $1.25 per person, children $.50 with advanced notice.*

DIRECTIONS: *Located on the outskirts of Chatsworth between Dalton and Chatsworth at the intersection of GA 225 and GA 52.*

ADDITIONAL INFORMATION: *Vann House Historical Site, Georgia Dept. of Natural Resources, Rt. 7, Box 7655, Chatsworth, GA 30705. (404) 659-2598.*

~**NEW ECHOTA.** [Fig. 10(7)] By 1825 the Cherokee Nation had discarded the tribunal council of chiefs as a ruling body and patterned their government on the republican form of the United States. In November, 1825, the legislature of the Cherokee Nation, which covered the area from eastern North Carolina westward through northern Georgia into northeastern Alabama and eastern Tennessee, established its capital at New Echota. Among the many buildings constructed there were a number of commercial buildings, a legislative hall, a supreme court building and a mission station.

Prior to 1827 Sequoyah created the first written form of the Cherokee language. In response to this, the American Board of Commissions for Foreign Mission, which was based in Boston, underwrote most of the cost of establishing a print shop in New Echota. A member of the board, Samuel A. Worcester, settled in the community in 1827.

New Echota Print Shop

Thirteen years after the establishment of New Echota, the United States Congress ordered the removal of the Cherokees to the West. This forced march in the winter of 1838-39 caused the death of 4,000 people and became known as the Trail of Tears. After this, the town quickly fell into disrepair, and by the 20th century the site was lost.

In the early 1950's a group of Calhoun citizens purchased 200 acres of the original site and deeded it to the state of Georgia. Five buildings have been reconstructed, and guided tours are available.

FACILITIES: *Guided tours, museum with slide show, nature trail, picnic area, bus parking.*

DATES/HOURS: *Open year round, 9-5 Tue.-Sat., 2-5:30 Sun.; closed Mon., Thanksgiving and Christmas.*

FEES: *Adults $1.50, children 6-12 $.75, group rates available.*

SPECIAL EVENTS: *Cherokee Festival, Oct.; New England Christmas, Dec.*

DIRECTIONS: *From I-75 take exit 131 (north of Calhoun) onto GA 225 and go east one mile.*

ADDITIONAL INFORMATION: *New Echota State Historic Site, Georgia Department of Natural Resources, 1211 Chatsworth Highway N.E., Calhoun, GA 30701. (404) 629-8151.*

~WILLIAM WEINMAN MINERAL MUSEUM. [Fig. 10(8)]

This museum, the largest mineral museum in the Southeast, was established in 1983 by the Cartersville Tourism Council with a donation from the family of William J. Weinman, a pioneer in barite mining in Bartow County. It is dedicated to the collection and exhibition of minerals, rocks, gemstones and fossils from Georgia and around the world. It provides lapidary and identification services. Part of the facility is set aside for lapidary research and classroom activities. A new wing and a library were added in 1987, and a new paleontology wing is being planned.

The Georgian Exhibit Hall features a simulated limestone cave with a waterfall that dramatizes the dynamics of cave formation. It also houses a local mining display, local fossil finds and other specimens from Georgia. Many of the exhibits throughout the museum may be touched.

Lectures by a museum consultant on a variety of topics including rock and mineral identification, birthstones, fossils and fossilization and the solar system may be scheduled by appointment.

FACILITIES: *Touch-and-feel exhibits, guided tours on request, film, special lectures by appointment, library, handicapped access, gift and book shop.*

DATES/HOURS: *10-4:30 Tue.-Sat., 2-4:30 Sun.; closed Mon. and holidays.*

FEES: *Adults and children 12 and over $2; seniors $1.50; children 6-12 $1; group rates for 15 or more; 50% discount for children under*

12; 2 free adults with grade school group. Reservations required for groups.

SPECIAL EVENTS: *Annual rock swap, second Sat. in Jun.*

DIRECTIONS: *On the southwest side of the intersection of US 411 and I-75, Exit 26.*

ADDITIONAL INFORMATION: *William Weinman Mineral Museum, Cartersville Tourism Council, P.O. Box 1255, Cartersville, GA 30120. (404) 386-0576.*

~ETOWAH MOUNDS. [Fig. 10(9)] The Etowah Mounds and Village of the Mississippian Indians were occupied between 700 and 1650 and flourished from about 1000 until 1500. Several thousand Indians may have lived in this fortified town at its peak. It was the center of political and religious life in the valley and home to the chiefs who directed the growth, storage and distribution of food.

Three flat-topped ceremonial mounds that served as platforms for temples or residences for chiefs and priests are located on the flood-plain at the juncture of the Etowah River and Pumpkinvine Creek. The village was surrounded by a stockade and deep ditch on all but the river side. It was linked to other Mississippian towns by the Etowah River. Visitors may take a self-guided tour of the mounds. The entire walk is a little over 0.5 mile.

An excellent museum explains the archeological interpretations of the lives of people of the community. Many artifacts, including cer-emonial objects, pottery tools and many shell beads, are on display. This is the only archeological site in northwest Georgia open to the public.

FACILITIES: *Archeological site, museum with audio visual show, maps and brochures, nature walks, bus parking, benches by the river.*

DATES/HOURS: *9-5 Tue.-Sat., 2-5:30 Sun.; closed Mon. (except some legal holidays), Thanksgiving and Christmas Day.*

SPECIAL EVENTS: *Indian skills day (spring); artifacts identification days (Apr. and Nov.); astronomy programs.*

FEES: *Adults $1.50; children 6-12 $.75; group rates available.*

DIRECTIONS: *From I-75 take exit 124 onto GA 61, go through Car-tersville to Indian Mound Road; follow signs to the mounds, six miles.*

ADDITIONAL INFORMATION: *Etowah Mounds Historic Site, Georgia Department of Natural Resources, 813 Indian Mounds Road, S.W., Cartersville, GA 30120. (404) 387-3747.*

MAP REFERENCES: *USGS 1:100,000 series: Chattanooga - Rome - Chickamauga - Cleveland - Dalton - Cartersville.*

Etowah Mounds

Large-flowered trillium
Trillium grandiflorum

The large, white flowers are held erect above the three leaves characteristic of trilliums. Where soils are basic, this trillium is often found in dense colonies.

THE BLUE RIDGE

The Blue Ridge, the Cumberland Plateau and the Valley and Ridge are all part of the Appalachian Mountains—also known as Appalachia.

The part of Appalachia known as the Blue Ridge is technically called the Blue Ridge Province, which should be distinguished from the Blue Ridge Mountains. The Blue Ridge Province, which stretches from northern Georgia to southern Pennsylvania, contains many different mountain ranges. Together, these ranges form what is literally the rooftop of eastern North America. The Blue Ridge Province is shaped somewhat like an elongated teardrop; it is twelve to fifteen miles wide in northern Virginia, but becomes much wider toward the southern end of the region where, across Georgia, North Carolina and Tennessee, the province is more than 70 miles wide.

Running down the eastern edge of the province is the region's namesake range, the Blue Ridge Mountains. This historic mountain range forms an almost unbroken wall which stretches from Georgia through Virginia. For much of its length, the crest of the Blue Ridge Mountains forms the drainage dividing line—known as the Eastern Continental Divide—which separates rivers flowing eastward into the Atlantic Ocean from those flowing westward to the Gulf of Mexico.

The western part of the Blue Ridge Province is made up of several other ranges known collectively as the Unaka Mountains. The Unakas include the Iron Mountains in southwestern Virginia and northeastern Tennessee, the Bald Mountains and Stone Mountains along the Tennessee/North Carolina border and, farther south, the famous Great Smoky Mountains. South of the Smokies are the Unicoi Mountains and, in Georgia, the southernmost component of the Unaka Range—the Cohutta Mountains.

While the Cohuttas, as one segment of the Unaka Range, are part of the Blue Ridge Province's western side, they are geologically and geographically independent of their counterpart range to the east— the Blue Ridge Mountains.

Geologically, the Eastern and Western Blue Ridge sections are divided by a break in the earth's surface called the Hayesville Fault. The Eastern Blue Ridge has more highly metamorphosed rocks (mostly schists and gneisses) than its counterpart. In addition, the Eastern Blue Ridge is more or less one continuous high ridge, while in the Western Blue Ridge the mountains tend to be in isolated groupings. Also, the Western Blue Ridge has a unique feature called the Murphy Syncline, a great trough stretching from the marble quarries near Tate through Ellijay to Blue Ridge, Georgia. This is a long, low, straight pass through the mountains and the easiest major access to the valleys and Tennessee River tributaries lying north of the Blue Ridge.

The Blue Ridge enjoys a botanically rich mixture of temperate climate plants. North meets South in Georgia's mountains, with northern species mixing with their southern kin. Many northern species are at their southern limits here. Within the Southern Highlands is contained the greatest mixture of temperate climate plants in the world, save eastern temperate Asia, located at about the same latitude.

The Blue Ridge is generally part of the Appalachian flyway for birds, especially warblers, tanagers, thrushes and vireos. Because the climate more resembles that of New Jersey than of Georgia, birds nest here that do not nest in the valleys below. Rose-breasted grosbeak, scarlet tanager, dark-eyed junco, chestnut-sided warbler, black-throated blue warbler and black-throated green warbler are but a few examples. These are all birds that nest in the North or in mountainous regions of the South.

Most of the mountain forests managed by the Forest Service lie in the Western and Eastern Blue Ridge, as does all of the wilderness. For details of the history and use of the wilderness, please consult Appendix H. Appendix I addresses the management plan by which the Chattahoochee-Oconee National Forest is currently administered. There the reader will find a brief explanation of how our national forest is zoned in Management Area categories, some being potential wilderness and others lying adjacent to established wilderness.

Scarlet tanager
Piranga olivacea

This beautiful red-bodied bird with black wings breeds only in the high mountains. It passes through the rest of Georgia on migration in the spring and fall.

The Western Blue Ridge

The area known as the Western Blue Ridge includes the Cohutta Mountains and Wilderness, Big Frog Wilderness, Lake Conasauga, Carters Lake, Fort Mountain State Park, Copper Basin, the Rich Mountains and much of the area drained by the lower reaches of the Etowah and Toccoa Rivers. Positioned between the Great Valley and the Eastern Blue Ridge, the Western Blue Ridge section of the Georgia mountains has a character and wildness all its own. Geologically, as part of the southern Unaka Range, some of these mountains have more in common with the Great Smokies to the north than with their immediate sandstone and limestone neighbors to the west or the highly metamorphosed crystalline rock to the east. Because of its diversity, this region offers some of the greatest possibilities for ecological rambling found anywhere in the mountains.

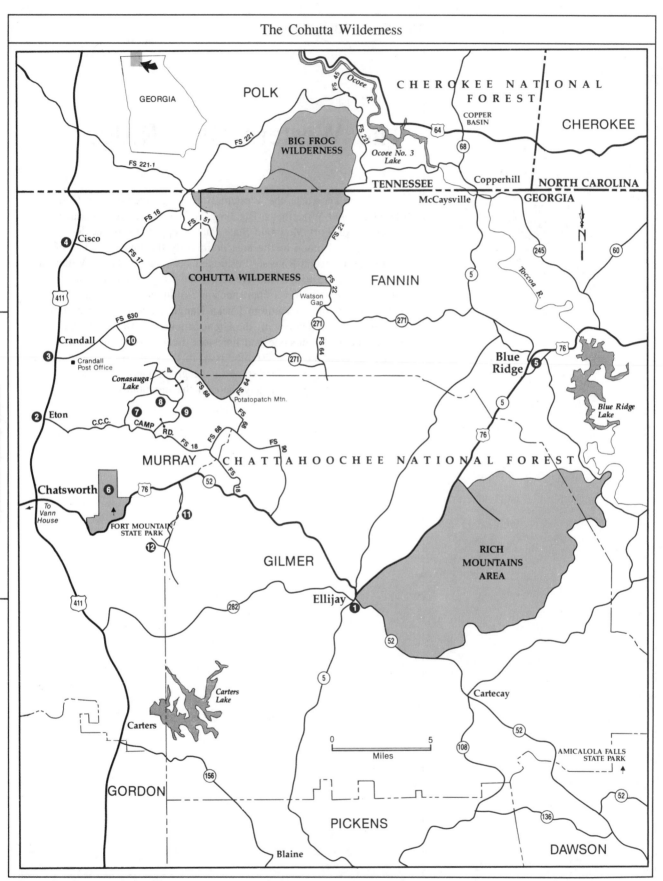

The Cohutta Wilderness

Figure 11 — **COHUTTAS ACCESS**

46

Fig. 11 - Cohuttas Access
(page references in parentheses)

1   Ellijay Access (49)
2   Eton Access (49)
3   Crandall Access (50)
4   Cisco Access (50)
5   Blue Ridge Access (50)
6   Fort Mountain State Park (65)
7   Windy Gap Cycle Trail (52)
8   Milma Creek ORV Trail (52)
9   Tibbs ORV Trail (52)
10   Rocky Flats ORV Trail (53)
11   Tatum Lead ORV Trail (53)
12   **Rocky Creek ORV Trail (53)**

The Cohutta Wilderness

The Cohutta Wilderness covers 37,000 acres (about 60 square miles) that spill over the Georgia/Tennessee border and lie within the 95,000-acre Cohutta Wildlife Management Area. It was designated as a wilderness in 1975. Hemp Top was added in 1986, making this the third-largest mountain wilderness area in the East.

The Cohuttas share a unique distinction with the Rich Mountains in having round, flat-topped ridges and peaks covered with deep, black soils. In most of the Eastern Blue Ridge, on the other hand, the higher the elevation, the rockier and thinner the soils. This characteristic of the Cohuttas profoundly affects the plant communities. Rich-soil ridges are often carpeted with lush ferns and knee-high herbs.

The wilderness is home to a variety of wildlife. Deer and black bears make their home here, as do wild boar and a variety of smaller creatures such as bobcats and squirrels.

T.P.'s Country Store (see Eton access below) and Greg's General Store (see Cisco access below) display the trophies of local hunters and are good places to get a close-up look at some of the kinds of creatures that inhabit the wilderness.

Few of the visitors who enjoy the Cohutta Wilderness realize its history of logging; seventy percent of the area was logged between 1915 and 1930. Three or four logging camps, each with 80 to 100 men, were operated simultaneously in the area. Railroads were built by hand and ran up the Jacks and Conasauga Rivers. Trestles built over the river often were washed away by floods. Bunk cars were winched up hillsides. Logs were skidded out with horses, and cable logging was done in the inaccessible areas. Logging was completed in the Conasauga River drainage in 1928 and started along the Jacks River in 1929. The Depression halted logging for about three years. During that time the loggers worked in the Civilian Conservation Corps building some of the facilities still used in the area. After the Depression, Beech Creek, Rough Creek, Rock Wall, Poplar Creek and Penitentiary Creek areas were logged. The railroads were dismantled and the rails removed in 1937. Remnants of ties and trestles can be found today. Also one can occasionally find dynamite drills in rocks, spikes, cables, steel support rods, horseshoes and old building foundations. While in operation, the Conasauga River Lumber Company sawmill sawed 80,000 board feet a day. It was from this company that the U.S. Forest Service acquired a large portion of the area in 1934 and 1935. Farms have converted back to forests, roads have been turned into hiking trails and the area is returning to the way it was when only native Americans lived here.

WESTERN BLUE RIDGE

The Cohutta Wilderness

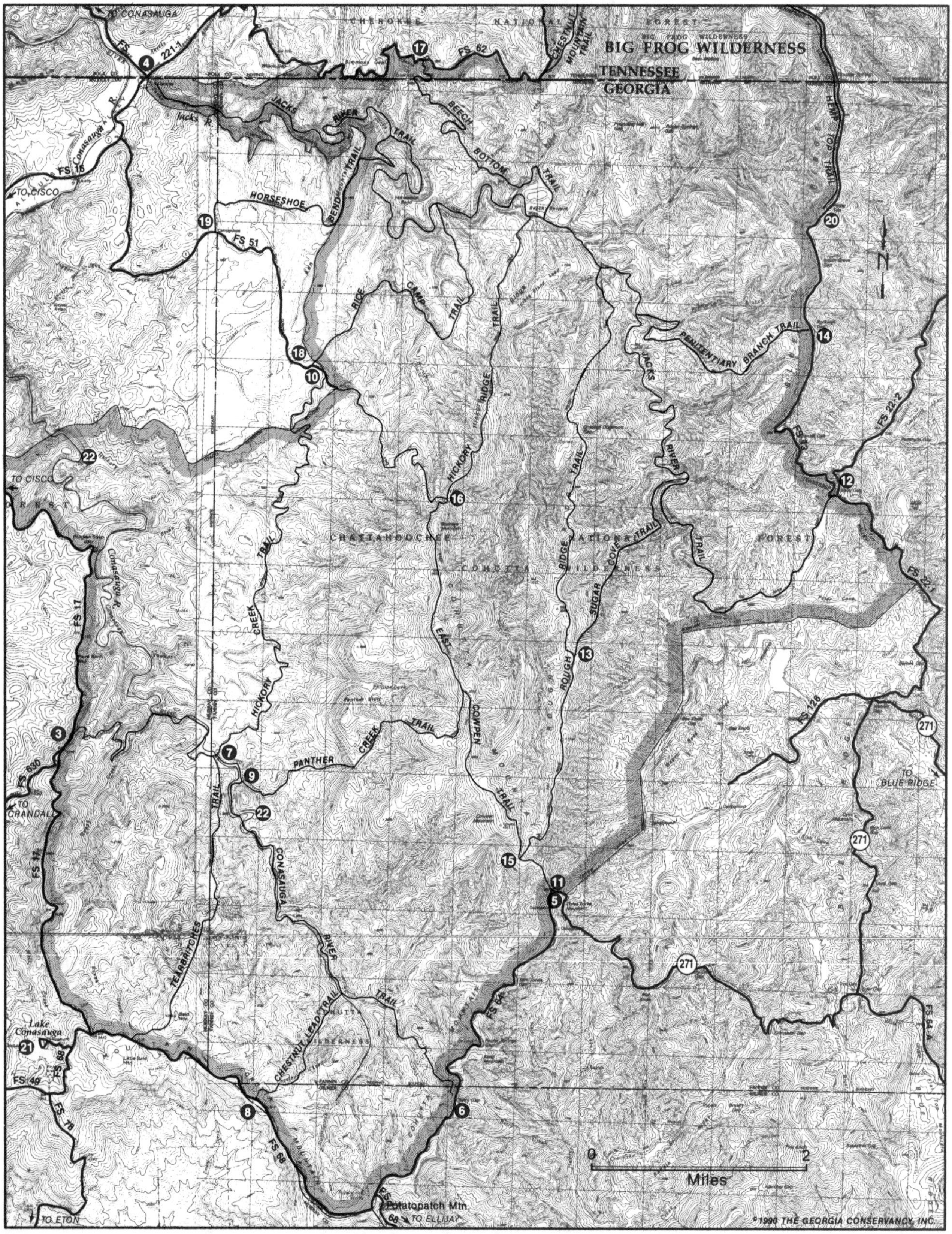

Figure 12 — **COHUTTA WILDERNESS**

Fig. 12 - Cohutta Wilderness
(page references in parentheses)

    3 Crandall Access (50)
    4 Cisco Access (50)
    5 Blue Ridge Access (50)
    6 Conasauga River Trail (51)
    7 Tearbritches Trail (51)
    8 Chestnut Lead Trail (51)
    9 Panther Creek Trail (51)
   10 Hickory Creek Trail (51)
   11 East Cowpen Trail (50, 51)
   12 Jack's River Trail (51)
   13 Sugar Cove Trail (52)
   14 Penitentiary Branch Trail (52)
   15 Rough Ridge Trail (52)
   16 Hickory Ridge Trail (52)
   17 Beech Bottom Trail (52)
   18 Rice Camp Trail (52)
   19 Horseshoe Bend Trail (52)
   20 Hemp Top Trail (52)
   21 Lake Conasauga Recreation Area (55)
   22 Conasauga River (57)

~ACCESS TO THE COHUTTA WILDERNESS. The following guide provides an overview of the Cohutta Wilderness, a way to approach the endeavor before beginning a detailed exploration of any one trail. The map provides information on access roads to the wilderness from five towns and villages on its border. Also shown are Forest Service roads bordering the area and designated trails which cross it. Trailheads are generally well marked and parking areas are provided. All of the roads that border the wilderness are one-lane dirt, sometimes with a coating of loose gravel. They are wide enough for two cars to pass cautiously. Curves are sharp and hard to see around.

Often rock breaks through the road surface, creating a washboard ride. Although a four-wheel-drive vehicle would be the ideal transportation on these surfaces, most cars in good condition will have little trouble. Some roads are closed depending on weather conditions, so it is recommended that one call the Cohutta Ranger District of the U.S. Forest Service at (404) 695-6736 in advance of a trip to check road conditions.

ELLIJAY ACCESS. [Fig. 11(1)] From the Ellijay Square go west on GA 52. At about 0.7 mile, take FS 90 north to FS 68, or go 9.2 miles to FS 18 north, then to FS 68. There is a sign for Lake Conasauga Recreation Area; turn right. After 1.3 miles the pavement ends. At the fork, take the left fork over a one-lane bridge. Continue on FS 18, which is marked just across the creek. At 3.5 miles is an intersection where FS 68 turns sharply to the right. Take FS 68 turning up a steep incline. At mile 4.5 is a nice level picnic or camping area, and at mile 5.7 is Holly Creek Checking Station. Soon, at mile 6, the road forks, with FS 90 going to the right; stay on FS 68. Find Barnes Creek Picnic Area for day use at mile 7.2; a wooden platform extends out over a small waterfall. At mile 9.5 is the intersection marked Potato Patch Mountain on the map.

ETON ACCESS. [Fig. 11(2)] From Chatsworth take US 411 north to Eton. Turn right at the only traffic light onto Fourth Avenue (GA 286 ends here). Set the odometer at 0.0 where Fourth Avenue begins at US 411. Mile 1.1, Grassy Mountain intersects from the left. Mile 1.5, the road forks at T.P.'s Country Store; bear left on the CCC Camp Road. Mile 3.8, Crandall Road intersects from left. At mile 4.2 Cool Springs Road intersects from right. At mile 5.1, the road, still CCC Camp Road, passes through a scenic valley with Fort, Beaver and Tatum Mountains in the background. The pavement ends at mile 6.1. Mile 7 is the start of a nice drive along a creek. At mile 7.2 the view looking upstream through the trees at Holly Creek is a fine sight. Mile 10.3 is the intersection of FS 18 and FS 68. (Note the CCC Camp Road and FS 18 at some point become the same road). From this point, refer to the Ellijay Access (above) beginning at mile 3.5. If there is time for exploring only one access point to the Cohutta Wilderness, this should be it. The valley drive and the drive along the creek make this one of the most visually rewarding ways to approach the wilderness.

CRANDALL ACCESS. [Fig. 11(3) Fig. 12(3)] From Chatsworth take US 411 north. Pass through Eton approximately 2.5 miles. Watch for a green and white sign marked "Crandall" on the right. Cross railroad tracks and turn right. Take first left at post office (note USFS sign for Lake Conasauga). Set the odometer at 0.0 here. The paved road ends at mile 0.5. Mile 6.7, Hickey Gap. Mile 8.9, intersection with FS 17.

CISCO ACCESS. [Fig. 11(4);Fig. 12(4)] GA 2 intersects US 411 here at Greg's General Store in Cisco. Set the odometer at 0.0 here. Go east toward the Cohuttas as if continuing on GA 2. At mile 0.7 pass county road 169 on the right. Mile 1 marks the end of the pavement. Take the right fork at the "Y" intersection at mile 1.6. (County road 210 bears left.) At mile 3.2, FS 17 comes in from the right, FS 16 goes left. Follow FS 16 just across the state line into Tennessee to the start of Jacks River Trail (note FS road 51 branches to right just after crossing the river. Stay left on FS 16).

BLUE RIDGE ACCESS. [Fig. 11(5), Fig. 12(5)] Set the odometer at 0.0 at the intersection of US 76 and GA 5 in Blue Ridge. Go north on GA 5. Take old SR 2, which turns to the left at mile 3.2. At mile 6.9 are Fightingtown Creek and McKinney Crossing. At mile 11.3 the pavement ends. At 13.3, after a long climb up the mountain, look for the sign, "Cohutta Wildlife Management Area, Watson Gap." Bear left on FS 64. Mile 17.6 marks Dyer Gap. Where FS 64-A forks to the left, stay on FS 64, the right fork. At mile 18.3, cross the south fork of the Jacks River. At mile 18.4, FS 64-B intersects on the left. At mile 20.2, the Mountain Town Creek Trail is on the left. At mile 22.9, reach Three Forks [Fig. 12(11)] and East Cowpen Trail.

~HIKING TRAILS OF THE COHUTTA WILDERNESS. With 95 miles of trails, the Cohutta Wilderness is a hiker's dream come true. All the trails are blazed and easy to follow, with the exception of Jacks River Trail downstream from the falls. After heavy rains, both the Jacks and Conasauga Rivers can become raging torrents, virtually impossible to cross safely. Those planning a hike to the Cohutta Wilderness should watch weather forecasts carefully. Use a walking stick or staff to help cross rivers, and if water is raging, do not even try. In bad weather a trip may get extended. Be prepared for this possibility with extra food. Make sure people know the route of the hike and expected time of return. Even in low water, plan on getting wet. For example, the Conasauga River Trail between Betty Gap and FS 17 has 38 river crossings. Hiking boots will quickly become soggy footweights. Many experienced hikers on

Bobcat
Felis rufus

Along with the red and gray foxes, the bobcat is a principal predator at the top of the food chain, which begins with colonization of a fallen leaf by bacteria and fungi on the forest floor. While the bobcat will occasionally attack deer, it cannot effectively control their numbers—a job once handled by cougars and wolves.

Rose-breasted grosbeak
Pheucticus ludovicianus

Fortunate bird watchers may see this spectacular bird in the summer. It breeds in our higher mountains in deciduous forests. The male is startlingly colored, with a large rose chest bib against a snow white breast, and with black head and back.

the Conasauga and Jacks River Trails wear old tennis shoes and simply resign themselves to having wet feet. Bring dry shoes for camp.

Camping is permitted anywhere except in the trails and at trailheads. The trick is to find a spot flat enough. Fires are permitted using dead and down wood only. No permits are required. Please obey wilderness regulations posted on bulletin boards at trailheads. Horses are prohibited on certain trails. These trails are also posted on bulletin boards.

Text mileages are from Tim Homan's book, *The Hiking Trails of North Georgia*. Homan's figures are regarded as accurate, since he walked and rewalked the trails using a measuring wheel.

Wilderness maps are available from the U.S. Forest Service District Office in Chatsworth or from patrolling Forest Service officers.

CONASAUGA RIVER TRAIL. [Fig. 12(6)] From Betty Gap to the parking area at Forest Service Road 17, 13.1 miles. A popular hiking trail. Bray Field [Fig. 12(7)] can accommodate perhaps 100 campers.

TEARBRITCHES TRAIL. [Fig. 12(7)]. From FS 68 to Hickory Creek Trail [Fig. 12(10)]. From the parking area at FS 68 to the Conasauga River Trail is 3.4 miles.

CHESTNUT LEAD TRAIL. [Fig. 12(8)] From the parking area at FS 68 to its junction with the Conasauga River Trail, 1.8 miles. Provides a good look at skeletons of giant chestnut trees that thrived in this forest before the chestnut blight.

PANTHER CREEK TRAIL. [Fig. 12(9)] From the Conasauga River Trail to the East Cowpen Trail, 3.4 miles. This popular trail passes a high waterfall.

HICKORY CREEK TRAIL. [Fig. 12(10)] From the trailhead at FS 51 to trailhead at FS 630, 8.6 miles.

EAST COWPEN TRAIL. [Fig. 12(11)] From the parking area at Three Forks to the trailhead at FS 51, 7 miles. A good high-elevation trail, it follows the former route of old GA 2, on which erosion control was done before it was closed. Though not necessarily a good destination trail, it can provide relatively quick access to other trails.

JACKS RIVER TRAIL. [Fig. 12(12)] From the parking area at Dally Gap to the trailhead in Alaculsy Valley, 16.7 miles. The longest and wettest trail in the Cohutta Wilderness, it crosses the river 40 times. It is often crowded at the falls. The least-used portion of the trail is from Alaculsy to Jacks River Falls. In the middle of Horseshoe Bend are several beautiful spots to camp.

SUGAR COVE TRAIL. [Fig. 12(13)] From Rough Ridge Trail to Jacks River Trail, 2.2 miles.

PENITENTIARY BRANCH TRAIL. [Fig. 12(14)] From the Hemp Top Trail to Jacks River Trail, 3.5 miles.

ROUGH RIDGE TRAIL. [Fig. 12(15)] From East Cowpen Trail to Jacks River Trail, seven miles.

HICKORY RIDGE TRAIL. [Fig. 12(16)] From East Cowpen Trail to Jacks River Trail, 3.5 miles. Not heavily used.

BEECH BOTTOM TRAIL. [Fig. 12(17)] From FS 62 to its junction with the Jacks River Trail, four miles.

RICE CAMP TRAIL. [Fig. 12(18)] From FS 51 to the Jacks River Trail, 3.9 miles.

HORSESHOE BEND TRAIL. [Fig. 12(19)] From FS 51 to the Jacks River Trail, three miles. Not heavily used.

HEMP TOP TRAIL. [Fig. 12(20)] From the trailhead at Dally Gap to Big Frog Mountain, six miles. Not heavily used.

~OFF-ROAD-VEHICLE TRAILS ON THE COHUTTA RANGER DISTRICT.

WINDY GAP CYCLE TRAIL. [Fig. 11(7)] five miles. Designed for experienced trail bikers. Take US 411 north from Chatsworth for four miles. Turn right (east) at the traffic light in Eton and go about five miles. Turn left on FS 218 (Muskrat Road) and travel three miles to the trailhead. The north portion is unsuitable for three- and four-wheelers. They must use Milma Creek to Tibbs Trail.

MILMA CREEK ORV TRAIL. [Fig. 11(8)] Four miles. Suitable for all-terrain vehicles. Connects Windy Gap Cycle Trail and Tibbs Trail. Access is by Windy Gap Cycle Trail. See directions above.

TIBBS ORV TRAIL. [Fig. 11(9)] Five miles. Suitable for all-terrain vehicles. Note that this trail is closed by a gate at both ends. Access through Windy Gap Cycle Trail and Milma Creek ORV Trail. See directions above.

ROCKY FLATS ORV TRAIL. [Fig. 11(10)] Five miles. Suitable for 4-wheel-drive vehicles. Trail is three miles east of Crandall off Mill Creek Road (FS 630) on the right.

TATUM LEAD ORV TRAIL. [Fig. 11(11)] Seven miles. Suitable for 4-wheel-drive vehicles, motorbikes and all-terrain vehicles. Trail deadends on private property with no outlet. Take GA 52 east from Chatsworth nine miles. The trail is located 0.5 mile past the Cohutta Lodge on the right.

ROCK CREEK ORV TRAIL. [Fig. 11(12)] Two miles. Reached from SR 52 off the Tatum Lead Trail, or take FS 3 past Peeples Lake. The trail is about 0.25 mile south of the low water bridge on Rock Creek. Suitable for all-terrain vehicles and cycles.

Hellbender
Cryptobranchus alleganiensis

This grotesque creature is Georgia's largest salamander, over 20 inches long. It lives under rocks in well-oxygenated mountain streams, but only in Tennessee River tributaries on the north side of Georgia's Blue Ridge.

WESTERN BLUE RIDGE

Jack-in-the-pulpit
Arisaema triphyllum

This common biennial with the unusual flowers has red berries which are similar to those of ginseng. Although called Indian turnip, the thick root contains needle-like crystals of calcium oxalate, which is extremely irritating.

Lake Conasauga

Nineteen-acre Lake Conasauga [Fig. 12(21)], located at 3,150 feet, near the summit of Grassy Mountain, is the highest lake in Georgia. The name Conasauga is derived from the Cherokee word *kahnasagah*, meaning "grass, sparkling water or strong horse," according to various sources. Grassy Mountain, at 3,682 feet, is one of the higher mountains in the area, and the grassy Ball Field is nearby.

Conasauga River and Lake Conasauga do indeed sparkle. The metaphor of a strong horse may come from the river overflowing its banks and flooding after heavy rain. Whatever the source, a river, lake and several ancient Indian settlements in the area share the name Conasauga.

Lake Conasauga, the picnic area and U.S. Forest Service roads 17, 18 and 68 were constructed by the Civilian Conservation Corps during the administration of Franklin D. Roosevelt.

A fully developed Forest Service campground is available. The 35 campsites have tent pads. Restrooms and cold running water are centrally located. Most of the sites are not on the lake, but are very close. This is a heavily used campground, and on busy summer weekends it is likely to be full. There is an overflow camping area. No water is available but there are portable toilets. The group camping area is a large grassy field without tables, grills or water.

The entire recreation area is accessible from the day-use area, which has a restroom, water, tables, grills, two covered shelters and a parking lot. The large, heavily used but rarely full picnic area offers quiet solitude a short walk from the car. Food and equipment must be carried to the picnic tables and shelters, which are some distance from the parking area. At the lake there is a developed swimming area with a dock and pea-gravel bottom. There is no beach for sunbathing, but a pleasant grassy ledge instead. Swimming is restricted to the marked swimming area. The water remains cool most of the summer, though by July 4 it is quite comfortable.

Off the picnic road is a boat ramp and parking-lot access road. The lake is limited to electric motors, rowing and paddling. It is a great place to canoe or raft.

Although the lake is heavily fished, some very large bass live in the deeps. Rainbow trout are stocked, and bream and crappie are also present.

~LAKE CONASAUGA RECREATION AREA. [Fig. 12(21)] A Song Bird Management Area, where the trees and other vegetation are managed to provide the best bird habitat. Over 100 species of birds can be seen. These include hawks, owls, woodpeckers, kinglets, thrushes, vireos, warblers, cuckoos, phoebes, flycatchers, chickadees, titmice, nuthatches, brown creepers, wrens, tanagers, grosbeaks,

Red-tail hawk
Buteo jamaicensis

Although the broad-winged hawk may be more common, the red-tail is more visible as it circles high above the mountain forests, often emitting a high-pitched, piercing whistle. The brick-red tail of the adult can often be seen as the hawk circles and dips. Its primary food is squirrels and other rodents. During cold fronts, thousands of these and other raptors ride the updrafts southward along the Appalachian escarpments and ridges to winter in the southeastern states.

Tractable and easily trained, it is the raptor of choice for beginning falconers.

The broad-wing is the only other hawk as commonly seen in the mountains as the red-tail.

indigo buntings and red crossbills. A checklist of the birds is available from the Cohutta Ranger District Office.

Like most of Georgia's highlands, the elevation, climate, vegetation and nesting birds of Lake Conasauga are similar to those in Pennsylvania. Georgia's mountains are the approximate southern limit for eastern hemlock and eastern white pine. This is an excellent area in which to see a wide range of trees, shrubs, herbs and flowers representative of the southern highlands, including the yellow and black birch and mountain camellias. A plant list is available from the Ranger District Office.

FACILITIES: *Parking, camping, picnicking, swimming, boating (electric motors only) canoeing, fishing, trails, drinking water, restrooms.*

DATES/HOURS: *Paid campsites open second Fri. in Apr.-last weekend in Oct. Overflow camping area open all year.*

FEES: *Campsite $5.*

DIRECTIONS: *From Chatsworth, take US 441 north four miles; turn right (east) at traffic light at Eton; follow this country road making no turns until the pavement ends and it becomes FS 18; turn left (northeast) on FS 68 for 10 miles. From Ellijay take US 52 west from the square for about seven miles to FS 18, marked with a sign for Lake Conasauga Recreation Area. Follow the paved road. Where the pavement ends, cross one-lane bridge. FS 18 marked here. Continue to the junction with FS 68; turn right and follow the signs to Lake Conasauga.*

ADDITIONAL INFORMATION: *U.S. Forest Service, Cohutta Ranger District, 401 Old Ellijay Road, Chatsworth, GA 30705. (404) 695-6736.*

~HIKING TRAILS AROUND LAKE CONASAUGA.

LAKE CONASAUGA TRAIL. 1.2 miles. An easy walk around the lake, passing through tunnels of rhododendron and crossing picturesque bridges. Interesting ferns, wild flowers, shrubs, trees, birds and scenic views of the lake are found along the trail.

GRASSY MOUNTAIN TOWER TRAIL. 1.6 miles. From the dam on Lake Conasauga to the old fire tower atop Grassy Mountain, this trail makes an easy ascent along the ridge. To the west are excellent views of the wilderness and valley.

SONGBIRD TRAIL. Two miles. This trail begins at the overflow, then runs along a small brook and around a beaver swamp through the Songbird Management Area, a series of clearcuts which provide a variety of vegetation valuable to many songbirds. Interpretive nature walks are offered on certain Saturday afternoons between Memorial Day and Labor Day.

Tufted titmouse
Parus bicolor

This is a small, vigorous sprite of a bird that inhabits deciduous forests, especially along streams. Its predominately gray color and topknot are good field characteristics. Since it nests in tree holes, it is an example of animal life that finds old-growth forests attractive.

~THE CONASAUGA RIVER. [Fig. 12(22)] The Conasauga River is born deep in the Cohutta Wilderness. From its inception, it flows north through a series of almost inaccessible steep gorges before reaching the Alaculsy Valley. Here it appears to rest for a couple of miles before its confluence with the Jacks River and return to whitewater. This upper section offers beautiful rough-country hiking. Considered uncanoeable by most, at very high water levels it provides a few hardy souls a wildwater experience hard to beat. The section beginning where the Conasauga leaves the valley at its confluence with the Jacks is much more suited to recreational paddling. Here the river turns westward to cut across several ridges before bending south to join the Coosawattee and eventually become part of the Coosa River system.

This is a crystal clear mountain stream which during the summer lacks sufficient water for easy navigation by canoe. Most of the rapids are intricate Class I or Class II mazes—excellent water to help sharpen water reading skills. There is one Class III rapid thrown into the middle of the run to keep paddlers alert on this exceptionally scenic river.

The Conasauga is normally high enough to run during the winter and spring months. Even at these higher levels it will remain clear. Since this river rises rapidly in time of flood, avoid putting in if it is cloudy and turbid. There are no specific hazards for intermediate or advanced canoeists, although the one Class III rapid could cause problems for less-experienced paddlers. Cold-weather paddling trips are for experienced groups only. Full wet-suit protection and complete safety and first-aid gear are essential.

DIRECTIONS: *Travel north on US 411 over the Georgia state line. The Conasauga River bridge, which is the take-out point, is just a couple of miles across the line in Tennessee. To return to the put-in, continue north on US 411 to the first paved road on the right next to a service station. This is Sheeds Creek Road; turn right. The pavement soon ends, but the roadbed is solid and will present no problems. Follow this same road for about seven miles over several ridges until it drops down into a small valley. Several camping areas as well as the river will be visible on the right, followed by a large steel bridge. This is the Jacks River Bridge and marks the confluence of the Jacks and Conasauga Rivers. There are several good launch sites in this area.*

WESTERN BLUE RIDGE

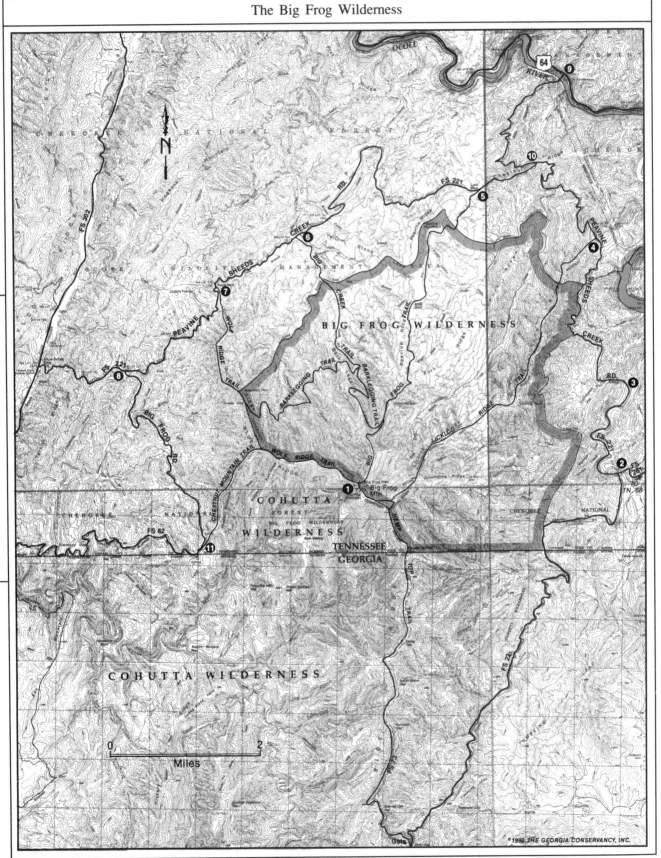

Figure 13 — **BIG FROG WILDERNESS**

Fig. 13 - Big Frog Wilderness
(page references in parentheses)

1   Big Frog Mountain (59)
2   FS 221 intersection with FS 251 (59)
3   Tumbling Creek Campground (59)
4   Licklog Ridge Trail (59)
5   Big Frog trailhead (59)
6   Big Creek trailhead (59)
7   Wolf Ridge trailhead (59)
8   Big Frog Road (59)
9   Ocoee River rafting put-in (59)
10 Intersection of FS 221 and Peavine-
    Sheeds Creek Road (59)
11 Chestnut Mountain Trail (60)

The Big Frog Wilderness

The Cohutta Wilderness extends into Tennessee as far as the Eastern Continental Divide. Protruding from it is the isolated hulk of Big Frog Mountain [Fig. 13(1)]. Big Frog is not a high mountain (4,224 feet), but like Grassy Mountain (3,692 feet) in the Cohuttas it appears more dominant because it stands alone. Lacking the protection of other mountains, it receives the full impact of cold fronts and other climatic events. In addition it receives high rainfall. Big Frog is a scenic mountain. The top is forested; northern hardwoods are present, as is a boulderfield on the north side.

Big Frog was designated a wilderness by Congress in 1984 and expanded in 1986. It totals 8,055 acres, 83 of which are in Georgia.

~ROAD ACCESS AND HIKING ACCESS TO BIG FROG WILDERNESS.

COPPERHILL ACCESS. From Blue Ridge take GA 5 north to the Tennessee line. Pass through Copperhill and in about two miles take GA 251 west. Cross the Ocoee River and continue on GA 251 for 5.8 miles. Cross Tumbling Creek and intersect FS 221 [Fig. 13(2)]. Turn north on FS 221, Peavine-Sheeds Creek Road. Off this road, pass five trailheads to Big Frog Mountain. Note that at each trailhead, the distance from the trailhead to Big Frog Summit is given. Set the odometer at 0.0. At 2 miles, pass Tumbling Creek Campground [Fig. 13(3)]; at 5.6 miles reach Licklog Ridge Trail [Fig. 13(4)] (5.6 miles to summit); at 8.4 miles reach Big Frog trailhead [Fig. 13(5)] (5.2 miles to summit); at 13.2 miles reach Big Creek trailhead [Fig. 13(6)] (5.2 miles to summit); at 14.8 miles reach Wolf Ridge trailhead [Fig. 13(7)] (7.6 miles to summit; at 17.2 miles pass the turnoff on Big Frog Road (gated) [Fig. 13(8)]; at 18.8 miles reach a fork in Alaculsy Creek Valley. Turn south on FS 221. Just north is the Sylco Campground. Continue down FS 221 but go straight when FS 221 turns west at 22.8 miles. One will reach Ciscoon on US 411 in 8 to 10 miles.

CHATSWORTH ACCESS. The Big Frog trails can be reached from Chatsworth by reversing the above directions.

OCOEE RIVER ACCESS. From Copperhill north on TN 68 go 28 miles to US 64 intersection. Take US 64 west and go eight miles. Take the first left road [Fig. 13(9)] after the highway begins running along the river. Just below this is the put-in for rafting the famous Ocoee River. After crossing the river one passes the USFS Thunder Rock Campground. Go four miles to intersect the Peavine-Sheeds Creek Road, FS 221 [Fig. 13(10)], between Licklog Ridge (east) and

Big Frog (west) trailheads. Note: It is well worth a few moments to drive down the Ocoee River Gorge just to watch the rafts go by. This whitewater trip rivals the Chattooga in excitement, but not as a wilderness experience, since US 64 closely follows the Ocoee.

CHESTNUT MOUNTAIN TRAIL. [Fig. 13(11)] Approximately 10 miles east of US 411 on FS 221, Peavine-Sheeds Creek Road, turn east on FS 62 and go six miles to the trailhead. Hike 3.2 miles to Big Frog summit along Chestnut Mountain and Wolf Ridge.

MAP REFERENCES: *For Cohuttas and Rich Mt., USGS 1:100,000 series: Cleveland - Dalton - Cartersville, USGS 1:24,000 series: Cashes Valley - Blue Ridge - Wilscot - Ellijay - Tickanetley - Noontootla. For Big Frog, USGS 1:24,000 series: Epworth - Ducktown - Hemp Top - Caney Creek. County Highway Maps: Gilmer - Murray - Fannin - Gordon.*

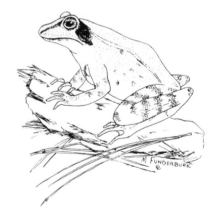

Wood frog
Rana sylvatica

This northern animal is found in our Blue Ridge at the extreme southern limits of its range. Its black head patches are characteristic. Key to the survival of this very shy frog is midwinter breeding, which gives it a head start in surviving both competition and predation.

Carters Lake

Located 12 miles south of Chatsworth off US 411, 3,500-acre Carters Lake [Fig. 14(1)] was constructed by the U.S. Army Corps of Engineers in 1977. The lake provides many recreational opportunities including boating, swimming, camping, hiking and fishing. A large area near the dam on the south shore has been developed by a concessionaire as the Blue Ridge Mountain Marina Resort. In a road cut below the dam one can see the Cartersville-Great Smoky Fault where Western Blue Ridge rocks rest against those of the Great Valley.

DATES/HOURS: *The Resource Manager's office and visitor center is open year-round Mon.-Fri. 8-4:30; summer, Sat. and Sun. 10-6.*
DIRECTIONS: *Access via GA 136 east from US 411. Follow signs.*
ADDITIONAL INFORMATION: *Contact the Resource Manager's office, Carters Lake, P.O. Box 86, Oakman, GA 30732. (404) 334-2248.*

~CAMPING AT CARTERS LAKE. A map is available at the Resource Manager's office. Here also, reservations can be made for campsites at Doll Mountain and Woodring Branch.

HARRIS BRANCH PARK. Group camping only. Shelter, 6 tables, large grill, 10 tent pads, running water, 2 comfort stations. Public beach open daily Apr. until mid Sept. Reservations required. Gates open at 9 and close at 9. Closed Oct.-Mar.

DOLL MOUNTAIN PARK. 65 campsites, 28 with electrical and water hookups; two comfort stations with shower facilities and a recreational dump station. Fee: $9 for those campsites with electrical hookups, $7 for those without. Gate open 9am-10pm. Closed Oct.-Mar.

RIDGEWAY PARK. 22 primitive campsites with pit toilets, boat ramp and dock. Accessible by dirt road only. No charge.

WOODRING BRANCH. 31 campsites, all with electrical and water hookups; comfort station and boat ramp. Another 12 campsites with pit toilets and a hand-operated water pump are available.
FEES: *$9 with water and electrical hookups; $7 without.*
DATES/HOURS: *Gate open 9am-10pm. Closed Nov.-Mar.*

~HIKING AT CARTERS LAKE. A map is available at the Resource Manager's office.

HIDDEN POND TRAIL. About 0.5 mile. The trail was constructed to provide access sites for bird watchers. Two bridges are

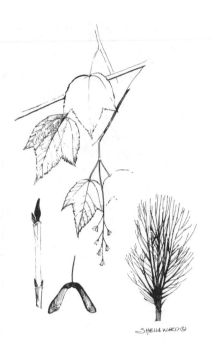

Striped maple
Acer pensylvanicum

This is the more common of our two high-altitude maples, seldom growing below 2,200 feet. It is a shrub, or small tree, with bright green bark striped with white lengthwise. Seeds, twigs and leaves are browsed by several kinds of animals.

WESTERN BLUE RIDGE

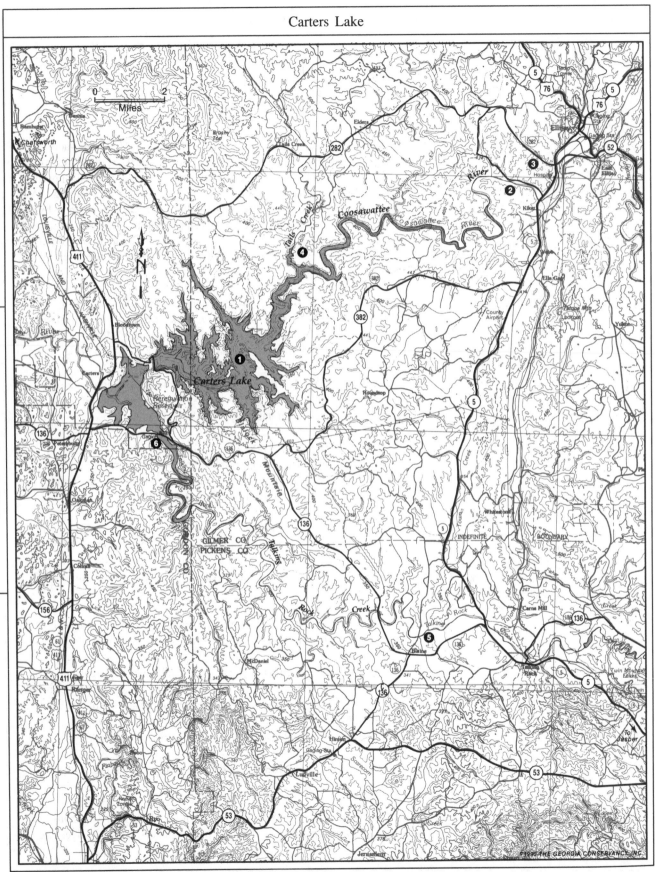

Figure 14 — **CARTERS LAKE**

Fig. 14 - Carters Lake
(page references in parentheses)

1 Carters Lake (61)
2 The Coosawattee River (63)
3 Gilmer County Park (64)
4 Tumbling Waters Nature Trail/Ridgeway access area (63, 64)
5 Talking Rock Creek (64)
6 Reregulation reservoir below Carters Lake dam (64)

part of the trail; one 20-foot bridge spans the stream near the entrance to the management area and a 210-foot structure goes across a beaver pond. An observation platform upstream at the edge of a second beaver pond provides a view of an active beaver lodge and offers an excellent opportunity for viewing water fowl. Located near the entrance to the management area.

TUMBLING WATERS NATURE TRAIL. [Fig. 14(4)] Approximately one mile through a secluded valley carved by a mountain stream. The trail includes two viewing platforms located above a cliff from which hikers can view Tails Creek cascading into Carters Lake. Trailhead located in Ridgeway Park.

BIG ACORN NATURE TRAIL. About 0.5 mile. Easy trail along a wood chip path. Signs identify trees and shrubs. The trailhead is at the Carters Lake Visitor Center.

~BLUE RIDGE MOUNTAIN MARINA RESORT.

Cabins and rooms, rental houseboats, convenience store, pontoon and fishing boat rental, guided fishing trips, snack bar and boat repair.

~CANOEING TRIPS.

THE COOSAWATTEE RIVER. [Fig. 14(2)] The Cartecay and Ellijay Rivers meet in the town of Ellijay to form the Coosawattee, one of the largest rivers in north Georgia. Once out of town, the river turns west through the southern Cohuttas, carving downward more than 500 feet in 22 miles through a spectacular gorge and emerging through a narrow breach into what geologists call the Great Valley. The highest earthen dam east of the Mississippi now fills that breach, and Carters Lake has inundated more than half the river, including the biggest rapids and the highest cliffs. This gorge was second only to Tallulah Gorge in grandeur. In fact, canoeing insiders believe that James Dickey's novel-turned-movie, *Deliverance*, which was filmed on the Chattooga, was actually written more with the Coosawattee in mind. A fine run of intermediate difficulty remains on the upper section, past forested bluffs. Because of the open nature of this river, with wide views of the surrounding trees, it is most scenic in April, when the woods are leafing out, and in October, during the fall color display. Although the river gradient is almost 30 feet per mile in places, the rapids do not exceed Class III and are separated by easy, flat sections which allow paddlers to relax and enjoy the scenery.

DIRECTIONS: *To find the put-in, first locate the GA 5 bridge over the Coosawattee south of Ellijay. On the north side of the bridge, turn west on Legion Road and drive about a mile to where the road comes just to the river's edge [Fig. 14(2)]. One can also put in a couple of miles upstream at the Gilmer County Park, just south of the intersection of GA 5 and GA 282 [Fig. 14(3)]. To reach the take-out, go back out Legion Road to GA 5, up to GA 282, and west about eight miles, watching for a large sign to the Ridgeway access area. Follow the signs to the boat ramp [Fig. 14(4)].*

TALKING ROCK CREEK. [Fig. 14(5)] Talking Rock Creek is a beautiful, clear mountain stream deeply etched into the canyon-like foothills of the Cohutta and Blue Ridge Mountains, just northwest of Jasper. Generally running northwest, it empties into the reservoir below Carters Lake Dam. Canoeists experience wild and remote country, high cliffs and primitive mountain scenery, as well as Class I - III rapids.

DIRECTIONS: *The put-in and take-out are about nine miles apart on GA 136. The put-in bridge is about two miles north of Blaine [Fig. 14(5)], and the take-out bridge is where the creek runs into the reregulation reservoir below Carters Lake Dam [Fig. 14(6)]. Total distance from bridge to bridge is about 15 miles. Steady paddling by experienced canoeists makes a six- to eight-hour trip feasible. Expect possible headwinds during the last three miles, which could extend the length of the trip.*

MAP REFERENCES: *For Cohuttas, Rich Mt. and Big Frog, USGS 1:100,000 series: Cleveland - Dalton - Cartersville, USGS 1:24,000 series: Cashes Valley - Blue Ridge - Wilscot - Ellijay - Tickanetley - Noontootla. For Big Frog, USGS 1:24,000 series: Epworth - Ducktown - Hemp Top - Caney Creek. County Highway Maps: Gilmer - Murray - Fannin - Gordon.*

Black-capped chickadee
Parus atricapillus

This irrepressible mite of a bird brings cheer to bird lovers everywhere. It breeds in the mountains and is an example of a species dependent on nest holes in hollow trees, many of which are excavated by small woodpeckers. Such relationships between animals are not unusual in most mature forest eco-systems.

Fort Mountain State Park

Fort Mountain State Park [Fig. 11(6)] is located on Fort Mountain, just southwest of the Cohutta Wilderness. The park derives its name from an ancient stone wall, measuring some 855 feet in length, which stands on the highest point of the mountain. Remains of circular depressions made of various-sized stones and measuring about 10 feet across occur in the wall at about 30-foot intervals. The wall ranges in height from two to six feet, although it was probably considerably higher in the past. Archeologists and historians have been unable to solve the puzzle of who, if anyone, built the wall or why or when they built it. There are many theories. A favorite explanation is that the wall was built by the Woodland Indians around 500 A.D. The east-west orientation of its end points would result in alignment at sunrise and sunset at the solar equinox in both spring and fall. The dramatic setting of the wall, offering expansive vistas to the east and west, would add to its religious significance. Ceremonial centers similar to this one were built by the Woodland Indians at Old Stone Fort, Tennessee and Rock Eagle Mound in Putnam County, Georgia. The Woodland Indians occupied the Southeast from several centuries B.C. to about 900 A.D.

A less probable but more romantic theory attributes the wall to a legendary Welsh prince named Medoc. He supposedly sailed into Mobile, Alabama, 500 years ago, then worked his way northward toward the Fort Mountain vicinity. Nothing else is known about Prince Medoc, except that his name is vaguely linked to several petroglyphs found in other parts of the Southeast.

Some geologists believe—and this is the least romantic explanation of all—that the "wall" is the result of natural weathering of a generally horizontal stratum of a hard caprock of quartzites and conglameratites which produced the present ring of boulders.

In the 1930's the Civilian Conservation Corps built a 38-foot stone observation tower at the mountain's summit 520 feet north of the wall. Its special feature is a heart-shaped stone which lies concealed just above the east window.

A portion of Fort Mountain State Park's 1,932 acres was donated to the federal government in 1929 by Ivan Allen, Sr., for the preservation of the stone wall and for the public's pleasure. In the 1940's it was turned over to the state of Georgia.

The hiking vistas and natural history are outstanding. The park has a spectacular cascade dropping 400 feet off the cliffs, an old gold mine [Fig. 15(5)] on streams feeding the lake and an underlay of vast mineral deposits.

The visitor to Fort Mountain may hear the activity of commercial mines in the bowels of the mountain. Fort Mountain is probably Georgia's leading talc producer. Large companies moved in around 1900. Mines surround the mountain on three sides; two can be seen

Fort Mountain Stone Wall

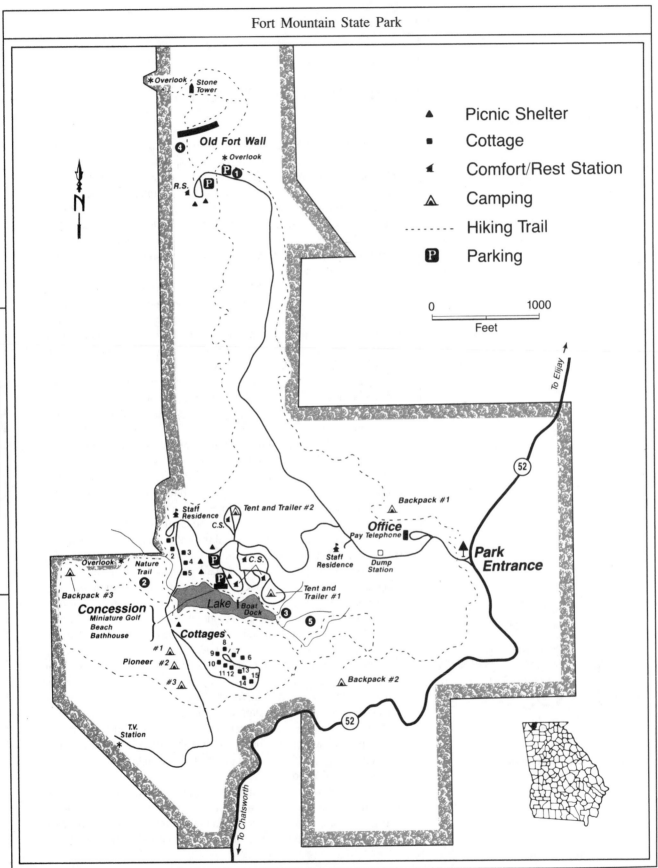

WESTERN BLUE RIDGE

Picnic Shelter
Cottage
Comfort/Rest Station
Camping
Hiking Trail
Parking

0   1000
Feet

N

Overlook   Stone Tower
Old Fort Wall
Overlook
R.S.

To Ellijay

52

Backpack #1

Office
Pay Telephone

Staff Residence
Tent and Trailer #2
C.S.
Staff Residence
Dump Station

Park Entrance

Overlook
Nature Trail
Backpack #3
Concession
Miniature Golf
Beach
Bathhouse

Lake   Boat Dock
Tent and Trailer #1

Cottages
Pioneer
#1
#2
#3

Backpack #2

T.V. Station

52

To Chatsworth

Figure 15 — **FORT MOUNTAIN STATE PARK**

66

Fig. 15 - Fort Mountain State Park
(page references in parentheses)

1 Gahuti Trail (67)
2 Big Rock Nature Trail (67)
3 Lake Loop Trail (67)
4 Old Fort Trail (67)
5 old gold mine (65)

from the Chatsworth overlook.

FACILITIES: *There are 15 two- and three-bedroom cottages; 70 tent and trailer sites; 12 miles of foot trails; swimming beach with bath house; paddle boats; 7 picnic shelters with 117 tables and miniature golf.*

DATES/HOURS: *Open all year round, 7am-10pm; office open 8am-5pm.*

DIRECTIONS: *Located 7 miles east of Chatsworth on GA 52. Take exit 136 off I-75.*

ADDITIONAL INFORMATION: *Fort Mountain State Park, Box 7008, Rt. 7, Chatsworth, GA 30705. (404) 695-2621. Or refer to the State Parks section, Appendix B.*

~FORT MOUNTAIN HIKING TRAILS. Inquire at the park office for detailed directions and a map.

GAHUTI TRAIL. [Fig. 15(1)] An 8.2-mile loop trail around Fort Mountain. Three limited-use camping sites are located along the trail for backpackers. One orange blaze, which is easy to see, designates the trail. Old logging roads crisscross the trail, and it is easy to mistake one of these for the trail. The first 0.3 mile looks out over the Cohutta Wilderness and is one of the finest views in Georgia. The trail begins at a gravel parking area marked "Cool Springs Overlook" in Fort Mountain State Park.

BIG ROCK NATURE TRAIL. [Fig. 15(2)] 0.7 mile. This trail provides hikers a glimpse of the rugged and diverse natural habitat found on Fort Mountain. Where the trail reaches the first branch, note the unusual occurrence of Catawba rhododendron. Then pass several rocky outcrops which form natural outlooks with chestnut oak as the dominant tree. One view is of a 400-foot cascade of Gold Mine Creek. Along this creek is ordinary rosebay, with mountain laurel, galax and wild ginger.

LAKE LOOP TRAIL. [Fig. 15(3)] Approximately 1.1 miles. This trail follows along the edge of 17-acre Fort Mountain Lake.

OLD FORT TRAIL. [Fig. 15(4)] 1.3 miles. This trail leads to the ancient stone wall from which Fort Mountain derives its name. The trail passes through a forest of alternating stands of scarlet oak, Virginia pine and gnarled white oak. Past the wall there is a stone tower which children will love. West of the tower, a short trail leads to the Chatsworth Overlook platform.

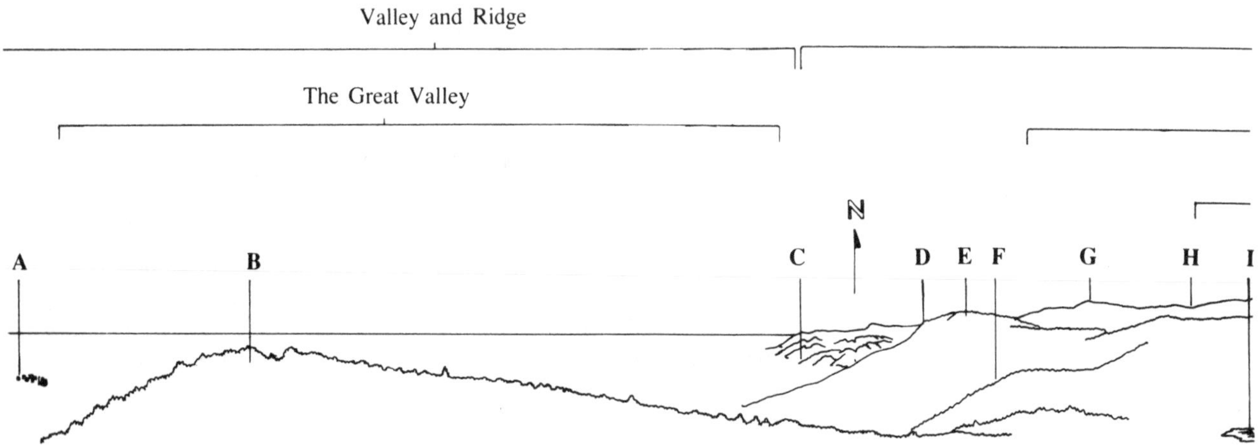

Valley and Ridge

The Great Valley

WESTERN BLUE RIDGE

A   B   C D E F G H I

N

NORTH VISTA

A - Chatsworth
B - Cohutta Mountain, NW flank
C - Cartersville-Great Smoky Fault

D - Chatsworth Overlook
E - Fort Mountain
F - Gold Mine Branch Ravine

G - Grassy Mountain
H - Lake Conasauga
I - Lake on Gold Mine Branch

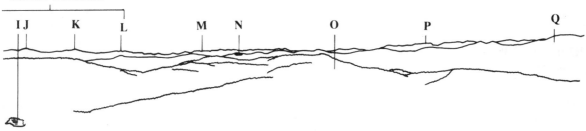

Western Blue Ridge

Cohutta Mountains

Cohutta Wilderness

I J   K   L   M N   O   P   Q

NORTH VISTA (Continued)

I — Lake on Gold Mine Branch
J — Bald Mountain
K — Cowpen Mountain (unseen)

L — Potato Patch Mountain
M — Flat Top Mountain
N — Cohutta Lodge

O — Cold Springs Mountain
P — Rich Mountain Wilderness
Q — Cold Spring Mountain

WESTERN BLUE RIDGE

COMPILED BY CHARLES WHARTON AND NELL JONES
ILLUSTRATED BY MOZELLE FUNDERBURK

Fort Mountain State Park

Cohutta Mountains

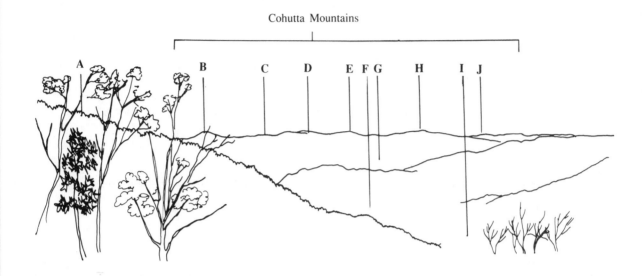

NORTHEAST VISTA
From Cool Springs Overlook

A - Fort Mountain, East flank
B - Grassy Mountain
C - Lake Conasauga

D - Bald Mountain
E - Cowpen Mountain
F - Mill Creek Watershed

G - Holly Creek Watershed
H - Potato Patch Mountain
I - Talc mine location
J - Flat Top Mountain

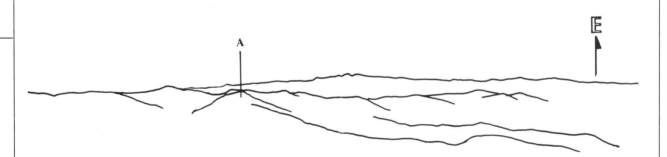

EAST VISTA

A - Cold Spring Mountain

WESTERN BLUE RIDGE

COMPILED BY CHARLES WHARTON AND NELL JONES
ILLUSTRATED BY MOZELLE FUNDERBURK

The Copper Basin

At the junction where east Tennessee, northwest Georgia and southwest North Carolina meet, the Copper Basin stands out in startling contrast to its surroundings—the epitome of man's disregard for nature. Its denuded red hills shimmer with glowing colors ranging from soft pastels to dark copper and reddish hues, surrounded by a ring of lush green mountains, thus giving the illusion of a bowl or basin. The Blue Ridge Mountains, with elevations reaching 4,200 feet, can be seen in every direction.

Approximately 35,000 acres of rolling hills, the Copper Basin has been described as a moonscape, a red desert or a beloved scar (by people who were born, raised and continue to live in this area) and is damaging testimony to the long-term effect of acid rain. However, unlike present-day acid rain, that which produced the Copper Basin fell close to its point of origin, was highly visible and had an immediate as well as long-range effect. Efforts to reclaim the proper balance of nature have been numerous and reportedly represent the most extensive reclamation project attempted in the United States.

Devastation of the Copper Basin is usually attributed to the copper mining industry. Other factors, however, also contributed. Burning by the Cherokee Indians, followed by early settlers' burning to clear land, established a pattern of land abuse early on. According to Tennessee historian J.B. Killebrew in 1874, the Copper Basin area was "a barren sterile region prior to 1850."

In the mid-1800's, the arrival of the copper mining industry was heralded with exuberance, as it provided much-needed livelihood for the local mountain people. During this period the Copper Basin was a veritable boom area, with people converging from every direction to participate in the mining, as well as the development of the railroad. The basin's forests were badly cut over to obtain fuel for copper smelting, then subjected to copper sulfide fumes generated by open-air roasting of copper ore. The fumes—spread further when high smoke stacks were added after 1907—hung close to the ground or mixed with frost, fog or rain, killing nearly every remaining tree, bush, shrub, weed and growing plant in the 35,000-acre area. At that time little thought was given to the effect on the land. Even today, in spite of the ravaged land that remains as a result of copper mining, the people who worked in the mines and their families are fiercely proud of their barren hills. The devastation was twofold when mining operations ceased. The land was exhausted, as was the morale of the people left with no source of income. Adding insult to injury long after the copper smelting fumes were controlled, Tennessee law permitted open-range cattle grazing. Lowland farmers drove and later trucked cattle up into the basin for free grazing, having burned the land indiscriminately to encourage springtime growth of thin sedge pasturage.

Hellebore
Veratrum viride

Unlike the smaller false hellebore (*V. parviflorum*), which occurs in the upper Piedmont along the Gainesville Ridges, this huge, robust plant (reaching five feet) is found in the highest parts of our mountains and under almost bog conditions. All parts are poisonous.

WESTERN BLUE RIDGE

71

Reclamation began with the help of the Civilian Conservation Corps in the early 1930's. It has continued through the efforts of at least three copper companies as well as the Tennessee Valley Authority (TVA), the U.S. Soil Conservation Service, U.S. Forest Service, the Tennessee Division of Natural Resources, other state agencies and the Universities of Tennessee, Georgia and North Carolina. The hillsides have been roughly regraded, partially terraced and thickly planted with pines, bush clover, weeping lovegrass, clumps of Japanese knotweed and kudzu. Rock check dams have been built and locust seedlings planted in the accumulated soil above the dams.

The Tennessee Chemical Company still operates a sulfuric acid plant in Copperhill. However, the area's future seems to point to tourism, with the proliferation of whitewater enthusiasts who pass through this area on the way to nearby rapids of the Ocoee River.

The Copper Basin is now listed on the National Register of Historic Places. The Tennessee Chemical Company has given the old abandoned Burra Burra mine, together with seventeen hilltop acres with old buildings, to the Ducktown Basin Museum. In 1988 the state of Tennessee purchased the museum to commemorate the copper mining area as the state's first historical industrial site.

DIRECTIONS: *From Blue Ridge go north on GA 5 for 11 miles to Copperhill, then north on TN 68 to US 64, which bisects the area from east to west.*

MAP REFERENCES: *USGS 1:100,000 series: Cleveland.*

The Rich Mountains

The 13,276-acre Rich Mountains are primarily wilderness (9,649 acres) and primitive back country (3,627 acres) which is not heavily used. The Rich Mountains are remarkable because many of the peaks and ridges are covered with a deep, black porter's loam, a characteristic shared with the Cohuttas. In the Eastern Blue Ridge such soils are confined to coves. On the Rich Mountains this soil-covering results in spectacular wildflower displays. On ridges and slopes alike, one finds lush summer herb growth and forests of basswood, ash and black cherry—trees that occur in the Eastern Blue Ridge mostly in high rich coves. Gaps—at least in the Turniptown area—have populations of the rare columbo, a most unusual plant. There is old-growth timber south of Turniptown Mountain. North-facing coves have boulderfields and rare northern wildflowers at the southern limit of their range. There is a large bear population, and one can find "licks" where deer have eaten clay-rich soil.

About 60 inches of rain falls here each year, May usually being the wettest month and April and July the driest.

Sites of old Indian camps can be found along the high ridge lines. Remnants of white settlements dating from about 1910 are just north of Rich Mountain. The largest gold nugget ever found in Georgia came from a creek draining this area. Marble, which is mined at the famous quarries near Tate and Marble Hill, can also be found exposed in the bottom of the syncline.

Elevation varies from approximately 2,000 feet near Little Rock Creek to 4,081 feet on Big Bald Mountain [Fig. 16(1)]. High peaks and lookouts from the Old Road (see below) offer panoramic vistas after leaves fall. Rugged mountain terrain with rock outcrops, and streams with many small waterfalls create a beautiful scenery.

US 76 [Fig. 16(10)] between Ellijay [Fig. 16(2)] and Blue Ridge [Fig. 16(11)], Georgia, generally follows the Murphy Syncline, which divides the highly metamorphosed rocks of the Blue Ridge proper from the moderately metamorphosed rocks of the Cohuttas. This remarkable geologic trough is clearly visible in satellite photographs. It is likely that the uninformed visitor driving up US 76 in the deep gash of the Murphy Syncline would pass the Rich Mountains area by, since the higher peaks and ridges are barely visible from the road. Hikers exploring the Rich Mountains area should be experienced and carry topographical maps, compass and other survival gear.

DIRECTIONS: *From the McDonald's Restaurant intersection in East Ellijay on US 76, travel north on US 76 (GA 2 and 5, Appalachian Hwy. 515) for 8.7 miles and turn left onto a county road. Take the first immediate right; turn back right again under a four-lane highway*

Silverbell
Halesia carolina

This small tree seldom exceeds two feet in diameter, yet it is a common feature of moist cove forests. From March to May, its showy, pendant, white flowers are a delight to the senses and give rise to a four-winged green fruit.

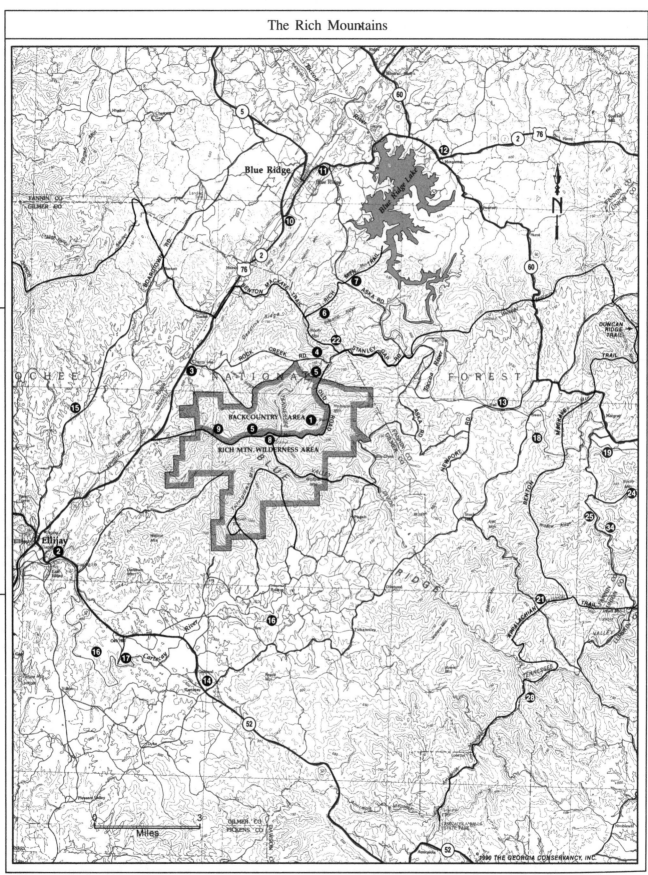

Figure 16 — **RICH MOUNTAINS**

Fig. 16 - Rich Mountain
(page references in parentheses)

1 Big Bald Mountain (73)
2 Ellijay (73)
3 Rock Creek Baptist Church
4 Stanley Gap (75)
5 Old Road (75)
6 Rich Mountain Trail (75)
7 Deep Gap (75)
8 Rich Mountain (73)
9 Aaron Mountain (75)
10 Murphy Syncline [US 76 between Elli-jay and Blue Ridge] (73)
11 Blue Ridge (73, 77)
12 Morganton (77)
13 Dial, Georgia (77)
14 Cartecay (77)
15 Boardtown Road (77)
16 The Cartecay River (77)
17 Cartecay River put-in (78)
18 Toccoa River (79)
19 Deep Hole Recreation Area (81, 83)
21 Three Forks (81)
24 Little Rock Creek Falls (82)
25 The Chattahoochee Forest National Fish Hatchery (82)
28 Springer Mountain (86)
34 Frank Gross Campground (83)

and take Rock Creek Road, which parallels Little Rock Creek. Proceed five miles to Stanley Gap [Fig. 16(4)]. The paved road becomes a moderately rough dirt road at 2.1 miles. Near Stanley Gap is a small parking area on the right at the intersection with FS 38.

ALTERNATE ACCESS: *Other than by the Rock Creek Road access, the Rich Mountains area can be approached from Aska Road and Stanley Creek Road. These roads are passable with two-wheel-drive vehicles. An old road leaves GA 5 near the gravel quarry at White-path and forms the boundary of the area as it winds around Aaron, Bee, Rich, and Little Bald Mountains. Turning north, it forms the northeast boundary of the area as it passes around Big Bald Mountain through Wolfpen Gap and over Stanley Creek to Stanley Gap Road. This boundary road is referred to as the Old Road [Fig. 16(5)]. It is passable with four-wheel-drive vehicles only.*

In order to reach Rich Mountain from Stanley Gap, walk south on a Gilmer County public road which starts by the bulletin board and borders the wilderness area to the base of Rich Mountain. From there several primitive, unmarked trails cross through the wilderness and back country area. One must be careful in order to avoid getting lost. This is a seven-mile hike with an elevation gain of over 2,000 feet.

~RICH MOUNTAIN TRAIL. [Fig. 16(6)] About 8.8 miles one way. Moderately difficult. The only well-marked trail in the area is the Rich Mountain Trail, designated with rectangular-shaped white blazes.

DIRECTIONS: *Begin at Stanley Gap (see directions above) and go north to the shores of Lake Blue Ridge. After about 0.5 mile, intersect with the diamond-shaped, white-blazed Benton MacKaye Trail and share the same route for about the next two miles. After that the Benton MacKaye Trail heads over the ridge toward Lucius, while the Rich Mountain Trail turns right and goes down the side of the ridge toward Lake Blue Ridge.*

ALTERNATE ACCESS: *From Blue Ridge go one mile on US 76 to Aska Road. Turn right and continue four miles to Deep Gap [Fig. 16(7)]. The trail crosses the road at the gap. To reach Stanley Gap, go on Aska Road four additional miles to Stanley Gap Road. Turn right on a gravel road and travel 3.9 miles to the trailhead.*

To reach the lake shore, from US 76 go three miles on the Aska Road and turn left on Campbell Camp Road; travel 2.4 miles to the trailhead.

~AARON MOUNTAIN. [Fig. 16(9)] This mountain has a rounded dome covered with rich, black soil and a wildflower display in spring. An old-timber growth (129 years) lies on the south face of Aaron Mountain. At Horse Cove, there are a good boulderfield and northern hardwood forest with some possible record-sized, second-growth trees, especially silverbell.

~**LAKE BLUE RIDGE.** The lake shimmers like a sapphire in a green granite setting. Most of the surrounding land is part of the Chattahoochee National Forest, which protects the lake from being overly developed. Except for a few water skiers, most of the aficionados come to camp and fish. It is the only lake in the state where one can battle the mighty muskie, a large game fish of the pike family, although the prime fishing attractions are walleye, bluegill and smallmouth bass. Thirty-five fish attractors—manmade feeding covers—have been scattered around the coves and creeks. Lake Blue Ridge is fed by the north-flowing Toccoa River. The river flows gently for about 15 miles north of the dam, then changes its name to the Ocoee and froths into one of the Southeast's most exhilarating whitewater streams for rafting and kayaking. Call for water level information and power generation schedules, which may affect fishing near the dam. (800) 251-9242, Mon.-Fri. 8:30 to 6, weekends 8:30 to 4:30.
ADDITIONAL INFORMATION: *Contact the U.S. Forest Service, East Main St., Blue Ridge, GA 30513. (404) 632-3031.*

LAKE BLUE RIDGE TRAIL. 0.6 mile. A loop trail that follows the shoreline of Lake Blue Ridge and offers a beautiful view of the lake.
DIRECTIONS: *From Blue Ridge take old US 76 east for 1.5 miles to Dry Branch Road; turn right; go three miles to the entrance to the Blue Ridge Recreation Area. The trail begins and ends in the picnic area.*

LAKE BLUE RIDGE CAMPSITES. 55 campsites in the area, several along the lake; bathrooms and showers; no hookups are provided. For availability around the lake, Memorial Day through Labor Day, contact the U.S. Forest Service, Toccoa Ranger District. (404) 632-3031.

LAKE BLUE RIDGE BOAT RENTAL. Fishing boats can be rented at the Blue Ridge Lake Marina (phone (404) 632-2618) on the northern side, near the dam. It is the only commercial outlet on the lake for gas, food and supplies. It also provides one of several boat-launch ramps. Others are at Morganton Point and the more remote Lake Blue Ridge Recreation Area (also known as Dry Branch or Green Creek). The U.S. Forest Service offers tent camping and picnic areas at both sites. (404) 632-8331.

LAKE BLUE RIDGE CABIN RENTAL. Most cabins are fully furnished, with fireplaces and decks. Some include breakfast and hot tubs. Contact Bed and Breakfast Hideaway Homes, P.O. Box 300,

Muskellunge
Esox masquinongy

This giant member of the pike family inhabits unpolluted tributaries of the Tennessee River system that drain the north slopes of the Georgia Blue Ridge. Huge examples are sometimes caught in Lake Blue Ridge and in the Little Tennessee River below Franklin.

Blue Ridge, GA 30513, (404) 632-2411. Or contact the Blue Ridge Visitor Center, P.O. Box 875, Blue Ridge, GA 30513. (404) 632-5680.

Morganton Point Recreation Area. Located on the shores of Lake Blue Ridge 0.5 mile from the town of Morganton, this campground contains 37 campsites, 8 picnic sites, a designated swimming area with a lifeguard on duty during the summer camping season and a boat-launch ramp. No showers or hiking trails are within this recreation area, and electricity is available only in the bathrooms.

DIRECTIONS: *From Blue Ridge [Fig. 16(11)] take old US 76 east and south of town to Lakewood Junction. Here GA 60 and US 76 join, with GA 60 continuing as the designated main road south and east to Morganton [Fig. 16(12)]. It is approximately five miles from Blue Ridge to Morganton. The drive is scenic, crossing the TVA dam with a splendid view of Lake Blue Ridge to the southwest. Also between the dam and Lakewood Junction is a U.S. Forest Service boat-launch ramp near Lakewood. At Morganton, look for the white-on-green sign to the recreation area, on the right side of the road just before the road turns east and south.*

~DRIVING TOURS

ASKA ROAD TO NEWPORT ROAD. Starting from the intersection of old US 76 and Aska Road, go south 13.8 miles. Turn left at the dead end onto a paved road to Dial, Georgia [Fig. 16(13)]. This road comes out on GA 60, where one can head for either Dahlonega or Morganton. For a picture-postcard alternative, turn right at the dead end onto Newport Road and go 4.5 miles to SR 1010. Turn right and go 12.2 miles to Cartecay [Fig. 16(14)].

BOARDTOWN ROAD BETWEEN ELLIJAY AND BLUE RIDGE. This 18.6-mile drive between Ellijay and Blue Ridge provides a good look at the intimacy and charm of the north Georgia countryside. Visitors will pass red barns and silver silos, small green fields with silver creeks running through them and cows wandering about, Christmas tree farms, doublewides and cedar homes. Pickup truck drivers will lift an index finger off the steering wheel to say "howdy" as they pass.

DIRECTIONS: *From the town square in the center of Ellijay, take GA 52 and GA 2 west (Dalton Street) to Boardtown Road [Fig. 16(15)], about 0.4 mile from the center of town. There is a road sign, as well as a sign to Sugar Creek Raceway.*

~THE CARTECAY RIVER. [Fig. 16(16)] The Cartecay is a small, intimate river located east of Ellijay. Flowing out of a long valley and past farmlands, it passes over a series of tight drops around upland ridges. It then returns to its more placid nature just prior to its confluence with the Ellijay River, where the two become

WESTERN BLUE RIDGE

the Coosawattee. This is a narrow, clear mountain stream with almost continuous Class I and II rapids for the first 5.5 miles of this section. Although level, it is fast-flowing along steep ridges and through shaded tree canopies for the final six miles. This is intermediate to advanced whitewater with one unavoidable Class III rapid. The river requires more skill than do the upper Chattahoochee and Broad Rivers. In places it is comparable to Section III of the Chattooga.

DIRECTIONS: *Put in on a dirt road located 2.5 miles east of Ellijay on GA 52 past Oak Hill Apple House. Turn right onto the dirt road and go 1.5 miles to the river [Fig. 16(17)]. Take out at a small roadside park along GA 52 east of Ellijay.*

MAP REFERENCES: *For Cohuttas and Rich Mt., USGS 1:100,000 series: Cleveland - Dalton - Cartersville. USGS 1:24,000 series: Cashes Valley - Blue Ridge - Wilscot - Ellijay - Tickanetley - Noontootla. County Highway Maps: Gilmer - Murray - Fannin - Gordon.*

Peregrine falcon
Falco peregrinus

Peregrines formerly nested in the cliffs and gorges of the Blue Ridge and northwest Georgia. They have even visited Atlanta's taller buildings and have used the Hurt Building, feeding on the pigeons that cross the park below. With controls on pesticides, these falcons are making a comeback.

Mountain laurel
Kalmia latifolia

The leaves of this heath are poisonous. It blooms after the flame azalea but before both the Carolina and rosebay rhododendron. Its most spectacular displays are found along streams where the plants get full sunlight. Known to mountain people as "ivy," it forms slicks on dry, rocky south-facing slopes.

The Etowah River and Toccoa River Watersheds

The Etowah River and the Toccoa River flow in different directions. The Etowah drains the south side of the Tennessee Valley divide, while the Toccoa drains the north side. In these watersheds, visitors will find the highest waterfall in Georgia, as well as the approach trail for the beginning of the Appalachian Trail. A fish hatchery allows one to see how the hundreds of thousands of rainbow trout stocked in Georgia's rivers and streams are raised to catching size. Two fine rivers provide canoeing opportunities for boaters of varying skills and experience.

~CANOEING.

ETOWAH RIVER. The upper section of the Etowah River is ideal for beginning canoeists, families and organized groups who want to run a brisk mountain river and also to be close to the scenic and historical attractions of Dahlonega. A 12-mile stretch can be canoed in one day of steady paddling or two leisurely days. (Those opting for the two-day version can break the trip at Castleberry Bridge and camp at the nearby Blackburn Park [Fig. 17(30)] 1.3 miles south of Auraria on GA 9E or go into Dahlonega seven miles south on 9E).

One hazard is Etowah Falls, 1.5 miles from the put-in. The canoeist must land on the rocks on the right bank and portage over or around them. Below Castleberry Bridge [Fig. 17(33)] is an old mine tunnel about seven feet in diameter and about 0.2 mile long. Scout this carefully. Run it only if light is visible at the other end; if the exit light is not clear and bright, the tunnel is likely to be too obstructed with debris and stumps to be safely passable.

DIRECTIONS: *Put in at the bridge on US 19 [Fig. 17(31)]. Castleberry Bridge is a good take-out, or the trip may be continued to the bridge at GA 136 [Fig. 17(32)].*

TOCCOA RIVER. Some knowledgeable canoeists have described the Toccoa [Fig. 17(18)] as Georgia's prettiest whitewater stream. It has its headwaters in Union County, flows into Fannin County and becomes the major feeder stream for Lake Blue Ridge. It resumes its flow below Blue Ridge and travels into Tennessee, where it is known as the Ocoee.

The stream's first couple of miles provide a startling contrast between undisturbed river banks and those touched by human hand. In apparent efforts to squeeze a little more yield from flood plains, some farmers have cleared to the edge of the water, removing vegetation which holds the soil. The unhappy consequence is that

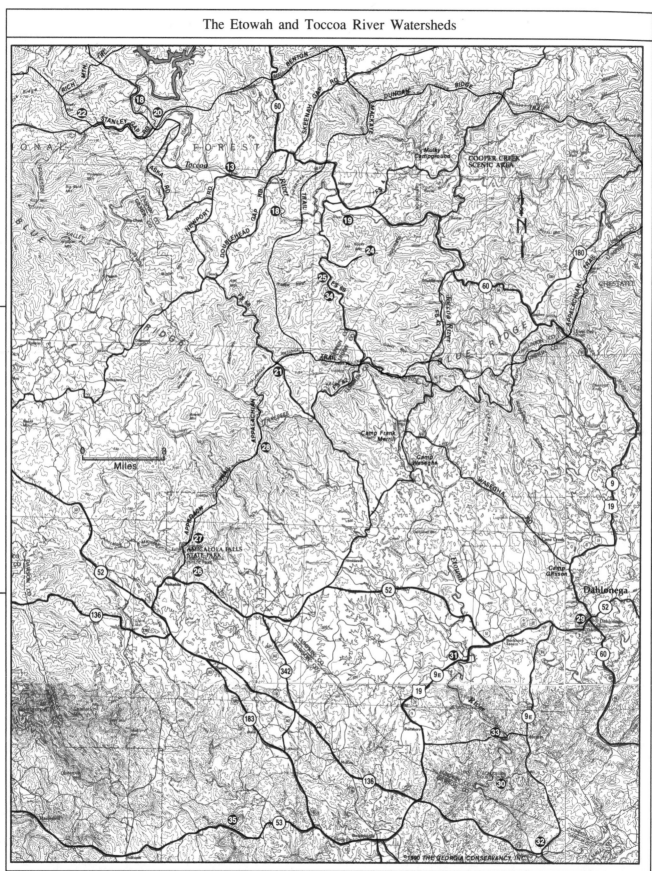

WESTERN BLUE RIDGE

Figure 17 — **ETOWAH RIVER AND TOCCOA RIVER WATERSHEDS**

Fig. 17 - Etowah and Toccoa
River Watersheds

(page references in parentheses)

13 Dial (81)
18 Toccoa River (79)
19 Deep Hole Recreation Area (81, 83)
20 Shallow Ford Bridge (81)
21 Three Forks (81)
22 Fall Branch Falls (double falls) (82)
24 Little Rock Creek Falls (82)
25 The Chattahoochee Forest National Fish
     Hatchery (82)
26 Amicalola Falls State Park (85)
27 Amicalola Falls (85)
28 Springer Mountain (86)
29 Dahlonega Gold Museum (87)
30 Blackburn Park (79)
31 Bridge on US 19 (79)
32 Bridge at GA 136 (79)
33 Castleberry Bridge (79)
34 Frank Gross Campground (83)
35 Amicalola Creek and Dawson Forest
     Wildlife Management Area (86)

the banks are rapidly eroding, dumping silt and any remaining vegetation into the water.

The river offers a variety of interesting forms of vegetation for each season. Early spring brings bluets in the moss, then azalea, laurel and—all around Deep Hole Campground—wild strawberries. In late spring abundant rhododendron garnishes the banks. Summer offers the richness of mature hardwood stands in full leaf. When autumn comes the hardwoods take on an incredible glow. Alternate leaf dogwood and deciduous holly sport their bright red berries right on into winter. When upper-story trees provide enough shade, galax carpets the banks, the waxy leaves dark green until December, then thriving coppery as pennies for the winter months. Galax is gathered frequently for use in floral arrangements. Sadly, this has led to its near-extinction in many areas.

The most beautiful section of the Toccoa River lies behind Toonowee Mountain. Small rapids, hemlocks trailing in the water and the beautifully clear stream itself combine to saturate the senses.

DIRECTIONS: *Put-in for the upper section is at Deep Hole [Fig. 17(19)], a U.S. Forest Service campground on GA 60, 27 miles north of Dahlonega. Driving from Deep Hole, continue north on GA 60 for 4.5 miles and then left onto an unmarked, paved road that goes between two buildings and looks at first like a driveway. Continue on mixed gravel/paved roads to Dial [Fig. 17(13)], where there are two bridges. On the way is the Chastain House, the oldest home in Fannin County. The old bridge at Dial is blocked to traffic and is the take-out, or if running the lower section, the put-in. If the put-in is at Dial, the take-out is at the Shallow Ford Bridge, reached on the east side of the river by continuing on the gravel road along the river and bearing left at a fork about midway; or cross the Dial Bridge to the west side of the river. Continue on the paved road to the first road on the right, turn right and continue until reaching the Shallow Ford Bridge [Fig. 17(20)].*

~WATERFALLS.

LONG CREEK FALLS. Picturesque falls and trail. Requires a 20-30 minute walk in each direction.

DIRECTIONS: *From Blue Ridge follow old US 76 to Aska Road across from Harmony Church. Turn south and go 13.8 miles to the end of the road. Turn right on Newport Road, go 4.3 miles to the end of the road. Turn left, cross bridge over Noontootla Creek, continue on gravel road. Pass a cemetery and come to an intersection 0.6 mile from the bridge. Turn hard right on FS 58 and go southeast into the forest along this road 6.6 miles to Three Forks [Fig. 17(21)]. Hike to the northeast up Long Creek to the falls. The trail corridor has an assortment of blazes designating three major hiking trails: the Appalachian (white vertical 2"x 6"), the Duncan Ridge National Recreational Trail (blue vertical 2"x 6") and the*

WESTERN BLUE RIDGE

Benton MacKaye Trail (white diamond 5"x 7"). The distance to the falls is 1.1 miles, ascending gradually along the way. A side trail to the falls is indicated with vertical blue blazes.

FALL BRANCH FALLS. [Fig. 17(22)] A fine double waterfall. **DIRECTIONS:** *From Blue Ridge follow old US 76 to Aska Road. Turn south and go approximately 8.2 miles to the intersection with Stanley Creek Road, entering from the right. Turn right onto Stanley Creek Road and go 3.2 miles to a small parking area just beyond an interesting farm owned by long-time Forest Service fire warden Garfield Stanley. Cross a wooden bridge over Fall Branch and park on the right. Hike up the hill on the Benton MacKaye Trail to double falls [Fig. 17(22)] on the right. There is a small picnic and/or camping spot 30 yards above the waterfall.*

SEA CREEK FALLS. **DIRECTIONS:** *From Blue Ridge follow old US 76 east five miles to the intersection with GA 60 South at Lakewood Junction. Continue 14.7 miles south on GA 60 through the small town of Morganton, past the entrance to Deep Hole Recreation Area to the junction with FS 4, entering from the left. Follow FS 4 an additional 3.3 miles to right-hand curve in the road just inside the U.S. Forest Service boundary. The road to the immediate left before curve is the access to the falls. Park in the area at the end of this spur (about 0.3 mile) and walk upstream 150 feet to view the falls.*

LITTLE ROCK CREEK FALLS. [Fig. 17(24)] There is a series of small falls just before reaching the main one. The walk is strenuous on a footpath leading along the left side of the creek and going only part of the way to the falls. There is not a footpath up the side of the main falls because of the dangerous slippery rocks in the area. Use extreme caution.
DIRECTIONS: *From Blue Ridge follow the directions above for Sea Creek Falls, but only as far as the crossing of Skeenah Creek on GA 60 south. Skeenah Creek is located about 11.3 miles south of Morganton. There is an old but still operational mill on the northeast side of the highway. A commercial campground is also located on this site. After crossing Skeenah Creek, continue south on GA 60 another 3.1 miles to the intersection with FS 69, Fish Hatchery Road, coming from the right. Turn onto this road and go about three miles to where the road crosses Little Rock Creek [Fig. 17(24)]. There is a bridge and a small pull-out area here.*

~CAMPING AND RECREATION.

THE CHATTAHOOCHEE FOREST NATIONAL FISH HATCHERY. [Fig. 17(25)] The hatchery produces rainbow trout for stocking in rivers, streams and lakes of the Chattahoochee National Forest and

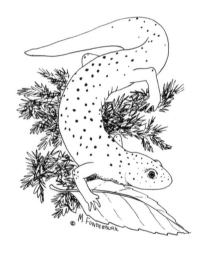

Northern red salamander
Pseudotriton ruber

It is always startling to turn over a rock and see these red creatures with black spots. Mountaineers call them "red dogs" and believe that trout prefer them to species of other colors. Red salamanders occur in quite dry locations on the floodplains of mountain streams.

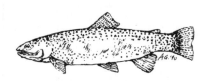

Rainbow trout
Onocorhynchus mykiss

Native to the Sierras and mountains of the West Coast, rainbow were introduced into north Georgia by the legendary forest ranger Arthur Woody. More aggressive than the native brook trout, and egg-eaters, they have displaced the native "specks" from all but the tiniest headwater streams.

other areas of north Georgia. While spawning operations are not conducted at this hatchery, fertilized eggs are shipped here and incubated under controlled conditions. Eggs hatch within three to four weeks, and the young fry are soon placed on a specially formulated dry feed. Upon reaching two to three inches in size, the fingerlings are moved to outside raceways for rearing to catchable size. The hatchery turns out about 850,000 trout each year. These fish are harvested from the raceways and distributed by truck for stocking into streams, lakes and reservoirs of north Georgia in cooperation with the State Game and Fish Department. There are signs located throughout the grounds to explain the hatchery and its operations, and there is a sheltered exhibit.

There is fishing in Rock Creek by the hatchery, and nearby Cooper Creek is an angler's paradise for trout fishing.

FACILITIES: *Group tours by arrangement, handicapped access, restrooms.*

DATES/HOURS: *7:30-4:30 daily.*

DIRECTIONS: *Located five miles off Ga 60, 26 miles south of Blue Ridge. Direction signs are posted near Fish Hatchery Road.*

ADDITIONAL INFORMATION: *U.S. Fish and Wildlife Service, Fish Hatchery Road (FS 69), Suches, GA 30572. (404) 838-4723.*

FRANK GROSS CAMPGROUND. [Fig. 16(34), Fig. 17(34)] A small campground located along Rock Creek near the Chattahoochee National Fish Hatchery. Fishing is allowed (at no charge) in the adjacent Rock Creek and also in the 13-1/2-acre Rock Creek Lake 1.7 miles further west on the right side of Fish Hatchery Road. The lake is managed by the National Fish Hatchery, and the creek and lake are stocked periodically with nine-inch rainbow trout.

FACILITIES: *Eleven campsites with picnic tables, drinking water and two chemical toilets. Trailers up to 22 feet can be accommodated.*

DATES/HOURS: *Late spring to early fall.*

FEES: *$5 per night.*

DIRECTIONS: *Take GA 60 north from Dahlonega for 27 miles; turn left (south) and go five miles on the Fish Hatchery Road (FS 69).*

ADDITIONAL INFORMATION: *Frank Gross Campground, U.S. Forest Service, Toccoa Ranger District, E. Main St., Box 1839, Blue Ridge, GA 30513. (404) 632-3031.*

DEEP HOLE RECREATION AREA. [Fig. 17(19)] A small campground located in an attractive mountain setting on a bend of the Toccoa River just north of the fish hatchery. Its name comes from a deep hole in the river by the campground. This is an excellent canoe launch for the Toccoa River.

FACILITIES: *Eight campsites suitable for tents or small trailers; restrooms; drinking water.*

DATES/HOURS: *Open late spring through early fall.*

FEES: *$5 per night.*

WESTERN BLUE RIDGE

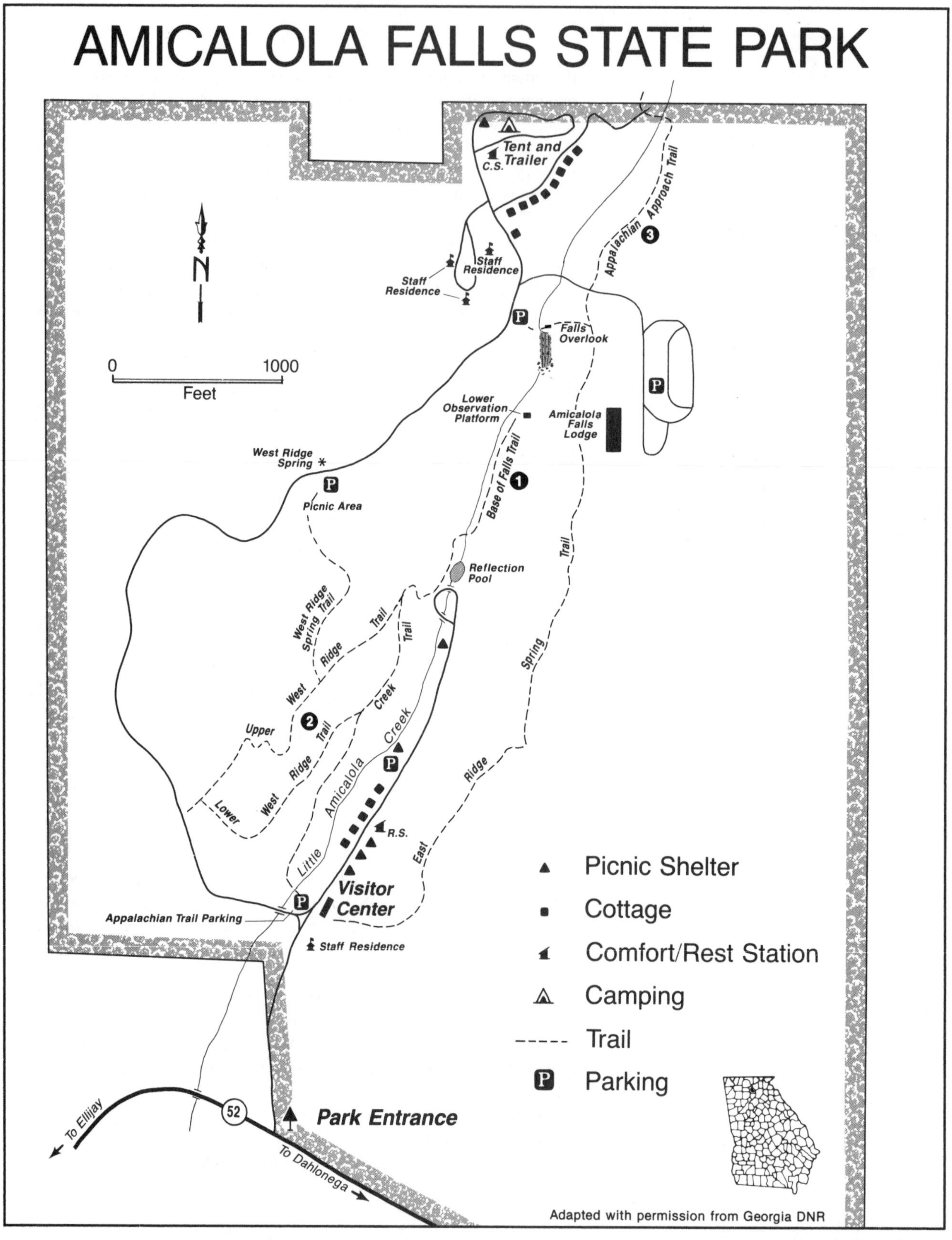

AMICALOLA FALLS STATE PARK

WESTERN BLUE RIDGE

N

0   1000
Feet

Tent and
Trailer
C.S.

Appalachian Approach Trail

3

Staff
Residence

Staff
Residence

Falls
Overlook

Lower
Observation
Platform

Amicalola Falls
Lodge

West Ridge
Spring *

Picnic Area

Base of Falls Trail

1

West Ridge
Spring Trail

West Ridge Trail

Trail

Creek Trail

Reflection
Pool

Spring Trail

Upper
West Ridge Trail

2

Lower
West Ridge Trail

Amicalola Creek

Little Amicalola Creek

East Ridge

R.S.

Visitor
Center

Appalachian Trail Parking

Staff Residence

▲ Picnic Shelter

▪ Cottage

◀ Comfort/Rest Station

⛺ Camping

----- Trail

🅿 Parking

52

To Ellijay

To Dahlonega

Park Entrance

Adapted with permission from Georgia DNR

Figure 18 — **AMICALOLA STATE PARK**

84

Fig. 18 - Amicalola Falls State
Park
(page references in parentheses)

1 Amicalola Falls Hiking Trail (85)
2 West Ridge Loop Trail (86)
3 Appalachian Trail Approach Trail (86)

DIRECTIONS: *27 miles north of Dahlonega on GA 60.*
ADDITIONAL INFORMATION: *Deep Hole Recreation Area, U.S. Forest Service, Toccoa Ranger District, E. Main St., Box 1839, Blue Ridge, GA 30513. (404) 632-3031.*

~AMICALOLA FALLS STATE PARK.

Amicalola is a Cherokee word meaning "tumbling waters," an appropriate label since the park's beautiful falls [Fig. 17(27)] slide and plunge 729 feet in seven cascades, making it the highest waterfall in Georgia. It tumbles southwest through a cove of Amicalola Mountain and forms part of the Amicalola Creek watershed. This, in turn, feeds into the Etowah, which joins the Oostanaula to form the Coosa near Rome.

The park, nestled along the southernmost edge of the Blue Ridge Mountain chain [Fig. 17(26)], consists of more than 900 acres surrounding the waterfall. The forest types include cove hardwood, upland oak/hickory and mixed pine and hardwood.

Both mountain and Piedmont flora and fauna can be found here, and most of the species native to this region inhabit the park. Here a small colony of pink lady slippers grows, pileated woodpeckers nest and the eastern milk snake reaches its southernmost range.

All seasons are beautiful at Amicalola Falls. Spring and summer offer an abundance of wildflowers, including dogwood, mountain laurel and rhododendron. Autumn offers brilliant colors in the forest, and the winter months hold a special magic as the deer and other wild animals seek refuge within the park. April and May are ideal times to enjoy the waterfall because of the unusually high volume of water. Little Amicalola Creek flows through the park and provides an opportunity for trout fishing.

FACILITIES: 900 acres; 17 tent and trailer sites; comfort station with hot showers, flush toilets and laundry facilities; 57-room lodge, restaurant and meeting center; 15 cottages, 3 playgrounds, 5 picnic shelters. Walk-in lodge accommodating 40 persons with family style meals; 5-mile hike from park to lodge; 3,000-foot elevation; trail crosses the Appalachian Trail and passes near Cochran's Falls.
SPECIAL EVENTS: *Jun.-Aug., naturalists' programs are provided Thur.-Sun. on topics dealing with the area's natural, cultural and historical resources. Other programs are scheduled throughout the year. A schedule is available in the park office.*
DATES/HOURS: *Daily 7am-10pm year round. Office open 8-5.*
DIRECTIONS: *15 miles northwest of Dawsonville and 18 miles west of Dahlonega on GA 52.*
ADDITIONAL INFORMATION: *Amicalola Falls State Park, Georgia Department of Natural Resources, Star Route, Box 213, Dawsonville, GA 30534. (404) 265-2885.*

~HIKING TRAILS AT AMICALOLA FALLS STATE PARK.

AMICALOLA FALLS HIKING TRAIL. [Fig. 18(1)] 0.25 mile. The most scenic trail in Amicalola Park leads to the base of

Amicalola Falls. The walk follows a rocky path uphill along cascading Amicalola Creek. Several large yellow poplars tower over the trail as it leads through a cove hardwood forest and ends at the lower observation deck.

DIRECTIONS: *The trailhead is in Amicalola Falls State Park near the reflection pool at the end of the main park road. The trail is marked with red blazes.*

WEST RIDGE LOOP TRAIL. [Fig. 18(2)] A 1.2-mile nature trail within the park. Virginia pine is the dominant tree along much of the trail.

DIRECTIONS: *There are three access points for the trail: 1) across the road and field from the visitor center; 2) to the right on the paved road to the top of the park; and 3) at the turnaround of the main park road, marked with nature trail signs. The access route across from the visitor center is the longest and most scenic, overlooking Amicalola Creek as it winds down the hillside.*

APPALACHIAN TRAIL APPROACH TRAIL. [Fig. 18(3)] 8.1 miles. Springer Mountain (3,782 feet) [Fig. 16(28), Fig. 17(28)], the southern starting point/terminus for the Appalachian Trail (A.T.), is reached by this hike from Amicalola Falls State Park. The trail is strenuous, up and down along the peaks and knobs of Amicalola Mountain, and is a good testing ground for those contemplating longer hikes on the A.T. itself.

DIRECTIONS: *The trailhead begins at the back of the park visitor center.*

~AMICALOLA CREEK AND DAWSON FOREST WILDLIFE MANAGEMENT AREA. [Fig. 17(35)].

South of Amicalola Falls State Park, on Amicalola Creek in the Etowah River Basin, the Georgia Department of Natural Resources operates a 4,700-acre wildlife refuge. Knowledgeable canoeists and naturalists consider the Amicalola to be one of Georgia's most beautiful and exciting waterways. More river than creek in size, the Amicalola was one of the top three candidates in the nationwide search for a river to be designated as the first National Wild River Park. Georgia Highway 53 crosses the midpoint of the Amicalola, approximately seven miles west of Dawsonville. Dawsonville can be reached from GA 400 by traveling west on GA 53.

On the southeast side of the GA 53 bridge is a guide marker which graphically depicts the river, access points, the more prominent rapids and difficulty ratings. First-time users in particular should pay close attention to the information on the marker.

There are several put-in points above the GA 53 bridge, including Six Mile and Devil's Elbow. Both are state maintained. Some parking is available, camping is allowed and launching is easy. Take-out for boating above the GA 53 bridge (and put-in for boating

Ruffed grouse
Bonasa umbellus

Even more so than the ground hog, the ruffed grouse is a creature of the mountains. Called "pheasant" by old time mountaineers, it is a prize game bird. Its drumming, a characteristic mountain sound, is made by the male, usually on a log or stump. The vibrations are of such low frequency and power that they are felt as much as heard.

below the GA 53 bridge) is near the DNR ranger's cabin on the northeast side of the bridge. Parking is not allowed at the cabin, but adequate parking is available on the shoulders of GA 53 at the bridge. There are no access points on the Amicalola below the GA 53 bridge until one reaches the Etowah River. Take-out is on the Etowah, two miles below the confluence with Amicalola Creek, at a concrete ramp near Kelley Bridge. Access to Six Mile and Devil's Elbow is reached by proceeding west on GA 53 approximately one mile and turning north at the first paved road (county road 192). Turn right at the first major intersection to reach Devil's Elbow. Continue north at the intersection and watch for the sign for the Six Mile put-in.

The GA Highway 53 bridge marks a dividing point in the Amicalola's difficulty. The section above the bridge is ideal for teaching and intermediate canoeing. This section begins as easy water and grows progressively more difficult. Several long "rock gardens", a five-foot drop, and a deceptive "roostertail" mark this section. Below the GA 53 bridge is the most difficult water on the river. Beginning with the Edge of the World, a Class IV rapid about 0.5 mile below the bridge, there are several Class II-IV rapids which should be attempted only by expert boaters. Low-water conditions usually are present after June. A foot trail leads down the east side of the river to Edge of the World.

The beauty of this river, with its steep banks, gorges and mountain vegetation, cannot be overemphasized.

~DAHLONEGA GOLD MUSEUM. [Fig. 17(29)] America's first gold rush took place not in California, but in the southern Blue Ridge Mountains in the vicinity of Dahlonega during the late 1820's. The town's name, in fact, comes from the Cherokee word for gold, *talonega,* which translates literally as "precious yellow color." Gold was first discovered by white men near Dahlonega in 1828. Four years later, large discoveries of the precious metal were made in nearby Auraria. It was not until 1848 that gold was discovered in California and that gold rush occurred. From 1837 until 1861, the U.S. government operated a mint in Dahlonega which manufactured a total of $6 million worth of gold coins from locally-mined ore. Samples of the precious metal, scale models showing old mining techniques and other relics of Dahlonega's golden era are on display in the museum. Constructed in 1836, the museum is Georgia's oldest public building.

DATES/HOURS: *Mon.-Sat. 9-5, Sun. 10-5.*
FEES: *Adults $1.50, 12 and under $.75, 5 and under free; group rates with advanced notice.*
DIRECTIONS: *On the town square in Dahlonega.*
ADDITIONAL INFORMATION: *(404) 864-2257.*

MAP REFERENCES: *USGS 1:100,000 series: Dalton - Toccoa.*

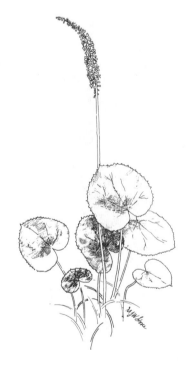

Galax
Galax aphylla

Galax, or "coltsfoot," is widespread in the mountains on dry, acid soils. It is evergreen but may turn purple or bronze in winter. It is frequently used as a Christmas decoration.

Cucumber magnolia
Magnolia acuminata

This is the largest of the mountain magnolias and has rough instead of smooth bark. Its cylindrical many-seeded fruits vaguely resemble cucumbers. The leaves are simple and do not have eared bases.

The Eastern Blue Ridge

The Blue Ridge Mountains, which form the spine of the Eastern Blue Ridge, were formed over 200 million years ago when the North American, European and African continents collided —a process called "plate tectonics." The movement of two continents against each other produced an intense pressure from the direction of what is now southeastern Georgia. Over millions of years the forces of nature have worn as much as five miles off the mountains, shaping them into the peaks, cliffsides and valleys we see today.

The changes that have gone on for millions of centuries continue today. For example, the Eastern Continental Divide running through much of Georgia, separating the waters that flow into the Gulf of Mexico from those that flow into the Atlantic, is currently moving northward at the rate of 3,000 feet every million years. Rivers continue to change course. Until recently (in geological terms) the Chattooga River, which originates in North Carolina and flows along the border between Georgia and South Carolina, was part of the headwaters of the Chattahoochee River and flowed into the Gulf of Mexico. The Savannah River, gradually cutting a path northward, eventually intersected with the Chattooga and diverted its flow southeastward into the Savannah and eventually into the Atlantic. This "river capture," one of the most interesting and easily visualized phenomenon of geological history, has occurred a number of times in Georgia and is an ongoing process. Topsoil—the thin, fragile covering of the hard gneiss and schist rock of the Blue Ridge—is forming at the rate of about one inch every 50 to 100 years. Visitors to the foot of Toxaway Dam can see how the flood of 1916 wiped away the topsoil down to bare rock in a matter of minutes.

Georgia's Blue Ridge Mountains, with their rich geological history and diverse recreational opportunities, are surprisingly undiscovered. When visiting the mountains, most of us stick to the main highways; towns such as Helen, Clayton and Dahlonega are familiar names. But few people have discovered the upper portions of the wild and scenic Chattooga River, much less explored the hundreds of scenic logging roads or, even less, walked the unmarked hiking trails known mostly to hunters and fishermen. The information on the Eastern Blue Ridge in the following pages is designed to help readers get off the main roads and onto the backroads and trails and to discover the diversity, beauty and surprising fragility of these ageless mountains.

Cooper Creek and Duncan Ridge

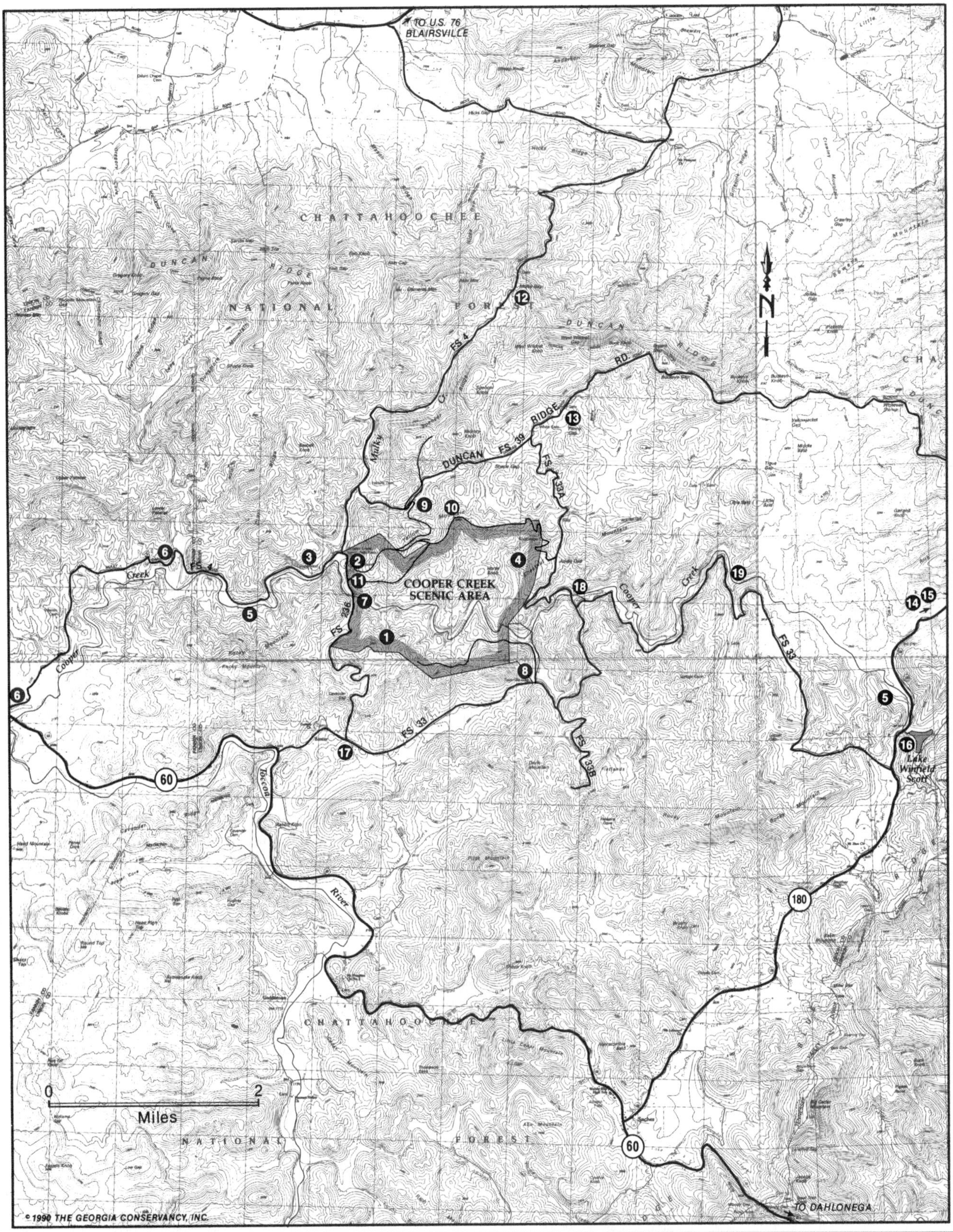

Figure 19 — **COOPER CREEK AND DUNCAN RIDGE**

Cooper Creek and Duncan Ridge

Fig. 19 - Cooper Creek and
Duncan Ridge

(page references in parentheses)

1 Cooper Creek Scenic Area (91)
2 Cooper Creek Recreation Areas and
   Mill Shoals Trail (91, 93, 94, 95)
3 Mulky Recreation Areas (91, 93, 96)
4 Bryant Creek (91, 93)
5 Cooper Creek (91)
6 FS Road 4 [off GA 60] (91)
7 Cooper Creek Bridge, Cavender Gap
   Rd, FS 236 [start Hemlock & White
   Pine Stands Hiking Trail] (93, 95)
8 Virgin Old-Growth Hike (93)
9 Duncan Ridge Road (94)
10 Top of Yellow Mountain (94)
11 Yellow Mountain Trail (94)
12 Mulky Gap [scenic drive] (91, 94)
13 Fanny Gap Drive [scenic drive] (95)
14 GA 180 [FS 39 ends] to Vogel (95)
15 Vogel State Park (95)
16 Lake Winfield Scott (95)
17 FS 33, Turkey Creek Road [Cavendar
   Gap Rd ends] (95)
18 FS 33A (95)
19 Access path leading to Cooper Creek
   [off FS 33] (96)

The 1,240-acre Cooper Creek Scenic Area [Fig. 19(1)], which ranges between 2,000 and 2,500 feet in elevation, is surrounded by more than 34,000 acres of the Cooper Creek Water Management Area and the slightly larger, overlapping Cooper Creek Wildlife Management Area. Within the latter are two U.S. Forest Service campgrounds, Cooper Creek [Fig. 19(2)] and Mulky [Fig. 19(3)] Recreation Areas. Cooper Creek Scenic Area is roughly a mile and a half long by one mile wide. Cooper Creek [Fig. 19(5)], a cold mountain trout stream, runs approximately two miles down the center of the scenic area. Numerous small branches join Cooper Creek. Two of these, Stillhouse Branch [Fig. 20(1)] and Deep Cove Branch [Fig. 20(2)], are completely contained within the boundaries of the scenic area. Bryant Creek [Fig. 19(4)], a larger tributary with its headwaters on the south face of Duncan Ridge, parallels the eastern boundary. There are stands of large hemlock and white pine, reaching three and four feet in diameter, along Cooper Creek (and to some extent, Bryant Creek) and a short way up its tributaries. These are of special interest because this is close to the southern geographical limit of the hemlock/white pine community. The only evidence of human occupation in the scenic area is a few rock piles on Deep Cove Branch, a possible former cabin site.

Cherry may have been cut for furniture manufacture in the past, and some dead chestnut was removed from among the giant poplars in the southeast corner. Otherwise, it is believed that the scenic area represents original untouched forest. Fire has apparently only rarely touched the hemlock/white pine habitat. Dense growth of uniformly-aged white pine on Chestnut Ridge and the ridge along the south boundary may attest to severe burns there in times past. The U.S. Army holds training exercises in Cooper Creek Wildlife Management Area.

In an arc crossing the northern part of Figure 19 is Duncan Ridge, perhaps the longest continuous ridge projecting from the main Blue Ridge itself. Part of Duncan Ridge is traversed by Duncan Ridge Road, accessible from the scenic area or off Highway 180 at Wolfpen Gap [Fig. 15(25)]. The Duncan Ridge Trail (see Blood Mountain) [Fig. 15(24)] is reached at several points off the Duncan Ridge Road or at Mulky Gap [Fig. 19(12)]. The north side of Duncan Ridge offers many opportunities to explore exciting environments such as boulderfields and northern hardwood forests in the coveheads, which also have spring wildflower displays.

DIRECTIONS: *Take GA 60 north from Dahlonega for 26 miles, turn east (right) onto FS Road 4 [Fig. 19(6)] and go six miles.*

ADDITIONAL INFORMATION: *U.S. Forest Service, Chestatee Ranger District, 1015 Tipton Dr., Dahlonega, GA 30533. (404) 864-6173.*

EASTERN BLUE RIDGE

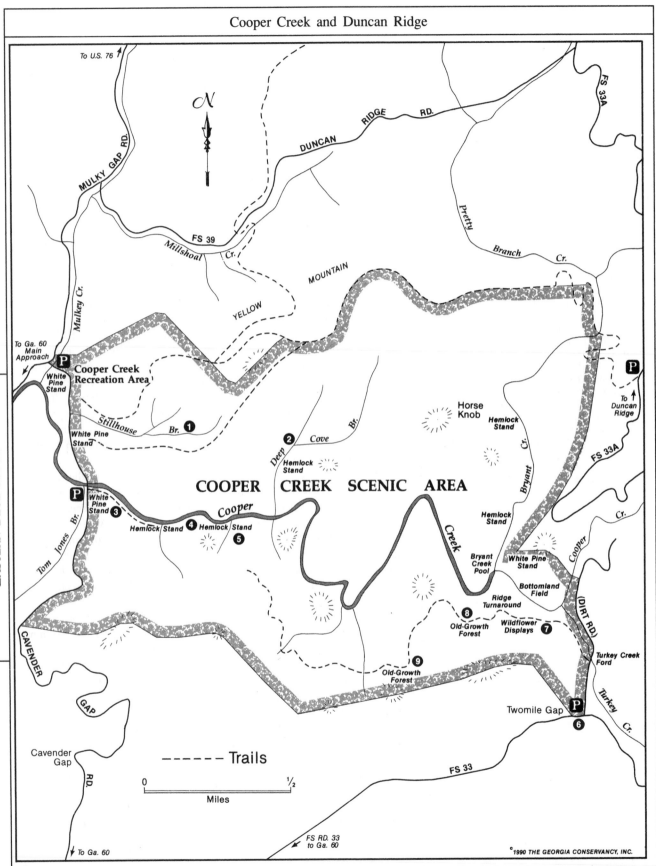

EASTERN BLUE RIDGE

Figure 20 — **COOPER CREEK SCENIC AREA**

Fig. 20 - Cooper Creek Scenic
Area

(page references in parentheses)

1 Stillhouse Branch (91)
2 Deep Cove Branch (91)
3 grove of white pines (93)
4 rhododendron & mountain laurel canopy
   (93)
5 second small feeder branch on Cooper
   Creek (93)
6 parking for hike to virgin old-growth
   timber (93)
7 log road - hike to virgin old-growth
   timber (93)
8 first big trees - hike to virgin old-
   growth timber (94)
9 largest poplars - "valley of the giants"
   (94)

~**MULKY CAMPGROUND.** [Fig. 19(3)] A small campground with 10 campsites. Camping is usually from the last Saturday in March through mid-October. There are sanitary facilities, drinking water, tent pads and picnic tables.

DIRECTIONS: *Same as for Cooper Creek, above. Once on FS 4, continue on this dirt/gravel road entering and leaving national forest property once before re-entering just before the campground sign.*

~**COOPER CREEK RECREATION AREA.** [Fig. 19(2)] Located along the banks of sparkling mountain streams stocked with trout, adjacent to the Cooper Creek Scenic Area. The 20 campsites can accommodate either tents or trailers up to 22 feet. There are sanitary facilities and drinking water. The Mill Shoals Trail originates in the Recreation Area and the Yellow Mountain Trail is nearby.

DIRECTIONS: *Same as for Cooper Creek and Mulky Campground, above. Continue less than a mile through the Mulky Campground to intersection with FS 236 entering from right. The recreation area is immediately ahead on this road.*

~**HIKING TRAILS.**

HEMLOCK AND WHITE PINE STANDS. A suggested walking route to see the streamside stands of hemlock/heath and white pine begins at the bridge over Cooper Creek on Cavender Gap Road, FS 236 [Fig. 19(7)], and follows the right (south) bank to at least the second small feeder branch coming in on the right side. Here there is a rough trail made by fishermen. It passes through a grove of white pines [Fig. 20(3)], then under an almost solid canopy of rhododendron and mountain laurel [Fig. 20(4)]. After 0.25 mile one begins to encounter the large hemlocks and white pines. At the second branch [Fig. 20(5)] is another intriguing grove in the tiny valley of the feeder stream. Farther up these small branch streams are cove hardwoods—oak, buckeye, hickory, cucumber tree and yellow poplar.

VIRGIN OLD-GROWTH HIKE. [Fig. 19(8)] About 1 mile. Park at a low gap [Fig. 20(6)] about 0.4 mile from the end of the pavement going east on FS 33. There will be an old road pitching steeply north, the first road to the left after leaving the pavement. Park along FS 33. Walk down this road and take the first left-hand log road [Fig. 20(7)] just before the Turkey Creek ford. This nearly level log road passes through several moist coves with wildflower displays. Across Cooper Creek is a six-acre bottomland that has been continuously in cultivation since early settler times and probably even in Indian days. After passing two small coves, watch for the first place that a vehicle could be turned around (the turn-around is on a ridge which leads down to a fine pool at the mouth of Bryant Creek [Fig. 19(4)]). From the turn-around ridge the first of the big trees [Fig. 20(8)] is only several hundred yards along the old log road. The old-growth forest has widely spaced specimens of large white and northern red oak and black birch, but the largest trees are giant tulip poplars with circumferences of up to 17 feet. Storms through the ages have broken the tops out of many of them. While many big trees can be seen from the log road, others must be searched for above and below the road. The log road continues, crosses a white pine ridge and in about 0.25 mile reaches the "valley of the giants" where the largest poplars grow [Fig. 20(9)]. The trail continues to parallel Cooper Creek for an undetermined distance.

MILL SHOALS TRAIL. [Fig. 19(2)] This trail is approximately two miles one way and considered moderate to strenuous. It is nearly impossible to follow without a map and detailed instructions. The starting point is well marked with a sign opposite the first entrance to the recreation area, but after that there are neither blazes nor signs. Stay to the right when entering the trail. It climbs steeply to a ridgetop, then descends through hardwoods to a jeep road, turns right onto the jeep road for 15 or 20 paces, then narrows and drops toward a stream on the left. It winds through an area with tall hemlock, white pine and dense vegetation, crosses three small streams, turns right on an old road and in about 50 feet turns left. At Duncan Ridge Road [Fig. 19(9)] it turns right, stays on the road for 350-400 yards and then continues on the left of the road. Leaving the roadside, it slowly goes up the side of a dry ridge on which one can see bracken fern, then goes straight and ends at the next jeep road.

YELLOW MOUNTAIN TRAIL. [Fig. 19(11)] This is mainly a ridge trail. It is 1.6 miles one way and is considered moderate. The trail entrance is marked by a yellow post on the northeast side of Cavender Gap Road, FS 236. The trail is marked with yellow blazes. At the start of the trail, one passes through a shady grove of hemlock on a hillside above a small stream; later there are several large remnant oaks. The trail gently ascends a ridge, which forms the northern boundary of Cooper Creek Scenic Area, for 1.2 miles to the top of Yellow Mountain [Fig. 19(10)]. Short leaf pine are common along the route. The trail then descends through an area scorched by fire and ends at the first dirt road.

~SCENIC DRIVES. There are three scenic drives which can be made through the area. Each drive begins at the entrance sign to Cooper Creek on FS 4.

MULKY GAP DRIVE. [Fig. 19(12)] The first drive continues on FS 4 north across Mulky Gap. It goes up along Mulky Creek, with a beautiful streamside zone of hemlock/heath. Soon after the gap, one can either turn right on FS 40—a dead-end road which in May and

Tulip poplar
Liriodendron tulipifera

Along with those of the white pine, the wind-borne seeds of the tulip poplar rapidly seed in to openings in mountain forests. Poplars often take over moist coves denuded by heavy logging or disease, such as the chestnut blight. They often attain a venerable age and large diameter; in Cooper Creek Scenic Area some poplars measure 17 feet in circumference. Unfortunately, there is little or no demand for poplar lumber.

June will reward the visitor with a display of mountain laurel in bloom—or continue on FS 4, which winds down to US 76 west of Blairsville.

FANNY GAP DRIVE. [Fig. 19(13)] Turn right (east) from FS 4 onto FS 39. It passes Fanny Gap before turning sharply to follow Duncan Ridge past Buckeye Knob, Coosa Bald (4,271 feet) and Wildcat Knob. The road ends at GA 180 [Fig. 19(14)], which goes east to Vogel State Park [Fig. 19(15)] and US 19/129 past Sosebee Cove Scenic Area, or goes west past beautiful trout-stocked Lake Winfield Scott [Fig. 19(16)] to GA 60 at Suches.

THE LOOP DRIVE. Turn right (south) near the Cooper Creek Recreation Area [Fig. 19(2)] onto the dirt Cavender Gap Road (FS 236) [Fig. 19(7)] which winds through a forest of large eastern white pine, eastern hemlock, oak, hickory and poplar and ends at paved FS 33, Turkey Creek Road [Fig. 19(17)]. Turn left (east) and proceed until the pavement ends after approximately two miles. Go on the gravel road for 0.4 mile to a low gap (Two Mile Gap) where a narrow road dips steeply at the left. This is the main entrance to the east end of the scenic area and the starting point for the short hike to the virgin old-growth area (see above). The gravel road continues to the point where FS 33 makes a hairpin curve to the right. Here go straight ahead onto FS 33A [Fig. 19(18)], which crosses Cooper Creek, Addis Gap and Bryant Creek before ending at FS 39. Turn left and go to the juncture with FS 4; turn left again and return to the starting point.

~A CANOEING GUIDE TO COOPER CREEK. Cooper Creek flows from the base of the dam on Lake Winfield Scott [Fig. 19(16)]. The dam is 14.5 miles south of Blairsville on GA 180. From its beginning, Cooper Creek twists and flows out of the mountains for 15 miles before it joins the Toccoa River along GA 60. The creek runs through three federally protected areas: the Chattahoochee National Forest and two areas within Cooper Creek Game Management Area and Cooper Creek Scenic Area. Cooper Creek has long been a popular trout-fishing stream and could well become one of Georgia's most popular canoeing streams as well.

The first four miles of Cooper Creek are too narrow and shallow to canoe, and the final four miles flow mostly through flat, privately-owned farmland. The seven-mile stretch in between, however, is as interesting a run of Class II whitewater as Georgia has to offer. The average gradient of Cooper Creek is a steep 40-plus feet per mile, which puts it in the "gradient class" with such mighty rivers as the Chattooga Section IV (45 feet per mile) and Alabama's Little River Canyon (31 feet per mile). However, because Cooper Creek has a smaller watershed area and a lower level of water, it is less difficult to canoe than either of these rivers. Cooper Creek is within the

Two-lined salamander
Eurycea bislineata

Often vividly yellow or reddish with two black lines down the sides, this small slender salamander lives under rocks along mountain streams. Large numbers, assumed to be breeding aggregations, have been found in Cooper Creek. An aquatic variety of this salamander occurs in watercress-choked springs of the Valley and Ridge Province.

EASTERN BLUE RIDGE

Class II-III difficulty range. Nevertheless, the creek is a steep little stream that requires experience and skill to negotiate. There are two waterfalls—one drops five feet and the other, eight feet—which are good Class III runs. A long slide of twisting channels and barrier rocks, which descends more than five feet, is, in high water, a Class III run as well.

DIRECTIONS: *To reach the put-in on Cooper Creek, go north out of Dahlonega nine miles on US 19/GA 60 to the point where the two roads separate. Bear left on GA 60, go seven miles to Suches and turn right (north) onto GA 180. Go north on 180 for 4.4 miles to Lake Winfield Scott Recreation Area. Turn left on FS 33 and go five miles. An access path leading down to the edge of the creek branches off FS 33 at the five-mile point [Fig. 19(19)]. Limited but adequate parking space is provided at this put-in. To reach the take-out, go west from the put-in on FS 33 for 1.4 miles to an intersection. (A right turn at this intersection and a 0.1-mile drive will lead to the Bryant Creek Road Bridge. The bridge offers a good view of the river and could serve as an alternate put-in, shortening the canoe trip by 1.7 miles.) At the intersection turn left and continue 3.5 miles on FS 33 to where it meets FS 236; turn right (north) on FS 236 and go 2.3 miles to the Cooper Creek Scenic Area and the Tom Jones Creek Bridge over Cooper Creek; cross the bridge and continue 0.5 mile through the campground; turn left (west) on FS 4; go another 0.5 mile to Mulky Creek Campground [Fig. 19(3)]. The total distance from put-in to take-out is about seven miles.*

MAP REFERENCES: *1:24,000 series: Suches - Neel's Gap - Mulky Gap - Coosa Bald.*

Dutchman's breeches
Dicentra cucullaria

Dutchman's breeches and squirrel corn (*D. canadensis*) look very much alike. Both are indicators of moist, rich high-elevation north-facing coves and boulderfields. They may be seen above the road at Sosebee Cove [Fig. 18 (6)]. Their delicate, filigreed foliage is distinctive.

Blood Mountain

Blood Mountain [Fig. 21(1)] is the highest peak on Georgia's portion of the Appalachian Trail. Some believe the name came from a bloody battle between the Cherokee and Creek Indians long before white men arrived in the area. Other theories derive the name from red lichen or Catawba rhododendron growing on the rocky summit. At 4,458 feet, it overlooks an area rich in streams, hiking trails and scenic recreation spots, one of which—Sosebee Cove [Fig. 21(2)]—is probably Georgia's only north-facing cove traversed by a paved road at such high elevation. It has an accessible boulderfield, northern hardwoods and large buckeyes and provides an example of how tulip poplar takes over following too-thorough logging of cove hardwood forests.

~DESOTO FALLS SCENIC RECREATION AREA.
[Fig. 21(14)] DeSoto Falls was named for the Spanish explorer DeSoto because a piece of armor attributed to his expedition was supposedly found in the area. The scenic area is located in rugged, mountainous country with exceptional views. Elevations in this 650-acre area of clear streams feeding Frogtown Creek vary between 2,000 and 3,400 feet. Visitors can hike to view five waterfalls.
FACILITIES: *Parking, restrooms, camping, picnicking, fishing, hiking.*
DATES/HOURS: *Open late spring to early fall.*
FEES: *Campsite $5 per night.*
DIRECTIONS: *Take US 129 north from Cleveland 15 miles.*
ADDITIONAL INFORMATION: *DeSoto Falls Scenic and Recreation Area, U.S. Forest Service, Chestatee Ranger District, 200 W. Main, P.O. Box 2080, Dahlonega, GA 30533. (404) 864-6173.*

DESOTO FALLS TRAIL. [Fig. 21(14)] Three miles. The lower 0.8 mile of the trail passes by the two lower cascades of DeSoto Falls [Fig. 21(16)] and is relatively easy. The last 2.2 miles leading to the uppermost falls on Frogtown Creek [Fig. 21(17)] are much steeper. The trailhead is in the Desoto Falls Recreation Area.
DIRECTIONS: *Follow the directions to DeSoto Falls Scenic Area (above). The trail begins at the bridge in the lower camping loop of DeSoto Falls Recreation Area.*

~DESOTO FALLS CAMPGROUND. [Fig. 21(15)] This is rugged, mountainous country with exceptional views and several beautiful waterfalls. It is adjacent to DeSoto Falls Scenic Area (see above).
FACILITIES: *Twenty-four campsites, six picnic sites, restrooms with cold showers, streams for wading and fishing.*
DIRECTIONS: *Take US 129 north from Cleveland 15 miles.*

EASTERN BLUE RIDGE

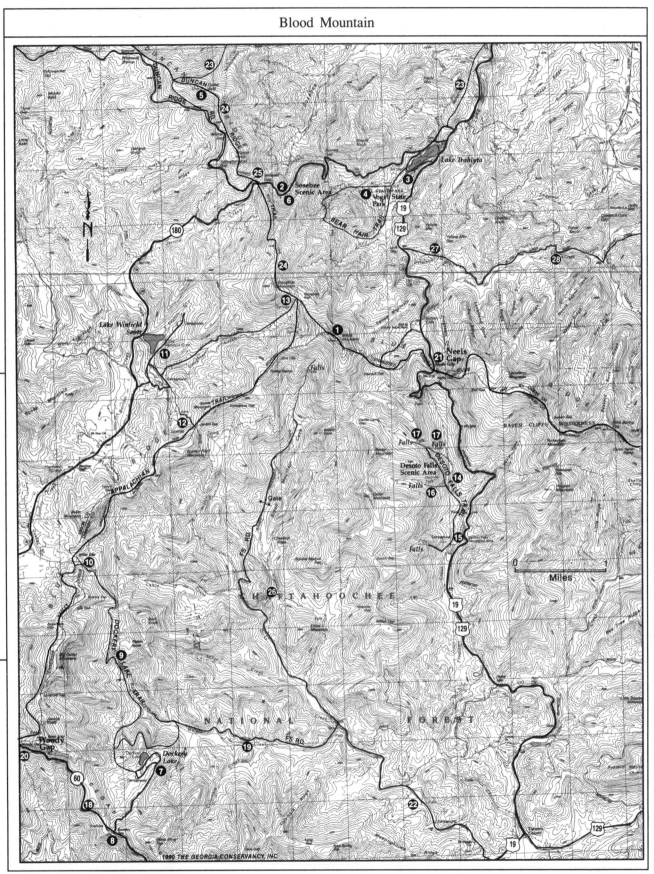

Blood Mountain

Figure 21 — **BLOOD MOUNTAIN**

98

Fig. 21 - Blood Mountain
(page references in parentheses)

1 Blood Mountain (97, 99, 102)
2 Sosebee Cove (97, 102)
3 Vogel State Park (99)
4 Bear Hair Trail (101)
5 Coosa Bald [Duncan Ridge] (101, 102)
6 Sosebee Cove Scenic Area & Hiking Trail (101)
7 Dockery Lake Recreation Area a/k/a Lakeshore Trail (103)
8 FS Road 654 [off GA 60 at Dockery Lake sign] (103)
9 Dockery Lake Trail (103)
10 Miller Gap [end Dockery Lake Trail] (103)
11 Lake Winfield Scott (102)
12 Jarrard Gap Trail (102)
13 Slaughter Creek Trail & Gap (102)
14 DeSoto Falls Scenic Recreation Area & Trail (97)
15 DeSoto Falls Campground (97)
16 DeSoto Falls two lower cascades (97)
17 Frogtown Creek and falls (97)
18 Chestatee Overlook (103)
19 Waters Creek [trophy trout stream] (103)
20 Woody Gap (102)
21 Walasi-Yi Interpretive Center (99)
22 Waters Creek Recreation Area (104)
23 Coosa Backcountry Trail (101)
24 Duncan Ridge Trail (91, 102)
25 Wolfpen Gap (91, 102)
26 Blood Mountain Falls (104)
27 Helton Creek Falls drive (101)
28 Helton Creek Falls (101)

~WALASI-YI INTERPRETIVE CENTER. [Fig. 21(21)]

The beautiful stone center was built from 1934 to 1938 of native rock by the Civilian Conservation Corps. It was placed on the National Register of Historic Places in 1977 and is now owned by the Department of Natural Resources. In the breezeway here is the only place where the 2,135-mile-long Appalachian Trail (A.T.) goes through a man-made structure. Approximately 1,000 hikers each year pass through the breezeway, hoping to hike the entire 2,000 miles from Georgia to Maine. There is a store here (owned by Jeff and Dorothy Hansen since 1983) with outdoor books, mountain crafts, gifts, maps, clothing and camping equipment.

DIRECTIONS: *At Neel's Gap on US 19 and 129, approximately 18 miles north of Cleveland and 21 miles north of Dahlonega.*

ADDITIONAL INFORMATION: *Mountain crossing at Walasi-Yi Center, Hwy. 129, Rt. 1, Box 1240, Blairsville, GA 30512. (404) 745-6095.*

~NEEL'S GAP TO BLOOD MOUNTAIN HIKE. [Fig. 21(1)]

About two miles. An enjoyable day trip with many scenic vistas is a climb up Blood Mountain (4,458 feet). The trail is generally steep and rocky in many places but easy to follow. Near the summit hikers will be rewarded with several picnic rocks and superb vistas from rock outcrops, including views of Mount Yonah, Tray Mountain, Lake Winfield Scott and Slaughter Mountain. An old stone cabin, built by the Civilian Conservation Corps in the 1930's as an Appalachian Trail shelter and listed on the National Register of Historic Places, sits near the top. This is the highest point on the Appalachian Trail in Georgia. It is perhaps the state's most-hiked portion of the Appalachian Trail.

DIRECTIONS: *To reach the trailhead follow directions to the Walasi-Yi Center, above. Parking for day hikers is 0.5 mile north of the center. Follow the blue blazes from the parking area along the Reece Access Trail. After about 0.8 mile the trail intersects with the white-blazed Appalachian Trail at Flatrock Gap (a 420-foot increase in elevation). Turn right onto the A.T. and proceed about 1.5 miles to the top of Blood Mountain.*

~VOGEL STATE PARK. [Fig. 21(3)]

One of the prettiest state parks in all of Georgia. It is over 2,500 feet in elevation, usually affording cool temperatures even during hot summer months. The park can be crowded in summer, and campsites fill up quickly. There are short hiking trails in the park as well as the trailhead for the challenging 12.5-mile Coosa Backcountry Trail (see below).

FACILITIES: *Thirty-six cottages, 95 tent or trailer sites with water and electrical hookups (15 sites without), picnic shelters and tables, grills, restrooms, hot showers, stocked trout lake, swimming beach, paddle boats for rent, playground, miniature golf. Maps are available at the visitor center near the entrance.*

EASTERN BLUE RIDGE

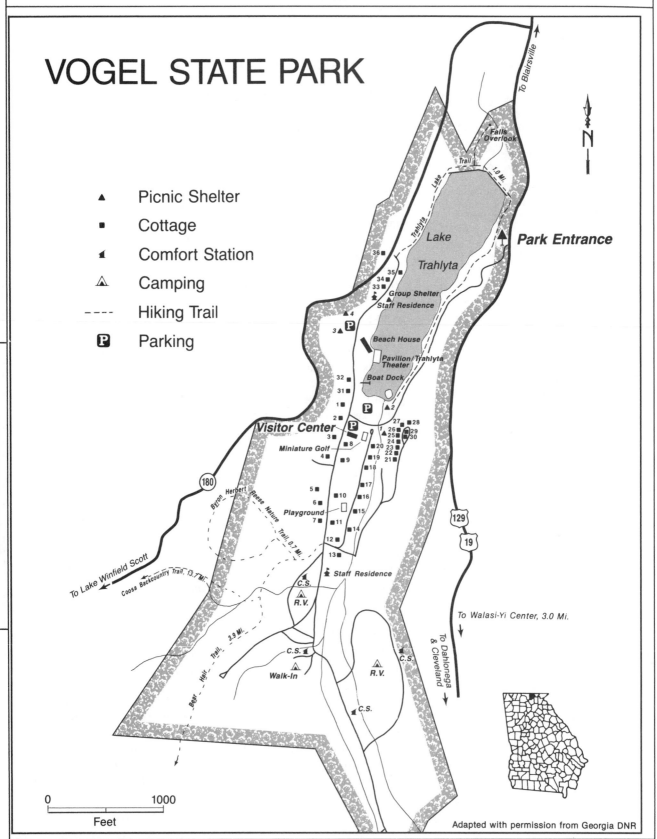

VOGEL STATE PARK

▲ Picnic Shelter
■ Cottage
◄ Comfort Station
⚠ Camping
- - - - Hiking Trail
🅿 Parking

Park Entrance

Falls Overlook

Lake Trahlyta

Lake Trahlyta Trail 1.0 Mi.

36
35
34
33
Group Shelter
Staff Residence
4
3
Beach House
Pavilion/Trahlyta Theater
Boat Dock
32
31
1
2
Visitor Center
27 28
26 29
25 30
24
23
8
20
22
4
19 21
9
18
3
Miniature Golf
5
10 17
6 16
Playground
7 11 15
14
12
13
Staff Residence
C.S.
R.V.

To Blairsville

To Lake Winfield Scott

Byron Herbert Reese Nature Trail 0.7 Mi.

Coosa Backcountry Trail, 13.7 Mi.

Bear Hair Trail, 3.9 Mi.

Walk-In

C.S.
R.V.

C.S.

C.S.

To Walasi-Yi Center, 3.0 Mi.

To Dahlonega & Cleveland

180
129
19

0   1000
Feet

Adapted with permission from Georgia DNR

Figure 22 — **VOGEL STATE PARK**

DATES/HOURS: *Open year round 7am-10pm, swimming Jun. 1 - Labor Day except on Mondays; office open 8-5.*
DIRECTIONS: *Eleven miles south of Blairsville on US 19/129.*
ADDITIONAL INFORMATION: *Vogel State Park, Rt. 1, Box 1230, Blairsville, GA 30512. (404) 745-2628.*

~HIKING TRAILS AT VOGEL STATE PARK.

BEAR HAIR TRAIL. [Fig. 21(4)] Four miles. This orange-blaze-marked loop trail is ideal for family hikes. It is of moderate difficulty, beginning and ending in Vogel State Park.
DIRECTIONS: *Follow directions to Vogel State Park, above. The trail begins behind the visitor center.*

COOSA BACKCOUNTRY TRAIL. [Fig. 21(23)] 12.5 miles. This difficult trail is marked with yellow blazes and signs and for the most part is easy to follow. It fords streams on its lower part and traverses the high Duncan Ridge, including Coosa Bald [Fig. 21(5)] at over 4,000 feet. It is recommended that hikers take more than one day to hike the entire route, although it can be done in one long day, particularly during the longer daylight hours of spring and summer. A permit is required and is available free, together with a trail map, at the Vogel State Park Visitor Center.
DIRECTIONS: *The trail begins in Vogel State Park (see directions above).*

~HELTON CREEK FALLS DRIVE. [Fig. 21(27)] About 1.5 miles south of Vogel State Park at Lark Gap, a rough dirt road (FS 118) goes down Helton Creek. With care, in 1.6 miles you can reach the very beautiful Helton Creek Falls [Fig. 21(28)] even in an average car. To continue on to this road's terminus at the Russell Scenic Highway requires great care. Because of potholes and creek fordings, it is recommended only for 4x4 and high-clearance vehicles. There are actually two falls, one about 30 feet high and visible from the road; the other, twice as high, is about 150 feet upstream.

~SOSEBEE COVE SCENIC AREA AND HIKING TRAIL.
[Fig. 21(6)] This 175-acre tract of prize hardwood timber is a memorial to Arthur Woody, who served as a Forest Service Ranger from 1911 to 1945. Ranger Woody, the "Barefoot Ranger," loved this peaceful cove and negotiated its purchase by the Forest Service. Rare and beautiful wildflowers and ferns abound. In the boulderfield above the road, there is rich high-altitude herb flora, including Dutchman's breeches, squirrel corn, waterleaf and others. Here also is found the rare yellowwood tree and representative northern hardwoods, such as yellow birch. A salamander-rich branch flows down the cove. There are several large buckeyes below the road, along with a stand of second-growth yellow poplar that followed heavy

EASTERN BLUE RIDGE

logging and destroyed the diversity of the cove forest. A 0.5-mile loop trail circles the area.

Woody, with his own funds, brought the first deer back into the mountains after they had been extirpated in 1895. He always claimed his father killed the last deer in north Georgia in that year.

DIRECTIONS: *Take US 129 south from Blairsville for 9.5 miles; turn right (west) on GA 180 and go two miles to the Sosebee Cove parking area [Fig. 21(2)] on the right.*

~DUNCAN RIDGE TRAIL. [Fig. 21(24)] On this trail, one can traverse the longest contiguous ridge line leading off the main Blue Ridge. Trail begins at Blood Mountain [Fig. 21(1)], crosses northwest through Slaughter Gap [Fig. 21(13)], Wolfpen Gap [Fig. 21(25)], and Coosa Bald [Fig. 21(5)], then goes westward to Mulky Gap (Cooper Creek section) and intersects with the Benton Mackaye Trail (Long Trails section).

~LAKE WINFIELD SCOTT. [Fig. 21(11)] This lovely, clear, 18-acre mountain lake, which is owned and managed by the U.S. Forest Service, is the source of Cooper Creek and contains a large population of rainbow trout. A nice hiking trail circles the lake.

FACILITIES: *Camping, picnicking, swimming, boating (electric motors only), fishing and hiking.*

DIRECTIONS: *Take US 19 south from Blairsville 9.5 miles; turn right (west) on GA 180 and go seven miles.*

JARRARD GAP TRAIL [FIG. 21(12)] AND SLAUGHTER CREEK TRAIL [FIG. 21(13)]. One mile and 2.7 miles, respectively. These two trails provide access to the Appalachian Trail from Lake Winfield Scott Recreation Area. The Jarrard Gap Trail follows an old logging road through cove hardwoods.

DIRECTIONS: *Follow directions to Lake Winfield Scott, above. The trails begin at the main bulletin board near the head of the lake and share the same path for a short distance. Parking is available near the campground host's cabin.*

~WOODY GAP. [Fig. 21(20)] The gap, with scenic vistas of Yahoola Valley, is marked with a large wooden sign. This is where the white-blazed Appalachian Trail crosses GA 60. A moderate one-mile hike to the north leads to a rock-outcrop overlook on the rocky face of Big Cedar Mountain (3,737 feet). A 1.5-mile hike to the south leads to a southerly view of the Yahoola Valley from atop Ramrock Mountain (3,200 feet). Both of these trail sections offer a pretty display of spring wildflowers on this richly wooded Blue Ridge Mountain range.

FACILITIES: *Large parking area with chemical toilets and trash cans; picnicking areas with 10 tables located on both sides of the road.*

Bloodroot
Sanguinaria canadensis

One of the earliest spring wildflowers, its characteristic large, round leaf with an irregular edge persists into summer. The tuberous red roots produce an orange dye that can color both skin and cloth.

DIRECTIONS: *Fourteen miles north of Dahlonega on GA 60.*

~CHESTATEE OVERLOOK. [Fig. 21(18)] The overlook offers a scenic vista of Blood Mountain Cove. There are hiking trails in the area (see below). The watershed in the foreground is the famous Waters Creek trophy trout stream [Fig. 21(19)].
FACILITIES: *Three picnic tables.*
DIRECTIONS: *Take GA 60 north from Dahlonega 12 miles.*

~DOCKERY LAKE RECREATION AREA. [Fig. 21(7)] Dockery Lake (2,388 feet), nestled within a large cove surrounded by ridgetops and small valleys, offers the forest visitor a wide variety of natural and scenic beauty. Deer and grouse are common sights. Purple rhododendron blooms in May at higher elevations, while the white variety blooms in mid-June at lower elevations. Native trees such as dogwood, sourwood, locust and laurel add more color to spring and brilliance to the fall leaf season. Trout fishing is available along the Pigeon Roost Creek and nearby Waters Creek, as well as in the six-acre Dockery Lake, which is stocked on a regular basis.
FACILITIES: *Eleven campsites (no electrical or water hookups or showers), restrooms, drinking water, fishing, hiking, six picnic sites.*
DATES/HOURS: *For picnicking and fishing, from the last Sat. in Mar.-Nov. 30; overnight camping usually extends from around May 1 through the end of Oct.*
FEES: *Campsite $5 per night.*
DIRECTIONS: *Follow GA 60 for 12.3 miles north of Dahlonega and turn right onto FS 654 opposite the Dockery Lake sign [Fig. 21(8)].*
ADDITIONAL INFORMATION: *Dockery Lake, U.S. Forest Service, Toccoa Ranger District, E. Main St., Box 1839, Blue Ridge, GA 30513. (404) 632-3031.*

DOCKERY LAKE TRAIL. [Fig. 21(9)] 3.4 miles. This trail provides access to the Appalachian Trail. It winds north three miles over an old logging road and terminates at Miller Gap [Fig. 21(10)]. The trail parallels a portion of Pigeon Roost Creek and provides scenic views of nearby mountain ridges and peaks. Twelve streams either parallel or cross the trail. Stands of hemlock, white pine, hickory, black walnut and magnolia cling to the mountain slopes of granite and milky quartz. Delicate mosses and colorful lichens adorn the boulders bordering much of the trail. In spring, the trail comes alive with blooming magnolias and wildflowers including wild iris, trillium, bloodroot and fleabane.
DIRECTIONS: *Follow the directions for Dockery Lake Recreation, above. The trail begins at the parking lot.*

LAKESHORE TRAIL. [Fig. 21(7)] 0.5 mile. This trail encircles Dockery Lake and is accessible to the handicapped. Footpaths provide access to fishing areas around the Lake.

EASTERN BLUE RIDGE

DIRECTIONS: *Follow directions for Dockery Lake Recreation Area, above. The trail begins at the parking lot.*

~WATERS CREEK RECREATION AREA. [Fig. 21(22)] Located along a beautiful mountain stream. The headwaters is a trophy trout stream.
FACILITIES: *Camping, picnicking, hiking and fishing.*
DIRECTIONS: *Take US 19 north from Dahlonega 12 miles, turn left (northwest) onto FS 34 [Fig. 21(22)] and go one mile.*

~BLOOD MOUNTAIN FALLS. [Fig. 21(26)] This waterfall is located on Blood Mountain Creek, which flows approximately 20 feet through a rock cut, creating a churning sluice of water. An unmaintained footpath leads to the falls. Picnic facilities are available at the Waters Creek Recreation Area (above).
DIRECTIONS: *Follow the directions to Waters Creek Recreation Area, above. After passing the game warden station the road narrows; go 2.5 miles to Blood Mountain Creek. The falls are located on the right.*

MAP REFERENCES: *USGS 1:24,000 series: Neel's Gap - Coosa Bald.*

White tail deer
Odocoileus virginianus

By the 1930's these deer were nearly exterminated in the Blue Ridge. They were reintroduced by Ranger Arthur Woody of Suches, Georgia. They are mainly browsers and eat a variety of shrubs and herbs. Acorns (and formerly chestnuts) are their primary food. They also eat lichens, as well as fallen dead leaves.

EASTERN BLUE RIDGE

Raven
Corvus corax

The subject of Edgar Allen Poe's famous poem, this very large, black bird, twice the size of a crow, sticks to the highest parts of the Georgia Blue Ridge, where it nests in cliffs. A hoarse, croaking call is usually the only evidence of a raven in the vicinity.

Raven Cliffs

Raven Cliffs Wilderness Area is located northwest of Cleveland. A number of trails with beautiful mountain streams and waterfalls, mountaintops, a wide variety of natural community types, rock outcrops and scenic vistas abound throughout the area.

Established in 1986, Raven Cliffs Wilderness is 9,649 acres. It is the first designated wilderness along the Appalachian Trail as the hiker heads north toward Maine.

~DUKE'S CREEK FALLS TRAIL. [Fig. 23(1)] About one mile. The large falls seen from the trail and parking lot [Fig. 23(4)] is called Duke's Creek Falls even though it is on Davis Creek. There are several smaller waterfalls in the area. The trail ends at the confluence of Davis Creek and Duke's Creek. Duke's Creek is a beautiful mountain waterway with large boulders and splashing water around foaming pools and riffles. Spray from the falls, which is about 250 feet high, cools the area and provides a pleasant relief for the hiker. Careful observers will notice the small wildflowers growing along the banks of the trail. Water seeps out of this bank at scattered locations and, with broken patches of sunlight, provides excellent habitat for a variety of flora. This is a west-facing slope with patches of mountain laurel and rhododendron all along the way. The upper part of the slope is drier, with mixed hardwoods, especially oaks, hickories and tulip poplar, forming a tree canopy about 50 feet high. Toward the bottom of the trail and along Duke's Creek, a cove forest of young hemlock and white pine is developing. Several large hemlocks provide an accent along the stream bank.
DIRECTIONS: *Take GA 75 north from Helen for 1.5 miles; turn left on GA 356 (75 Alt); go 2.3 miles to the Richard Russell Scenic Highway; turn right and go two miles to the Duke's Creek Falls parking area [Fig. 23(4)]. An alternate access is to go approximately one mile farther north on Richard Russell Scenic Highway to a Forest Service road which intersects the highway [Fig. 23(3)] to the southwest and travel along the southern boundary of the Raven Cliffs Wilderness Area. If the gate is open, one can drive 0.6 mile, park and then follow an unmarked trail over a small ridge and down to the top of Duke's Creek Falls. The falls can be clearly heard from the FS road, and the hike is only about 1,200 feet from the road.*

~RAVEN CLIFFS FALLS TRAIL. [Fig. 23(5)] About 2.5 miles. Marked with blue blazes. Dodd's Creek is one of the most beautiful mountain streams easily accessible in north Georgia. It splashes and winds through the mountain valley with an abundance of whitewater, riffles and pools, moss-covered seepages and overhanging tangles of laurel. At numerous points along the trail the hiker can

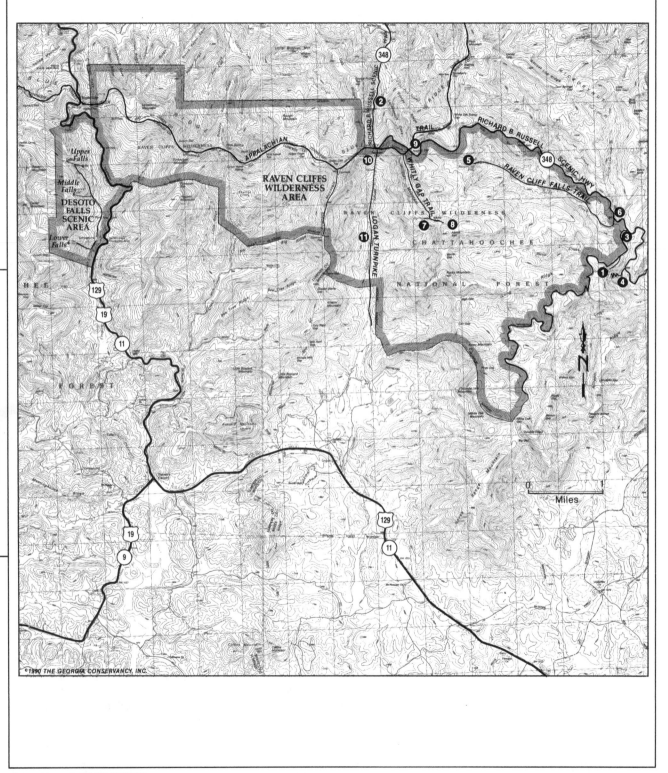

Fig. 23 - Raven Cliffs
(page references in parentheses)

1 Duke's Creek Falls Trail (105)
2 Richard Russell Scenic Highway (109)
3 Forest Service Rd to Raven Cliffs Wilderness Area [intersects Russell Scene Hwy] (105)
4 Duke's Creek Falls parking lot (105)
5 Raven Cliffs Falls (105)
6 Raven Cliffs Falls trailhead and parking area (107)
7 Wildcat Mountain, Whitly Gap Trail (107)
8 Adams Bald (107)
9 parking area [north of Russell Hwy access to Wildcat Mountain] a/k/a Hogpen Gap (108, 109)
10 Tesnatee Gap (108, 109)
11 Logan Turnpike Trail (108)

approach the stream for a closer view. There are five or six lesser falls to observe along the way, and one of these is impressive enough to make many visitors think it is Raven Cliffs Falls itself. Near the falls the trail climbs about 40 feet and moves a little away from Dodd's Creek, then returns at Raven Cliffs. Directly ahead, the visitor encounters a massive cliff face of solid rock that rises vertically from the landscape about 80-90 feet. The cliff appears from the trail as two large blocks with a narrow crevasse between. Raven Cliff Falls results from the water of Dodd's Creek falling straight down between the blocks back inside the crevasse and into a dark pool at the bottom. Although the water flow is not great this high in the drainage basin, the sound of it is amplified by the cliff face and gives the visitor an overall impression of the powerful forces at work sculpting the mountain landscape.

Even though no signs identify the trail, it is a heavily visited area. On a November weekend, for example, 42 vehicles were parked at the trailhead and six camps were in use nearby. At Raven Cliffs, two mountain climbers were rappelling from the cliff face and several hikers were sitting on top of the cliff. In spite of such a level of activity, this is one of the best trails anywhere for a great hiking experience with the whole family.

DIRECTIONS: *Take GA 75 north from Helen 1.5 miles; turn left on GA 356 (75 Alt) and go 2.3 miles to the Richard Russell Scenic Highway; turn right and go 2.8 miles to the trailhead and parking area [Fig. 23(6)].*

~WILDCAT MOUNTAIN, WHITLY GAP TRAIL. [Fig. 23(7)]

Whitly Gap Trail is about 1.1 miles long; if the visitor wants to visit Adams Bald [Fig. 23(8)], another 0.5 mile is added to the trip. The best part of the trail, however, is to the top of Wildcat Mountain, which is only about 0.5 mile. The climb up the north slope is about 300 feet. This trail is fun for children and adults alike. It ascends from the road first through a stand of sweet birch and some hardwoods and then through a laurel thicket of rhododendron and mountain laurel. This type of heath growth is typical on the north-facing slope of higher peaks in this area. Whitly Gap Trail is an easily accessible example of this fairyland growth form. Children are amazed by this natural community type. Everything is their size and everything is green and pretty. There are moss-covered rocks, ferns and wildflowers along the trail. Small gnarled limbs of the laurel thicket arch over the path, making it a small secret passageway. The trail emerges from the evergreen thicket near the ridgetop of Wildcat Mountain at an elevation just under 3,800 feet. This is the highest peak in the vicinity and provides an outstanding scenic view in all directions, especially west and south. The fairyland theme continues on the Wildcat Mountain ridgeline. White oaks, chestnut oaks, scarlet oaks and several sweet birch, which normally grow into tall dominant trees, are gnarled and stunted on the mountaintop. Limbs

EASTERN BLUE RIDGE

start about two feet from the ground and children can't resist climbing them to get an adult's view of the surrounding mountain ranges.
DIRECTIONS: *About seven miles northwest of the junction of the Richard Russell Scenic Highway and GA 75 Alt. The Appalachian Trail crosses Richard Russell Scenic Highway at Hogpen Gap. Whitly Gap Trail branches off the A.T. on the north slope of Wildcat Mountain. A parking area [Fig. 23(9)] on the north side of the Russell Highway provides convenient access to Wildcat Mountain.*

~LOGAN TURNPIKE TRAIL. [Fig. 23(11)] About two miles. The Logan Turnpike is an abandoned toll road which was privately maintained and used during horse-and-buggy days as a corridor through the mountains. It is difficult to imagine anyone pulling an empty wagon, much less a fully loaded one, straight up this steep trail through Tesnatee Gap [Fig. 23(10)]. About 1,200 feet down the trail and near the bottom of the steep part of the slope, one of the most interesting aspects of this trail begins to appear. Here is an excellent location to observe firsthand the formation of a natural stream in the forest. Tiny springs of water begin to appear along the lower slopes to the right and left of Logan Turnpike. Crystal clear water seeps up from points along the ground and flows so gently that it does not push aside the leaf litter to make a visible path. These small trickles would go unnoticed in the woods except that several coalesce and travel along the trail underfoot. Eventually, the small trickles join others, making small but noisy brooks less than a foot wide. Several of these turn and run along the trail before crossing it to the west side and forming the beginning of Town Creek. The beautiful stream which results contains clear, cold water with moss-covered rocks through the stream bed and no silt to be found. Contrast this with the striking difference seen in an urban/suburban community where after a rain, the warm muddy water rushes along gullies from the roadside and fills the streams first with a torrent of erosive force and then with mud and silt as the storm water subsides. The trail extends 2.6 miles almost due south from the trailhead and drops about 1,270 feet in that distance—700 feet in the first half-mile, a part of the trail that is steep and rocky.
DIRECTIONS: *At the highest point on the Richard Russell Scenic Highway, 7.6 miles from the junction with GA 75 Alt., the scenic drive passes close to Tesnatee Gap, then turns due north. The Logan Turnpike goes south through Tesnatee Gap [Fig. 23(10)]. There is a marker here for the Gap. A parking area provided on the south side of the Russell Highway provides easy access. The Logan Turnpike begins on the east side of the parking lot and goes south down the draw. To reach the southern trailhead for the turnpike, take US 19 north from Dahlonega for 13.5 miles to Turners Corner; turn right and proceed south on US 129 for 2.8 miles; turn left on Town Creek Road (gravel road) and go 2.5 miles. This road becomes very rough past the old tollkeeper's house near the trailhead; a high-clearance*

Christmas fern
Polystichum acrostichoides

Our most common evergreen fern grows in clumps, in moist, shaded soil. It is said to have been used as Christmas decoration by early New England settlers.

vehicle is recommended. Park off the road and walk 0.2 mile to the trailhead. The trail begins at the junction of the county road and the Forest Service property line. An historical marker on the approach road to the trailhead designates the tollkeeper's house.

~RICHARD RUSSELL SCENIC HIGHWAY DRIVING TOUR.

[Fig. 23(2)] This scenic route crosses the Blue Ridge and provides scenic overlooks. It forms the northern boundary of the eastern half of the Raven Cliffs Wilderness, giving access to Raven Cliffs' trails, Duke's Creek Falls and the Appalachian Trail at two places. To arrive at the start of the driving tour, take GA 356 (75 Alt.) out of Helen 2.3 miles. Watch for GA 348 turning west where it dead ends into GA 356. Set the odometer on zero. The first overlook is at 1.4 miles. The entrance to Duke's Creek Falls parking is 0.8 miles farther, and the trail to Raven Cliffs, about a mile beyond that. One encounters white pines about mile 2.4; it is a common tree until mile 4.7, when deciduous (oak/hickory) forest continues to the gap. The road begins to climb steeply at 3.2 miles.

The Tray Mountain vista (pages 110, 111) is to the right at 4.1 miles. The foreground ridge bears white pine mixed with hardwoods, while red maples grow close below the parking area. At mile 4.2 the road bank has a remarkable covering of Christmas fern and primitive club moss. Vistas to the left, such as at miles 5.1, 6.0 and 6.7, overlook the Raven Cliffs Wilderness. One is able to gaze across the flat Dahlonega Gold Belt to Yonah Mountain (see vista) and the distant Piedmont. At milepost 6.0 one begins to see in the road cuts the structure of the most common rock making up the eastern Blue Ridge, a banded gneiss. This rock becomes more noticeable at mile 6.3 and at the Hogpen Gap [Fig. 23(9)], just beyond the crossing of the Appalachian Trail. Here, at 7.0 miles, the large cut on the left offers a study in the wavy banding of dark and light that characterizes metamorphic rock (see vista). Starting down the colder north slope of the Blue Ridge there is parking at 7.5 miles and close access to the Appalachian Trail at Testnatee Gap [Fig. 23(10)]. At this point one crosses the old Logan Turnpike, which came through Tesnatee Gap, one of the earliest crossings of the Blue Ridge by the early settlers. From this point the highway parallels the old Logan Turnpike, descending rapidly down the Nottely River headwaters—in this case, Lordamercy Cove. At 8.9 miles one encounters a hemlock-heath community along the creek, and at 9.4 miles in the floodplain south of the highway is a white pine/tulip poplar forest indicating the site of an abandoned field. One should anticipate a settlement ahead, and after passing through a mix of white pine and Virginia pine, one reaches the first house at 10.5 miles. At mile 10.8, by looking across the floodplain, one can see the extent of former hillside pastures so common in the early days of settlement. Note how the growth of white pines in the old

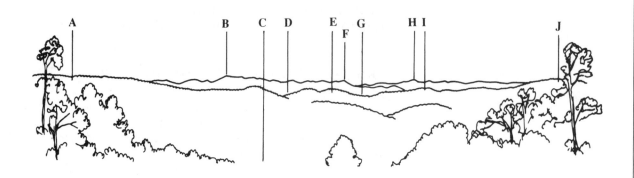

EAST VISTA
View at 4.1 miles

A - Locust Log Ridge
B - Tray Mountain
C - Bear Den Creek Valley

D - Little Low Gap
E - Blue Knob
F - Chimney Mountain

G - Saddle Gap
H - Tallulah Mountains
I - Little Blue Knob
J - Stoney Knob

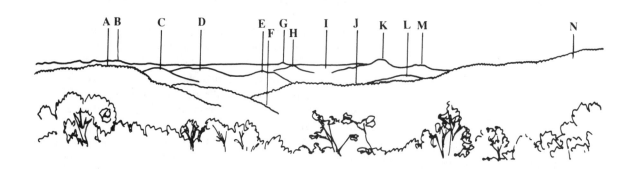

SOUTH VISTA
View at 6 miles

A - Piney Mountain
B - Blue Ridge Escarpment
C - Stony Mountain
D - Hickory Nut Mountain

E - Little Hickory Nut Mountain
F - Dodd's Creek
G - Currahee Mountain
H - Sal Mountain
I - Piedmont Mountain

J - Dukes Creek Falls
K - Yonah Mountain
L - Allison Ridge
M - Pink Mountain
N - Ridge to Adams Bald

EASTERN BLUE RIDGE

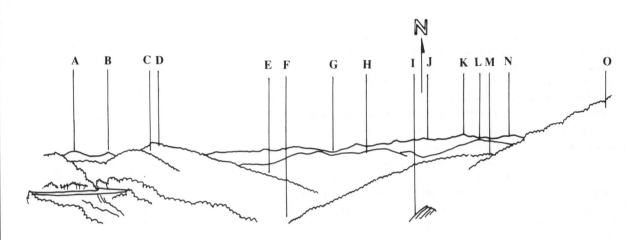

NORTH VISTA
View at 7 miles

A - Slaughter Mountain
B - Coosa Bald
C - Turkey Pen Flats
D - Double Poplar Top
E - Nottely River Valley

F - Lordamercy Cove
G - Trackrock Gap
H - Cass Mountains
I - cliff
J - Arkaqua Ridge

K - Brasstown Bald
L - Jack's Gap
M - Grassy Ridge
N - Sheep Rock Top
O - Wolfpen Stamp

EASTERN BLUE RIDGE

COMPILED BY CHARLES WHARTON AND NELL JONES
ILLUSTRATED BY MOZELLE FUNDERBURK

pasture is sharply delineated from the hardwoods above it. Highway 348 deadends into GA 180 at 13.6 miles. Turn east on GA 180. In about four miles, the road enters the ring of ultrabasic rock surrounding Brasstown Bald and in which Indian carvings are preserved at Trackrock Gap nearby. Continue and cross Jack's Gap where the Jack's Gap Trail crosses and the road to Brasstown begins its very steep ascent. Dropping down the east side from the gap, one descends Soapstone Creek, leaving the soapstone and other peculiar rocks at the Owl Creek road turnoff. Continue on, deadend into GA 17 and turn south. Almost immediately the High Shoals Falls Scenic Area road turns east, and in another mile the very steep road to Indian Grave Gap and Tray Mountain (FS 283) also turns east. Continuing on GA 17, one should reach Unicoi Gap in approximately three more miles. Unicoi Gap was the boundary between Indian and white lands until the Dahlonega gold rush. It was one of the first gaps crossed by a highway. Continuing down the south side of the Blue Ridge, watch for the sign marking Andrews Cove on the left. Here Andrews Creek follows the westernmost part of the famed geologic anomaly, the Warwoman Shear, which cuts across Lake Burton to the Chattooga River country. Past Andrews Cove, one descends to the Chattahoochee headwaters and the starting point at Helen.

MAP REFERENCES: *USGS 1:24,000 series: Cowrock - Neel's Gap.*

Ballooning at Helen

Helen And The Upper Chattahoochee

The north Georgia town of Helen [Fig. 24(1)] developed around the Byrd-Matthews Sawmill, which was built in 1912. The town was named for the daughter of John McCombs, a prominent citizen of that era, who was part owner of the mill and of the newly built railroad through the valley. The sawmill operated continuously until the late 1920's, when the virgin pines and hardwoods, once plentiful here, had been cut down and run through its blades. It was subsequently demolished. For the next 40 years Helen's fortunes declined. Bypassed by the major transportation routes through the mountains, it got little benefit from the steady increase in tourism that the mountain region as a whole experienced during that period, and the town's few citizens found jobs scarce. A new women's apparel plant, Orbit Manufacturing, opened in the early 1960's run by a man named Jim Wilkins, and a few people were hired. But the town was almost a ghost town in 1968, when the business district consisted of one run-down motel and 16 concrete block buildings, nine of them empty. Then things began to change.

Three men were the prime movers behind born-again Helen. One of them was Jim Wilkins, the founder of Orbit Manufacturing, who owned most of the west side of the business district. Another was Pete Hodgkinson, who lived in nearby Clarkesville, worked with Wilkins in the management of Orbit and also owned land in Helen. They added their ideas and resources to those of the third member of the triumvirate, John Kollock, an artist who lived nearby and who had a passion for the architecture and landscape of the Bavarian Alps. Within a week of their first meeting, these three drew up the initial plan for putting a new face on Helen—one calculated to be alluring to the mountain tourists. Kollock drew a series of sketches depicting his vision of what the town would look like after its projected transformation, and the other two wasted no time in convincing their fellow businessmen and property owners in town to cooperate with the effort. Hodgkinson was later killed in 1976 in an accident while hot air ballooning, a sport he brought to Helen and which later developed into one of the area's major promotional attractions as the Helen-to-the-Atlantic Balloon Race.

In the years since, Helen has developed into a major north Georgia tourist attraction, drawing visitors from Atlanta as well as from all over the Southeast. Outside entrepreneurs have opened new businesses, all in keeping with the Bavarian Alpine theme, and have bought up slices of the surrounding woodlands for development as second home sites. Visitors to Helen can wander through the Alpine-style shops to browse for antiques, brownies, books, Indian jewelry, cigars, backpacks and Christmas ornaments or sit on a restaurant deck overloooking the Chattahoochee to dine on anything from pizza to knockwurst.

EASTERN BLUE RIDGE

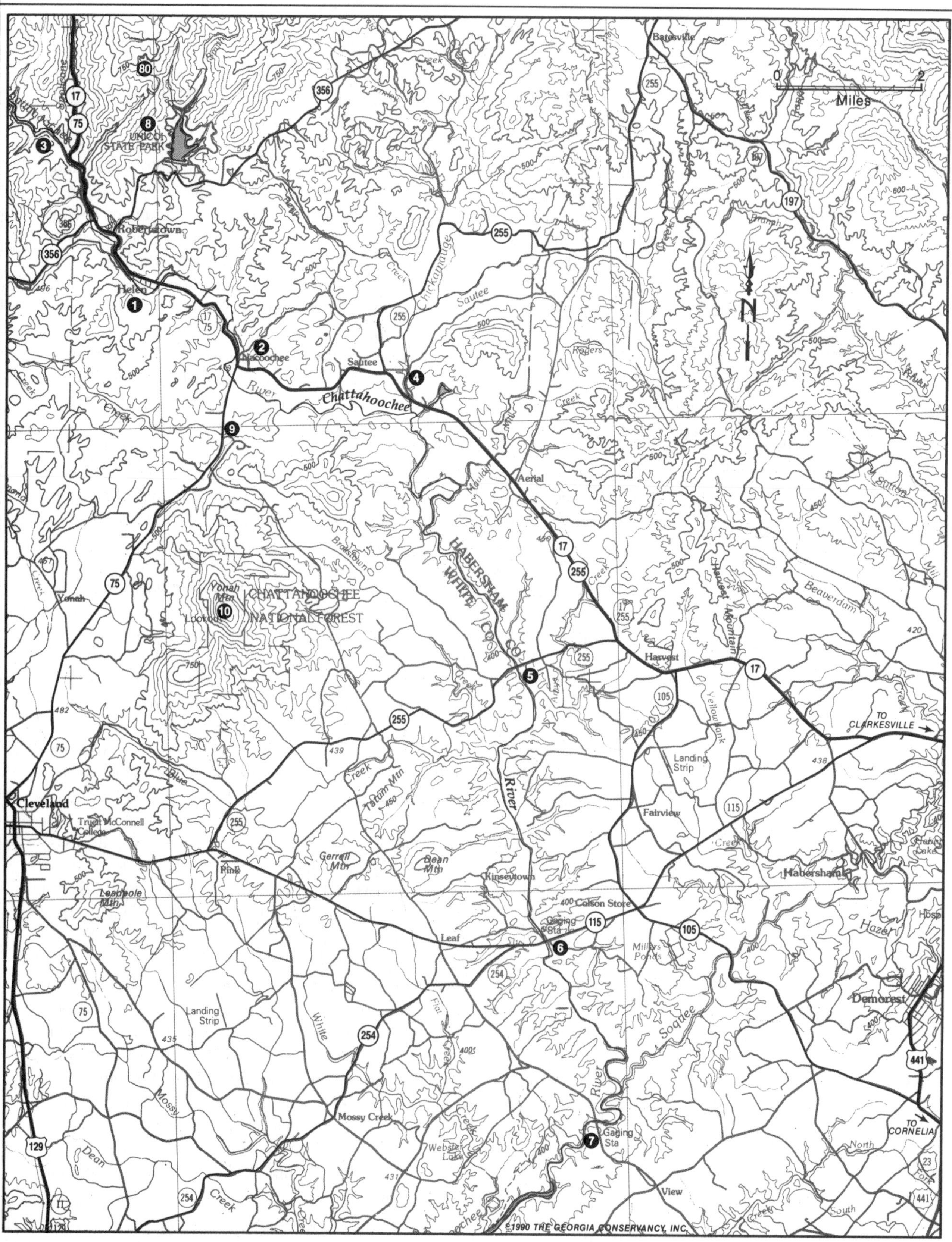

Figure 24 — **HELEN AND THE UPPER CHATTAHOOCHEE**

EASTERN BLUE RIDGE

Fig. 24 - Helen and the Upper Chattahoochee

(page references in parentheses)

1 Helen (113)
2 Nacoochee Valley aka West End (115)
3 Upper Chattahoochee (115)
4 Sautee Creek (115)
5 GA 255 (115)
6 Section between GA 255 and GA 115 (115)
7 Duncan Bridge (115)
8 Unicoi State Park (117)
9 State Historic Marker [Gold discovered here] (115)
10 Yonah Mountain (118)
80 Anna Ruby Falls Scenic Area (125)

~**NACOOCHEE VALLEY.** [Fig. 24(2)] Just north of the junction of GA 75 and GA 17, the Nacoochee Valley extends to the east. In the foreground is the Nacoochee Indian Mound, rising from the flat pastureland and crowned with a white latticework gazebo. A much larger, wooded mound stands in the floodplain to the east. At the time of the first European contact with this area—Hernando de Soto's 1540 expedition in search of gold—this was the center of civilization in the region, a Cherokee town called Guasili, or Guaxale. The mound, however, predates even the Cherokees; it was built by their predecessors in this valley, the Uchee Indians. The name "Nacoochee," in fact, comes from the Uchee word for this small temple mound, *Nagutsi*.

~**WEST END.** [Fig. 24(2)] Just north of the GA 75/17 junction is the impressive Italianate Victorian house known as West End. One of the oldest surviving structures in the valley, it was built in 1870 for retired Confederate Colonel John Nichols and was later occupied by Lamartine Griffin Hardman, Georgia governor from 1927 to 1931.

~**DUKE'S CREEK GOLD MINING.** The first bridge south of the Chattahoochee River crosses Duke's Creek on GA 75 [Fig. 24(9)]. This is the site of the first discovery of gold in White County (see state historical marker). In the flood plain east of the bridge, there is a series of narrow ponds. These are ponds associated with mining the placer deposits (gold in stream gravel). In some river floodplains, huge dredges were floated in ponds of their own digging, digging out in front and filling in behind.

~**CANOEING THE UPPER CHATTAHOOCHEE.** The section of the Chattahoochee River above Helen is a tight, difficult and rapidly descending mountain river [Fig. 24(3)]. This section can usually be run only after a rain, and water levels vary almost hourly. It should be run in the spring only by experts paddling in small parties.

The Upper Chattahoochee, from Nacoochee Valley to GA 255, is a nice float on moderate rapids. Near the end of the valley, Sautee Creek [Fig. 24(4)] enters from the left. Many paddlers put their boats into Sautee Creek on Lynch Mountain Road, an unpaved county road next to the GA 17 bridge over the creek. This is a short float across the valley to the main stream of the Chattahoochee.

As noted in *North Georgia Canoeing* by Bob Sehlinger and Don Otey, from the Sautee Creek junction down to GA 255 [Fig. 24(5)] is one of the longest undisturbed stretches of the river. The terrain is heavily forested, with large white pines and frequent rock outcroppings. Rapids are fairly frequent but are of the mild Class I and II category

The section between GA 255 and GA 115 [Fig. 24(6)] contains some Class III water. From GA 115 to Duncan Bridge [Fig. 24(7)] is the section most appealing to whitewater buffs. None of the

EASTERN BLUE RIDGE

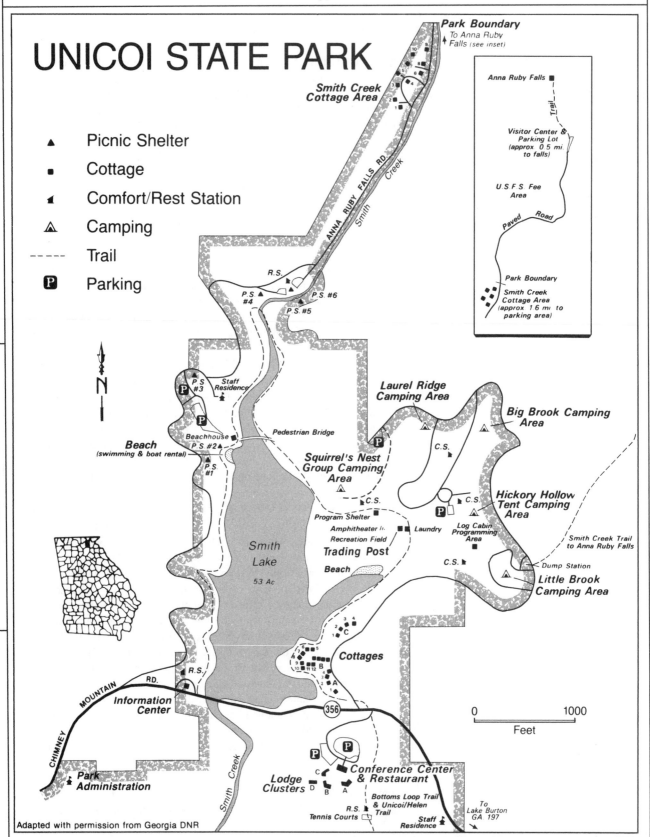

UNICOI STATE PARK

Legend:
- ▲ Picnic Shelter
- ■ Cottage
- ◄ Comfort/Rest Station
- ⛺ Camping
- - - - Trail
- 🅿 Parking

Park Boundary
To Anna Ruby Falls (see inset)

Smith Creek Cottage Area

Inset:
Anna Ruby Falls ■
Trail
Visitor Center & Parking Lot (approx. 0.5 mi. to falls)
U.S.F.S. Fee Area
Paved Road
Park Boundary
Smith Creek Cottage Area (approx. 1.6 mi. to parking area)

ANNA RUBY FALLS RD.
Smith Creek

R.S.
P.S. #4
P.S. #6
P.S. #5

N

P.S #3
Staff Residence

Beach (swimming & boat rental)
Beachhouse
P.S. #2
P.S. #1

Pedestrian Bridge

Laurel Ridge Camping Area

Big Brook Camping Area

C.S.

Squirrel's Nest Group Camping Area

C.S.

Hickory Hollow Tent Camping Area

C.S.

Log Cabin Programming Area

Smith Creek Trail to Anna Ruby Falls

Program Shelter
Amphitheater
Recreation Field
Laundry
Trading Post
Beach

C.S.

Dump Station

Little Brook Camping Area

Smith Lake
53 Ac.

3 4
2 C 1
6 5
8 7 B
9
10 11 12
A
Cottages

R.S.
MOUNTAIN RD.
CHIMNEY
Information Center

356

0   1000
Feet

Park Administration

Lodge Clusters
C
D B A
Conference Center & Restaurant

Bottoms Loop Trail & Unicoi/Helen Trail
Tennis Courts
R.S.
Staff Residence

To Lake Burton GA 197

EASTERN BLUE RIDGE

Adapted with permission from Georgia DNR

Figure 25 — **UNICOI STATE PARK**

116

rapids is particularly difficult; but combined, they provide interesting and challenging canoeing.

DIRECTIONS: *In Helen there is a take-out point across from the Wildewood Outpost. There is a put-in spot where Sautee Creek enters the river from the northeast. One can put in to Sautee Creek on Lynch Mountain Road, an unpaved county road next to the GA 17 bridge over the creek. Other put-in, take-out points: 1) The GA 255 bridge, on the left or Habersham County side of the river only. The property owner on the right side should not be disturbed. Use the public highway right-of-way. 2) The GA 115 bridge. Enter on the White County side at the small county park on the left side of the highway, as one approaches the river from Cleveland. 3) Duncan Bridge. The distance from Jasus Creek to Helen is about eight river miles; approximately six hours should be allowed for the run. From Helen to the GA 255 bridge is approximately 13 miles; from the GA 255 bridge to the GA 115 bridge is 4.2 miles, and from there to Duncan bridge is about four miles. The Wildewood Outpost runs a parking lot at Duncan Bridge; there is a fee.*

~UNICOI STATE PARK. [Fig. 24(8)] Just two miles north of Helen, Unicoi is a 1,081-acre park with a beautiful 100-room lodge plus a wide range of other accommodations and a buffet-style restaurant. Popular activities include hiking on 12 miles of trails, group camping and walk-in tent campsites, mountain culture programs and a craft shop in the lodge.

FACILITIES: *100-room lodge and conference center, 30 cottages, 80 tent and trailer sites, 53-acre lake and beach, 4 lighted tennis courts, buffet style restaurant.*

SPECIAL EVENTS: *Fireside Arts and Crafts Show-Feb., Mountain Eatin's & Squeezin's-Jul.*

DATES/HOURS: *Park, 7am-10pm; office 8-5.*

DIRECTIONS: *Located two miles northeast of Helen via GA 356.*

ADDITIONAL INFORMATION: *Unicoi State Park, P.O.Box 849, Helen, GA 30545. (404) 878-2201 (office and group reservations), 878-2824 (lodge and cottage reservations), 878-3366 (campground and shelter reservations).*

~HIKING TRAILS OF UNICOI STATE PARK.

UNICOI LAKE TRAIL. This is a 2.4-mile loop trail around Unicoi Lake, across the dam and returning to the information center.

DIRECTIONS: *Follow directions to Unicoi State Park (above). The trail begins at the information center.*

BOTTOMS LOOP TRAIL. 2.1 miles. A pleasant trail past streams, fields, low ridges and wildflower displays.

DIRECTIONS: *Follow directions to Unicoi State Park (above). The trail begins near the lodge and conference center.*

EASTERN BLUE RIDGE

~**YONAH MOUNTAIN.** [Fig. 24(10)] This landmark peak, featured on the cover of this guidebook, is a monolith of granite gneiss. It and its companion, Pink Mountain, are highly visible from the Richard Russell Scenic Highway (see South Vista, p. 111) and stand as isolated peaks in the Dahlonega Gold Belt. Yonah's convenient cliffs provide mountaineering experience for U.S. Army Ranger Units as well as other climbers. Most of Yonah (*bear* in Cherokee) is in the Chattahoochee National Forest.

DIRECTIONS: *The turnoff to Yonah is less than one mile on SR 75 north of Cleveland.*

MAP REFERENCES: *USGS 1:100,000 series: Toccoa.*

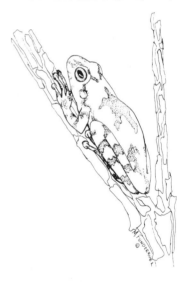

Gray treefrog
Hyla versicolor

Following the mid-winter calls of the wood frog and the shrill cries of the spring peeper, the hoarser calls of the gray treefrog come in late May and June from areas near standing water.

Tray Mountain

This is rugged backcountry combined with some fine state parks and easy-to-reach waterfalls and hikes, including the Appalachian Trail. Access is available to most parts of this area by car. The Tray Mountain area includes unique sites such as the incomparable Ramp Cove, with the finest stand of giant buckeyes in Georgia (if not the Southeast) and a wildflower paradise. Exciting boulderfields are common here just under the Appalachian Trail (A.T.) and off the Kelly Ridge. The Kelly Ridge spur provides a superb hike similar to the great Duncan Ridge in the Blood Mountain area. The huge rock outcrop at the Mill Creek Roughs is worth exploring. Tray Mountain itself, with its superlative boulderfield, is one of the major overlooks in the Georgia Blue Ridge. The southern part of this area is the 9,702-acre Tray Mountain Wilderness.

Tray Mountain [Fig. 26(50)] ranks among Georgia's highest peaks (4,430 feet). Because of its elevation and the fact that it stands as a sentinel in a great sweeping arc of the Appalachian Trail from west to north, Tray Mountain is a magnificent grandstand from which to view the Nantahalas and the Georgia Blue Ridge. Southward one can see the Piedmont. On clear days it is said that even Kennesaw and Stone Mountain are visible. Closer is the flat terrain of the Dahlonega Gold Belt, bordered on the west by the Hayesville Fault, from which the mountains of the Raven Cliff Wilderness rise abruptly. In the foreground, also, is the lovely peak of Yonah Mountain. Yonah's abrupt cliffs provide the best easily accessible area for rock climbing in the Georgia mountains.

~**MAIN ACCESS ROUTES TO TRAY MOUNTAIN.** The first is to take SR 356 east from Robertstown (one mile north of Helen) for five miles. Turn left at Bethel Church onto Chimney Mountain Road and follow it for two miles to FS 79. This is Tray Mountain Road, which is maintained for four-wheel-drive vehicles and pickup trucks. Travel FS 79 [Fig. 26(51)] north for seven miles to Tray Mountain Gap [Fig. 26(60)] at the intersection of FS 698 and the A.T. crossing.

The second route, a steep incline with switchbacks, is to take GA 75 north from Robertstown for one mile. Turn right on FS 79 across from the Hooch Trading Post. Travel in a northerly direction 6.5 miles to a fork. The left fork goes to a landmark called Indian Grave Gap [Fig. 26(52)], a high wide saddle between Rocky Mountain (4,017 feet) and Tray. On either side are "hanging valleys" of great scenic beauty. Also crossing here are the trails up High Shoals Creek [Fig. 26(53)] and from Andrews Cove [Fig. 26(54)]. Here the last remnant of the great gash of Warwoman Shear [Fig. 26(56)] makes its final appearance, lining up the head of High Shoals Creek [Fig. 26(55)] with Andrews Creek. The right fork goes past the little

Buckeye
Aesculus octandra

The buckeye, or "horse chestnut," is among the last trees to bear foliage in the spring and the first to color in the fall. It grows in high mountain coves above 2,500 feet. Large buckeyes stand below the road in Sosebee Cove [Fig. 21(6)], near Blood Mountain. A magnificent forest of huge buckeyes occupies the upper end of Ramp Cove north of Kelly Ridge.

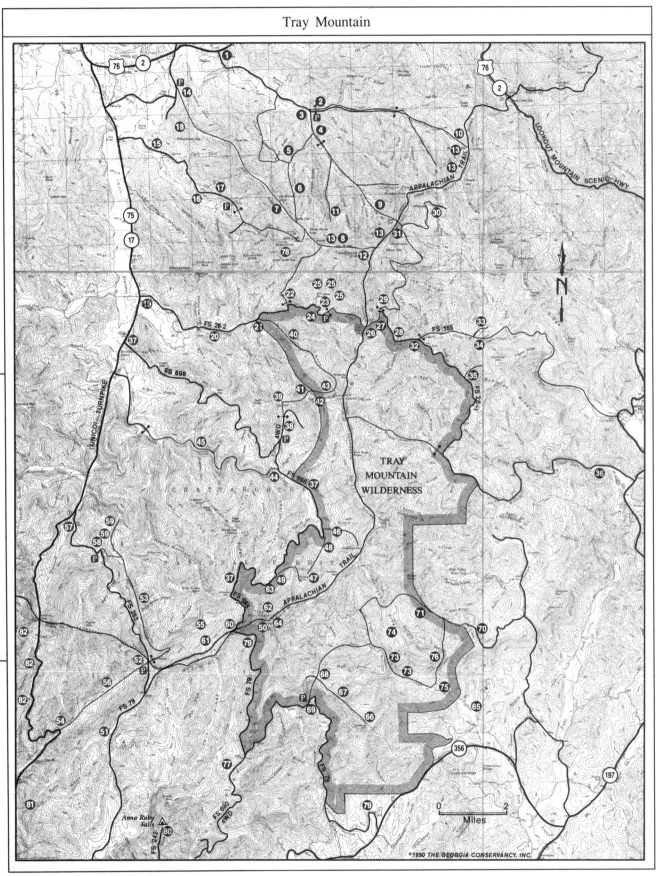

EASTERN BLUE RIDGE

Figure 26 — **TRAY MOUNTAIN**

Fig. 26 - Tray Mountain
(page references in parentheses)

1 Lower Hightower Church (122)
2 gate at end of road to Swallow Creek (122)
3 Swallow Creek parking (122)
4 Swallow Creek ford (122)
5 Ramp Cove ravine (122)
6 Ramp Cove (121, 122)
7 Kelly Ridge (122)
8 Stroud Cove (122)
9 Dismal Cove (122)
10 Swallow Creek (122)
11 Stroud Creek falls & cascades (122)
12 Kelly Knob (122)
13 boulderfields, Kelly Ridge & AT (122)
14 SR 88 parking (122)
15 Cynth Creek (122)
16 Dyer Family trout farm (122)
17 Cynth Creek Road (122)
18 Schoolhouse Gap (122)
19 Mill Creek Road (122)
20 Mill Creek (122)
21 Sassafras Creek (122)
22 gated road - Sassafras Creek (122)
23 Mill Creek Roughs (123)
24 waterfall, Mill Creek (123)
25 roughs, Mill Creek (123)
26 Addis Gap (123)
27 Addis Family Farm (123)
28 Wildcat Creek Road (123)
29 FS 675 (123)
30 White Oak Stamp (123)
31 Deep Gap (123)
32 Park's Gap (123)
33 Dick's Creek Road (123)
34 Moccasin Creek Trail (123)
35 Fuller Gap (123)
36 Wildcat Creek Road (123)
37 Corbin Creek Road (121)
38 log road to Tripp Gap (123)
39 Tripp Gap (123)
40 Sassafras Branch Cove (124)
41 rock outcrop, High Top (124)
42 white oak forest (124)

(continued on page 123)

meadow [Fig. 26(61)] called "Cheese Dairy," the former site of a goat cheese factory. There is a spring here at this popular camping spot. Continue to Tray Gap [Fig. 26(60)], the intersection of FS 698 and the A.T. The trail to Tray Mountain begins here at Tray Gap.

The third route, the shortest, is to take GA 75 north from Helen 11 miles (two miles north of Unicoi Gap). Turn right onto FS 283. Proceed in a southerly direction for about four miles. Turn east at the junction with FS 79 and go two miles to arrive at the intersection of FS 698 and the A.T. crossing. At 1.3 miles on FS 283, pass the High Shoals trailhead [Fig. 26(58)] to a bridge over High Shoals and a trail down to two sets of exceptional falls where, because of several deaths, viewing platforms [Fig. 26(59)] have been built.

~**APPALACHIAN TRAIL.** It is an exhilarating experience to hike the 0.9-mile portion of the Appalachian Trail that climbs 600 feet to the summit of Tray Mountain. The ridges at Tray Gap and upward bear red oak ridge forest; near the summit, the oaks become dwarfed and gnarled. There are patches of lily of the valley and other interesting plants on the way. Near the top, there is a veritable garden of purple, or Catawba, rhododendron which—unlike the common or rosebay—blooms in spring rather than summer. It surrounds rock outcrops on which grow patches of high-altitude spike moss.

Just below the top of Tray on the north side is one of the best-developed boulderfields in north Georgia [Fig. 26(62)]. It is hazardous walking, but one can drop down through it to Corbin Creek Road [Fig. 26(37)] or go up the third cove [Fig. 26(63)] two miles or more north of Tray Gap. It is characterized by two high-altitude maples—striped and mountain—together with holly and Catawba rhododendron. Two herbs here—the beautiful rosy twisted stalk and an elderberry—are at their southernmost limits. Just down the A.T., north from the top a few hundred yards, there is a side trail to the south leading to an exceptional overlook [Fig. 26(64)] of the southern part of the Tray Mountain area and the headwaters of the Soque River.

~**SWALLOW CREEK.** The northern portion of the Tray Mountain area is largely the watershed of Swallow Creek. While not designated wilderness, much of this area is wild and primitive. It has two outstanding high ridges—the Blue Ridge (from Dick's Gap to Kelly Knob—4,276 feet) and the Kelly Ridge. The walking along both is easy, and the scenery is rewarding. The Swallow Creek watershed, tucked away in the Blue Ridge, is hardly known at all. There is a high cove of huge old-growth buckeyes (Ramp Cove) [Fig. 26(6)] and the heaviest growth of the fabled mountain garlic (ramps) in Georgia. The abundant north-facing coves offer boulderfields and wildflower assemblages. The advantage of this area is that one can hike up one creek, hit the ridge, go around and down

EASTERN BLUE RIDGE

another creek and arrive back at the starting point, creating a hike suited to individual desires.

The basic approach to the area is by turning off US 76, two miles east of where GA 17/75 dead ends into it. Turning here [Fig. 26(1)] at the lower Hightower Church, drive several miles to the end of the pavement to park [Fig. 26(3)]. If the gate [Fig. 26(2)] straight ahead is open, proceed another mile or so. Most visitors park at the end of the pavement [Fig. 26(3)]. Of the two dirt roads to the right, select the left-hand (a jeep can drive another 0.25 mile on FS 300, but it is not recommended.) From the end of the pavement, go up the dirt road and take the first old road to the right that fords the creek [Fig. 26(4)] (there are two old roads; take the one most traveled). Follow this old logging road, which shortly climbs a long ravine [Fig. 26(5)]. High up in this ravine, one finds smooth-barked, black and crooked trunks of the rare yellowwood tree. Cross a flat area, follow the road on up and soon enter what may be the grandest old-growth forest in the mountains [Fig. 26(6)]. The buckeyes here reach four feet in diameter and exceed those in Sosebee Cove. Moreover, the herbaceous ground is extremely rich in species, including abundant ramps for which the cove is named. The soil is rich black Porter's loam. One can continue up to the top of Kelly Ridge [Fig. 26(7)], walk around and come down Stroud [Fig. 26(8)], or Dismal [Fig. 26(9)] Coves (note that Stroud and Dismal are not marked on the ground and can be difficult to locate) or take the A.T. to Moreland Gap and come down Swallow Creek itself [Fig. 26(10)]. There is a series of small falls and cascades along Stroud Creek [Fig. 26(11)]. Kelly Knob itself is a high scenic point [Fig. 26(12)]. As one walks east along Kelly Ridge and on the A.T., almost every cove has a boulderfield at its head [Fig. 26(13)]. Some can be seen from the A.T.

One obvious easy way to reach Kelly Ridge is from Dick's Gap on US 76, which cuts out some of the climbing. West on Kelly Ridge one can drop off to a parking area on SR 88 [Fig. 26(14)]. Normally, one could drop off at Schoolhouse Gap [Fig. 26(18)], but a clearcut presently blocks the way. Another access to Kelly Ridge is by way of the Cynth Creek [Fig. 26(15)] Road which turns east at the first bridge over the Hiawassee River south of the GA 17/US 76 junction. This road [Fig. 26(17)] passes around one of the Dyer family's four trout-rearing stations [Fig. 26(16)], which sell trout for stocking and as bait for striped bass in Lakes Burton and Lanier.

South of Kelly Ridge is an area of interest. The western access is by the Mill Creek Road [Fig. 26(19)], which is 3.5 miles north of Indian Grove Gap Road or 3.4 miles south of the junction of GA 17 and US 76. The pavement ends above the Dyer Trout Farm on Mill Creek [Fig. 26(20)]. The road climbs through nice oak/hickory slope forest and passes a trailhead for Sassafras Creek [Fig. 26(21)] and a north-turning gated road [Fig. 26(22)] which can lead the hiker to Kelly Ridge. About 0.25 mile before a locked gate (9.1 miles from GA 17) on the main road one crosses three small branches at

Ramp
Allium tricoccum

These wild garlic-type onions are found only above 3,000 feet—and then usually only in north-facing coves and on sites with deep, rich soils. When their leaves first appear in the spring, ramps are gathered and eaten by mountain people. This spring ritual, a celebration of nature, has developed into ramp festivals, drawing even Presidents. By summer, both leaves and flowers are gone and no trace remains.

Fig. 26 - Tray Mountain

(continued from page 121)

43 boulderfield, yellow birch, Dismal
   Mountain (124)
44 Miller Branch Road (124)
45 Corbin Creek (124)
46 Double Branch to Steeltrap Gap (124)
47 Spring Cove (124)
48 blocked log road to Spring Cove (124)
49 ridge trail to Spring Cove (124)
50 Tray Mountain (119)
51 FS 79 (119)
52 Indian Grave Gap (119)
53 High Shoals Creek (119)
54 Andrews Cove Recreation Area
   (119, 126)
55 Andrews Creek (119)
56 Warwoman Shear (119)
57 FS 283 (125)
58 High Shoals trailhead to Blue
   Hole/High Shoals Falls (121, 125)
59 viewing platforms, falls below High
   Shoals (121, 125)
60 Tray Mountain Gap (119, 121)
61 "Cheese Dairy" (121)
62 boulderfields, north top of Tray Mountain (121)
63 third cove north of Tray Gap (121)
64 overlook, south Tray Mtn & Soque
   River headwaters (121)
65 private land - blocks access to Soque
   River (124)
66 top of Chimney Mountain (124)
67 ridgeline to Chimney Mountain (124)
68 Deep Gap (124)
69 Rich Cove Trail (124)
70 Skelton Branch Road (124)
71 trail to Soque River/Chimney Mountain
   (124)
73 waterfalls, left fork of Soque River
   (124)
74 Wolfpen Ridge (125)
75 old tram railroad up Soque River (125)
76 see 71 (125)
77 FS 690 (125)
78 Buzzard Knob (125)
79 FS 79
80 Anna Ruby Falls/Smith Creek Trail
   (125, 126)
81 Lost House Branch Falls (127)
82 three falls on Spoil Cane Creek (127)

the Mill Creek Roughs [Fig. 26(23)]. Just below the juncture of the last two branches is a beautiful waterfall [Fig. 26(24)]. Up the tiny branches are about a quarter of a mile of "flats" ideal for picnicking. At the head of the flats, one encounters the "roughs," [Fig. 26(25)] and trails cease. A dense, unbanded rock outcrops here near the surface over many acres. Streams cascade off it through rhododendron thickets. The huge area of rough is most unusual in northern Georgia. Soil has difficulty forming over this immense outcrop. Because of its roughness, it has not been logged since horse-logging days—and then perhaps sparingly. Some old trees might reward exploration. A rattlesnake den is reported in the vicinity of Buzzard Knob [Fig. 26(78)].

~ADDIS GAP. [Fig. 26(26)] The gap cannot be reached by vehicle, as the old road has been gated. The gap was named for the Addis Family who farmed the rocky slopes 0.25 mile east of the gap [Fig. 26(27)].
DIRECTIONS: *Addis Gap is reached from the east by the Wildcat Creek Road (26-1) [Fig. 26(28)], which turns off GA 197 one mile north of LaPrades or 1.5 miles south of Moccasin Creek State Park (also GA 197). It is the first left road past Wildcat Creek going north on GA 197. It is marked FS 26. Just north of the old Addis homestead a gated road, FS 675 [Fig. 26(29)], serves as a trail at least as far as White Oak Stamp [Fig. 26(30)] on the head of Chastain Creek. There is an easy connection with the A.T. at Deep Gap [Fig. 26(31)], where the trail up an old logging road also terminates.*

~TRAILS. At [Fig. 26(32)] the Park's Gap to Dick's Creek Road begins [Fig. 26(33)]. A gated road, it can be hiked to the Dick's Creek watershed. In just a short distance, the trail down Moccasin Creek [Fig. 26(34)] by the Moccasin Creek Falls begins. At Fuller Gap [Fig. 26(35)] another "trail," really an old log road, joins this one at the vicinity of the Moccasin Creek Falls. The Moccasin Creek Trail is a renowned hike of great beauty. It is actually the roadbed of the old railroad by which the watershed was logged in the early 1900's. Hiking up from Moccasin Fish Hatchery to the high falls located between Falls Mountain and Pig Pen Ridge takes about one hour. There is a smaller set of falls below the large one. Exploration of these falls can be dangerous.

Approximately four miles back down the Wildcat Creek Road [Fig. 26(36)], a gated log road runs up Wildcat Branch.

~NORTHERN ACCESS. The principal access to the northern half of the Tray Mountain area from the west is the Corbin Creek Road which turns east off GA 17/75 about one mile south of the Mill Creek Road. Take this gravel road (698) 4.2 miles to where it crosses Miller Branch. One can park here and walk a gated log road (FS 698-A) [Fig. 26(38)] to Tripp Gap [Fig. 26(39)]. There is a trail here that turns right up the ridge towards High Top, passing it to the north and continuing into and around the head of Sassafras Branch Cove [Fig. 26(40)]. On the northwest face of High Top is a very fragmented rock outcrop [Fig. 26(41)] with much lichen growth and with occasional seeps with sphagnum moss and saxifrage. The flat on the south side [Fig. 26(42)] is a white oak forest. Many of the trees are quite old. On the north slope between the two tops of Dismal Mountain is a poorly developed boulderfield with some yellow birch [Fig. 26(43)]. About 0.5 mile south from Miller Branch, one encounters the terminus [Fig. 26(44)] of the old road up Corbin Creek [Fig. 26(45)]. The other end begins as a gravel road about 0.5 mile south of the main Corbin Creek Road.

The next trail of consequence goes up Double Branch [Fig. 26(46)] to Steeltrap Gap.

~**SPRING COVE AREA.** [Fig. 26(47)] Spring Cove has a nice spring surrounded by stately older (80-year) forest with ash, buckeye and hemlock with diameters up to 36 inches. It is reached on foot along a blocked log road [Fig. 26(48)], where Corbin Creek Road crosses Corbin Creek, or by a trail up the ridge [Fig. 26(49)].

~**THE HEAD OF THE SOQUE RIVER AND CHIMNEY MOUNTAIN.** The wilderness south of the A.T. is rough and steep terrain. It is not well known at all. Private land [Fig. 26(65)] currently blocks easy access up the Soque River. The most interesting hike is to the top of Chimney Mountain [Fig. 26(66)], reached by the ridgeline [Fig. 26(67)] from a gap [Fig. 26(68)] and an access trail up Rich Cove [Fig. 26(69)]. To get to this trailhead, one either comes down 4.4 miles on FS 79 [Fig. 26(79)] east out of Tray Gap or up a similar distance from GA 356. Four-wheel drive is advisable on FS 79. The views from Chimney Mountain (3,357 feet) are exceptional. The trail to the top passes through high-quality pitch pine and scarlet oak ridge forest and is very pleasant walking. The south and west faces of Chimney Mountain have extensive rock outcrops. The southern outcrop is surrounded by red cedar which appears to be quite old. It is unusual for red cedar to appear on mountaintops. The summit is a flat lichen/sedge-covered outcrop. There are three rather hollow rock cairns about four feet high on the summit of Chimney Mountain. They are of unknown origin.

The other access to this portion of the wilderness is by way of the Skelton Branch Road [Fig. 26(70)], reached by taking GA 197 to the first left turn after GA 356 deadends into it. Go two miles on paved road and take the first main (gravel) road to the left for 0.5 mile; there, take the right fork; then the first road to the left should be Skelton Branch. The best trail [Fig. 26(71)] crosses Wolf Pen Branch and strikes the north prong of the Soque, from which point one can go up the left prong to Deep Gap [Fig. 26(68)] or down the left fork to two waterfalls [Fig. 26(73)]. There is no verification of

Rosy twisted stalk
Streptopus roseus

This unusual plant occurs in boulderfields on the north face of our highest peaks. It is one of a host of plants at the southernmost extension of their range in our Georgia mountains and able to survive only in cold, moist forests at high elevations.

the trail [Fig. 26(76)], but it is marked on 1957 topographical sheets. The old timers ranged cattle on the Wolfpen Ridge [Fig. 26(74)]. There was an old tram railroad up the Soque [Fig. 26(75)] during the early logging era. While one can find occasional large trees in the Soque watershed, most of the timber is young (around 30 years), owing to the disastrous Hickory Nut Ridge fire that swept 10,000 acres of the basin in 1953. Another fire ravaged the Wildcat watershed in 1958. Fortunately, the wetter north side of the Blue Ridge did not burn. There is one road one should not attempt without four-wheel drive and perhaps a chain saw; that is FS 690 [Fig. 26(77)] south to Unicoi Park.

~**HIGH SHOALS TRAIL.** 1.2 miles. High Shoals Scenic Area is comprised of 170 acres with five waterfalls, luxuriant banks of rhododendron and laurel and sparkling mountain streams. The only way to see the two major attractions, Blue Hole and High Shoals Falls, is to hike the steep, moderately difficult 1.2-mile trail [Fig. 26(58)]. The trail, marked by blue blazes, is in good condition, but reaching the trailhead can be difficult. The road is rough, and fording the stream may cause trouble. When the road is frozen or very muddy, only a four-wheel-drive vehicle can negotiate it.

The trail descends from 2,880 feet to 2,560 feet by many switchbacks through a predominantly hardwood forest. After reaching the bottom, the trail follows High Shoals Creek downstream, crosses the water on a wooden bridge, then descends steeply more than 300 feet as the creek cascades downward in a series of five waterfalls. Side trails lead to two observation decks [Fig. 26(59)]. The first deck overlooks Blue Hole, a pool more than 20 feet deep created by the churning of the water and rock falling from 30 feet above. Farther downstream is the grander High Shoals Falls, which tumbles more than 100 feet over jagged rocks, splashing and spraying water into the air.

DIRECTIONS: *Go 11 miles north of Helen on GA 75 to the dirt and gravel Indian Grave Gap Road, FS 283 (the first road to the right after Unicoi Gap) [Fig. 26(57)]; make a sharp right turn (east); proceed ahead, ford the usually shallow stream and continue up the hill. Parking for the trail is approximately 1.3 miles from GA 75.*

~**ANNA RUBY FALLS SCENIC AREA.** [Fig. 24(80), Fig. 26(80)] Anna Ruby Falls, high on the slopes of Tray Mountain, is formed at the junction of Curtis and York Creeks. Both creeks originate atop Tray Mountain and are fed by underground springs, rain and snow. Curtis Creek then drops 153 feet, and York Creek drops 50 feet, forming the double falls. At the base of the falls, where there is an observation deck, the water becomes Smith Creek and tumbles downhill to Unicoi Lake. The U.S. Forest Service purchased the land surrounding the falls in 1925. The 1,600-acre scenic area adjacent to and surrounding part of Unicoi State Park

EASTERN BLUE RIDGE

was established in 1964. The falls were named for Anna Ruby Nichols, the only daughter of Col. John H. Nichols, who purchased the surrounding land in 1869. His Victorian-style mansion, West End, still stands at the junction of GA 17 and 75. He also built Crescent Hill Baptist Church and the gazebo atop the Indian Mound, both of which are still standing along GA 17.

A paved 0.4-mile trail leads from the parking lot to the foot of the falls.

FACILITIES: *Picnicking, drinking water, restrooms, trails, fishing, parking, group tours by arrangement, vending machines, information.*

FEES: *Parking - cars $2, buses $4.*

DATES/HOURS: *9-8 daily.*

DIRECTIONS: *Take GA 75 north from Helen one mile; turn right onto GA 356 and go 1.5 miles; turn left at the entrance to the falls; follow this road 3.6 miles to the parking area, which accommodates 140 cars and two tour buses.*

ADDITIONAL INFORMATION: *Anna Ruby Falls Scenic Area, U.S. Forest Service, Chattooga Ranger District, Burton Road, Hwy 197, Clarkesville, GA 30523. (404) 754-6221.*

~SMITH CREEK TRAIL. [Fig. 26(80)] 4.6 miles. This trail provides hikers with a nice walk through dense patches of rhododendron, mountain laurel, hemlock and fern. The trail goes up and over Hickory Nut Ridge through hardwood stands and crosses several small mountain streams before ending at Unicoi State Park Campground.

DIRECTIONS: *Follow the directions to Anna Ruby Falls Scenic Area, above. The trail begins at the right of the observation bridge.*

~DESOTO FALLS SCENIC RECREATION AREA AND TRAIL. See Blood Mountain section.

~UNICOI STATE PARK. See Helen and the Upper Chattahoochee section.

~ANDREWS COVE RECREATION AREA. [Fig. 26(54)] This recreation area is located along a beautiful mountain stream in a heavily wooded area. It is two miles from Andrews Cove to the Appalachian Trail over an easy to moderate trail.

FACILITIES: *Toilets, drinking water pump, camping, hiking.*

DATES/HOURS: *Apr. 1-Nov. 1, 7am-10pm.*

DIRECTIONS: *On GA 75, five miles north of Helen and 14 miles north of Cleveland.*

ADDITIONAL INFORMATION: *Andrews Cove Recreation Area, U.S. Forest Service, Chattooga Ranger District, P.O. Box 196, Burton Road, Clarkesville, GA 30523. (404)754-6221.*

~**LOST HOUSE BRANCH FALLS AND SPOIL CANE CREEK FALLS.** There is a beautiful falls [Fig. 26(81)] on Lost House Branch, reached by trail from GA 75 three miles south of Andrews Cove. Between the recreation area and Unicoi Gap are three falls [Fig. 26(82)] on Spoil Cane Creek west of GA 17/75. The upper two falls are visible from the highway.

MAP REFERENCES: USGS 1:24,000 series: Macedonia - Tray Mountain.

Red elderberry
  Sambucus pubens

Sometimes called the mountain elderberry, this plant occurs only at high elevations such as in the Tray Mountain boulderfields [Fig. 26(50)]. The common elderberry, *S. canadensis*, which grows in moist places throughout, has purple berries from which elderberry wine is made.

EASTERN BLUE RIDGE

127

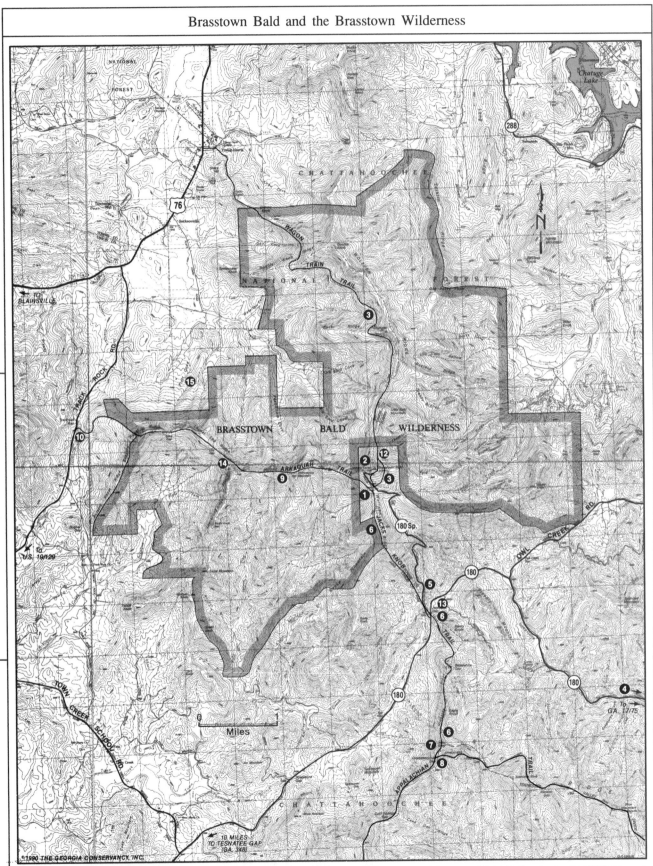

Figure 27 — **BRASSTOWN BALD AND BRASSTOWN WILDERNESS**

Fig. 27 - Brasstown
(page references in parentheses)

1 parking, Brasstown Bald Visitor Center (129, 131)
2 Brasstown Bald Visitor Center (129)
3 Wagon Train Trail (129, 132)
4 GA 180/GA 66 (131)
5 GA 180 spur (131)
6 Jack's Knob Trail (131)
7 Jack's Knob (131)
8 Chattahoochee Gap (131)
9 Arkaquah Trail (131)
10 Track Rock Gap Archeological Area (131, 132)
12 cloud forest & boulderfield (129, 132)
13 Jack's Gap (131)
14 Blue Bluff Overlook (132)
15 Plott Cove Research Natural Area (132)

Brasstown Bald and the Brasstown Wilderness

Brasstown Bald is Georgia's highest mountain. From its summit at 4,784 feet there are breathtaking views of four states. On a clear day it is possible to see as far south as Atlanta.

In 1986, 11,405 acres within the Chattahoochee National Forest were designated by Congress as the Brasstown Wilderness. The bald itself, which is not within the wilderness area, is only three-quarters of an acre. A narrow ring of ultrabasic rocks (soapstone, dunite and olivine) completely surrounds Brasstown Bald and the ridges leading to it. This is the southernmost habitat for many northern plant and animal species, including the red-back vole. A northern hardwood "cloud forest" of huge, old birches covers the north face. Rhododendron and mountain laurel are among the few shrubs that can survive on these thin, cold soils. The wildflower displays are particularly outstanding in the north-facing coves and down the east side of Wolfpen—one of the longest, highest ridges in Georgia.

Brasstown Bald was so named because of confusion between the Cherokee words *itse-yi,* meaning "new green place," and *untsaiyi,* meaning "brass."

Cherokee legend regarding bald mountains described a horrible, sharp-clawed, winged beast who attempted to steal and eat Indian children. The Cherokees cleared the forest to capture the monster and prayed to their Great Spirit, who killed the beast, restored the children and has kept the mountaintops clear of trees ever since. A steep, paved 0.5-mile trail leads from the parking area [Fig. 27(1)] to the visitor center [Fig. 27(2)] on the bald. For a fee, a shuttle bus carries visitors from the parking area to the visitor center.

The trail from the parking area to the summit [Fig. 27(2)] is well worth walking. One first crosses the old wagon road [Fig. 27(3)] to Young Harris, which leads east then north into the fantastic "cloud forest" [Fig. 27(12)] of northern hardwoods on the north side of the mountain, below the visitor center. The huge old yellow birch are festooned with old man's beard lichen because of the continuous moisture from cloud condensation. Rosebay rhododendron may be found near the parking lot, followed by purple rhododendron as the major heath shrub. As one ascends, the trees gradually get shorter. One soon enters a dwarfed red oak and white oak forest where the trees are very old, twisted and limby. The top is a shrub bald with unique mountaintop species such as dwarf willow and the red-berried mountain ash.

~**THE VISITOR CENTER COMPLEX.** The center, built of stone, offers interpretive programs, including the exhibit "Man and the Mountain," tracing human and natural history of the Southern

Brasstown Bald

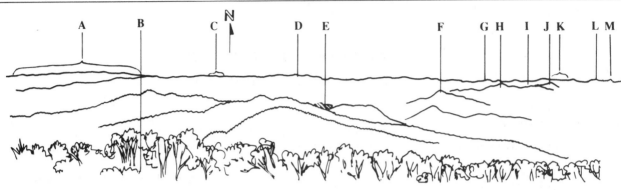

NORTH VISTA

A - Unicoi Range
B - Wolfpen Ridge
C - Snowbird Mountains
D - Tusquittee Bald

E - Lake Chatuge
F - Bell Mountain
G - Kimsey Bald
H - Eagle Mountain

I - Yellow Mountain
J - Hightower Bald
K - Standing Indian Mountain
L - Little Bald
M - Ridgepole Mountain

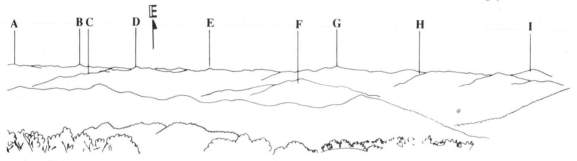

EAST VISTA

A - Ridgepole Mountain
B - Rabun Bald
C - Kelly Ridge

D - Kelly Knob
E - Dismal Mountain
F - Spaniard Mountain

G - Tray Mountain
H - Unicoi Gap
I - Yonah Mountain

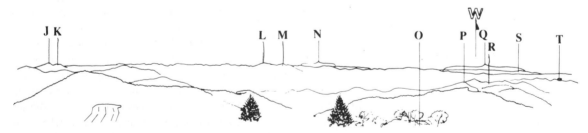

SOUTH AND WEST VISTA

J - Yonah Mountain
K - Pink Mountain
L - Blood Mountain

M - Slaughter Mountain
N - Duncan Ridge
O - Arkaqua Ridge
P - Chimney Top Mountain

Q - Cohutta Mountains
R - Track Rock Gap
S - Big Frog Mountain
T - Lake Nottely

COMPILED BY CHARLES WHARTON AND NELL JONES
ILLUSTRATED BY MOZELLE FUNDERBURK

EASTERN BLUE RIDGE

Appalachian region. The Mountaintop Theater features continuous video programs. An outside observation deck provides a 360-degree view of the surrounding area. Here visitors may be awed by the view but unprotected from the wind. Because of its height, Brasstown Bald gets much weather that misses the valleys. Strong wind, rain and lower temperatures are not uncommon. In winter there is often snow and ice. The fire lookout tower is not open to the public.

FACILITIES: *Video show, picnic area, bookstore and gift shop, hiking trails, parking lot ($1 fee), restrooms, exhibits, observation deck, brochures, concessions, shuttle bus.*

DATES/HOURS: *10-5:30 daily Memorial Day-Oct., weekends in early spring (depending on the weather); parking lot, observation deck and trails are open year-round.*

DIRECTIONS: *From Cleveland take GA 75 north through Helen to GA 180; turn left (west) onto GA 180 (also GA 66) [Fig. 27(4)]; go six miles; turn right onto GA 180 spur [Fig. 27(5)]; continue three miles to Brasstown Bald parking lot [Fig. 27(1)].*

ADDITIONAL INFORMATION: *Brasstown Bald, U.S. Forest Service, Brasstown Ranger District, GA 129/19 South, P.O. Box 9, Blairsville, GA 30512. (404) 745-6928.*

~HIKING TRAILS FROM BRASSTOWN BALD. There are four hiking trails, including the paved summit-access trail. All start from the parking area at the bald, but only three of the trails are marked with signs. Simple maps and descriptions of the Arkaquah Trail and Jack's Knob Trail are available in the Forest Service brochure, *Trail Guide to the Chattahoochee-Oconee National Forests*. The 1:24,000-scale topographical maps of the area (Hiawassee, Jack's Gap and Blairsville quadrangles) show three of the trails — Arkaquah Trail, Wagon Train Trail and part of Jack's Knob Trail.

JACK'S KNOB TRAIL. [Fig. 27(6)] About 4.5 miles. Built in the 1930's by the Civilian Conservation Corps and reconstructed in the 1980's by the Forest Service, Jack's Knob Trail is limited to foot traffic. Descending southward from the parking lot along a ridge following the boundary of Towns and Union Counties, it crosses GA 180 in Jack's Gap [Fig. 27(13)] at an elevation of 3,000 feet and ascends Hiawassee Ridge past Jack's Knob [Fig. 27(7)], elevation 3,805 feet. Jack's Knob Trail joins the Appalachian Trail in Chatta-hoochee Gap near the source of the Chattahoochee River [Fig. 27(8)].

ARKAQUAH TRAIL. [Fig. 27(9)] About 5.5 miles. There is a difference of 2,500 feet in elevation as the trail descends westward along a ridgetop from its beginning in the Brasstown Bald parking area to its end at Track Rock Gap Archeological Area [Fig. 27(10)]. With a difficulty rating of moderate to strenuous, this is not consid-

Cloud forest

The highest elevations on the north face of many of our highest peaks bear a distinctive forest of northern hardwoods including yellow birch, beech, basswood and, sometimes, sugar maple. Because they are frequently "in the clouds," they drip with condensed moisture; lichens such as old man's beard (*Usnea strigosa*) drape from trees such as yellow birch (*Betula lutea*).

ered a beginner's trail. Blue Bluff Overlook [Fig. 27(14)] is on the trail. Hikers pass Chimney Top Mountain and will be able to see Rocky Knob to the south. Plott Cove Research Natural Area [Fig. 27(15)], which is rich in herbs, wildflowers and northern hardwoods, is north of the trail at Cove Gap. To reach the western end of the trail at Track Rock Gap, go east of Blairsville on US 76 for six miles, turn right onto Track Rock Road and go three miles.

WAGON TRAIN TRAIL. [Fig. 27(3)] This trail is unmarked at both beginning and end. To find it, go between the bookstore and the concession stand located in the parking area. Take the paved trail and turn right (east) onto a dirt road. This trail is a wide path originally intended to be GA 66, and on some state maps still shown as such. It is an easy seven-mile walk with fine views. Near the summit, the trail passes remarkable cliffs and boulderfields [Fig. 27(12)] where rock tripe, lichens, reindeer moss, old-man's beard and club moss flourish. In early spring, silverbell, service-berry, mountain buttercups, white saxifrage, toothwort, cinquefoil, bluets, hi-bush and low-bush blueberries, white and purple violets, Solomon's seal and plume, pussytoes and four varieties of trillium can be seen blooming along the trail. The trail ends behind the women's dormitory on the Young Harris College campus.

~TRACK ROCK ARCHEOLOGICAL SITE. [Fig. 27(10)] Like

the Mayan hieroglyphics of southern Mexico and Central America, the ancient petroglyphs carved into three large soapstone boulders on the west side of the road here have resisted translation. Referred to by the Cherokees who inhabited the area at the time of the white settlement as *degayelunha,* or "printed place," the rocks have been enclosed in metal cages to protect them from vandals and graffiti scrawlers. Though the stones are weathered, their mysterious inscriptions are still discernible to travelers who take time to stop here at the foot of Brasstown Bald. Similar examples of ancient picture writing can occasionally be found on rocks and on very old beech trees in the Southern Appalachians.

DIRECTIONS: *On Track Rock Road off US 76, four miles southwest of Young Harris.*

MAP REFERENCES: *USGS 1:24,000 series: Jack's Gap - Hiawassee -Blairsville.*

Solomon's seal
  Polygonatum biflorum
Solomon's plume
  Smilacina racemosa

The two-foot-long fronds of these plants are common in the herb layer of moist cove forests. Solomon's plume has flowers borne on the end of the stalk rather than dangling from the axils of each set of leaves, as in the Solomon's seal.

The Hightower Area of the Southern Nantahala Wilderness

Yellowwood
Cladrastis lutea

This very rare tree grows in a few ravines and boulderfields on the north face of our higher peaks and ridges. Its leaves and flowers resemble black locust. The trunk is often twisted and the bark, smooth and almost black —quite different from the deeply-furrowed gray locust bark. Yellowwood occurs in Sosebee Cove, Ramp Cove and abundantly in Loggy Branch Cove on Hightower Bald.

As one drives US 76 between Hiawassee and Dick's Creek Gap, the east-west trending high ridge or lead to the north is the western portion of the Southern Nantahala Wilderness. Visible are the cliffs near the top of Hightower Bald (4,568 feet), the highest peak in the area. This long, high ridge links a series of peaks with stunning views both north and south. It is an area for the backcountry hiker and explorer. Getting up on the high lead involves considerable climbing, beginning at the head of deep coves and flats.

On the northern approach there is a wealth of logging roads by which one can hike up to the edge of boulderfields in both Loggy Branch and Giesky Creek watersheds. The western approach up Sim's Branch passes east of the prominent Bell Knob, with its landmark quartz mine on top, visible for miles around. Of the eight access approaches, six are through private lands whose owners have been friendly to hikers and campers (though not necessarily to hunters), providing they are courteous and considerate. If possible ask permission. Both the Scataway and Shoal Branch (see below) accesses, unlike Hall Creek access, have a buffer area of Forest Service land before the wilderness boundary. Accordingly, both parking and camping areas are provided. Thus these latter two accesses are recommended for the average visitor.

This area is not well known, and the old settler trails across Skut and Lemons Gap are hard to find, but sometimes that is half the fun. There is little evidence of logging roads above 4,000 feet in the zone of northern hardwoods.

Plans for the management of the Southern Nantahala Wilderness are in process and will include signs and trails. The trails throughout the area are largely old logging roads, currently unmaintained and unmarked.

~**LOGGY BRANCH AND HIGHTOWER BALD.** The easiest approach to Hightower Bald is the Loggy Branch access [Fig. 28(3)]. How far to drive on these rough roads will be a matter of personal judgment. A jeep road turns and goes south up the hillside west of Loggy Branch, swings right and passes by an enormous red maple at the foot of a large boulderfield [Fig. 28(5)]. Nearby there is a government corner marked in red paint. The road then extends to Loggy Branch [Fig. 28(4)] a short distance below the wilderness boundary. If so inclined, one can locate the famous Montgomery Corner and/or 30-mile post where the state line takes a large jog north and south.

Loggy Branch Cove itself is a botanical paradise. According to Georgia's eminent botanist Wilbur Duncan, it compares favorably

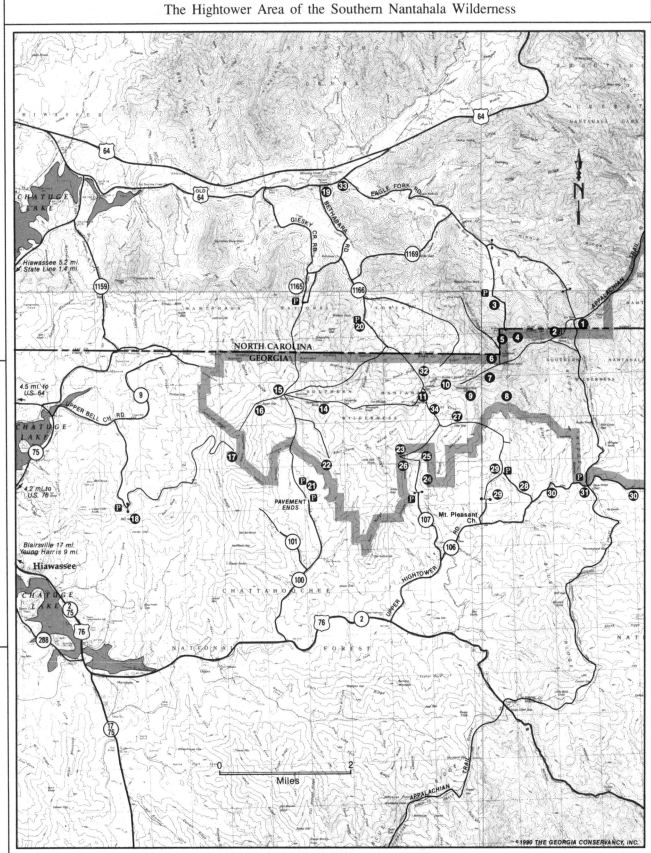

Figure 28 — **HIGHTOWER AREA OF SOUTHERN NANTAHALA WILDERNESS**

Fig. 28 - Hightower Area of Southern Nantahala Wilderness
(page references in parentheses)

 1 Bly Gap (138)
 2 Rich Knob (138)
 3 Loggy Branch (133, 136)
 4 Loggy Branch, lower cove
    (133, 135, 136)
 5 boulderfield, Loggy Branch (133)
 6 east face, Hightower Bald (135, 138)
 7 south face cliffs, Hightower Bald
    (135, 138)
 8 Buckhorn Ridge approach (no trail) (138)
 9 Shooting Creek Bald (135)
10 High Cove Ridge (135, 136)
11 Rattlesnake Knob (136, 138)
14 Sassafras Knob Cliffs (135)
15 Skut Gap (135, 136, 137)
16 Egypt Gap (135)
17 Eagle Mountain (137)
18 gate, trail to Eagle Mountain (137)
19 Bethabara Road (136)
20 parking, Beech Flats & Lemons Gap
    (136)
21 log road trail to Scataway Creek (137)
22 Bluff Cove Cliffs (137)
23 origin, Shook Branch Trail (137)
24 Hall Creek Falls subdivision (137)
25 Shook Branch, waterfall (138)
26 dirt road, Hall Creek access (137)
27 Eller Gap (138)
28 gorge on Shoal Branch (138)
29 Shoal Branch trail (138)
30 fork to Blue Ridge Gap (138)
31 Blue Ridge Gap (138)
32 Lemons Gap (136)
33 Eagle Fork Creek Road (136)
34 Owensby Cove (135, 138)

with anything in the Smokies. Up and down Loggy Branch, one can find the black, twisted trunks of the rare yellowwood tree. This is Georgia's largest colony, and one of the largest aggregations of yellowwood in the Blue Ridge. Most of this area is privately owned.

Higher up in the cove, one encounters a northern hardwood forest of beech, sugar maple and yellow birch. In mountain gaps and below them can be found the southern limit of the "Beech Gap" phase of this community, where high altitude varieties of beech predominate. On the cold, high side of Hightower [Fig. 28(6)] just under the top, there is a refuge for two plants normally associated with the spruce/fir forest: a beautiful viburnum and a type of oxalis clover. This is the only place in Georgia where this particular viburnum (*Viburnum alnifolium*) is known to grow.

The 150-foot cliffs on the south side [Fig. 28(7)] are dominated by moss and lichen, primitive rock spike moss, the rare Blue Ridge St. John's wort and the federally listed and very rare Biltmore sedge. The boreal red-back vole, another Pleistocence relict, has been found here. On top is a dwarfed oak forest of white and red oak with a remarkably extensive growth of beaked hazelnut which, with mountain raspberry, dominates the understory. Large hawthorn trees grow here and there. One can climb a dwarfed oak, as if walking up a ladder, and obtain fine views.

The ridgeline is supported by massive gneiss and amphibolite. A walk west down the ridge to Tom's Gap is rewarding; after a climb up a little cliff just west of Tom's Gap, one gets excellent vistas of the Hightower cliffs and the watershed below. Dwarf willow grows here in abundance on the cliff edge, and purple rhododendron is common.

The most difficult section of the ridgeline is between Shooting Creek Bald (4,317 feet) [Fig. 28(9)] and along the High Cove Ridge [Fig. 28(10)], an almost continuous series of rock outcrops, cliffs and rhododendron. One can walk around under the cliffs; bear hunters prefer to burrow along the top. There is extensive rhododendron on the north face of Rattlesnake Knob. Otherwise the ridge is a fairly easy walk all the way to Eagle Mountain. Oak ridge forests to the east of Skut Gap [Fig. 28(15)] are dominated by northern red oak; those west, by white oak. Just south of Egypt Gap [Fig. 28(16)], a series of small cliffs is covered with marginal wood fern, alum root, rock cap fern and, nearby, monkshood. The Sassafras Knob Cliffs [Fig. 28(14)] have bush honeysuckle. The coves, especially lower Owensby Cove [Fig. 28(34)] and Loggy Branch [Fig. 28(4)], often have beautiful open stands of poplar or oak/hickory slope forest, waterfalls and wildflower assemblages.

Much is to be learned from this relatively unexplored area. Early settlers lived remarkably high and far back in the mountain coves. On the Loggy Branch Road a family named Davenport lived on rocky soil at about 3,000 feet. It is said that sledloads of mayapple, used for medicinal purposes, came out of Loggy Branch Cove and

EASTERN BLUE RIDGE

were sold for two cents a pound. There are reported Indian petroglyphs on a rock on the trail to Lemons Gap [Fig. 28(32)].

~ACCESS ROUTES

LOGGY BRANCH COVE ACCESS. Northern access to Loggy Branch Cove, Hightower Bald and the eastern part of the wilderness. On old US 64 east, pass Bethabara Road [Fig. 28(19)] 0.4 mile; turn right at a sign on paved Eagle Fork Creek Road [Fig. 28(33)]; go 2.1 miles to the third bridge; turn left on a dirt road just before the bridge. (At 0.4 mile a gated road turns left. This is a very rough jeep road. If chosen, take all other right turns and eventually reach Bly Gap on the Appalachian Trail. The gate opens November 1.) Past this gated road go about two miles from the paved road and follow the most developed road (through some private lands) to reach a U.S. Forest Service sign. Do not cross the branch but turn up the ridge following an old logging road which goes by a huge red maple and on to Loggy Branch [Fig. 28(3)], well up in the cove. Whether four-wheel drive is needed will depend on logging activities and rain. Certainly past the government boundary, one will need four-wheel drive, but at that point the short distance to the lower cove [Fig. 28(4)] can be hiked.

NORTHERN ACCESS. To Beech Flats, Lemons Gap and the central part of the wilderness. From GA 75 north out of Hiawassee, dead end at old US 64; turn east and go four miles; turn south at the sign, Bethabara Road (1166) [Fig. 28(19)]; go two miles; take the last road (dirt) to the right (west) just before the bridge; go about 0.4 mile through an apple orchard; turn left; ford a creek and park [Fig. 28(20)]. Continue south about 0.6 mile to where the road is blocked at a branch. Walk up the road on the left side of the branch. The wilderness boundary is very close. Climb southeast through Beech Flats until coming to the ridgeline where, with luck, one will find oneself in the vicinity of Rattlesnake Knob [Fig. 28(11)]. To dodge difficult cliffs [Fig. 28(10)] of High Cove Ridge, avoid striking the ridge east of Lemons Gap. It is said that an old trail to, or close to, Skut Gap [Fig. 28(15)] leaves the entrance road (turns south) just past the last house after the creek ford.

OLD SKUT GAP TRAIL. Northern access to Old Skut Gap Trail and the western part of the wilderness. From the junction of GA 75 north, turn east on old US 64; go 3.2 miles to the Giesky Creek sign (1165); turn right (south); at 2.4 miles, in a U-shaped curve, cross the bridge over Nattie Branch. The landowner here, John Robbins, lives just north of the bridge and says to park on the west side of the branch where the old log road follows the route of the old trail to Skut Gap by way of Burnt Cabin Cove.

Beaked hazelnut
Corylus cornuta

While the American hazelnut occurs statewide, the beaked hazelnut is confined to the higher mountain ridges beneath the dwarfed red oak. It forms thickets atop Hightower Bald. The nuts are sweet and relished by wildlife. Along with the chinquapin and beech, it contributes to the smaller mast supplementing the fruits of the oaks and hickories.

EASTERN BLUE RIDGE

EAGLE MOUNTAIN ACCESS. [Fig. 28(17)] The western end of the wilderness. Off GA 75 north of Hiawassee, turn east on Upper Bell Creek Road (Rd. 9) just before a bridge crosses an arm of Lake Chatuge; go 1.2 miles; turn right (south) on SR 78. At about 1.6 miles, stop at a gate [Fig. 28(18)]; hike up the log road past Ben Gap (1.3 miles); reach another gate at two miles; walk up switchbacks to Eagle Mountain summit [Fig. 28(17)] (about 3.2 miles total from the parking area).

SCATAWAY CREEK ACCESS. Southern entrance to the wilderness. Go north on GA 17/75 from Helen; turn right on US 76 and go 3.2 miles; turn north on a paved road (SR 100). At 1.2 miles, a paved road (SR 101) to the left goes up Jack Hooper Branch. It is possible to hike up to Eagle Mountain [Fig. 28(17)] by this route, but there is no trail over the last mile of very steep terrain. The right fork (SR 100) continues toward the southern access trail to Skut Gap. After leaving the pavement, park and hike up an old log road trail [Fig. 28(21)] which does not follow the creek, but in 0.5 mile turns east up the slope and enters a clearcut. Instead, head steeply uphill (north) through a small stand of pine trees, coming to an old road. This road climbs steeply, rounds the end of a ridge and joins a more open road. Approximately 1.2 miles from the US Forest Service boundary, a trail turns right and goes southeast to the top of Bluff Cove Cliffs [Fig. 28(22)]. The old trail to Skut Gap [Fig. 28(15)] continues but is grown up and extremely hard to follow.

HALL CREEK ACCESS. This is the southern entrance to the central ridge of the wilderness and to the Maney Branch (Maney Cove) and Shook Branch (Owenby Cove) watersheds. It is the shortest route to the easternmost crossing of the main ridge by the old settlers' trail through Lemons Gap. A slightly longer hike is via the Shoal Branch access.

On the west side of the U.S. 76 bridge over Hightower Creek, turn north on Upper Hightower Road. Take the first paved left, at 1.4 miles. The pavement ends in another 0.8 mile. After passing a flood control reservoir on the right, be prepared to park along the gravel road anywhere south of the first mailbox on the left before reaching signs (another 0.2 mile) indicating private land, the Hall Creek Falls Wilderness community [Fig. 28(24)]. The public road ends a little south of these signs; walk up about 3,700 feet of graveled private road. Do not leave the road; it is a public right-of-way. After fording the creek twice, take the first old dirt road to the left [Fig. 28(26)], which leads to the red-blazed wilderness boundary. Follow the old road up the east side of the creek, Maney Branch. In less than 1,000 feet, watch for an old road or trail to turn eastward, sharply up a ridge [Fig. 28(23)]. This is the Shook Branch Trail. After about 1.25 miles on Shook Branch, Hall Branch Falls

EASTERN BLUE RIDGE

137

[Fig. 28(25)] lies due east about 600 feet and barely within the wilderness boundary. About one mile up the Shook Branch Trail, the trail from Eller Gap Trail [Fig. 28(27)] intersects from the east. The "trail" up Owensby Cove [Fig. 28(34)] to Lemons Gap may be indistinct. Most trails in this area are currently unmaintained and unmarked. It is about 3500 feet from the junction with the Eller Gap Trail to Lemons Gap, just east of Rattlesnake Knob [Fig. 28(11)].

NOTE: Accesses described below are the principal means of reaching Hightower Bald from the south and east.

SHOAL BRANCH ACCESS. To go up Shoal Creek, continue east on the main Upper Hightower Road (SR 105, blacktop). At about two miles, past the Hall Branch Road, turn left on the narrow but paved Jack Branch Road. After crossing Hightower Creek, continue past the first house on the left, then turn abruptly left onto a dirt road that goes around and behind the house. This road is a public access to Shoal Branch. It passes through its narrow, scenic gorge [Fig. 28(28)], then by a flood control reservoir and through a meadow. At the meadow's end, enter the Forest Service boundary where parking and camping is permitted. The Shoal Branch trail [Fig. (28(29)] continues northward 2,000 feet before swinging west to cross the creek and continue through Eller Gap [Fig. 28(27)] to intersect the Shook Branch trail in Owenby Cove. For those who wish to climb to Hightower Bald, it is easy but steep bushwhacking due north from where the Shoal Branch trail turns west and crosses the creek. Upon encountering the base of the cliffs [Fig. 28(7)], turn left and work around to Tom Gap; then follow the ridgeline to the top or turn right and proceed until reaching Buckhorn Ridge [Fig. 28(8)]. Follow it to the summit. If the Buckhorn Ridge route is chosen, it may be necessary to crawl through heath thickets the last 100 yards or so before breaking out into the dwarfed "orchard" oak community on top.

A route with far less climbing but more walking is the eastern approach to Hightower Bald [Fig. 28(6)] via the Appalachian Trail. Past the Shoal Branch Road turn-off, the main road becomes gravel. About 2,000 feet beyond the Shoal Branch Road, bear right at a fork [Fig. 28(30)]; go 1.2 miles to reach Blue Ridge Gap [Fig. 28(31)] (four-wheel drive recommended). At either Rich Knob [Fig. 28(2)] or Bly Gap [Fig. 28(1)], pick up the main ridge west to Hightower Bald.

MAP REFERENCES: *USGS 1:24,000 series: Shooting Creek - Macedonia - Rainbow Springs - Hightower Bald.*

Alum Root
Heuchera sp.

The leaves of alum root resemble a hairy-stemmed variety of the more common foamflower *(Tiarella cordifolia)*. The alum root seems to prefer growing on or near rocks; some species prefer basic rock outcrops.

White Oak Stamp

White Oak Stamp, together with Buck Creek and Chunky Gal Mountain (next section), is so unusual that parts of this area are classified and protected as "special interest areas" by the U.S. Forest Service. White Oak Stamp and adjacent areas of Chunky Gal and the Buck Creek watershed offer not only one of the very best examples of old-growth, high-altitude forest areas to explore, but also vistas as exciting as any area within the scope of this book.

It is rare to find a large "flat" area such as White Oak Stamp at high elevations along the Blue Ridge. Most of the forest above 4,200 feet is virgin old-growth. A good part of it, especially on slopes and ridges, is high-altitude northern red oak forest [Fig. 29(56)], with many trees exceeding two feet in diameter. Shrubs here include flame azalea, several viburnums and three species of blueberry. Mixed northern red oak/white oak forest occurs in certain areas [Fig. 29(76)]. Perhaps the most exciting environment is the area of northern hardwoods [Fig. 29(57)], especially in the Big Laurel cove heads, through which the Buck Creek access trail [Fig. 29(64)] passes. Here are giant old yellow birch between two and three feet in diameter. Subdominants are buckeye and beech, the latter predominating on slight ridges with a rare pure beech forest lower down [Fig. 29(77)]. Just above it is a large stand of rare chokecherry [Fig. 29(78)].

The trail bisects one of the strikingly beautiful gneissic boulder-fields. The northern herb/wildflower display is outstanding, with perhaps the largest colonies of the edible ramp and the poisonous large hellebore that visitors will ever see. This forest continues on the east side of Chunky Gal as far as Bear Gap [Fig. 29(72)].

In a low area not far from the Appalachian Trail [Fig. 29(70)]—[Fig. 29(58)] is the old trail, now rerouted—lies a remarkable high-altitude heath bog on the head of Muskrat Branch [Fig. 29(53)]. While the dominant shrubs are rosebay rhododendron and mountain laurel, purple rhododendron does occur. This thicket is difficult to penetrate, but bears love it and native brook trout are common in the tiny crystal clear streams. Yellow birch, hemlock and red maple make up a scattered overstory. The rare bog turtle may be present. Two small areas are open sedge marshes with cinnamon fern. Approaching the bog from the north is an old "burl road" [Fig. 29(54)] formerly used to haul out rhododendron root burls. These burls were used in the manufacture of pipe bowls when supplies from the Mediterranean were cut off during World War II.

There is a spring at the Muskrat Creek shelter [Fig. 29(50)] on the Appalachian Trail. Not far south of it are two clifftop vistas (no trails) which overlook the Tallulah watershed [Fig. 29(66), Fig. 29(69)].

Bog turtle
Clemmys muhlenbergii

This palm-sized turtle is the smallest of our mountain turtles, is now extremely rare and lives only in bogs —which, themselves, are endangered. Bog turtles, like wood frogs, seem to occur only on the north side of the Georgia Blue Ridge. An orange temple patch is characteristic.

EASTERN BLUE RIDGE

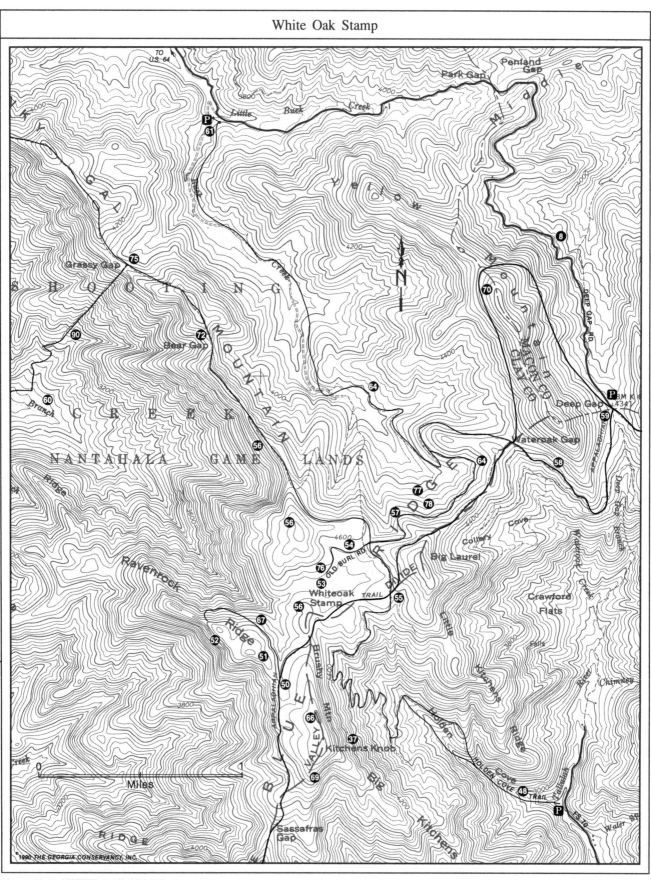

Figure 29 — **WHITE OAK STAMP**

Fig. 29 - White Oak Stamp
(page references in parentheses)

  8 Deep Gap Road (141)
 37 Kitchens Knob
 48 Holden Cove Trail (141)
 50 Muskrat Creek shelter (139)
 51 little top (141)
 52 Raven Rock Cliff (141)
 53 Muskrat Branch (139)
 54 old "burl road" (139)
 55 Appalachian Trail (141)
 56 northern red oak forest (139)
 57 Big Laurel cove heads (139)
 58 Appalachian Trail (unofficial old
       route) (139, 141)
 59 Deep Gap (141)
 60 Muskrat Branch (143, 144)
 61 junction with Little Buck Creek (141)
 64 Buck Creek Trail (139, 141)
 66 clifftop vista (139)
 67 old cattle and pig trail (141)
 69 clifftop vista (139)
 70 Appalachian Trail (new route) (139)
 72 Bear Gap (139)
 75 Grassy Gap (143)
 76 northern red/white oak forest (139)
 77 pure beech forest (139)
 78 stand of chokecherry (139)
 90 old Macon Trail (143, 144)

Hikers who walk west on the ridge opposite the shelter and are able to find the old cattle and pig trail [Fig. 29(67)] can follow it down, around and north of a little top [Fig. 29(51)], then back out southeastward to the top of Raven Rock Cliff [Fig. 29(52)], which has fine vistas.

DIRECTIONS: *Four trails converge at White Oak Stamp. The easiest access may be from Deep Gap [Fig. 29(59)] via the old A.T. loop south of Yellow Mountain [Fig. 29(58)]. Deep Gap Road [Fig. 29(8)] is reached off old US 64, which is paved and turns off new US 64. Those who relish the exertion of a two-hour climb can come up the scenic Holden Cove Trail [Fig. 29(48)] to where it crosses the Appalachian Trail [Fig. 29(55)] and continues on down Buck Creek. The Buck Creek Trail [Fig. 29(64)] is reached off the Deep Gap Road near the junction of Buck Creek and Little Buck Creek [Fig. 29(61)], [Fig. 30(61)].*

MAP REFERENCES: *USGS 1:24,000 series: Rainbow Springs.*

EASTERN BLUE RIDGE

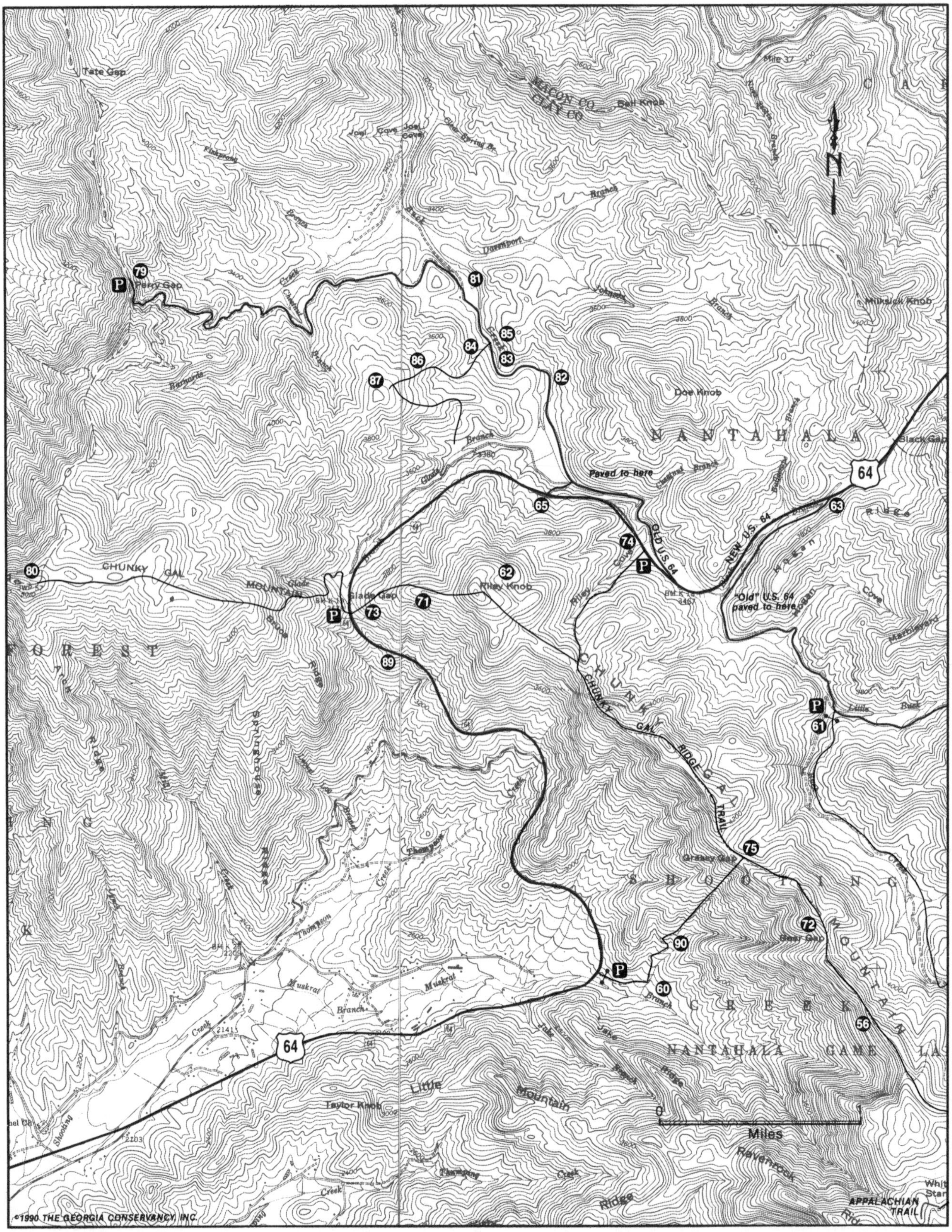

Figure 30 — **BUCK CREEK AND CHUNKY GAL MOUNTAIN**

Fig. 30 - Buck Creek and
Chunky Gal
(page references in parentheses)

60 Muskrat Creek (143, 144)
61 junction with Little Buck Creek (141)
62 Riley Knob (143)
65 montane deciduous forest (144)
71 trail from Glade Gap (143)
72 Bear Gap (143)
73 Glade Gap (143)
74 Riley Cove (143)
75 Grassy Gap (143)
79 Perry Gap trailhead (144)
80 Boteler Peak/Shooting Creek Bald (143)
81 fork, Buck Creek Road (144)
82 Buck Creek bridge (144)
83 olivine/dunite rocks (144)
84 Buck Creek rocks (144)
85 corundum mine shaft (144)
86 roads to Corundum Knob (144)
87 Corundum Knob (144)
89 Shooting Creek Overlook (144)
90 old Macon Trail (143, 144)

Buck Creek and Chunky Gal Mountain

Buck Creek and Chunky Gal Mountain, together with White Oak Stamp (previous section), are so unusual that parts of them are classified and protected as "special interest areas" by the U.S. Forest Service. Buck Creek is a renowned site of ultrabasic rocks of great interest to those studying minerals, gems or botany. Chunky Gal Mountain gets its name from the Cherokee legend of a plump Indian maiden who fell in love with a brave and followed him over this mountain after her parents had banished him from camp. With its long ridgetop scenic trail and noteworthy Riley Knob botanical area, Chunky Gal is considered by conservationists to be worthy of Wilderness Area designation.

~**CHUNKY GAL MOUNTAIN.** Chunky Gal is a long, eight-mile-high, remote, ridgelike mountain connecting the Blue Ridge and the Appalachian Trail with the Tusquittee and Fires Creek ranges. For hikers going north, there is a scenic overlook to the west from a cliff said to contain garnets and olivine. This is about 1.5 miles before Bear Gap. The trail's end south of Bear Gap [Fig. 30(72)] has most interesting vegetation in a near-original state. At Grassy Gap [Fig. 30(75)], a cove forest reaches the trail with lush herb flora including monkshood and purple-fringed orchid. A rare plant—wolfsmilk—occurs as far south as Grassy Gap, the southern limit of its growing range in the United States. Grassy Gap apparently was the crossing of the old Macon Trail [Fig. 30(90)] used by the Indians and was also a horseback mail route before the construction of US 64. It was a short cut from Shooting Creek to the headwaters of the Nantahala River. Accessible from Muskrat Branch [Fig. 30(60)], it may, nevertheless, be difficult to find.

~**THE RILEY KNOB/CHUNKY GAL SPECIAL INTEREST AREA.** [Fig. 30(62)] This area covers 215 acres between 3,600 and 4,400 feet and is an outstanding example of an extensive old-growth, high-altitude white oak forest. There is some cove forest and red oak ridge forest. Much of the rock in the Riley Knob area is amphibolite, which supports a rich herb flora. The knob and the Chunky Gal Ridge Trail are reached from US 64 at Riley Cove [Fig. 30(74)] or at a blue-blazed trail [Fig. 30(71)] from Glade Gap access point [Fig. 30(73)]

From this latter point, according to Allen de Hart's trail guide, one can cross US 64, turn left on old US 64, then right at 0.2 mile from Glade Gap on an old jeep road. Eventually one reaches Boteler Peak (also called Shooting Creek Bald, 5,010 feet) [Fig. 30(80)] at about 2.8 miles from Glade Gap. Here a blue-blazed trail descends northward to Perry Gap and continues on to link with the

Rim Trail on the east rim of the Fires Creek Basin, a noted bear refuge.

~**THE BUCK CREEK PINE BARRENS.** These pine barrens are geologically and botanically unique. Basic magnesium-rich rocks such as olivine and dunite [Fig. 30(83)] predominate. At the first little creek [Fig. 30(84)], about 0.5 mile past the bridge [Fig. 30(82)], one is treated to an assortment of unusual rocks. The creek bed is littered with pieces of olivine, gabbro, chlorite schist, talc (with which one can write) and other mineral specimens—a smorgasbord of basic and ultrabasic rock. The Buck Creek Barrens contain the largest single outcrop of dunite in the entire Georgia and North Carolina olivine belt.

Back 0.1 mile is a pullout by Buck Creek, a good place to picnic. Across the creek is a "tailings pile" or mine dump. The old corundum mine shaft [Fig. 30(85)] is above it in an area of dunite rock [Fig. 30(83)]. In the late 1800's, mining for the abrasive corundum, which has a hardness next to the diamond's, was carried out throughout the corundum belt. Old roads [Fig. 30(86)] go back to Corundum Knob [Fig. 30(87)], where corundum was also mined. Here it is possible to find tiny rubies in a matrix of green stone, a type of amphibole called *smaragdite*.

Because of the unique plant life here, 103 of the 346 acres in the Buck Creek Barrens have been proposed as a botanical preserve. Before leaving US 64, note the presence of a normal montane deciduous forest [Fig. 30(65)]. After crossing the bridge [Fig. 30(82)], one almost immediately enters an area dominated by pitch pine with scrubby, scattered white oak. The soil moisture and temperature are such that some prairie grasses have become established. The Forest Service recognizes three unique plant communities here: 1) pitch pine/witherod, 2) the only location of pitch pine bluestem grass and prairie dropseed south of Pennsylvania and 3) one of two sites for pitch pine/little bluestem grass in North Carolina. Two unusual wildflowers are big-leaf grass of parnassus and fringed gentian.

The weird rocks, the unusual vegetation and the chance of panning a piece of ruby corundum out of Buck Creek make this area a prized one. After passing through the mineralized zone, one quickly reaches a fork [Fig. 30(81)]. The left-hand turn goes 2.8 miles west to the Perry Gap trailhead [Fig. 30(79)]; the right-hand turn is into what was the old Buck Creek Lodge, which is still private property. After a return to new US 64, it is 2.3 miles to the Shooting Creek Overlook [Fig. 30(89)] (with picnic tables). The next gated road on the left goes only a short distance up Muskrat Branch [Fig. 30(60)] where, with luck, one can locate the old Macon Trail [Fig. 30(90)].

MAP REFERENCES: *USGS 1:24,000 series: Rainbow Springs - Shooting Creek.*

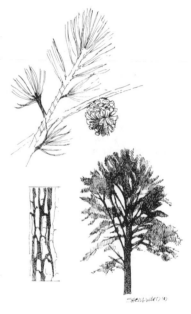

Pitch pine
Pinus rigida

This is the common mountain ridge-top pine, which occurs at moderate elevations. At higher elevations, it is often replaced by the table mountain pine, especially in the Rabun Bald area and on the Highlands Plateau [Fig. 47(21)]. Oddly, it sometimes grows in bogs over deep peat. It is easily seen on the ridge west of Patterson Gap [Fig. 37(9)].

EASTERN BLUE RIDGE

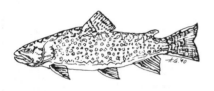

Brook trout
Salvelinus fontinalis

Brook trout, along with lake trout, are classified as chars. They are our only native species and occupy every stream and rivulet, except above significant waterfalls. They are colored like flowers—sides dotted with red spots surrounded by blue rings and with white-edged red fins. The flesh of chars is pink-to-orange in color.

The Nantahala Basin

Rivers in the Nantahala and the Tallulah Basins, separated from each other by the Eastern Continental Divide, run in opposite directions. Water flowing north in the Nantahala follows a much longer path via the Mississippi to the Gulf of Mexico, while water in the Tallulah Basin reaches the Atlantic more directly via the Savannah River. Because the route to the Atlantic is a shorter, steeper one, downcutting is heavier on the south side of the Blue Ridge. This may be one reason why the Tallulah River is nearly 1,000 feet lower than the bed of the Nantahala River.

At 3,000 feet, Nantahala Lake, into which the Nantahala River flows, is one of the highest large lakes in the mountains. Because of the coldness of Nantahala Lake, the Nantahala River experiences two fish-spawning runs—a run of Kokanee salmon in the fall (stocked by Bob Humphries in the early 1960's) and a run of large rainbow trout (steelhead) in the winter. The river may be the only one in the Southeast experiencing a salmon run.

The Nantahala watershed has an extensive system of trails of different lengths and varying degrees of difficulty. There are at least three horse trails and a special horse camp. There are fascinating plant communities, including bogs and some virgin forest.

Because of its soils and elevation, the Nantahala watershed had original timber of a size and density which brought visitors from as far away as Asheville, even when virgin timber was widespread.

The area was logged until the 1920's. Ritter Lumber Company had its logging camp where the main campground for the area is today [Fig. 31(5)]; and at Rainbow Springs [Fig. 31(40)], Ritter had a band-saw mill to saw the huge trees. Narrow-gauge railroads ran up and down the Nantahala River and went up its tributaries until stopped by waterfalls. The route of the dismantled railroad is marked on topographic sheets (Rainbow Springs quadrangle).

The Nantahala is known for large brown trout, and its headwaters still support native brook trout populations. It has also been a black bear refuge for years.

DIRECTIONS: *Go north on US 441 to Franklin, NC; turn left onto US 64; go 12 miles and turn left onto old US 64; go 1.8 miles to Wallace Gap [Fig. 31(1)] and turn right onto FS Road 67/1, which is the road into the basin.*

~A DRIVING TOUR OF THE BASIN. For those interested in combining driving and short walks, there is a marvelous tour of the area to see an immense poplar tree, two waterfalls and vistas from Pickens' Nose.

From the turnoff at Wallace Gap (above), go 0.4 mile to a parking area on the left [Fig. 31(3)]. It is directly adjacent to the

EASTERN BLUE RIDGE

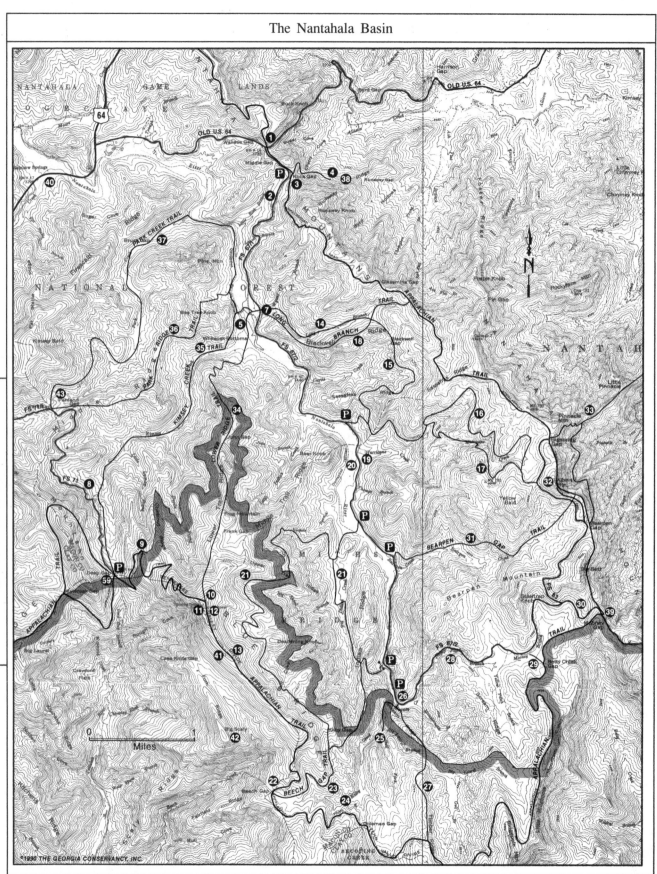

Figure 31 — **NANTAHALA BASIN AND STANDING INDIAN**

Fig. 31 - Nantahala Basin/Standing
Indian
(page references in parentheses)

1 Wallace Gap (145)
2 FS 67/1 (147)
3 parking (145)
4 John Wasilik Memorial Tree (147)
5 White Oak Bottoms Campground
    (145, 149)
7 Backcountry Information Site
    (147, 151)
8 FS 71 (148)
9 Appalachian Trail (148)
10 Standing Indian (148)
11 cliffs, top of Standing Indian (148)
12 mine pits, Standing Indian (148)
13 ridgeline, Standing Indian (148)
14 horse trail (151)
15 horse trail (151)
16 horse trail (151)
17 horse trail (151)
18 Long Branch horse trail (149, 150)
19 Hurricane Creek (151)
20 Nantahala Valley flood plain (147)
21 Big Indian Loop horse trail
    (149, 151)
22 Beech Gap (149, 150)
23 Beech Gap Trail (149, 150)
24 Kilby Creek (147, 149)
25 Big Laurel Falls (147)
26 Big Laurel Falls parking (147)
27 trailhead for Timber Ridge Trail (147)
28 Mooney Falls (147)
29 Betty Creek Gap connector (150)
30 FS 83 (147)
31 Bearpen Gap Trail (149)
32 Albert Mountain fire tower
    (147, 149, 150)
33 Pinnacle Mountain Trail (147)
34 Lower Ridge Trail (149, 150)
35 Kimsey Creek Trail (149, 150)
36 Park Ridge trail (150)
37 Park Creek Trail (150)
38 Runaway Knob Special Interest Area
    (147)
39 Mooney Gap (147, 150)
40 Rainbow Springs (145)
41 connector trail, Beech Creek (149)
42 Big Scaly (149)
43 Park Gap (150)
59 Deep Gap (148, 149, 150)

Appalachian Trail (A.T.), so that one can park here for walks in either direction on the A.T. This is also the trailhead for the short (1.4-mile round-trip) walk on a graded trail to the John Wasilik Memorial Tree [Fig. 31(4)], which is the second largest yellow poplar in the United States. It is eight feet in diameter, 25 feet in circumference and was 135 feet tall until topped by a storm. The tree is in one of a series of north-facing coves, called the Runaway Knob Special Interest Area [Fig. 31(38)], where over 100 plant species have been identified. Lying between 3,200 and 4,400 feet, the 140-acre area is the location of an exceptionally beautiful spring wildflower display. The forest below the Wasilik Poplar contains North Carolina's largest reproducing population of the rare yellow-wood tree, which occurs in only a few localities in Georgia and North Carolina.

Continue on FS 67/1 [Fig. 31(2)] to a fork at about 1.1 miles; take the left fork, FS Road 67/2, about 0.2 mile to the Back Country Information site [Fig. 31(7)]. In the valley upstream are flat areas of flood plain and alluvial fill with some open areas [Fig. 31(20)]. Some of these are wildlife openings and others are rare wetland bogs—some as large as 20 acres, lying between 3,400 and 3,500 feet in elevation. This is the second largest bog complex in western North Carolina and the subject of paleobotanical studies of the peat underlying them. The bogs should not be entered.

Continue 4.7 miles on FS 67/2 to the parking area for Big Laurel Falls [Fig. 31(25)] (1.2 miles round trip), an easy hike for the whole family [Fig. 31(26)]. This is also the trailhead for the Timber Ridge Trail [Fig. 31(27)], which connects with the A.T.

Continue on FS 67/2 for 0.8 mile to the pull-off area for Mooney Falls. The trail is a 0.2-mile round trip to the falls [Fig. 31(28)].

Continue on FS 67/2 until its intersection with FS 83 [Fig. 31(30)]. Turn right and continue past Mooney Gap [Fig. 31(39)], a station for acid rain studies by University of Georgia students, and crossing of the Appalachian Trail. At 0.7 mile past Mooney Gap, park on the north and walk south one mile to Pickens' Nose (5,000 feet). Vistas are to the east, west and south into the Betty Creek Basin. An optional walk is to Albert Mountain. Backtrack on FS 83 as far as it will go north, then hike up to the Albert Mountain fire tower [Fig. 31(32)] which provides an exceptional 360-degree view. (Pickens' Nose and Albert Mountain can also be reached by Buck Creek Road through the Coweeta Hydrologic Laboratory off US 441 north of the Georgia/North Carolina state line). At Big Spring Gap, the Pinnacle Mountain Trail [Fig. 31(33)] descends to the northeast.

~**KILBY CREEK.** The best virgin timber in the area lies above the falls of Kilby Creek [Fig. 31(24)], a challenge for wild-country devotees. This is largely cove hardwood with big hemlock/rhododen-

EASTERN BLUE RIDGE

dron forests along the streams. Above the falls there are eastern brook trout, the only native species.

This is wild and rough country, a true wilderness. Visitors to it should take no chances.

~**STANDING INDIAN.** [Fig. 31(10)] At 5,499 feet, this is the highest peak in the Nantahala Mountains. Its Indian name translates literally, "the place where man stood." Cherokee mythology relates the story of a winged monster that stole a child and carried him to the cliffs on top of the mountain [Fig. 31(11)]. The Indians prayed to the Great Spirit, who answered their prayers by sending a lightning bolt that destroyed the monster and the trees on the summit, but also killed a lone Indian sentry and turned him to stone.

The easiest way to reach the summit is via US 64 and FS 71 [Fig. 29(8), Fig. 31(8)], a long gravel road to Deep Gap [Fig. 31-(59)]. Along this road is dense roadside growth of an extremely primitive plant, a species of horsetail or scouring rush, whose silica content was useful to the early settlers for scrubbing pots. From Deep Gap it is a 2.5-mile walk to the summit, climbing 1,200 feet and passing a good spring and shelter about one-third of the way up. The first large northern loop of this trail [Fig. 31(9)] goes over and around a flat, wet, sheltered ridge with a deep stable soil, which may explain the white oak ridge forest here with flame azalea and fern understory. It also shows the effect of exposure. The white oak goes downslope only 30 feet to the east, but it goes down the western slope 120 feet. The summit of Standing Indian is heath or shrub bald, principally of purple rhododendron. Formerly, a fire tower stood here and a telephone wire ran up from the Tallulah Valley. The Fraser fir nearby were planted. There are two springs northeast of the summit. South of the ridgeline in the ridge forest (not on the Appalachian Trail) are some pits [Fig. 31(12)], relics of the period when mica was mined in the area. These may be discovered by diligent explorers. The Appalachian Trail here tunnels through rhododendron and flame azalea and is quite dramatic in early summer. Traveling on down the 1.5-mile ridgeline, one sees Little Bald directly south and passes through several environments, principally red oak ridge forest and areas of shrub bald vegetation [Fig. 31(13)] dominated by mountain laurel, with some purple rhododendron. Some drier areas have grasses, while other almost-bare-soil areas are covered with a rare tundra species—the three-leaved cinquefoil, a threatened species at the southern periphery of its range. The effects on the soil of ice heavage—that is, the repeated freezing and thawing of the earth—and the results of wind shear on the shrubs are evident. There has been much scientific debate on the origin of balds such as this which cap many of the Appalachians' highest peaks. Here on the southwest slope, one can see the bald area grading into dwarf northern red oak/evergreen heath, which within several hundred feet grades into northern red oak/deciduous

Horsetail
Equisetum sp.

This extremely primitive plant is rare in the mountains, occurring along the road to Deep Gap [Fig. 31(8)] and in Beech Creek Gorge [Fig. 32(15)]. Because of its high silica content, it has been used to scour pots; hence, the common name "scouring brush."

Three-leaved cinquefoil
Potentilla tridentata

This rare plant is restricted to rock crevices and balds at high elevations, such as on the Standing Indian ridgeline [Fig. 31(13)]. The common cinquefoil has five leaves and yellow flowers, while the three-leaved variety has white flowers.

heath (azaleas and blueberries). On the opposite side (the northeast slope) the bald areas grade into a beautiful northern red oak/fern community that in turn grades into a northern hardwood forest.

To the west lies Big Scaly (5,200 feet) [Fig. 31(42)] in the immediate foreground. The Girl Scouts had a connector trail [Fig. 31(41)] leading down to Beech Creek through the rhododendron and virgin red oak ridge forest with flame azalea understory, but the entrance is difficult to find. There are two other accesses to Beech Creek—one an old log road, the other a steep trail (see Tallulah Basin)—both beginning at Beech Gap.

The upper portion of the Big Indian Loop horse trail [Fig. 31(21)] passes through a succession of cove hardwoods, northern hardwoods and boulderfields.

Loop trail possibilities are numerous. If two vehicles are available, a shuttle can be set up. For example, one vehicle may be left at Deep Gap [Fig. 31(59)] and another at either White Oak Bottoms Campground [Fig. 31(5)] or at the Beech Gap Trail junction with FS 67. Then one could hike to the summit of Standing Indian and down the Lower Ridge Trail [Fig. 31(34)], or down the long spine of Standing Indian to Beech Gap [Fig. 31(22)] and down the Beech Gap Trail [Fig. 31(23)], with a side visit to the Kilby Creek virgin forest [Fig. 31(24)].

~HIKING TRAILS IN THE NANTAHALA BASIN. There are seven trails from the valley up to the Appalachian Trail (A.T.). They can be combined in a number of ways to create interesting loop hikes. One warning: the weather here can change rapidly. In particular, the hiker should beware afternoon thunderstorms on the high ridges and peaks in the summer months.

KIMSEY CREEK TRAIL TO STANDING INDIAN. Ten miles round trip. One favorite hike is to walk to Standing Indian Mountain starting from the Back Country Information Center on the Kimsey Creek Trail [Fig. 31(35)], a wonderfully varied path along creeks and through wildlife meadows with many wildflowers. The trail connects with the A.T. at Deep Gap [Fig. 31(59)]. Follow the A.T. to the top of Standing Indian, which is a strenuous climb. There is a junction at which one spur goes from the A.T. to the top for a vista. Return to the A.T. and continue a very short distance (10 yards or so) to the Lower Ridge Trail [Fig. 31(34)], which returns to the Back Country Information Center in four miles.

LOOP TRAIL. 10.9 miles round trip. Another loop might be to hike up the A.T. on the Long Branch Trail [Fig. 31(18)] from the Back Country Information Center (1.9 miles). Hike south (to the right) 3.1 miles on the A.T. to the Albert Mountain lookout tower (5,280 feet) [Fig. 31(32)] for views in all directions. Continue on the A.T. 0.3 mile to Bearpen Gap Trail [Fig. 31(31)]; descend 2.4

miles on Bearpen Gap Trail to FS 67/2; turn right and return 3.2 miles to the Back Country Information Center.

PARK CREEK AND PARK RIDGE TRAILS. Ten-mile loop. This interesting hike away from the A.T. (which means it is less crowded) combines the Park Creek [Fig. 31(37)] and Park Ridge Trails [Fig. 31(36)]. One begins at the Back Country Information Center. This beginning is the same as for the Lower Ridge Trail and the Kimsey Creek Trail. About 0.5 mile from the bridge in the campground, the Park Ridge Trail goes left up the ridge and climbs to Park Gap [Fig. 31(43)] at FS 71/1. Cross the road and descend on Park Creek Trail along a lovely stream to the Nantahala River; turn right and walk about 1.5 miles to the junction with Park Ridge Trail and retrace the path to the Back Country Information Center.

ACCESS TO DAY HIKES. Another access to day-hike trailheads is from FS 71/1. Take US 64 west from Franklin, past the turn-off at 12 miles onto old US 64; go about 2.5 miles and turn left onto FS 71; go about 2.5 miles to reach Park Gap [Fig. 31(43)]; park in this area and walk the Park Ridge and Park Creek loop trail. Driving another three miles past this parking area, one reaches the end of the road at Deep Gap. Here is access to the Kimsey Creek Trail, the A.T. east to Standing Indian Mountain (2.8 miles one way), a primitive trail south to the Tallulah River, and the A.T. west to White Oak Stamp and Bly Gap.

THREE-DAY WALK. Twenty-four miles. A good backpacking trip starts at the Back Country Information Center, on the Long Branch Trail [Fig. 31(18)] to the A.T. Turn right (south) onto the A.T. and follow it over Albert Mountain [Fig. 31(32)], through Bear Pen Gap, over Big Butt, down to Mooney Gap [Fig. 31(39)], passing Carter Gap and Beech Gap [Fig. 31(22)], climbing Standing Indian Mountain and descending to Deep Gap [Fig. 31(59)]. Turn right on Kimsey Creek Trail and return to the Back Country Information Center. This is a pleasant three-day (24-mile) walk. There are shelters at Big Spring Gap, Carter Gap and Standing Indian (near Deep Gap). This is a popular loop, so shelters may be filled. Walked in early June, the stretch up Standing Indian Mountain is a botanical garden. The Catawba rhododendron and mountain laurel arch over the trail to form a floral tunnel.

OTHER TRAIL POSSIBILITIES. Many other combinations are possible using the following trails in conjunction with the Appalachian Trail: Kimsey Creek Trail [Fig. 31(35)], Lower Ridge Trail [Fig. 31(34)], Long Branch Trail [Fig. 31(18)], Beech Gap Trail [Fig. 31(23)] and Betty Creek Gap connector [Fig. 31(29)].

EASTERN BLUE RIDGE

~HORSE TRAILS IN THE NANTAHALA BASIN. A series of special horse trails [Fig. 31(14), Fig. 31(15), Fig. 31(16), Fig. 31(17)] covers the Long Branch and Hurricane Creek watersheds. The Long Branch Trail [Fig. 31(14)] begins at [Fig. 31(7)] on Fig. 31. There is a horse camp near the mouth of Hurricane Creek [Fig. 31(19)]. For further information, ask the ranger. There is also a long horse trail [Fig. 31(21)] on the east slopes of Standing Indian.

ADDITIONAL INFORMATION: *The U.S. Forest Service has prepared a recreational opportunities guide (which they refer to as ROG) in which many of the hiking trails in the area are summarized along with directions to the trailheads. The public may view this guide at the Wayah Ranger District Forest Service office or order copies of the pages of the guide for the cost of copying and mailing. Topographical maps of the area are also available here. U.S. Forest Service, Wayah Ranger District, 8 Sloan Rd., Franklin, NC 28734. (704) 524-6441.*

MAP REFERENCES: *USGS 1:24,000 series: Prentiss - Rainbow Springs.*

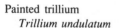

Painted trillium
Trillium undulatum

This species likes acid soils at high elevations, as do rhododendron and hemlock. The flower's reddish markings near the center distinguish this from all other trilliums.

EASTERN BLUE RIDGE

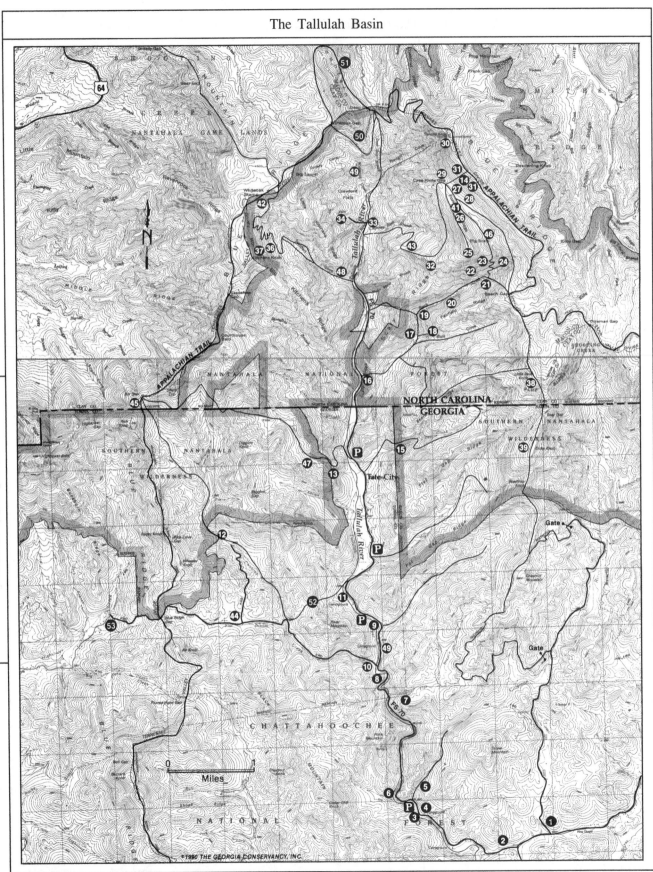

Figure 32 — **UPPER TALLULAH BASIN**

Fig. 32 - Upper Tallulah Basin
(page references in parentheses)

P trailhead parking
1 Coleman River Road [FS 54] (157)
2 FS 70 (153)
3 Tallulah Campground (155)
4 mini-gorge containing the "strainer hole"
5 Coleman River Scenic Area   (157)
6 Rock Mountain Gorge (start) (153)
7 Flat Branch Falls (153)
8 Rock Mountain Gorge (end) (153)
9 Tate Branch Campground (155)
10 Charlie's Creek Road (153)
11 Sandy Bottom Campground (155)
12 amethyst mine (153)
13 Fall Branch Falls (155)
14 Appalachian Trail connector trail (155)
15 Denton Creek Falls (153, 155)
16 Beech Creek - Chimney Rock Loop
     (153, 154, 155)
17 Beech Creek ford (154)
18 Bull Cove Branch Falls (154)
19 Bear Creek Falls (154)
20 Beech Creek Gorge (154)
21 rock crusher (154)
22 Big Scaly Mountain cliffs (154)
23 Tate corundum mine (154)
24 High Falls (154)
25 Big Scaly Mountain (154, 155)
26 trail to Big Scaly Mountain summit
     (154)
27 "Indian Stomp Ground" (154)
28 Beech Creek Spring (154)
29 boulderfield (155)
30 Standing Indian (154, 155)
31 shrub bald area (155)
32 Chimney Rock (155)
33 Girl Scout former camping area and Deep
     Gap Trail (155)
34 Thomas Falls (155)
36 Chimney Rocks (157)
37 Brush Mountain cliff (157)
38 Little Bald (155)
39 Dick's Knob (155)
41 beech, yellow birch & hop hornbeam
     forest (154)
42 White Oak Stamp (157)
43 gap overlook—waterspout watershed
     (155)
44 road to Charlie's Creek headwaters (153)
45 Bly Gap (155)
46 Beech Creek Flat (154)
47 Bly Gap Trail (155)
48 Holden Cove Trail (153, 157)
49 New Falls (155)
50 Appalachian Trail (old route)
51 Appalachian Trail (new route)
52 Powerline Trail
53 western approach up Hightower
     Creek Valley

The Tallulah Basin

If one had to select a national park site in Georgia, this land of gorges, waterfalls and scenic splendor would be it. Hunters of bear and hog have used the area for years. Only now are horseback riders and hikers discovering this watershed and its myriad trails, many of them connecting with the Appalachian Trail. There was no easy way for the early settlers to reach the remote valley called Tate City, a pastoral setting rimmed by a great northward flex of the Blue Ridge. Tate City was once a busy corundum mining community and later a logging town with stores and churches. Now only two churches and a handful of homes remain. Most of the original mountain people who lived by subsistence agriculture are gone. The bears and perhaps even the cougar have returned.

~UPPER TALLULAH BASIN SCENIC DRIVE. [Fig. 32(2) to Fig. 32(48)] This drive up the Tallulah's upper gorge is spectacular. It begins at the bridge over the Coleman River. At this bridge is the trailhead for an exciting, short (less than a mile) trail up the gorge of the Coleman River through the Coleman River Scenic Area [Fig. 32(5)], described on a sign just north of the bridge. FS 70 dead ends in the heart of the Southern Nantahala Wilderness. The major access point for the Tallulah River basin, it follows beside the Tallulah through the three-mile-long Rock Mountain Gorge [Fig. 32(6)] to [Fig. 32(8)], on the old railroad bed, which was blasted out of solid rock by the lumber company logging the valley in virgin timber days. This lovely road crosses the Tallulah four times. The picturesque gorge has been the site of television commercials and postcard vistas. One can picnic on the rocks or fish the pools stocked weekly with eating-size rainbow trout. In the gorge grow a number of the beautiful and rare flowering tree, the mountain camellia or *Stewartia*, which blooms in June and July. The best place to see it is in a stand at a wide place in the road at the extreme southern end of the Tate Branch Campground [Fig. 32(49)]. At Line Branch, one can look back, high up at the Flat Branch Falls [Fig. 32(7)]. Just below the Tate Branch Campground, Charlie's Creek Road fords the river [Fig. 32(10)]. When this road emerges on a flat near the A.T., a north-turning fork [Fig. 32(44)] leads one to the main Charlie's Creek. Across the creek and up the road a few hundred yards, there is bare dirt and a trail up to an amethyst mine [Fig. 32(12)] that has produced some of the finest gem amethysts in the United States.

~THE BEECH CREEK - CHIMNEY ROCK LOOP.
[Fig. 32(16)] A 12-mile loop. This hike has been a favorite of scout groups for many years. Skirting private property, the lower trailhead

is at the "Glory Patch" [Fig. 32(16)] and crosses a low gap in Scaly Ridge before descending to the Beech Creek log road trail at an old homesite. Shortly thereafter, this main road crosses Bull Cove Branch. A striking cliff and falls with rich herb growth lies just out of sight upstream [Fig. 32(18)]. The road then fords Beech Creek to enter [Fig. 32(17)] the stunningly beautiful Beech Creek Gorge [Fig. 32(20)] (a trail to the left [Fig. 32(19)] leads to Bear Gap). In about two miles, the log road trail reaches an old ore-crusher foundation of packed rock [Fig. 32(21)] and begins switch-backs up through the vast cliffs [Fig. 32(22)] on the face of Big Scaly Mountain [Fig. 32(25)]. At about the second switchback left, a prominent trail goes off east and down to the creek, where it reaches beautiful High Falls [Fig. 32(24)], probably 200 feet high. Trail length is less than 0.25 mile. The old Tate corundum mine is high in the cliffs [Fig. 32(23)], and the remains of the old oxen haul road (with dead-packed, or mortarless, rock) up to the mine may be found to the left (west) at about the third switchback to the east. If one goes west through the cliffs, there are perhaps 50 acres of virgin slope forest. It is possible to hike through this to Chimney Rock. Bears raise and den in these cliffs [Fig. 32(22)] and are often seen in the gorge below if the visitor can remain quiet. After gaining the "top" of the cliffs on the main road, one enters an incredibly long "flat" [Fig. 32(46)]. After 1.5 miles arrive at the Beech Creek Spring [Fig. 32(28)], once the site of an Adirondack shelter. Approaching the spring on the left, pass through an unusual climax variety of northern hardwood forest of beech with yellow birch and hop hornbeam [Fig. 32(41)]. This is possibly a relict Ice-Age forest of the Pleistocene era 15,000 to 20,000 years ago. At this point, the hiker is about 4,600 feet above sea level. Upslope, at about 4,700 feet, enter a totally different environment—a high-altitude or north-ern oak ridge forest which can best be experienced on the trail [Fig. 32(26)] to the top of Big Scaly. Near Beech Creek Spring, the forest of rich black soil was once principally northern red oaks. Trees were wide apart, and the area resembled an orchard. Trunks were short and limby. One can find a few of these ancient speci-mens missed by loggers. There are numerous small chestnut sprouts. Fraser's fir are also here, planted, as they are on top of Standing Indian [Fig. 32(30)]. The Beech Creek Flat [Fig. 32(46)] is a mecca for wildflower lovers. The highly prized ramps or "mountain garlic" grow in profusion and are found nearly to Bear Creek Falls in the gorge below.

Just north of the spring is an area of naked red earth, clay-rich soil which deer eat. This is the "Indian Stomp Ground" [Fig. 32(27)]. It is certainly possible that the Indians danced here, but early settlers may have invented this name as an explanation for the naked ground. Several hundred yards beyond, a log road turns left. Here a gentle nature trail [Fig. 32(26)] leads through virgin northern red oak ridge forest to the rocky summit of Big Scaly

SHEILA WARD ©

Hop hornbeam
Ostrya virginiana

The leaves of this small sub-canopy tree resemble the beech, with which it sometimes occurs at high elevations. Its dark, rough, scaly bark distinguishes it from both the beech and the ironwood, the latter growing on river floodplains.

(5,200 feet) [Fig. 32(25)], surrounded by dense purple rhododendron and yielding magnificent vistas to the northwest and southwest.

One can take the very steep and poorly marked Appalachian Trail connector trail [Fig. 32(14)] to the A.T., where one will find areas of shrub bald [Fig. 32(31)]. To the left (north) is Standing Indian Mountain (5,499 feet) [Fig. 32(30)]. To the right (south) is Little Bald (5,015 feet) [Fig. 32(38)], which one can also reach from the loop trail [Fig. 32(16)]. Just south of Little Bald is Dick's Knob [Fig. 32(39)], the third highest peak in Georgia. Just before Case Knife Gap, a few feet past the turnoffs of the Big Scaly and A.T. connector trails, the north-facing cove to the right has a boulderfield [Fig. 32(29)] with some northern hardwoods. Go down past a spring and follow the small branch. Down the loop road and through Case Knife Gap is the Chimney Rock watershed. This section is not nearly as steep as the Beech Creek section. Descending, watch carefully the ridgeline that comes down westerly from Big Scaly. Sticking slightly above it will be Chimney Rock [Fig. 32(32)]—a climbable (with great care) rock formation that affords a tremendous view of the watershed and is reached by a short (less than 0.25-mile), indistinct, trail winding up through huge scenic rocks. The trail turns south in a flat about 200 yards below the last fork of Chimney Rock Branch that is forded. The main log road trail continues down, passing through a gap [Fig. 32(43)] overlooking the Waterspout watershed and then meeting the Deep Gap Trail in a serene pasture. The Girl Scouts' primitive camping area was located here [Fig. 32(33)]. A trail leads to Thomas Falls from the Deep Gap Trail [Fig. 32(34)], and New Falls [Fig. 32(49)] is at the bluff where Wateroak Creek leaves Collary Cove.

FACILITIES: *Three campgrounds are located on the upper Tallulah River: Tallulah [Fig. 32(3)], 17 campsites ($7 fee); Sandy Bottom [Fig. 32(11)], 12 campsites ($5 fee); and Tate Branch [Fig. 32(9)], 19 campsites and 10 picnic shelters ($6 fee).*

~**WATERFALLS.** Many of the streams entering the Tate City Valley have waterfalls.

DENTON CREEK FALLS. [Fig. 32(15)] A sheer drop easily reached about 0.25 mile upstream from the first ford (where the road is blocked).

FALL BRANCH FALLS. [Fig. 32(13)] Best visited from the top by way of the Bly Gap Trail [Fig. 32(47)], a long trail which at Bly Gap [Fig. 32(45)] intersects both the Appalachian Trail and a road down into the Shooting Creek Valley. Park at the trailhead [Fig. 32(P)].

Pygmy shrew
Microsorex hoyi

One of the world's smallest mammals, this tiny shrew barely enters Georgia in the headwaters of the Tallulah River. Even here it is rare and difficult to trap.

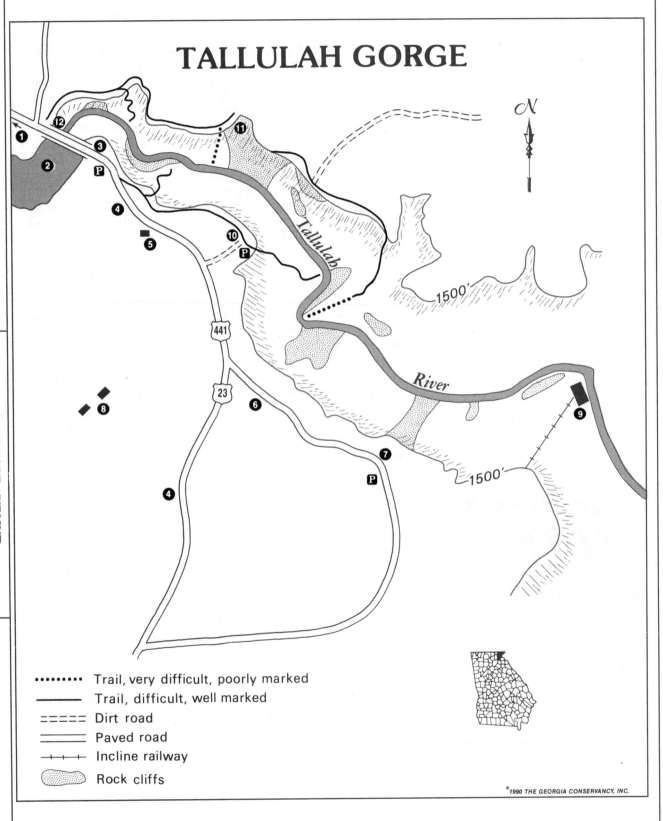

TALLULAH GORGE

Legend:
- •••••••• Trail, very difficult, poorly marked
- ———— Trail, difficult, well marked
- ===== Dirt road
- ———— Paved road
- +++++ Incline railway
- Rock cliffs

©1990 THE GEORGIA CONSERVANCY, INC.

Figure 33 — **TALLULAH GORGE**

156

Fig. 33 - Tallulah Gorge
(page references in parentheses)

 1 Terrora Park (160, 161, 162)
 2 Tallulah Falls Lake
 3 Tallulah Gorge Park (160, 162)
 4 US 441-23
 5 Old Tallulah Falls Railroad Station
 6 Old US 441-23 [scenic route]
 7 The Overlook (162)
 8 Tallulah Falls School
 9 Power Plant
10 Wallenda Cable Anchor & Vista
11 Cascade Falls
12 Tallulah Falls Dam and Bridge (161)

~THE HOLDEN COVE TRAIL. [Fig. 32(48)] This trail offers a number of smaller falls. Generally moderate, it is difficult in one place. Halfway up, a logging road intercepts the trail, making the rest of the climb easy and providing a view of Chimney Rocks [Fig. 32(36)], the formidable Brushy Mountain cliff [Fig. 32(37)] and rhododendron slicks. It proceeds to intersect both the A.T. and the Chunky Gal Trail at White Oak Stamp [Fig. 32(42)].

~COLEMAN RIVER ROAD. [Fig. 32(1)] This road provides access to the wilderness and to the Coleman River headwaters. **DIRECTIONS:** *Take the Persimmon/Patterson Gap road to the right off of US 76 7.5 miles west of Clayton. Continue 0.5 mile past the Tallulah River Road (FS 70) and turn left onto FS 54.*

~COLEMAN RIVER SCENIC AREA. [Fig. 32(5)] This picturesque 330 acres encompassing the lower Coleman River was dedicated in 1960 to "Ranger Nick" Nicholson following his 40 years of public service. A mile-long trail passes up the gorge with its pools and falls. Some large examples of evergreen trees, especially hemlock, can be seen. Fraser's magnolia is common and *Stewartia* occurs. Carolina rhododendron is unusually abundant. Between the Tallulah Campground and the Secenic Area trailhead is a mini-gorge containing the "strainer hole" which, prior to dynamiting, had a hydraulic or "keeper" at its input which drowned several people.

DIRECTIONS TO UPPER TALLULAH BASIN: *From the center of Clayton proceed west on US 76 7.5 miles, turn right (north) on a paved road and in 2.2 miles pass cemetery in community of Persimmon. Continue 1.8 miles and left at first paved road. Follow this road (FS 70) which becomes gravel. At one mile past parking area for canoe put-in (to float down to Lake Burton). The Forest Service's Tallulah River Campground is only 0.3 mile further. The Coleman River Scenic Area and bridge are 0.1 mile past the campground. The drive up the Rock Mountain Gorge begins 0.2 mile past the Coleman River bridge and continues for about 1.9 miles. The gorge ends just south of a shallow ford across the Tallulah, which leads to the four-wheel-drive road to Charlie's Creek. Continuing up the main road it is 0.3 mile to the second Forest Service campground at Tate Branch. From Tate Branch it is 0.8 mile to the third official campground at Sandy Bottoms. From there it is 0.5 mile to Mill Creek (and its trail) and another mile to Denton Creek, then another 0.5 mile to the Beech Creek Bridge. Shortly north of this bridge is the North Carolina state line. From there it is about 0.4 mile to the parking area and trailhead for the Beach Creek gorge trail. Watch for a flat, cleared area on your left. Signs are to be installed. The road ends about 0.2 mile farther and is the other end of the Beech Creek/Chimney Rock trail loop. Holden Cove Branch and its trail are several hundred yards back down the road from the deadend.*

~**TALLULAH GORGE.** [Fig. 33, Fig. 36(65)] At 600 feet in depth, Tallulah Gorge is one of the deepest and most spectacular gorges in the east. It is geologically unique, being cut down in resistant quartzite, quite unlike the gneisses and schists of the surrounding mountains. It is a textbook example of stream capture. Originally, both the Chattooga and Tallulah Rivers were headwaters of the Chattahoochee River. The Savannah River, downcutting more rapidly, eventually cut back and robbed the Chattahoochee of these two streams. Over millions of years, the increased flow has carved out the gorge.

The rare persistent trillium and a wealth of other flora are found in the gorge, as is the green salamander, a rare crevice-dweller. The bird density is low, consisting mainly of vultures, phoebes and swallows. Both the rare Carolina hemlock and table mountain pine grow around the gorge rim. Carolina rhododendron is unusually abundant. This is one of the few areas where the rare fringed polygala may be found.

Until the turn of the 19th century, Tallulah Falls and Tallulah Gorge were relatively unchanged by man. For centuries only the Cherokee Indians inhabited the area, and few whites penetrated the wilderness. The few white hunters and traders who wandered through the area told stories about the gorge and its mysterious thundering waters. Even the Cherokees seldom ventured into the gorge, believing it to be inhabited by a strange race of "little people" who were alleged to live in the nooks and crannies of the cliffs overlooking the falls. The Cherokees also believed that one of the caves in the gorge was the entrance to the Happy Hunting Grounds; if an Indian ever entered, he would never return.

After the Cherokees were driven out in 1819, white adventurers began to explore the region. Within a year of the Cherokees' departure, spectacular accounts were circulated concerning this natural wonder in the northeast Georgia mountains. Although great stamina was required to make the trip, tourists began forging their ways through the mountains to see this curiosity of nature. Clarkesville was the closest point where pack horses could be obtained to begin the 12-mile trek through the mountains to the gorge.

Interest in Tallulah Falls and Gorge had spread beyond Georgia. During the 1830's and 1840's foreign and American dignitaries began to make pilgrimages to the region. The area's attraction is not hard to understand. The gorge itself is a three-mile-long gash in the earth that reaches a depth of almost 600 feet, bordered by rocky, vertical walls. The Tallulah River carries runoff from a watershed area of over 200 square miles. In those days, this mighty river roared into the gorge over a series of spectacular cataracts, creating a continuous, thundering sound that echoed through the gorge day and night.

At the head of the gorge, the bed of the Tallulah River suddenly became narrow, creating a swift current headed toward the first falls. Tourists named this narrow bed Indian Arrow Rapids. The first of

Persistent trillium
Trillium persistens

This rare trillium was named by Georgia botanist Wilbur Duncan. The flower is erect, standing on a stalk above the three leaves. It grows under or near rhododendrons, and only in the Tallulah/Tugaloo River system of northeast Georgia and northwest South Carolina.

the great falls over which the Tallulah poured into the gorge was named Ladore; then came the 76-foot-high Tempesta Falls; then, the 96-foot Hurricane Falls. The fourth of the great falls was named Oseana. Next was Bridal Veil Falls, with a drop of 17 feet. And last was Sweet Sixteen Falls, with a 16-foot fall. Beyond the falls, deep in the canyon, was a great bend in the river called Horseshoe Bend, from which visitors liked to gaze upward to guess the height of the towering cliffs. Many streams and creeks poured over the canyon rim into the gorge below and were given appropriate names—no one knows exactly by whom. The pool at the bottom of Ladore Falls was named Hawthorne Pool, in memory of a man who fell to his death there. A natural water slide on the side of the gorge was named Hank's Sliding Place, in memory of a native of the region who slipped and fell more than 100 feet into the raging river below and lived to tell about it. The thundering waters beneath an overhanging rock reminded someone of the voice of Satan, so that rock was named Devil's Pulpit—probably the most popular tourist site at the gorge, then and now. An outcropping that reminded someone of a profile was given the name Witch's Head and was a popular spot for photographers in the nineteenth century.

As tourists grew impatient with making the long trek from Clarkesville and with having to camp at the gorge, inns sprang up near the attraction. Fine hotels were built, able to accommodate as many as 300 guests. Tallulah Gorge became a mecca for summer vacationers, offering cool temperatures, great views and accommodations for rich and poor.

The old Tallulah Falls Railroad, which reached the gorge in 1882, ran along its western rim. The cuts may still be seen, and the old train station at Tallulah Falls Dam is now a craft store. This railroad, which ran from Cornelia to Franklin, was the principal means of bringing visitors to the gorge in the early years. Before the right of way was sold in the 1950's and the many wooden trestles were demolished, it was the setting for Walt Disney's film *The Great Locomotive Chase*.

On July 24, 1886, a crowd estimated at 3,500 to 6,000 people assembled to watch Professor Leon walk across the gorge on a tightrope. His historic feat began on the north rim at Inspiration Point, the highest point in the gorge at 1,200 feet. When he was near the center, one of his guy lines broke and the professor fell. Luckily, he caught the cable and sat on it for 25 minutes, before completing his walk.

In 1905, the state legislature made an effort to buy and preserve the land around Tallulah Gorge, but could not raise the $100,000 needed to make the purchase. Three years later, what was to become Georgia Power Company was organized by E. Elmer Smith of York, Pennsylvania, and Eugene Ashley of Glens Falls, New York. In 1909, these two men obtained the $108,960 necessary to purchase the strategic tract of land around the head of the gorge.

Efforts were made to rescue the Tallulah River and Gorge from

development. In the first large environmental battle in the state's
history, a group of citizens led by the widow of Confederate General
James Longstreet appealed to officials of Rabun County, to the state
legislature, to the governor, to the Georgia Supreme Court and even
to President Taft. But it was too late. Work on Tallulah Dam
began.

Throngs of people came to the gorge area to watch this remarkable engineering feat. But more came in 1912 to view Tallulah Falls
for the last time.

In September of 1913, with the dam at the head of the gorge
completed and the river diverted through its powerhouses, electricity
flowed for the first time over the wires to Atlanta—to run the city's
trolley cars. The "terrible" Tallulah River, as the Cherokees had
called it, had been tamed and reduced to a trickle, dripping through
Tallulah Gorge.

The decline of Tallulah Gorge as a tourist attraction was rapid
thereafter. Many hotels closed. Others were burned in a fire of
1922 that almost destroyed the little tourist town of Tallulah Falls.
Two years later, the construction of US 441 bypassed the town of
Tallulah Falls altogether.

The moaning of the wind is the only sound that comes from the
gorge now, although the place has enjoyed a few brief moments of
notoriety. On July 18, 1970, Karl Wallenda duplicated Professor
Leon's tightrop walk across the gorge, completing the distance in
under forty minutes and breaking the professor's record for speed, if
not for distance. In 1972, scenes from the movie *Deliverance* were
shot in the canyon.

From its mile-high beginnings on the southwest slopes of Standing
Indian Mountain in North Carolina, the Tallulah bounded southward
through the north Georgia mountains, falling more than 4,700 feet
during the 46-mile journey to its confluence with the Chattooga
beyond the end of Tallulah Gorge, at the South Carolina border. Its
last four miles, beginning at the falls, were the most dramatic. Over
these falls the river plunged downward a total of 600 feet in less
than a mile.

What remains of the once terrible Tallulah? Although the river
and the lakes which now impound it are nothing like the scene of
100 years ago, the Tallulah today is an exciting and unusual experience.

~HIKING IN TALLULAH GORGE.

~**HIKING IN TALLULAH GORGE.** The hike into the gorge is
strenuous but rewarding. It can also be dangerous, especially when
the rocks are wet. Much of the gorge is privately owned, and access
to major trails is in private ownership.

The gorge can be seen when looking south from the US 441
bridge atop the dam. Approximately 200 feet deep at this point, it
becomes deeper downriver. Much of the gorge can be seen from the
rim or rim trails. The north rim trail begins in Terrora Park

Carolina rhododendron
Rhododendron minus

The Carolina rhododendron's leaves closely resemble mountain laurel, but its flowers do not. The purplish blooms come after mountain laurel has flowered. Rhododendron is best identified by the smooth bark—unlike the lightly-furrowed and shreddy bark of the mountain laurel. Carolina rhododendron is very common in the vicinity of Tallulah Falls and Panther Creek.

[Fig. 33(1), Fig. 34(v)] and goes under the highway bridge to an overlook. The south rim trail begins at Tallulah Gorge Park [Fig. 33(3)Fig. 35(65)]. Both trails include spectacular overlooks.

Access to the gorge is limited, although several unmarked trails lead into it. Most of these trails are very steep and dangerous and should not be attempted when wet.

The three best routes into the gorge are as follows:

THE CABLE TOWER TRAIL. The most accessible trail is just south of the Wallenda cable tower on the south rim [Fig. 35(64)]. Proceeding south on US 441, take the first left turn 0.35 miles south of the bridge, into a dirt parking area. Wallenda's south tower is at the end of this area, on the gorge rim. After enjoying the view, turn right to find the trail, which proceeds down an extensive boulder field to the gorge bottom. At its foot is Sliding Rock, which provides an exhilarating waterslide into a pool below. Across the top of Sliding Rock, on the far side, a trail can be found heading upstream. Be *very* careful crossing here, as moss and lichens make an extremely slippery surface.

THE GORGE PARK TRAIL. The other trail on the south rim is reached by the south rim trail originating in Tallulah Gorge Park, on the east side of US 441, just south of the bridge [Fig. 36(65), Fig. 33(12)]. The trail to the bottom begins at a left turn just a short distance along the main trail from the park. Unfortunately, this route to the bottom is currently closed, as it is in need of maintenance.

THE NORTH RIM TRAIL. A trail down from the north rim is reached by the north rim trail originating in Terrora Park and proceeding under the bridge until the trail into the gorge appears as a faint right turn, about 0.35 mile from Terrora Park [Fig. 33(1)]. Bear consistently to the right to avoid missing this trail. This trail does *not* reach the bottom of the gorge.

A convenient day trip can be made by descending into the gorge by the cable tower trail, then following the north-side trail upstream (or "rock-hopping" from boulder to boulder up the middle for the more adventurous.) When further progress is blocked by a large pool with a high, narrow waterfall at its end, the bottom of the gorge park trail can be found at the downstream edge of a huge rock outcrop on the south side. This trail leads into the south rim trail originating in the park. Allow at least four hours for the round trip.

Because of the many dangers that exist in the gorge, check with Georgia Power's Terrora Visitor Center before making a decision to enter the gorge. They strongly recommend seeing a short video and reading a brochure that explains the beauty and dangers of the gorge. Flash flooding in the gorge could happen at any time *without warning*. If a flash flood occurs, get to high ground immediately. You

EASTERN BLUE RIDGE

may or may not hear a warning siren before water is released into the gorge from above the dam.

~TERRORA PARK AND VISITOR CENTER. [Fig. 33(1)]

Terrora Park includes a park, picnic areas, campground and visitor center. It is owned and operated as a public service by Georgia Power Company.

FACILITIES: *Fifty campsites with water and electrical hookups, restrooms, picnic area with shelters, rest areas, swimming beach, tennis courts, playground, bathhouse with hot and cold showers, and audiovisual displays about the Georgia Power lake system. A short nature trail and the beginning of the north rim trail above Tallulah Gorge, which has an offshoot trail part-way to its bottom, are also found here.*

HOURS/DATES: *Terrora Park: Nov.-Mar., 8:30 - 5 Mon.-Fri.; Apr.-May, 8:30-5 Mon.-Sun.; Jun.-Aug., 8:30-7 Mon.-Sun.;Sep.-Oct. 8:30 - 5 Mon.-Sun; Visitor Center: Mon.-Sat. 9-5, Sun. 1-5; Campground: Apr.-Oct., Mon.-Sun.*

FEES: *$8 per tent, $9 per RV.*

DIRECTIONS: *Terrora Park is immediately north of the bridge over Tallulah Gorge on the west side of US 441, in the town of Tallulah Falls.*

ADDITIONAL INFORMATION: *Georgia Power Company, Terrora Park, US 441, P.O. Box 9, Tallulah Falls, GA 30573. (404) 754-3276 (visitor center) or (404) 754-6036 (camping and day use area).*

~TALLULAH GORGE PARK. [Fig. 33(3)]

Tallulah Gorge Park consists of a concession stand and small museum and includes the entrance to the scenic south rim trail. It is owned and operated by Tallulah Falls School.

FACILITIES: *A short (less than 0.25 mile) trail overlooking the gorge.*

DATES/HOURS: *Open every day, Apr.-Oct., 10-5.*

FEES: *Adults $2, children $.75.*

DIRECTIONS: *The park is located just south of the highway bridge on the east side of US 441, within the town limits of Tallulah Falls, 12 miles south of Clayton.*

ADDITIONAL INFORMATION: *Tallulah Falls School, Tallulah Falls, GA (404) 754-3181.*

~THE OVERLOOK. [Fig. 33(7)]

The Overlook is a privately owned concession stand. Outside and free of charge is a scenic view of the gorge.

FACILITIES: *An overlook into the gorge, with concession stand.*

DATES/HOURS: *Open summer - closed winter.*

FEES: *None.*

DIRECTIONS: *Proceed on US 441 0.6 mile south of the Tallulah Gorge bridge. Turn left on the first paved road (SR 15/Old US 441). The Overlook is on the left at 0.35 mile after turn.*

Red Squirrel
Tamiasciurus hudsonicus

About half as large as gray squirrels, red squirrels have white and black stripes down their sides. These frisky squirrels prefer evergreens, especially spruce-fir, but have been found as far south as Jacks Gap on the Georgia Blue Ridge (Brasstown Bald section). Red squirrels have been seen in the city limits of Clayton, where they feed on the cones of the Virginia pine.

EASTERN BLUE RIDGE

Pilot black snake
Elaphe obsoleta obsoleta

This slow-moving reptile is the second most common snake in the mountain forests, after the garter snake. It is a rodent eater and climbs well. A better name is black rat snake. It is docile and should be left alone to play its role in forest ecology.

~A CANOEING GUIDE AND DRIVING TOUR OF THE TALLULAH RIVER BASIN. The destinations below, whether reached by car, canoe, foot or a combination thereof, provide a rare opportunity for visitors to view the mountains from scenic lakes, run the rapids of what remains of Tallulah Gorge and pay tribute to what was once one of the mightiest rivers in Georgia. The guide [Fig. 34] which follows provides directions for canoeing 31.5 miles of the Tallulah River, including its scenic impounded lakes and sections of the river where Class I-IV rapids provide hints of what the river once was. The trip can be divided into six parts or done as one long trip. The driving directions to put-ins and take-outs provide an opportunity for visitors to see much of the same terrain by car.

THE FIRST 10 MILES. Although the first 10 miles of the Tallulah are uncanoeable, driving streamside is worthwhile for the mountain scenery alone. See directions for the scenic drive in the previous section.

THE UPPER TALLULAH—SECTION I. This section begins 10 miles from the source of the river. It offers miles of Class I-III whitewater paddling on a relatively untouched area of the river beside the Coleman River Wildlife Management Area, and two miles of paddling on the backwaters of Lake Burton.
DIRECTIONS: *The put-in for Section I is at the Tallulah River Recreation Area Campground [Fig. 34(a)]. Put in either at the campground or just up the road at the Coleman River Bridge. The take-out is on US 76, 9.2 miles west of Clayton on Jones Bridge over the Tallulah River finger of Lake Burton. The best take-out point is not at Jones Bridge itself, but 0.2 mile up Vickers Road [Fig. 34(h)], which starts at the northwest corner of the bridge.*

LAKE BURTON—SECTION II. Lake Burton, the largest of the five reservoir lakes on this trip, impounds almost 10 miles of the Tallulah River in its 2,775 acres. A many-fingered mountain lake with 62 miles of shoreline, Burton serves as a reservoir, controlling the water flow to Lakes Seed, Rabun, Tallulah and Tugalo below. It is a favorite spot for fishermen. Impounded in 1919 upon completion of Burton Dam, it was named after the town of Burton, which once occupied the site on which the lake now stands. Lake Burton is a large, deep lake, and canoeists must be alert for rapidly rising winds and thunderstorms. Paddling near the banks is recommended. Follow the map carefully to avoid making a wrong turn into one of its dead-end fingers.
DIRECTIONS: *This section is a 4.5-mile paddle down the lake's main Tallulah River channel, from the Jones Bridge put-in [Fig. 34(h)] to the Murray Cove take-out [Fig. 34(i)], the nearest public landing to Burton Dam. To reach Murray Cove from Jones Bridge, go east on*

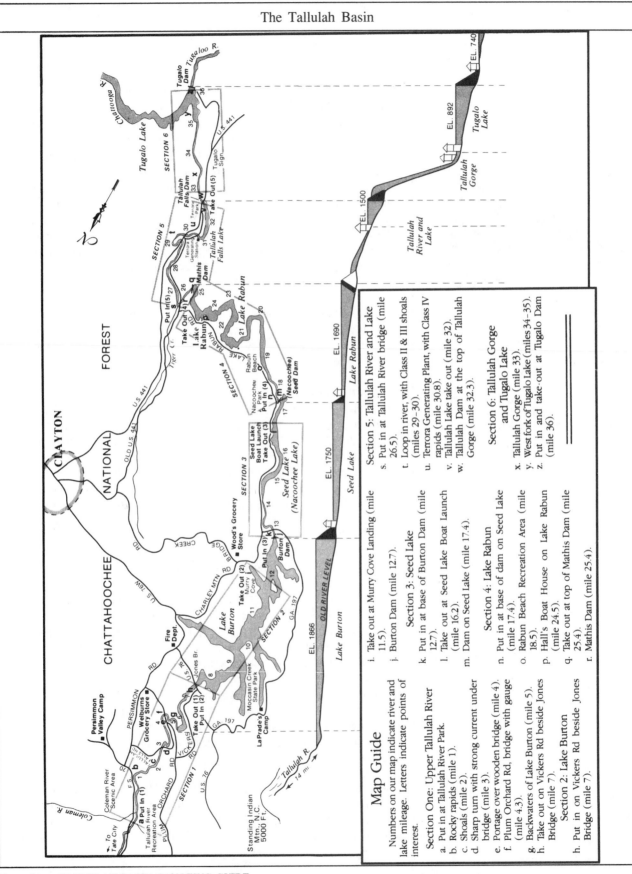

The Tallulah Basin

Map Guide

Numbers on our map indicate river and lake mileage. Letters indicate points of interest.

Section One: Upper Tallulah River
a. Put in at Tallulah River Park.
b. Rocky rapids (mile 1).
c. Shoals (mile 2).
d. Sharp turn with strong current under bridge (mile 3).
e. Portage over wooden bridge (mile 4).
f. Plum Orchard Rd, bridge with gauge (mile 4.3).
g. Backwaters of Lake Burton (mile 5).
h. Take out on Vickers Rd beside Jones Bridge (mile 7).

Section 2: Lake Burton
h. Put in on Vickers Rd beside Jones Bridge (mile 7).
i. Take out at Murry Cove Landing (mile 11.5).
j. Burton Dam (mile 12.7).

Section 3: Seed Lake
k. Put in at base of Burton Dam (mile 12.7).
l. Take out at Seed Lake Boat Launch (mile 16.2).
m. Dam on Seed Lake (mile 17.4).

Section 4: Lake Rabun
n. Put in at base of dam on Seed Lake (mile 17.4).
o. Rabun Beach Recreation Area (mile 18.5).
p. Hall's Boat House on Lake Rabun (mile 24.5).
q. Take out at top of Mathis Dam (mile 25.4).
r. Mathis Dam (mile 25.4).

Section 5: Tallulah River and Lake
s. Put in at Tallulah River bridge (mile 26.5).
t. Loop in river, with Class II & III shoals (miles 29–30).
u. Terrora Generating Plant, with Class IV rapids (mile 30.8).
v. Tallulah Lake take out (mile 32).
w. Tallulah Dam at the top of Tallulah Gorge (mile 32.3).

Section 6: Tallulah Gorge and Tugalo Lake
x. Tallulah Gorge (mile 33).
y. West fork of Tugalo Lake (miles 34–35).
z. Put in and take-out at Tugalo Dam (mile 36).

Figure 34 — **TALLULAH BASIN CANOEING GUIDE**

164

US 76 for 2.2 miles and turn right (south) onto paved Charlie Mountain Road. Follow this road for 3.5 miles and turn right onto paved Bridge Creek Road. Go 0.3 mile and turn right onto Murray Cove Road.

LAKE SEED—SECTION III. Lake Seed, sometimes called Lake Nacoochee, offers a canoeing experience entirely different from that offered by Lake Burton. Burton's wide and many-fingered layout provides breathtaking views of distant mountains. Seed, on the other hand, is tight and narrow and follows the original bed of the Tallulah River quite closely. Seed is 4.5 miles long, impounded by the 75-foot-high Nacoochee Dam, completed in 1926. The lake has a 13-mile shoreline. The canoe route goes 3.5 miles, from the put-in at the base of Burton Dam [Fig. 34(k)] to the public boat ramp on Lake Seed [Fig. 34(l)].

DIRECTIONS: *Put-in for this 3.5-mile trip is at the base of Burton Dam [Fig. 34(k)] (mile 12.7 on the map). Take Murray Cove Road to its intersection with Bridge Creek Road, turn right and go 1.6 miles to Lake Rabun Road. Turn right (west) and go 0.5 mile to the bridge over the Tallulah River at the base of Burton Dam.*

LAKE RABUN—SECTION IV. Lake Rabun has been a most popular recreation area for many years. Houses and cottages were built on its shores as early as the 1930's, and today its 25-mile shoreline is dotted with homes. Georgia Power Company, which owns most of the shoreline and leases land for homes, limits development, so sprawling motel complexes are not present. This eight-mile trip is winding and scenic, offering a stop at the popular Rabun Beach Recreation Area [Fig. 34(o)] located just off Lake Rabun Road. On the lake, stick close to shore to avoid heavy motorboat traffic. The Nacoochee Park Recreation Area [Fig. 34(n)] offers picnic tables and restrooms.

DIRECTIONS: *Put-in for Lake Rabun is at the base of the dam on Lake Seed at the Nacoochee Park Recreation Area [Fig. 34(n)] just off Lake Rabun Road. Take-out is at Hall's Boat House in the little town of Lakemont [Fig. 34(p)].*

TALLULAH RIVER AND LAKE TALLULAH—SECTION V. The special feature of this 5.5-mile stretch is that it follows for four miles the original bed of the Tallulah River, offering significant rapids, including a Class IV. The final 1.5 miles are on a lake complete with waterfalls and mountain streams trickling along its banks. This small lake, only 63 acres, is impounded by the 130-foot-tall Tallulah Dam. Completed in 1912, it was the first dam built on the Tallulah River. Its construction on the rim of Tallulah Gorge cut off most of the water for Tallulah Falls. Unlike its sister lakes, it is full of yellow perch.

DIRECTIONS: *The take-out for this stretch is in Terrora Park behind the Terrora Visitor Center [Fig. 34(v)] off US 441 at Tallulah Dam [Fig. 34(w)]. To reach the put-in, leave Terrora Park, turn left onto old US 441 and go four miles to the put-in bridge. At 1.6 miles into the shuttle, old US 441 joins the current US 441 for about 100 yards; turn left at this intersection. Stay on old US 441, which leaves the new road at the signs pointing to Lake Rabun. The put-in, located 1 mile downstream from Mathis Dam at the junction of the Tallulah River and Tiger Creek [Fig. 34(s)], is steep. Best access is at the northwest corner of the bridge.*

To scout the river, take the road that leads across the river to the Terrora Generating Station [Fig. 34(u)] 0.8 mile from Terrora Park, and to a bridge over the Tallulah River 0.9 mile beyond the park. These are good places from which to scout the four dangerous rapids in this section, one of them rated Class IV.

TALLULAH GORGE AND LAKE TUGALO—SECTION VI. The last two miles of canoeable water on the Tallulah River are in Tallulah Gorge, on the west finger of Lake Tugalo [Fig. 36(60)]. This section is canoed as a four-mile round trip, using the same point as put-in and take-out. The Tugaloo River begins where the Tallulah and Chattooga Rivers meet, and its name, in Cherokee, means "fork of a stream." Lake Tugalo was formed with the completion of the Tugalo Dam [Fig. 36(63)] and Hydroelectric Plant on the Tugaloo River in 1922.

Lake Tugalo covers 597 acres and has 18 miles of shoreline. The property around the lake is undeveloped. Tugalo is surrounded by a mixed pine-and-hardwood forest that has been relatively undisturbed by logging because of its steep shoreline.

Tugalo is a beautiful lake for both fisherman and canoeist. Catfish and bass fishing are good. Tugalo is one of the few lakes in Georgia where canoeing and slow boat traffic are the norm (boat motors are restricted to 10 HP or less). On a leisurely day's paddle around the lake a canoeist can explore many spots only accessible by water. Paddling up the Tallulah River arm of the lake leads into the Tallulah Gorge; paddling on the eastern side leads into the Chattooga Gorge [Fig. 36(61), Fig. 45(61)]. Waterfalls cascade into the lake at several points, and spring and summer wildflowers are abundant. Wildlife in the area include deer and turkey. There are plenty of places to stop along the shore to stretch, have a picnic or explore. Fires and camping are allowed only in Tugalo Park.

On the South Carolina side the ramp [Fig. 36(31), Fig. 45(31)] is very steep and difficult to navigate with a big boat and trailer. The parking lot here is often full during rafting season, this being a popular take-out point for rafters completing Section IV of the Chattooga River. There are no restroom facilities at the parking area. Tugalo Park [Fig. 36(62)] has primitive campsites level and big enough for a tent or small trailer. There is no reservation system.

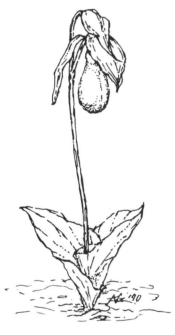

Pink lady slipper
Cypripedium acaule

This beautiful orchid, with two basal leaves, is most common beneath conifers, especially white pines. The much rarer yellow lady slipper prefers deciduous forest. Bulb diggers have severely reduced wild populations of our native orchids—especially lady slippers, which frequently die when transplanted.

The boat ramp in the park is level and graveled, giving access to the northern end of Lake Yonah.

FACILITIES: *Primitive camping, picnic tables, non-flush restrooms, boat ramps, parking.*

DATES/HOURS: *Check with the Georgia Power office at Terrora Park, (404) 754-6036 for date of opening of Tugalo Park. It will be closed for construction during 1990.*

DIRECTIONS: *Access to Lake Tugalo from the South Carolina side is at Long Creek, SC. Take US 76 east from Clayton approximately 10.7 miles to Long Creek; go south on Orchard Road (S37-538) for 2.6 miles to Battlecreek Road; turn right and go 2.5 miles to Damascus Church Road; turn right again. Just past Damascus Church (1.2 miles) turn right on Tugalo Lake Road (gravel); go 3.9 miles (the last mile is paved) to the boat landing on Lake Tugalo below the Chattooga River [Fig. 36(31), Fig. 45(31)].*

For access from Georgia to Tugalo Park, turn east onto GA 15 Scenic Loop off US 23/441 south of Tallulah Falls. Turn south onto Tugalo Plant Road (the sign says, "Georgia Power No. Ga. Hydro Group Hdq's Office"). Go three miles, then turn left through a gate onto a gravel road (sign says "Tugalo Plant"). The park is approximately two miles ahead on a steep, winding gravel road.

For directions and a U.S. Forest Service map of the Chattooga River Corridor ($2), stop at the Chattooga Whitewater Shop on US 76 in Long Creek.

ADDITIONAL INFORMATION: *Georgia Power Company, Terrora Park, US 23/441, P.O. Box 9, Tallulah Falls, GA 30573. (404) 754-6036.*

~RECREATION AREAS AND HIKING TRAILS

MOCCASIN CREEK STATE PARK. [Fig. 35(12)] This is a small park, 32 acres, built on a floodplain flat at the mouth of Moccasin Creek on the shore of Lake Burton. It is an excellent base of operations for area sightseeing, hiking and other recreational activities.

FACILITIES: *Fifty-three campsites, boat ramp and dock, wheelchair-accessible fishing pier, stream and lake fishing, lakeside picnic area, playground, open-air pavilion, trout hatchery, laundry facilities, comfort stations.*

DATES/HOURS: *Daily 7am-10 pm year round; office open 8am-5pm.*

SPECIAL EVENTS: *Daily interpretive programs Jun.-Aug.; annual special events include Lake Burton Fun Run, All About Mountain Trout and Lake Burton Arts and Crafts Festival.*

DIRECTIONS: *Located 20 miles north of Clarkesville on GA 197 and 17 miles west of Clayton (take US 76 west to GA 197).*

ADDITIONAL INFORMATION: *Moccasin Creek State Park, Georgia Department of Natural Resources, Rt 1, Box 1634, Clarkesville, GA 30523. (404) 947-3194.*

EASTERN BLUE RIDGE

TO HIAWASSEE
HELEN

Clayton

76

23

441

① Jones Bridge Park

② Timpson Cove Beach

⑫ Moccasin Creek State Park

⑬

BRIDGE CREEK RD.

CHARLIE MOUNTAIN RD.

Lake Burton

197

③ Murray Cove Boat Ramp

Burton Dam & Generating Station

TO CLARKESVILLE

BURTON DAM RD.

④ Lake Seed Boat Ramp

Lake Seed Campground

⑤

Lake Seed (Nacoochee Lake)

Rabun Beach Recreation Area U.S. Forest Service

Mathis Dam

LAKE RABUN RD.

Nacoochee Park

⑥

⑭

Terrora Generating Station

Nacoochee Dam & Generating Station

Lake Rabun

Tallulah River and Lake

Terrora Park Education Center & Campground

⑦

Tallulah Gorge

Tallulah Generating Station

Chattooga R.

Tallulah Dam

⑧

Tallulah Point

Lake Tugalo

Tugalo Dam & Generating Station

⑨

Panther Creek Recreation Area U.S. Forest Service

⑪

23

441

Lake Yonah

⑮

Yonah Boat Ramp

Tugaloo R.

Yonah Park

⑩

Yonah Dam & Generating Station

Georgia Power Public Use Areas

(1) **Jones Bridge Park**
Hwy. 76 on Lake Burton
• Two sheltered picnic tables

(2) **Timpson Cove Beach**
Charlie Mountain Rd. on Lake Burton
• White sand beach • Picnic Area • Restrooms

(3) **Murray Cove Boat Launch Area**
Bridge Creek Rd. on Lake Burton
• Paved boat ramp for small and medium boats

(4) **Lake Seed Boat Launch Area**
Lake Rabun Rd. on Lake Seed
• Gravel boat ramp for small boats

(5) **Lake Seed Campground**
County Rd. on Lake Seed (follow signs)
• Wilderness campsites
• White sand beach • Picnic area
• Latrines • No water available

(6) **Nacoochee Park**
Lake Rabun Rd. on Tallulah River just below
Nacoochee Dam
• Picnic area • Restrooms

(7) **Terrora Park and Education Center**
Hwy 23/441 on Tallulah Lake
Camping Area
• Fifty campsites with electrical and water hook-
ups, tables and grills
• Bath house with hot showers
• Playground • Pavilion

Park
• White sand beach with lifeguard in season
• Lighted tennis courts • Pavilion • Playground
• Picnic area • Restrooms • Fishing pier
• Nature trails and Tallulah Gorge overlook
• Playing field

Education Center
• Exhibits on electricity and North Georgia Hydro
system
• Displays on mountain habitat, area history,
pioneer culture and crafts
• Information on Georgia Power recreation areas

(8) **Tallulah Point**
Off Hwy 23/441 on hill overlooking Tallulah Gorge
(follow signs)
• Two sheltered picnic areas • Restrooms

(9) **Tugalo Park**
Off Hwy 23/441 below Tugalo Dam (follow signs)
• Primitive camping area • Restrooms
• Boat launch area

(10) **Yonah Park**
Ga. Hwy 184 to Yonah Dam Rd. on Lake Yonah
• Picnic area

17

225

Clarkesville

17

TO TOCCOA GA. 184

© 1990 THE GEORGIA CONSERVANCY, INC.

0 ___ 3
Miles

Figure 35 — TALLULAH BASIN RECREATION AREAS

Fig. 35 - Tallulah Basin Recreation Area

(page references in parentheses)

10 Lake Yonah Park (171)
11 Panther Creek Recreation Area & Hiking Trail (171)
12 Moccasin Creek State Park (167)
13 Moccasin Creek Trail & Non-Game Wildlife Trail (169)
14 Rabun Beach Recreation Area & Hiking Trail (169)
15 Lake Yonah (171)

NON-GAME WILDLIFE TRAIL. [Fig. 35(13)] 1.2-mile loop trail. Along the way are grassy fields, areas of old field pines—that is, white, Virginia and pitch pine—and old field scrub lacking a tree canopy. There is an extensive area of deciduous hardwoods with poplar, red oak and occasional sycamore. In this community along Moccasin Creek, alders dominate the creek bank along with dog hobbles and some American holly. Yellowroot, a mountain medicinal herb, occurs along the stream.

DIRECTIONS: *Trailhead is at the trout hatchery intake across the highway from the Moccasin Creek State Park entrance (see above).*

MOCCASIN CREEK TRAIL. [Fig. 35(13)] 6.2 miles. This trail follows Moccasin Creek, a beautiful trout stream with several waterfalls. It eventually passes several log roads which lead to FS road 26/1 and to Addis Gap and the northern edge of the Tray Mountain Wilderness. A hardwood-rhododendron community with hemlock and white pine prevails along the creek. The canopy is mostly poplar, red oak, white pine, black birch and hemlock. Fraser's magnolia occurs. The beautiful high falls is about a one-hour walk from the trailhead.

DIRECTIONS: *The trailhead is the same as for the Non-Game Wildlife Trail, above.*

RABUN BEACH RECREATION AREA AND HIKING TRAIL. [Fig. 35(14)] Located amidst lovely mountain scenery of 934-acre Lake Rabun, the hiking trail starts from camping area number two on Joe Branch and goes 0.5 mile to Panther Falls and 1.0 mile to Angel Falls. From late spring until July the trail travels through an outstanding display of flowering rhododendron.

FACILITIES: *Two camping areas on the opposite side of the road from the beach contain 80 campsites, restrooms, hiking, boating, fishing, swimming.*

DATES/HOURS: *7am-10pm Mon.-Thu, 7am-11pm Fri.-Sun., May 15-Nov. 1.*

FEES: *$5 per campsite.*

DIRECTIONS: *Take US 23/441 north from Clarkesville for 14.4 miles or south from Clayton 9.6 miles to the National Forest, and Rabun Beach Recreation Area signs. Turn west on unnumbered county road and go 2.6 miles; turn left (south) on unnumbered road (old US 441) and go 4.8 miles.*

ADDITIONAL INFORMATION: *Rabun Beach Recreation Area, Chattahoochee National Forest, Tallulah Ranger District, Chechero/Savannah St., P.O. Box 438, Clayton, GA 30525. (404) 782-3320.*

MINNEHAHA TRAIL. This 0.4-mile trail follows **Fall Branch** until it dead ends at 50-foot-high **Minnehaha Falls.**

EASTERN BLUE RIDGE

169

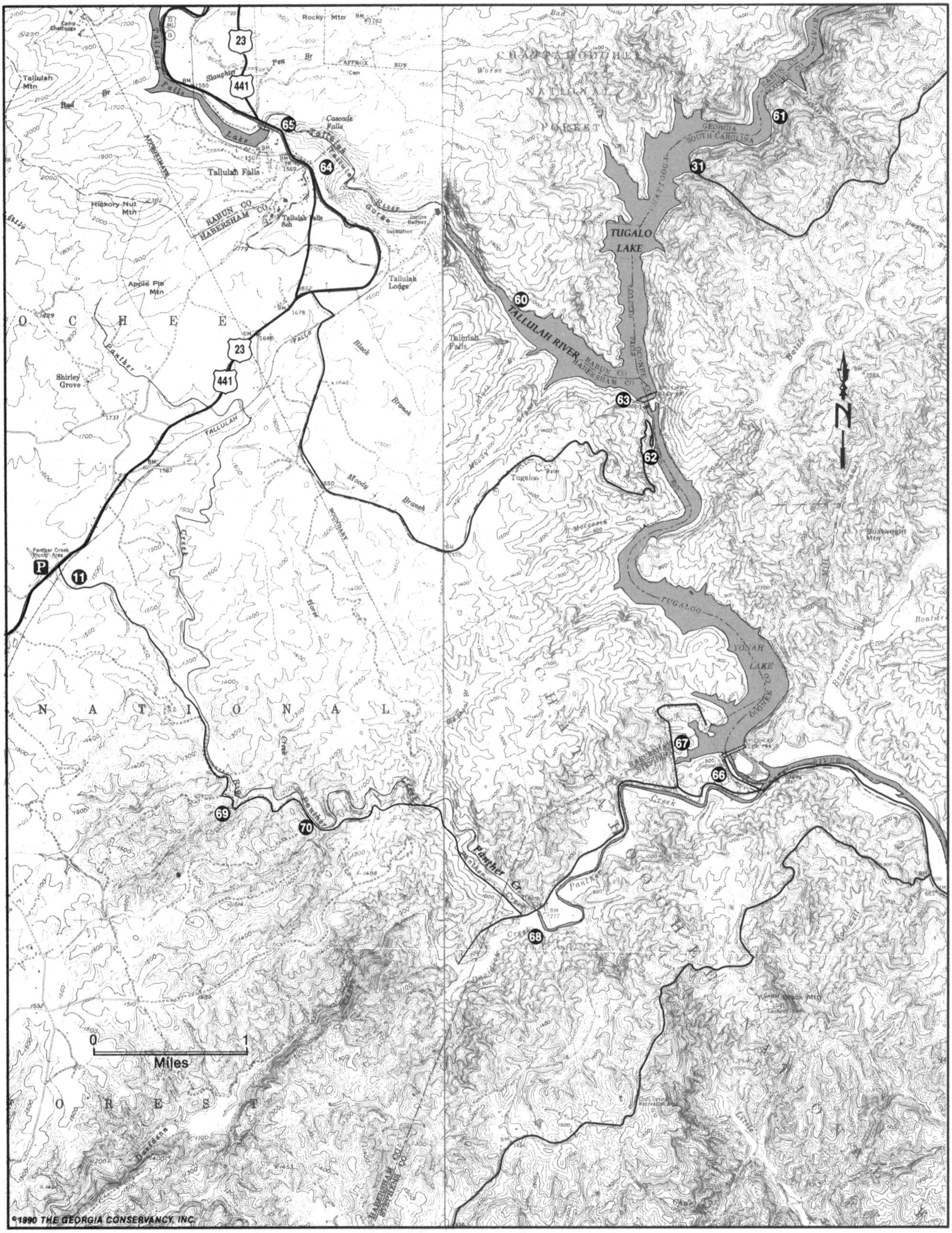

Figure 36 — **LOWER TALLULAH BASIN AND PANTHER CREEK**

EASTERN BLUE RIDGE

Fig. 36 - Lower Tallulah
Basin/Panther Creek
(page references in parentheses)

11 Panther Creek Recreation Area
   (171, 172)
31 Lake Tugalo, S.C. ramp (166, 167)
60 Lake Tugalo (166)
61 Chattooga Gorge (166)
62 Tugalo Park (166)
63 Tugalo Dam (166)
64 Cable Tower Trail (160)
65 Tallulah Gorge Park (162)
66 Lake Yonah Park (171)
67 Walker Creek boat ramp/Yonah boat
   ramp (171)
68 Davidson Creek (172)
69 Mill Shoals (172)
70 pool below Mill Shoals (172)

DIRECTIONS: *From the Rabun Beach Recreation Area above, continue past the recreation area for 1.0 mile and turn left, crossing the river below Lake Seed Dam. Follow the left fork of the road for 1.7 miles to a sign marking the trail on the right side of the road.*

~**LAKE YONAH.** [Fig. 35(15)] Lake Yonah, one of six lakes managed by Georgia Power Company, was formed when the Yonah Dam and Hydroelectric Plant was completed on the Tugalo River between Georgia and South Carolina in 1925. Yonah, meaning "big black bear" in Cherokee, is immediately south of Lake Tugalo and covers 325 acres. The land adjacent to the lake being very steep, there has been little timber harvested here. Happily, there remains an undisturbed heavy forest of pines and hardwoods. This area has a great diversity of plant life, including many wildflowers. Other than the common Georgia wildlife, including deer and turkey, there is an occasional bear. Private homes are built around the nine miles of shoreline, leaving the only public access to the lake at the boat ramps. The Lake Yonah boat ramp is paved and level. There is a small dock. The parking lot will hold approximately 15 cars and trailers. A dumpster is provided for trash. There are no restroom facilities.

The lake is popular year-round for canoeing and fishing for catfish and bass and in the summertime for waterskiing. Canoeists must use caution on the lake in warm weather because of the fast and constant ski traffic. The lake can be paddled easily in a day. A put-in spot to the right of the dam has many seasonal wildflowers and is good for picnicking.

~**LAKE YONAH PARK.** [Fig. 35(10), Fig. 36(66)] Located below the dam overlooking Tugaloo River, it has three picnic tables, trash cans and limited parking. The river banks are steep and overgrown, making access to the river difficult.
FACILITIES: *Picnic tables, parking, boat ramp, trash cans, dumpster, nature trail access.*
DIRECTIONS: *Yonah Dam road turns off GA 184 near its intersection with GA 17. Follow signs to Walker Creek boat ramp, Yonah boat ramp [Fig. 36(67)] and Lake Yonah Park [Fig. 36(66)].*
ADDITIONAL INFORMATION: *Georgia Power Company, Terrora Park, US Hwy 23/441, P.O. Box 9, Tallulah Falls, GA 30573. (404) 754-6036.*

~**PANTHER CREEK RECREATION AREA AND HIKING TRAIL.** [Fig. 36(11), Fig. 35(11)] Panther Creek originates on the southern slope of Stony Mountain at an elevation of 2,440 feet, meanders down 940 feet before crossing US 23 and 441 at the recreation area and empties into the Tugaloo River, which forms the border between Georgia and South Carolina. According to scientists who have studied the area, the natural features of Panther Creek

Gorge have changed little during the past million years.

The six-mile Panther Creek Hiking and Nature Trail [Fig. 36(11)], marked with blue blazes, begins at the Panther Creek Recreation Area. It winds through a forest of poplar, hemlock, white pine, oak, hickory and red maple, with an occasional birch, as it follows the steep, rocky bluffs of the creek. The trees, some of which are over 100 feet tall, provide shade in the summer and a display of colorful foliage in the fall. There are many rock cliffs with mosses and ferns growing in the moist crevices. In early spring trout lilies appear, followed by violets and trillium. Trailing arbutus, dwarf iris and gay-wings grow low to the ground. Spring flowering shrubs along the trail include serviceberry and horse sugar. There are masses of mountain laurel blooming in May, and the white and pink blossoms of the rhododendron are present well into June. The flowers of the dogwood and silverbell trees add to the beauty of the spring display.

The creek itself drops in a series of cascades. Little Panther Creek enters Panther Creek .6 mile before the stream turns sharply east at Mill Shoals, a former mill site [Fig. 36(69)]. Approximately 0.5 mile farther, 3.6 miles from Panther Creek Recreation Area and 2.4 miles from the eastern end of the trail, the creek falls 60 to 70 feet into a pool [Fig. 36(70)]. The trail leads down to the pool where there is a grand view of the falling water. This waterfall is preceded by an impressive Mill Shoals Falls which could be mistaken for the more dramatic falls farther on. The trail ends at a dirt road near the point where Davidson Creek joins Panther Creek. [Fig. 36(68)]. The road continues for two miles to Lake Yonah Dam and Park. Do not plan to hike out and return to Panther Creek Recreation Area by road from Lake Yonah. It would be a very long walk.

The eastern, or lower, end of the trail is designated a Protected Botanical Area [Fig. 36(68)] by the U.S. Forest Service because of the richness and diversity of its plant life. This area is unique because it is within the Brevard Fault Zone. A relatively narrow band of limestone within the fault supports vegetation not commonly found in north Georgia. The soil allows calcium-loving plants, such as chinquapin oak, to thrive here. The herbs, in particular, are remarkable.

Panther Creek Trail is recommended for day use only, since overnight camping areas are limited and water along the trail is not safe for drinking. The trail is moderately difficult to hike, with a few steep places. Hikers carrying heavy packs should be aware of the rocky overhangs and narrow trails.

Panther Creek, home to rainbow trout and redeye bass, is classified as a secondary trout stream. Fishing schedules are available on Georgia fishing licenses, which are renewable annually.

FACILITIES: *Recreation area, parking, restrooms, picnic tables with some shelters, hand pump for water, blazed hiking and nature trail.*
DATES/HOURS: *Trail open all year; recreation area closed in winter.*

Gay-wings
Polygala paucifolia

This rare and beautiful little wild-flower normally occurs at high elevations but is locally abundant along the rocky rim of Tallulah Gorge and along the Panther Creek Gorge.

DIRECTIONS: *Panther Creek Recreation area is nine miles north of Clarkesville and 3.6 miles south of Tallulah Falls on US 23/441. A four-lane highway parallel to the existing one is scheduled to be completed by 1992.*

For access to the eastern end of Panther Creek Trail, drive 0.6 miles from Yonah Dam Park on Yonah Dam Road to a dirt road and turn to the left. This road follows the creek approximately two miles to the small parking area at the end of the trail (no sign, but blue blaze marks the trail). The road is hard-packed dirt but is rocky and requires a four-wheel-drive vehicle in wet weather. The parking area is not secure for overnight parking. See Fig. 36.

ADDITIONAL INFORMATION: *Panther Creek, U.S. Forest Service, Chattahoochee National Forest, Burton Road, Clarkesville, GA 30523. (404)754-6221.*

MAP REFERENCES: *USGS 1:24,000 series: Tallulah Falls - Tugaloo Lake - Rainbow Springs - Hightower Bald; Brown's Guide, May 82.*

EASTERN BLUE RIDGE

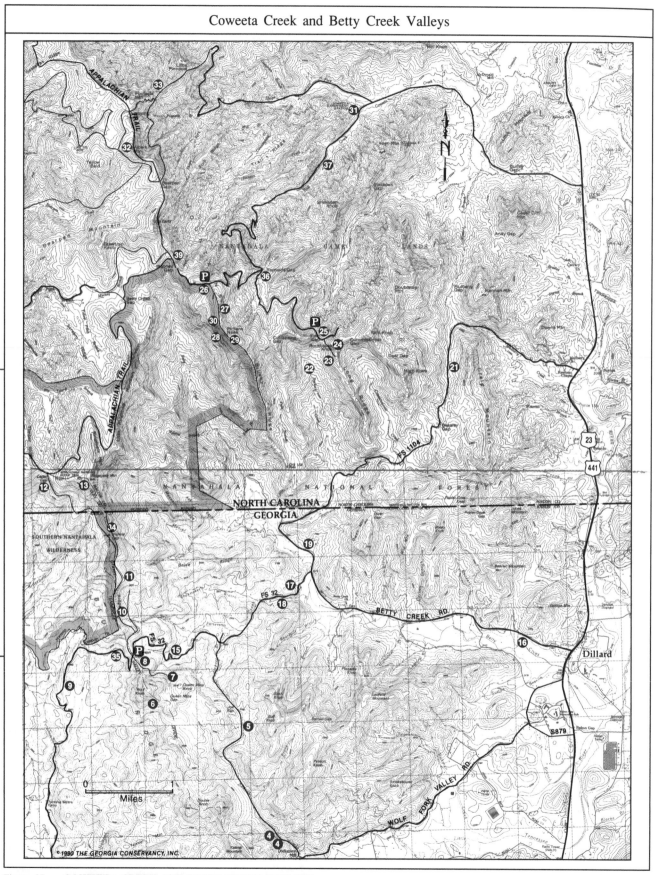

Figure 37 — **COWEETA CREEK AND BETTY CREEK VALLEYS**

Fig. 37 - Coweeta Creek and Betty Creek Valleys

(page references in parentheses)

4   waterfalls, Keener Creek (176)
5   Keener Creek Hiking Trail (176)
6   Wolf Knob (176)
7   herb flora, Wolf Knob (176)
8   Patterson Gap (176)
9   pitch pine ridge, Patterson Gap Road (176)
10 Till Ridge Cove (176)
11 Grassy Ridge Trail (176)
12 Carter's Gap (176)
13 Ridgepole Mountain (176)
15 tulip poplar coves, Patterson Gap Road (176)
16 Betty Creek Valley/Betty Creek Road (175)
17 FS 32 to Patterson Gap (176)
18 Patterson Creek Falls (176)
19 The Hambidge Center (175)
21 Mulberry Creek (175)
22 Barker's Creek (177)
23 boulders below Rockhouse Knob (177)
24 Rockhouse Knob (177)
25 pull off, Wolfpen Gap (177)
26 Wolfpit Gap (177)
27 spur to overlook on Pickens' Nose Trail (177)
28 Pickens' Nose Cliffs (177)
29 Pickens' Nose (177)
30 Pickens' Nose Trail (177)
31 Coweeta Hydrologic Laboratory (176)
32 Albert Mountain (177)
33 Pinacle Mountain Trail
34 Nichols' Gap (176)
35 hardwood forest cove, Patterson Gap (176)
36 Reynolds Gap (177)
37 Ball Creek (177)
39 Mooney Gap

Coweeta Creek and Betty Creek Valleys

~BETTY CREEK VALLEY. [Fig. 37(16)] This entrance to the eastern boundary of the Southern Nantahala Wilderness is one of the most beautiful valleys in north Georgia. Combining good hiking, scenic views and pleasant driving tours with the possibility of visits to the Hambidge Center or the Coweeta Hydrologic Laboratory, it will appeal to visitors with recreational, scientific or cultural interests.

Betty Creek Road [Fig. 37(16)] offers a scenic drive through this serene valley. The total distance from the turn off at Dillard to the North Carolina state line where the pavement ends is about six miles. The continuation of the road (NC 1104) crosses Beasley Gap and descends Mulberry Creek [Fig. 37(21)] to a beautiful early spring wildflower area which is accessible by car. It eventually comes out on US 441 south of Otto, NC.

~THE HAMBIDGE CENTER. [Fig. 37(19)] The creation of Mary Hambidge, a feminist, environmentalist and preserver of mountain culture who was 50 years ahead of her time. She helped her husband, Jay Hambidge, codify his ideas pertaining to classical art design principles, which they labeled Dynamic Symmetry. Their work gained international recognition. Mary encouraged local crafts, particularly dyeing and weaving, done in the large loom room at the center. She perfected a range of vegetable dyes which has never been duplicated. She decorated President Truman's yacht, designed costumes for dancer Isadora Duncan and opened a successful shop on Madison Avenue in New York. Elliott Wigginton, who went on to found *Foxfire*, a hugely successful series of publications dedicated to the preservation of mountain culture, was a protege of hers. In later years she became reclusive.

Today the Hambidge Center, which consists of an office building, gallery, workshop, dining hall and a number of cabins on 600 picturesque acres, organizes workshops, seminars, and film and concert series. Approximately 20 different programs are offered during the months of May to October. In addition, each year the center awards 20 to 25 resident fellowships to encourage creative exploration and inner self-renewal.

The center is open daily Monday through Friday from nine to five. Visitors are asked to register in the office and are welcome to walk the center's nature trails. There is also a water-powered grist mill known as the Barker's Creek Mill, restored for the third time in 1988. It is usually open on Fridays and Saturdays for grinding grains brought by local residents.

DIRECTIONS: *On Betty Creek Road approximately four miles west of Dillard.*

ADDITIONAL INFORMATION: *The Hambidge Center, P.O. Box 33, Rabun Gap, GA 30568. (404) 746-5718.*

~PATTERSON GAP. [Fig. 37(8)] The road to Patterson Gap (FS 32) [Fig. 37(17)] turns left off Betty Creek Road about 3.5 miles from US 441 and crosses a bridge. As one climbs a steep grade, off to the left is Patterson Creek Falls [Fig. 37(18)]. FS 32 passes through Moon Valley. After entering U.S Forest Service land, the road is steep but scenic through great coves of tulip poplar [Fig. 37(15)] which have come in after the death of the chestnut in the 1930's and following logging in the early 1900's. Crossing Patterson Gap, one circles a cove hardwood forest [Fig. 37(35)], then descends along a pitch pine ridge [Fig. 37(9)]. Along the road banks grows the rare sweetfern. This road eventually joins Persimmon Road, which dead ends at US 76.

~GRASSY RIDGE TRAIL. [Fig. 37(11)] At Patterson Gap [Fig. 37(8)], a well-known trail goes up Grassy Ridge, forking off to the right to Till Ridge Cove [Fig. 37(10)], considered by many to be one of the finest botanical areas in the state. From over 1,000 trillium nodding their heads in the spring to dazzling displays of golden witch hazel blooms in late October, the cove offers a constant pageant of wildflowers. The left fork eventually crosses the west side of the ridge at Nichols' Gap [Fig. 37(34)] and encounters the Appalachian Trail at Carter's Gap [Fig. 37(12)]. Hikers along this trail can look up at Ridgepole Mountain [Fig. 37(13)] (5,007 feet), with its heath thickets out of which emerge some evergreens. South of Patterson Gap stands Wolf Knob [Fig. 37(6)] (3,329 feet). North-facing coves in this area have lush and interesting herb flora [Fig. 37(7)].

~KEENER CREEK HIKING TRAIL. [Fig. 37(5)] A nice trail goes up Keener Creek from the Wolffork Valley loop road past two o waterfalls [Fig. 37(4)] in a gorge to the left, at or near the U.S. Forest Service boundary. Adventurous hikers equipped with topographic maps (the Dillard quadrangle) will notice a large flat area at the head of Keener Creek which should be interesting botanically. This area can be reached either from Patterson Gap or up an old log road turning off the paved Wolf Fork Valley Road just east of the junction with the graveled Blue Ridge Gap Road.

~COWEETA HYDROLOGIC LABORATORY. [Fig. 37(31)] The Coweeta Hydrologic Laboratory, site of a long-term ecological research program, is studying several watersheds for the effects of logging and other forest management practices on water yields and quality. Roadside signs indicate the experimental areas and explain the experiments. It is advisable to stop at the office to obtain a map of the area before beginning any exploration. The 14-mile driving

Witch hazel
Hamamelis virginiana

Witch hazel is fond of quite moist sites. It has the curious habit of blooming after its leaves have fallen, often in cold weather. Oil of witch hazel has scented a number of commercial liniments.

tour past the station continues as a loop to US 64 via the Standing Indian Campground and takes approximately one hour.

DATES/HOURS: *The laboratory is open 7:30 to 4, Mon.-Fri., closed holidays. The road to hiking trails, Pickens' Nose and Cherokee Cave is closed intermittently during periods of bad weather between Jan. 1 and Mar. 15.*

DIRECTIONS: *From Dillard, go north on US 441 4.3 miles to Coweeta Hydrologic Laboratory sign. Turn left and follow signs 2.9 miles to the parking lot.*

~DRIVE UP BALL CREEK [FIG. 37(37)] TO PICKENS' NOSE TRAILHEAD [FIG. 37(26)].

This long and curvy climb leads first to Reynolds Gap [Fig. 37(36)]. Take the left fork at Reynolds Gap to the first place one can see down the slope both north and south of the road. From the pull-off [Fig. 37(25)] here at Wolfpen Gap, a short and fairly level trail leads south to the famed "Cherokee Cave," a huge overhanging rock ledge on the west side of Rockhouse Knob [Fig. 37(24)]. Mountain legend holds that three Cherokees hid out here to avoid being driven to Oklahoma during the Indian removal known as the Trail of Tears. Below is a veritable rock city [Fig. 37(23)] of gigantic boulders fractured and fallen from the cliff above. Growing on them are some plants characteristic of boulder-fields—a vine-like gooseberry, for example. Farther down the cove of Barkers Creek [Fig. 37(22)] is a rich area with spring seeps and abundant herbs such as turks cap lillies. This is a nice hike, but the lower end is private, so visitors should inquire.

The right fork at Reynolds Gap [Fig. 37(36)] leads to Wolfpit Gap [Fig. 37(26)], where parking is obvious on the right. The Pickens' Nose Trail [Fig. 37(30)] begins here on the left. It is a relatively gentle climb of less than a mile to the top [Fig. 37(29)]. The vegetation and views make it a very attractive hike. At 0.3 mile, watch for a short spur trail to a rock cliff on the left [Fig. 37(27)], with a great view to the east. The trail runs through northern red oak ridge forest but gradually changes more to rhodo-dendron and shrubs. Watch for purple rhododendron and the rarer minniebush, *Menziesia*, along with the common mountain laurel. At the Pickens' Nose Cliffs [Fig. 37(28)] is one of the best views in the eastern part of the wilderness as one gazes out over the vast Betty Creek valley, 2,000 feet below, to Ridgepole and beyond. Outward Bound and others teach cliff climbing here. With care, exploration is possible down, around and under the cliffs. Plants that grow only on cliffs are found here. One, St. John's wort, is found only on high rock outcrops in the Southern Appalachians.

Albert Mountain [Fig. 37(32)] can be reached by continuing on FS 83 with a short hike on the Appalachian Trail. It affords fine views.

MAP REFERENCES: *USGS 1:24,000 series: Prentiss - Dillard.*

Strawberry bush
Euonymus atropurpureus

Also known as "bleeding heart" or "hearts a' bustin'," this large, straggl-ing shrub is sometimes cultivated as an ornamental. Its bristly, purple-pink fruits burst open and expose brilliant red seeds in the fall. One vine-like species is characteristic of boulderfields and large rocks, as below the Cherokee "cave" in the Coweeta section [Fig. 37].

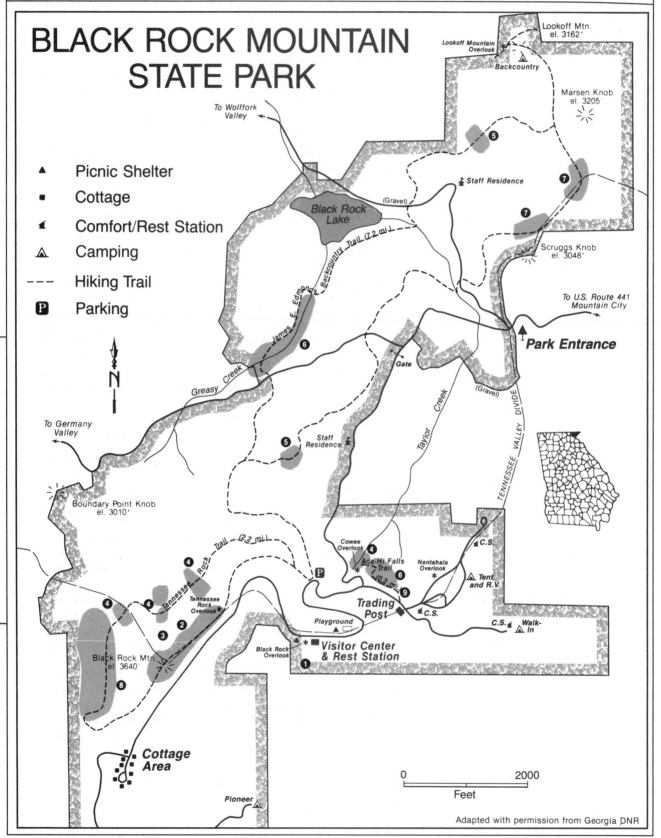

BLACK ROCK MOUNTAIN STATE PARK

Picnic Shelter

Cottage

Comfort/Rest Station

Camping

Hiking Trail

P Parking

Eastern Blue Ridge

Lookoff Mtn. el. 3162'

Lookoff Mountain Overlook

Backcountry

Marsen Knob el. 3205'

Staff Residence

Scruggs Knob el. 3048'

To Wolffork Valley

Black Rock Lake

(Gravel)

To U.S. Route 441 Mountain City

James E. Edmonds Backcountry Trail (2.2 mi.)

Greasy Creek

Gate

Taylor Creek

(Gravel)

Park Entrance

Staff Residence

To Germany Valley

Boundary Point Knob el. 3010'

TENNESSEE VALLEY DIVIDE

C.S.

Cowee Overlook

Ada-Hi Falls Trail (0.2 mi.)

Nantahala Overlook

Tent and R.V.

Tennessee Rock Trail (2.2 mi.)

Tennessee Rock Overlook

Playground

Trading Post

C.S.

C.S. Walk-In

Black Rock Mtn. el. 3640'

Black Rock Overlook

Visitor Center & Rest Station

Cottage Area

Pioneer

N

0   2000

Feet

Adapted with permission from Georgia DNR

Figure 38 — **BLACK ROCK MOUNTAIN STATE PARK**

178

Fig. 38 - Black Rock Mountain
State Park

(page references in parentheses)

4 poplar cove below boulderfield (179)
5 hemlock forests, James Edmonds Backcountry Trail (180)
6 red oak/rhododendron, James Edmonds
   Backcountry Trail (180)
7 mountain laurel, James Edmonds
   Backcountry Trail (180)
8 white pine stand (180)

Black Rock Mountain State Park

Black Rock Mountain State Park, named for its sheer cliffs [Fig. 38(1)] of dark granite, has the distinction of being Georgia's highest state park. It stretches over three miles along the Eastern Continental Divide, the spine of the Southern Blue Ridge Mountains. Containing six different peaks above 3,000 feet in elevation, it covers more than 1,500 acres. From park overlooks on a clear day, visitors may enjoy views extending for more than 80 miles. Among the areas of the Southern Appalachians visible are the Nantahala Mountains, the Cowee Range and, on especially clear days, the Great Smoky Mountains.

The park is noted for its many spring wildflowers, including several varieties of trillium, violets, bloodroot and flame azalea. In early summer, masses of mountain laurel and rhododendron are in bloom. In the fall, leaves of oak, maple, sourwood and other deciduous trees and shrubs create a spectacular blaze of yellow, orange and red. Evergreens present a contrasting note. Goldenrod and other fall blooms add to the show. The most common natural environment in the park is a deciduous hardwood slope forest with red oaks dominant. Chestnut oaks in drier places and white oaks in certain areas lend diversity.

Animals in the park include gray squirrels, chipmunks, opossums, black bears, foxes, woodchucks, bobcats, skunks and occasional deer. There are wild turkey, ruffed grouse and, in season, many songbirds.

The park's visitor center features an observation deck, wildlife exhibits, a log cabin exhibit, trail maps and wheelchair-accessible restrooms. Nature guides, raised-relief maps, hiking trail guides, and books about mountain culture and area attractions are also available. Park rangers are on duty to answer visitors' questions.

FACILITIES: *1,502 acres, 53 tent and trailer sites, 11 walk-in campsites, 10 rental cottages, playground, 2 picnic shelters, 17-acre lake, 6 scenic overlooks and 10-mile trail system.*

DATES/HOURS: *Daily 7am-10pm year round; office open 8am-5pm.*

SPECIAL EVENTS: *Spring wildflower program, May or June; overnight backpacking trip, fall.*

DIRECTIONS: *In Mountain City, three miles north of Clayton via US 441.*

ADDITIONAL INFORMATION: *Black Rock Mountain State Park, Mountain City, GA 30562. (404) 746-2141.*

~TENNESSEE ROCK TRAIL. 2.2 miles. In a relatively short distance, this trail passes through several distinct environments. The entire trail is above 3,000 feet in altitude, and the first mile is located on the north side of the Blue Ridge. This cool, moist environment nourishes the growth of a variety of wildflowers, including lady-slippers and umbrella leaf. Three poplar coves [Fig. 38(4)]

EASTERN BLUE RIDGE

are found along this section of the trail. As it passes through the second of these coves, the trail lies immediately below the summit of Black Rock Mountain (3,640 feet), which is just high enough to have on its north face a small boulderfield [Fig. 38(3)] containing herbs, such as blue cohosh, which are indicative of moist, high elevations. The trees among the rocks are primarily basswood and black birch, and the area provides fine wildflower displays in the spring and summer. After leaf fall, clumps of intermediate wood fern and alum root are visible.

Near the western border of the park, the trail passes through an almost pure stand of white pine [Fig. 38(8)] which seeded in after intensive logging of hardwoods prior to the establishment of the park. After leaving this pine forest, the trail climbs rather steeply to the summit of Black Rock Mountain, then follows the Blue Ridge crest [Fig. 38(2)] to Tennessee Rock Overlook. This entire section of trail is above 3,600 feet in altitude. There is much rock, and the red oaks are stunted and lichen-covered; rosebay rhododendron is prevalent. Beyond Tennessee Rock, the trail remains on the crest of the ridgeline for several hundred yards before descending back to the trailhead parking area.

~JAMES EDMONDS BACKCOUNTRY TRAIL. 7.2 miles.

Along this trail there are two patches of hemlock forest [Fig. 38(5)] and more extensive areas of red oak/rhododendron [Fig. 38(6)] in moist places, with mountain laurel replacing rhododendron in drier locations [Fig. 38(7)]. Where the rhododendron is thin, large patches of evergreen galax, or coltsfoot, are present.

A short side-trail leads hikers to the summit of 3,162-foot Lookoff Mountain, the northernmost peak in the park. Several granite cliffs are visible from the trail, and the scenic overlook on Lookoff Mountain is atop a similar outcrop. Cliff faces drop several hundred feet straight down, and granite surfaces are often surprisingly slippery. Hikers are cautioned to remain on the trail and not be tempted to explore more closely these beautiful, but potentially deadly, cliff faces.

While the name "Greasy Creek" may not be particularly poetic, the section of trail that follows this mountain stream [Fig. 38(6)] is nonetheless very scenic, with numerous small shoals and cascades framed with rhododendron and hemlock.

~ADA-HI FALLS TRAIL. 0.2 mile.

Ada-Hi (pronounced Uh-day'-he) is the Cherokee word for forest. This hike begins in the most common natural environment in the park—a deciduous hardwood slope forest dominated by red, chestnut, and white oaks. This forest then phases into a red oak/rhododendron environment with huge patches of the evergreen galax in open places. The trail ends in a cove of tulip poplars at a wooden overlook platform which allows hikers to view the falls safely and easily.

EASTERN BLUE RIDGE

Because Ada-Hi Falls is located so high in the Taylor Creek watershed, the falls are small; during extended periods of dry weather the flow of water diminishes to a trickle. Even so, with dense thickets of rhododendron arching over the trail and colorful displays of wildflowers to view, most hikers find the trail quite enjoyable.

MAP REFERENCES: USFS *Black Rock State Park map.*

Flame azalea
*Rhododendron
calendulaceum*

This deciduous rhododendron with showy yellow, orange or red blossoms gloriously dominates mountain forests in the spring, following the serviceberry. Red Oaks are common companions at high elevations.

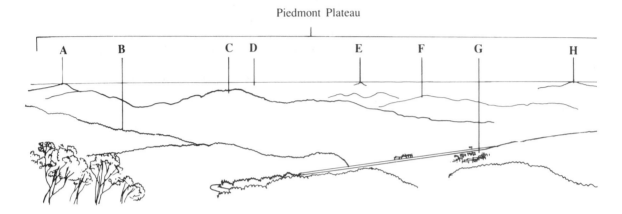

Piedmont Plateau

A B C D E F G H

SOUTH VISTA
View from Black Rock Overlook
Elevation 3,446 feet

A - Rainy Mountain
B - Warwoman Valley
C - Screamer Mountain

D - South Carolina Piedmont
E - Pine Mountain
F - Stroud Mountain

G - City of Clayton
H - Cliff Mountain

SOUTH VISTA — This view is the park's most expansive. The flat horizon far beyond the city of Clayton is the Piedmont Plateau or "foothill" section of Georgia and South Carolina. On a very clear day, points up to 80 miles away are visible and dormitory buildings at Clemson University in South Carolina are easily seen to the east.

The mountains to the south and southwest are known as the Tallulah Mountains and are an eastern extension of the main Blue Ridge crest. These mountains, located along the Rabun/Habersham County line, form a corridor which channels the flow of the southern Tallulah River before it reaches Tallulah Gorge.

Far to the southwest can be seen 3,156-foot Yonah Mountain, the highest point in Georgia's Piedmont region.

EASTERN BLUE RIDGE

Black Rock Mountain State Park

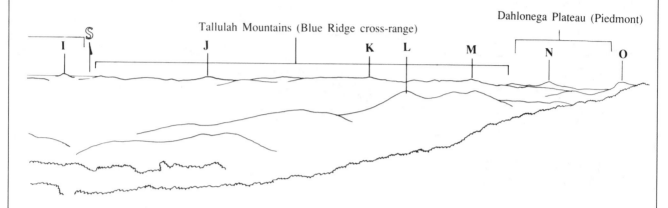

Tallulah Mountains (Blue Ridge cross-range)

Dahlonega Plateau (Piedmont)

I   S   J   K   L   M   N   O

SOUTH VISTA (Continued)
View from Black Rock Overlook

I - Currahee Mountain   K - Joe Mountain   M - Oakey Mountain
J - Hickory Nut Mountain   L - Tiger Mountain   N - Yonah Mountain
                                                               O - Glassy Mountain

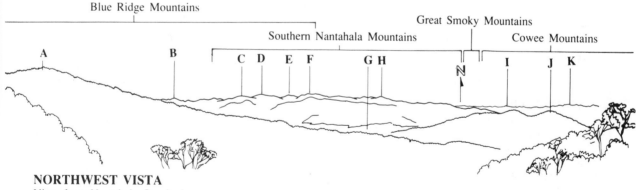

Blue Ridge Mountains

Great Smoky Mountains

Southern Nantahala Mountains   Cowee Mountains

A   B   C   D   E   F   G H   N   I   J   K

NORTHWEST VISTA
View from Nantahala Overlook
Elevation 3,276 feet

A - Black Rock Mountain, north summit   D - Little Bald   H - Pickens' Nose
B - Hightower Bald   E - Standing Indian Mountain   I - Cowee Bald
C - Dicks Knob   F - Ridgepole Mountain   J - Marsen Knob
                                               G - Wolffork Valley   K - Fishawk Mountain

EASTERN BLUE RIDGE

COMPILED BY ANTHONY LAMPROS
ILLUSTRATED BY MOZELLE FUNDERBURK

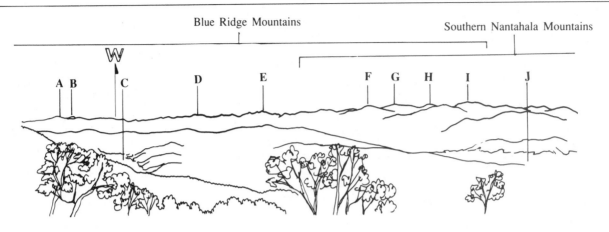

Blue Ridge Mountains

Southern Nantahala Mountains

NORTH AND WEST VISTA
View from Tennessee Rock Overlook
Elevation 3,625 feet

A - Kelly Knob
B - Brasstown Bald
C - Germany Valley

D - Eagle Mountain
E - Hightower Bald
F - Dick's Knob

G - Little Bald
H - Standing Indian Mountain
I - Ridgepole Mountain
J - Wolffork Valley

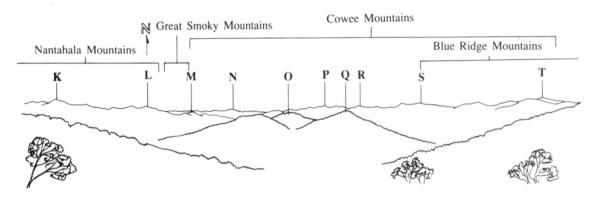

Nantahala Mountains

Great Smoky Mountains

Cowee Mountains

Blue Ridge Mountains

NORTHEAST VISTA
View from Cowee Overlook
Elevation 3,195 feet

K - Pickens' Nose
L - Doubletop Mountain
M - Hannah Mountain

N - Cowee Bald
O - Lookoff Mountain
P - Fishawk Mountain

Q - Marsen Knob
R - Jones Knob
S - Scaly Mountain
T - Rabun Bald

EASTERN BLUE RIDGE

COMPILED BY ANTHONY LAMPROS
ILLUSTRATED BY MOZELLE FUNDERBURK

Rabun Bald

Rabun Bald (4,696 feet) [Fig. 39(11)] is the second-highest peak in Georgia; only Brasstown Bald (4,784 feet) is higher. An observation tower on the summit provides hikers with what many people believe is the most spectacular view from any one point in the Georgia mountains. Into the Georgia and South Carolina Piedmont, views on clear days extend for more than 100 miles. In other directions, the views of the Blue Ridge, Nantahala, Cowee, and Great Smoky Mountains are outstanding.

Rabun Bald's main ridgeline, which is indicated by the Bartram Trail on the map, is the Eastern Continental Divide, dividing waters draining northward into the Tennessee/Mississippi Gulf system from those draining southward to the Atlantic Ocean. Most of Rabun Bald's streams are located on the mountain's southeast flank and drain via Warwoman Creek to the Chattooga River, then to the Savannah, and finally to the Atlantic.

The Rabun Bald area rates among Georgia's leading botanical sites; spring wildflowers are exceptional. Near the summit is a zone of dwarf oak heath (mainly scarlet oak and purple rhododendron). Look for the striking red berries of mountain ash. In some places there is a thick ground cover of blueberries. Together with the Chattooga River to the southwest and the Cowee Mountains to the north, the region is a prime habitat for deer, black bear, wild boar and even mountain lion.

DIRECTIONS: *Take US 441 north from Clayton for one mile past Dillard; turn right onto GA 246 toward Highlands, NC; continue on GA 246 and NC 106 for seven miles; turn right onto Hale Ridge Road (FS 7), which is beside the Scaly Post Office; go 2.1 miles and take the right fork (FS 7 goes left); go 1.3 miles and take a left fork on a steep dirt road toward Beegum Gap [Fig. 39(22)]; after 1.6 miles, park and walk two miles to Rabun Bald. There is an observation platform on the summit. Note the northern hardwood cove, boulderfield and wildflower area [Fig. 39(17)].*

~SCENIC DRIVES.

WARWOMAN ROAD. A scenic drive which follows Warwoman Shear, a geologic "path" which provided Indians and early settlers in the region with their principal east-west trading route.
DIRECTIONS: *From US 441 in Clayton, go east at the light where US 76 turns left.*

TUKALUGEE CREEK ROAD [FIG. 39(2)] AND SARAH'S CREEK ROAD (FS 156) [FIG. 39(3)]. All-weather roads providing a 10-mile scenic loop drive. Gate closed Dec.-Mar.

Wild boar
Sus scrofa

The European wild boar was first introduced into the Tallulah River watershed in the 1950's with breeding stock from the Knoxville Zoo. If kept within reasonable limits by hunting, the boar's damage to wildflowers with tuberous roots is minimal. Boars compete with native game for acorns and other foods. Like deer and beaver, they carry the intestinal parasite *Giardia*. Drinking surface water in the southern mountains is, therefore, not advisable.

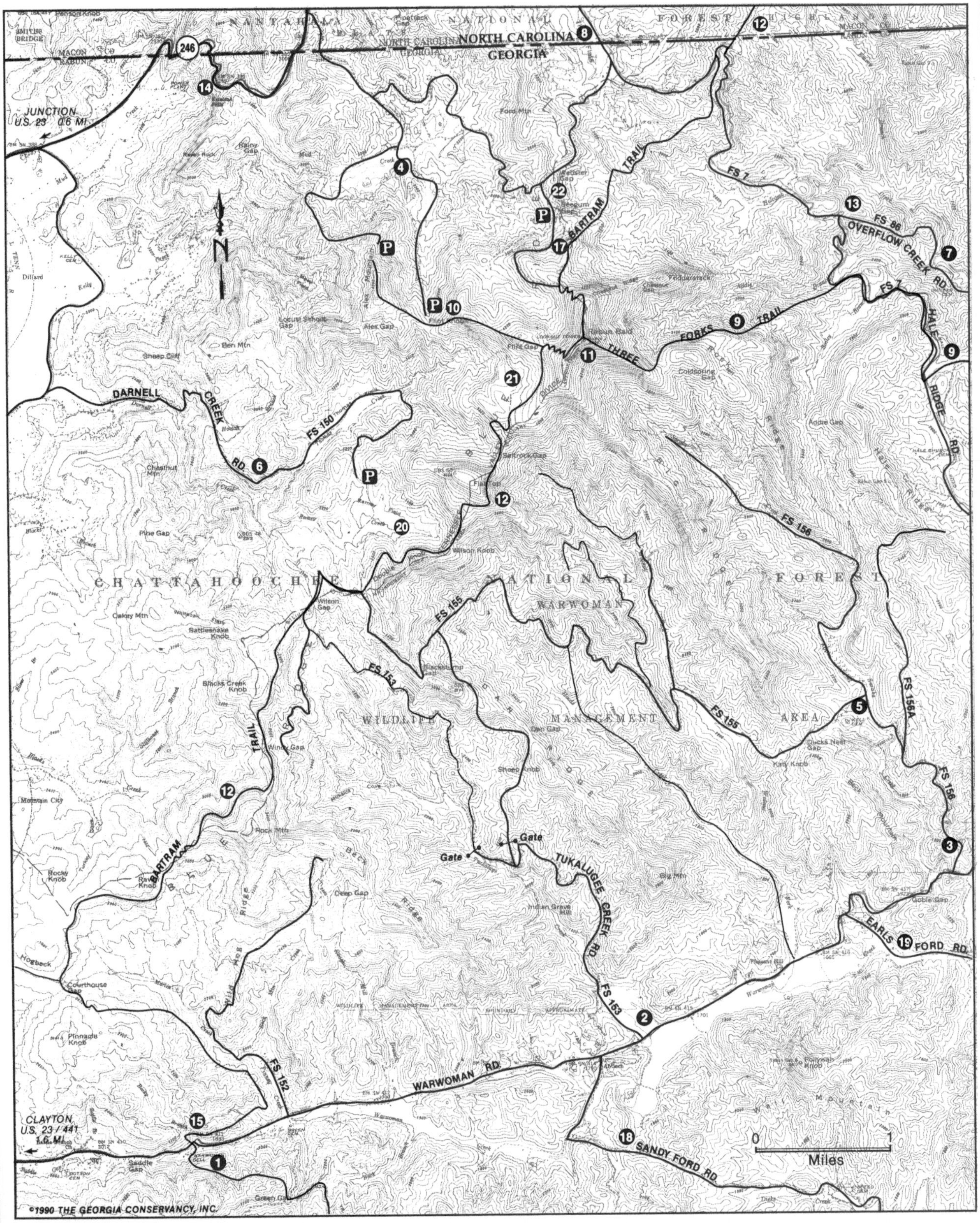

Figure 39 — **RABUN BALD**

Eastern Blue Ridge

Fig. 39 - Rabun Bald
(page references in parentheses)

 1 Warwoman Dell (187)
 2 Tukalugee Creek Road (185)
 3 Sarah's Creek Road (185)
 4 Sky Valley (187)
 5 Apple Valley (187)
 6 Darnell Creek Road (187)
 7 Overflow Creek Road (187)
 8 The Flats (188)
 9 Three Forks Trail (188)
10 Alex Mountain, Flint Knob Trail (188)
11 Rabun Bald (185)
12 Bartram Trail (189)
13 Holcomb Creek Trail & Falls/Ammons
     Creek Falls (188)
14 Estatoah Falls (188)
15 Becky Branch Falls (188)
17 hardwood cove, boulderfield & wild-
     flower area, Rabun Bald (185)
18 Sandy Ford Road (187)
19 Earl's Ford Road (187)
21 Laurel Slick (188)
22 Beegum Gap (185)

DARNELL CREEK ROAD (FS 150). [Fig. 39(6)] This scenic drive is especially pretty after leaf fall, when cascading Darnell Creek and surrounding mountains are more visible. The all-weather road is rough in spots, but certainly passable. While travel is not limited to trucks or four-wheel-drive vehicles, cars with low ground clearance should be driven with care.

OVERFLOW CREEK ROAD (FS 86). [Fig. 39(7)] This very scenic, all-weather road is open year round. The lower sections of the road run parallel to the West Fork of the Chattooga River, providing access at several places for fishermen, hikers and campers.

SANDY FORD ROAD. [Fig. 39(18)] One of only two unpaved-road access points to the Chattooga River on the Georgia side (Earl's Ford, below, being the other). Good canoe put-in point for Section III of the river. Not a four-wheel drive road, but difficult in bad weather.

EARL'S FORD ROAD. [Fig. 39(19)] Old county road that once provided major access from South Carolina to Georgia by crossing the Chattooga River. It parallels and crosses Warwoman Road. Four-wheel drive is advisable.

~POINTS OF INTEREST.

WARWOMAN DELL. [Fig. 39(1)] This recreation area was developed in the 1930's by the Civilian Conservation Corps. Cuts of the old Black Mountain Railroad can be found here. This railroad was partially constructed but never operated before the Civil War. An interpretive trail with 25 numbered posts and an accompanying pamphlet identify many plants common to the region. Several rare ferns, including the walking fern, are found here.
FACILITIES: *Two picnic pavilions, outdoor restrooms with facilities for handicapped.*
DATES/HOURS: *Open Memorial Day through Labor Day. Gate locked Fri. and Sat. at dark.*

APPLE VALLEY. [Fig. 39(5)] Popular, dispersed camping-and-fishing area managed by the U.S. Forest Service. Sarah's Creek is heavily stocked with trout. Off GA 246.

SKY VALLEY. [Fig. 39(4)] Centered around Georgia's highest valley (3,100 feet), Sky Valley is one of the highest incorporated cities in the Eastern U.S., with elevations inside the city limits exceeding 4,200 feet. Sky Valley Resort includes an 18-hole golf course, swimming pool, restaurant and condominiums, as well as year-round and rental homes. Sky Valley is best known as Georgia's only ski area, with runs up to 2,200 feet in length and a vertical

EASTERN BLUE RIDGE

drop of 250 feet. A rope tow serves the "bunny hill," and a double chairlift serves intermediate and advanced slopes. Located just off GA 246.

ALEX MOUNTAIN, FLINT KNOB TRAIL. [Fig. 39(10)] From the summit of 4,080-foot Alex Mountain are good vistas to the west and southeast. A Georgia Power microwave tower is located on the northern end of the mountain.
DIRECTIONS: *From Flint Gap on the Bartram Trail, or take the Sky Valley exit from GA 246 and take either the Alex Mountain or Flint Knob forks.*

THE FLATS. [Fig. 39(8)] A remarkable, high, flat area forming the western rim of the Highland Plateau. Formerly this was the location of a number of unique peat bogs. Among the rarest of mountain environments, these bogs occur at the heads of valleys where seeps and springs keep the soil consistently wet and produce rare plants such as bog laurel, swamp pink and cotton grass. Unfortunately, most of the bogs here have been drained or bulldozed.
DIRECTIONS: *See above.*

LAUREL SLICK. [Fig. 39(21)] Very dense thickets of rhododendron are found at the 4,000-foot level of Rabun Bald's southwestern flank.

~WATERFALLS.

BECKY BRANCH FALLS. [Fig. 39(15)] This 20-foot-high cascade is reached by a 0.25-mile trail that crosses Warwoman Road just upstream from the Warwoman Dell Recreation Area.

ESTATOAH FALLS. [Fig. 39(14)] This wide falls, located just inside the western city limits of Sky Valley, is best viewed from GA 246, approximately one mile west of Dillard.

HOLCOMB CREEK TRAIL AND FALLS AND AMMONS CREEK FALLS. [Fig. 39(13)] The one-mile trail to Holcomb Creek Falls is rated easy to moderate. This very scenic falls drops approximately 120 feet. The trail continues approximately 0.5 mile to Ammons Creek Falls, where an observation deck allows easy viewing.
DIRECTIONS: *Take Warwoman Road east from Clayton for 10 miles. Turn left (north) on FS 7 (Hale Ridge Road), or south on Hale Ridge Road from NC 106, and go nine miles.*

~HIKING TRAILS.

THREE FORKS TRAIL. [Fig. 39(9)] 9.5 miles. The trail begins at the summit of Rabun Bald (4,696 feet) and ends at Three Forks on the West Fork of the Chattooga River. Steep descents. See also Chattooga River, Section I, West Fork.

DIRECTIONS: *Hikers can also begin the trail from John Teague Gap. To start from there, take Warwoman Road east from Clayton for 16 miles to Overflow Creek Road (FS 86); turn left (northwest) and go four miles to John Teague Gap, where the trail crosses.*

BARTRAM TRAIL. [Fig. 39(12)] This National Recreational Trail stretches from the Georgia/North Carolina line over the summit of Rabun Bald to the Chattooga River. It is named for William Bartram, a naturalist who explored and wrote about this area in the 1770's. See also Long Trails section, Bartram Trail.

DIRECTIONS: *Take US 441 north from Clayton for one mile past Dillard; turn right onto GA 246 toward Highlands, NC. Continue on GA 246 and NC 106 for seven miles, then turn right onto Hale Ridge Road; go 2.1 miles, then take FS 7 for 1.1 miles.*

MAP REFERENCES: *USGS 1:24,000 series: Rabun Bald.*

Walking fern
Asplenium rhizophyllum

So named because its long, narrow leaf-tip takes root when it touches the ground and produces a new plant. It lives on mossy boulders and in rock crevices. Since it prefers calcium-rich rocks, it is relatively rare. It can be found at Warwoman Dell [Fig. 39(1)].

EASTERN BLUE RIDGE

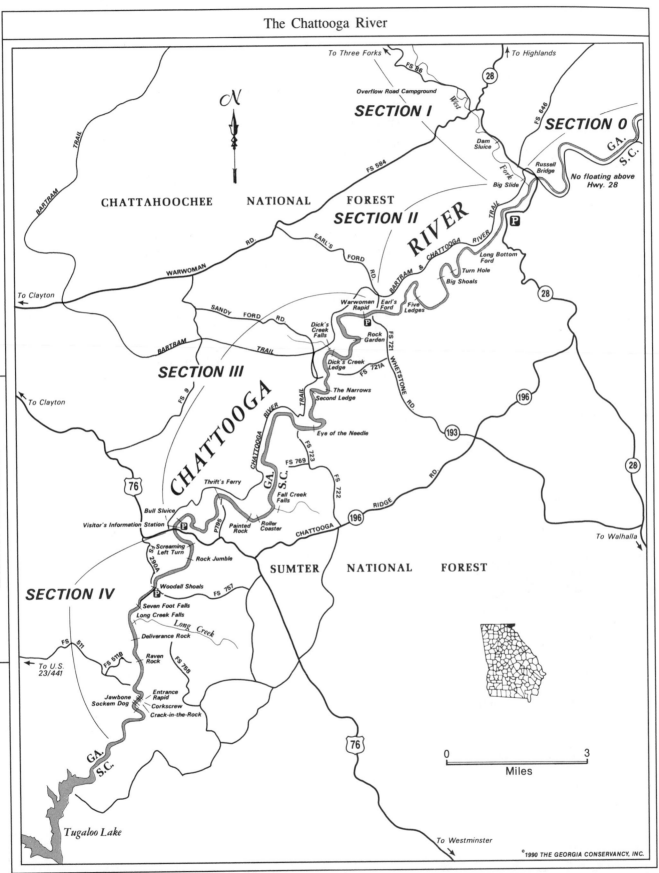

The Chattooga River

SECTION I

SECTION 0

To Three Forks

To Highlands

28

Overflow Road Campground

FS 86

FS 646

GA.
S.C.

Dam
Sluice

Russell
Bridge

No floating above
Hwy. 28

Big Slide

West

Fork

CHATTAHOOCHEE   NATIONAL   FOREST

SECTION II

RIVER

FS 584

BARTRAM

TRAIL

BARTRAM & CHATTOOGA

RIVER

TRAIL

Long Bottom
Ford

28

EARL'S

RD.

FORD

Turn Hole

Big Shoals

WARWOMAN   RD.

Warwoman
Rapid

Earl's
Ford

Five
Ledges

To Clayton

SANDY   FORD   RD.

Dick's
Creek
Falls

Rock
Garden

BARTRAM   TRAIL

Dick's Creek
Ledge

FS 721A

FS 721

WHETSTONE   RD.

SECTION III

The Narrows
Second Ledge

To Clayton

FS 9

CHATTOOGA

RIVER

TRAIL

Eye of the Needle

196

193

FS 723

FS 769

Thrift's Ferry

GA.
S.C.

Fall Creek
Falls

FS 722

76

Bull Sluice

Painted
Rock

Roller
Coaster

RIDGE   RD.

CHATTOOGA

196

To Walhalla

Visitor's Information Station

FP95

SUMTER   NATIONAL   FOREST

28

Screaming
Left Turn

FS 290A

Rock Jumble

SECTION IV

Woodall Shoals

FS 757

Seven Foot Falls

Long Creek Falls

Long   Creek

Deliverance Rock

FS 511

Raven
Rock

FS 758

To U.S.
23/441

FS 511B

Jawbone
Sockem Dog

Entrance
Rapid

Corkscrew

Crack-in-the-Rock

76

0   3
Miles

GA.
S.C.

Tugaloo Lake

To Westminster

©1990 THE GEORGIA CONSERVANCY, INC.

Figure 40 — **CHATTOOGA RIVER RAPIDS**

The Chattooga River

The Chattooga River is the crown jewel of southern whitewater rivers and a symbol for wilderness river lovers throughout the United States and Canada. Its high rainfall, unusual geology (with many cliffs, gorges and waterfalls) and steep gradient place it in the "world class" category of rivers. Most remaining rivers of the Chattooga's quality are tucked away in western gorges or West Virginia mountains. The river is arguably the area's prime single natural attraction, luring some 100,000 visitors a year for hiking, rafting, canoeing, kayaking, tubing, fishing, swimming or plain and simple river watching.

Headwaters of the Chattooga are in the Nantahala National Forest and private lands in North Carolina. Flowing southward out of North Carolina, they form approximately 40 river-miles of boundary between Georgia and South Carolina. The river drops from approximately 3,000 feet elevation at its headwaters to 950 feet at its termination into Lake Tugalo. It is under the control and protection of the Sumter National Forest in South Carolina, the Chattahoochee National Forest in Georgia and the Nantahala National Forest in North Carolina.

The names of the river's rapids and other landmarks bear witness to the area's early inhabitants. Indian names translated into English have become Sock'em Dog, Shoulder Bone and Cutting Bone Creek. Local settlers' humor shows in the names of two feeder creeks—Bad Creek and Worse Creek—both now covered by Lake Tugalo. Between those two streams is Sinking Mountain, named because of instability of the soil and underlying decayed rock.

The Chattooga was designated a Wild and Scenic River by Congress in May of 1974. As a result, no motorized vehicles are allowed within a quarter-mile of its banks. In addition, man-made facilities are minimal, consisting primarily of maintained hiking trails. Primitive toilet facilities and water are available at camping areas. As a result of the minimal disturbance by man, the Chattooga and its corridor provide a clean, litter-free hiking or rafting experience. However, the growth in population in the mountain areas and resulting activities could pose a multifaceted danger to the river in the future.

The Chattooga is divided into five sections, Section 0—Section IV. Section 0 includes the entire headwaters region from Whiteside Mountain southward to Russell Bridge (GA 28). Sections I-IV cover the portions of the river open to boating, including the West Fork (Section I) southward to Section IV and the river's end at Lake Tugalo.

Brown trout
Salmo trutta

Unlike the spring-breeding rainbow and brook, the brown trout spawns in the fall. Introduced from northern Europe, it can live in warmer water than the other two species. It hides during bright daylight, being best seen (and caught) in early morning or late afternoon.

EASTERN BLUE RIDGE

191

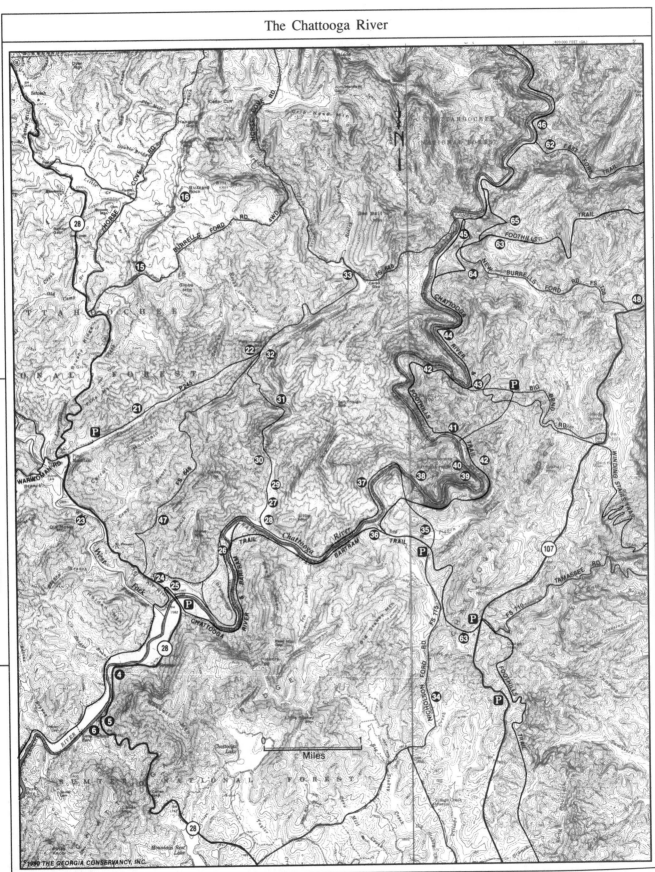

EASTERN BLUE RIDGE

Miles

© 1990 THE GEORGIA CONSERVANCY, INC.

Figure 41 — **CHATTOOGA RIVER/SECTION 0—THE HEADWATERS**

Fig. 41 - Chattooga River/
Section 0

(page references in parentheses)

15 Old Burrell's Ford Road (199)
21 Laurel Creek corundum mine (200)
22 Persimmon Gap trailhead (200)
23 Dam ruins (200)
24 river road from Russell Bridge/Adline
    Branch (194, 200)
25 Russell Bridge (194, 195, 201)
26 camping, Russell Bridge to Reed Creek
    (195)
27 Reed Creek Bottoms (195)
28 Reed Creek (194)
29 White pine with club moss & pink lady
    slippers (195)
30 Reed Creek Gorge (195)
31 Reed Creek Falls (195)
32 Persimmon Gap (195)
34 Nicholson Ford Road (195)
36 Lick Log Falls (194, 195)
37 road above Reed Creek (195)
38 approach to Gorge (195)
39 Rock Gorge (194, 195)
40 waterfall, SC Chattooga River Trail
    (195)
41 section above waterfall (195)
42 Big Bend Falls (194, 195)
43 Big Bend (194, 195)
44 "Steps" (195)
45 Burrell's Ford Bridge (Ellicott Rock Wil-
    derness trailhead) (193, 212, 213)
46 Chattooga River Trail (211, 213)
63 Foothills Trail (212)
64 King's Creek Falls (213)
65 Spoon Auger Falls (213)

SECTION 0 - THE HEADWATERS

~ACCESS TO RIVER CROSSINGS.

BURRELL'S FORD BRIDGE. FS 646 begins 0.5 mile west of Russell Bridge. Follow FS 646 for approximately 5.5 miles to the bridge. See Ellicott Rock section [Fig. 41(45), Fig. 46(45)].

BULL PEN BRIDGE. Follow SC 107 south from the intersection of US 64 in Cashiers, NC. Turn west on Bull Pen Road and follow it to the bridge. See Highlands section [Fig. 46(18), Fig. 48(18)].

~HIKING TRAILS AND ACCESS POINTS.

CHATTOOGA RIVER TRAIL. The southern end of the Chattooga River Trail begins in Georgia in the parking area at the west end of the US 76 bridge and continues north for 10 miles, where it intersects and combines with the Bartram Trail. The combined trails continue another 10 miles to the GA 28 bridge, where the hiker must cross the bridge and pick up the trails on the South Carolina side. At a point 3.7 miles above the bridge, the Bartram Trail branches off to the east with the Foothills Trail, while the Chattooga River Trail joins with the Foothills Trail and parallels the river closely for another 6.7 miles to Burrell's Ford Campground and Burrell's Ford Road. One-half mile north of Burrell's Ford Road, the trail enters the Ellicott Rock Wilderness. Here the hiker must register. The Foothills Trail branches off to the east at this point and the trail to Ellicott Rock continues upstream for 2.1 miles, where it joins with the East Fork Trail, which continues 2.5 miles to Walhalla Fish Hatchery. The trail continues 1.7 miles upstream to Ellicott Rock where Georgia, North Carolina and South Carolina boundaries meet [Fig. 46(30), Fig. 48(30)]. Ellicott Rock can also be reached by foot from North Carolina (see Ellicott Rock Wilderness section). The only camping area with restroom and water facilities is the Burrell's Ford Campground. Other camping areas are primitive, and in some areas in the Ellicott Rock Wilderness camping is forbidden.

THE CHATTOOGA ABOVE BULL PEN ROAD. The upper Chattooga River harbors some of the river's most scenic and rugged stretches. Closed to boats, the area must be reached by foot. Major access points are Bullpen Road [Fig. 48(13)] and primitive roads off Whiteside Cove Road [Fig. 48]. Both Bullpen Road and Whiteside Cove Road are gravel and accessible by car.

This section of the river is known for the steep, remote "Chattooga Cliffs" [Fig. 48(27)] and for a small gorge area called the Upper Narrows. Both areas can be reached from the Bullpen Road Bridge [Fig. 46(18), Fig. 48(18)], known locally as the "metal" or "government" bridge. It is recommended that the hiker have a car

EASTERN BLUE RIDGE

193

waiting at the bridge before beginning the walk upstream. There are two approach points, which are shown on the Highlands/Whiteside map [Fig. 48].

Along this stretch the Chattooga is narrow and wild. Farther up-river is relatively flat, but the adjacent cliffs and overhangs provide constant interest. Here the rare Biltmore sedge, a northern clubmoss, and forests of giant mountain laurel up to 30 feet tall are present at the base of the cliffs. Further downstream one reaches the Upper Narrows, where the rushing water is compressed into a stream about six feet wide. Only the most skilled rock climber can maneuver through the gorge. For a safer route, it is recommended that the hiker walk the gorge's edge. Downstream from the Upper Narrows a loop trail is reached. This trail consists of a lower and upper section. The lower section affords good views of the boulder-strewn gorge which is found just upstream from the Bullpen Road Bridge. Car-sized boulders and unusual potholes are present, as well as several nice swimming pools.

Below the bridge the river is less scenic but still worth the visit. Two trails off Bullpen Road lead to Ellicott Rock.

THE CHATTOOGA HEADWATERS FROM GA 28, BURRELL'S FORD BRIDGE TO RUSSELL BRIDGE. [Fig. 46(45)] Unlike some parts of the river, this section is relatively accessible. Old log roads up the East Fork and the splendid trail up the entire South Carolina side afford all degrees of hiking and fishing experiences (See Ellicott Rock section).

While the river itself is not constant whitewater, areas are breath-takingly wild and scenic. The area between the Big Bend [Fig. 41(43)] and Licklog Falls [Fig. 41(36)] is a challenge for the most intrepid fisherman, since there are no riverside trails. Crossing the river back and forth is essential and is risky in winter and spring high water. The wild isolation of the Rock Gorge [Fig. 41(39)] and the magnificence of the Big Bend Falls [Fig. 41(42)] make it worth-while. Prior to the construction of FS 646 (New Burrell's Ford Road), major accesses were at the Russell Bridge [Fig. 41(25), Fig. 42(25)] and from SC 28 near Big Creek (Old Burrell's Ford Road, seven miles of torturous mountain road). This was part of the "mystery river" (see West Fork section), the area known for large brown trout. The river is open for fishing year round.

For easy hiking and fishing, the section of the Chattooga between Russell Bridge and Reed Creek [Fig. 41(28), Fig. 42(28)] is hard to beat, for there is a trail (or log road) on either side. At the north side of the Russell Bridge one looks out over a marsh with ponds and wood-duck boxes. This was the old Whitmire place, formerly a fertile cornfield. When it was acquired by the Forest Service, beavers promptly dammed up Mose Branch, creating a marsh domi-nated by alder shrub, sedges and marsh grasses. One can go up the river by climbing down the bridge riprap or, more easily but less speedily, by taking the first road (gated) [Fig. 41(24), Fig. 42(24)] that turns off west of the bridge. About a mile up this

Golden eagle
Aquila chrysaetos

It is not generally known that this great bird winters in north Georgia. Like the raven, it frequents the higher peaks and ridges. Recently, young birds have been conditioned to the wild (hacked) and released at select places, such as Sam's Knob, in an effort to reestablish a breeding population.

EASTERN BLUE RIDGE

road (1.75 miles by river) are some beautiful pools and camping places [Fig. 41(26), Fig. 42(26)]. Further on there is an old field, called Reed Creek Bottoms, planted in loblolly pine [Fig. 41(27), Fig. 42(27)], which is rare in the mountains unless planted. Here one can turn up a trail on the west side of the field that leads up Reed Creek. Soon there will appear one of the most beautiful stands of white pine in north Georgia with abundant patches of club moss and pink lady slippers [Fig. 41(29), Fig. 42(29)]. Farther on one enters Reed Creek Gorge [Fig. 41(30), Fig. 42(30)]. There are no trails on this section. The cascades, falls and pools are extremely scenic and not too difficult to negotiate. With luck the visitor will see the highest of the falls, Reed Creek Falls [Fig. 41(31), Fig. 42(31)] before a more tranquil section leading up to Persimmon Gap [Fig. 41(32), Fig. 42(32)].

On the main river above Reed Creek there is more entrancing scenery, especially beginning at Lick Log Falls [Fig. 41(36)]. This area is most easily reached from the old Nicholson Ford Road [Fig. 41(34)]. Above this, around a long "square" bend, the road is fairly high above the river. The observant visitor may see signs of wild hogs rooting [Fig. 41(37)]. This is truly back country, in spite of the old log roads which soon will turn up the mountain, skipping the rock gorge entirely. On the approach to the gorge [Fig. 41(38)] one may see the beautiful mountain camellia, whose large white blossoms appear in late summer. This is a plant found in streamside zones and on most bluffs. It is difficult to negotiate the gorge [Fig. 41(39)], even with non-slip shoe soles. This can be a danger-ous section. Towering cliffs appear, and the only way out is at least one mile upstream by wading and rock hopping. Where the main Chattooga River Trail on the South Carolina side comes down to the river after going high around the gorge, there is a waterfall with a beautiful falls and pool below [Fig. 41(40)]. Although unnamed, this falls and the section above it [Fig. 41(41)] are alone worth the trip. At the next huge pool upstream there is a trail [Fig. 41(41)] leading up to an east-west ridge. Big Bend Road leads off to SC 107, the easiest access to the river above the rock gorge. Above this pool (and branch) is another 1.5-mile section which has no trail. The main trail cuts across a ridge and comes down just above Big Bend Falls [Fig. 41(42)]. A side trip down to the falls is worth the exer-tion. At the Big Bend [Fig. 41(43)], one will see pieces of truck axle sticking out of the rock, evidence of a former logging bridge. As unlikely as it may seem, trucks with light loads were able to haul logs up the steep ridge on the South Carolina side, now an access trail. Farther upstream the remaining several miles of river up the "Steps" [Fig. 41(44)] are a pleasant riverside hike and quite beautiful, with more whitewater and fewer huge pools than above Burrell's Ford Bridge.

~CANOEING AND BOATING. All boating is prohibited up-stream of the GA 28 bridge [Fig. 41(25), Fig. 42(25)].

EASTERN BLUE RIDGE

195

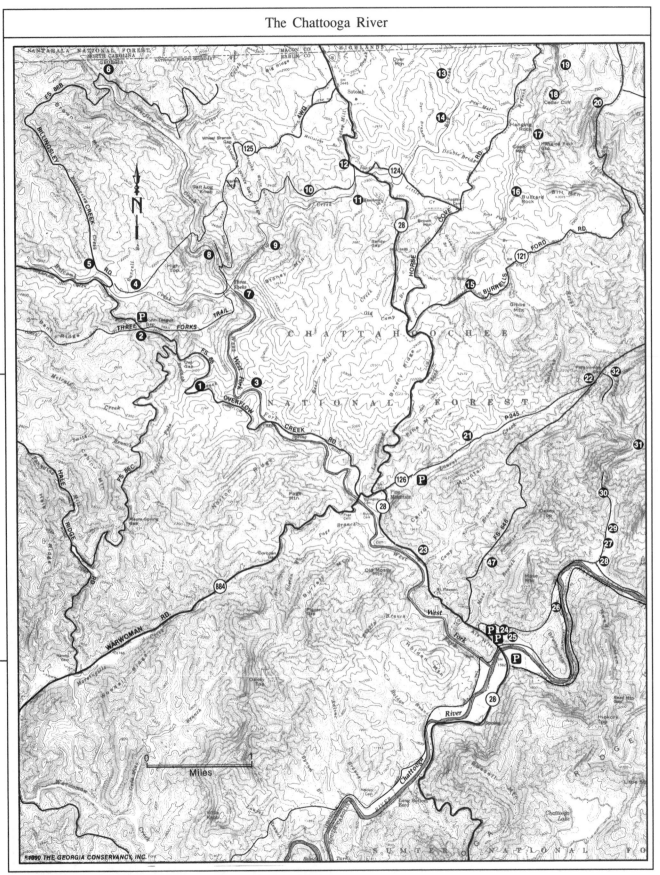

Figure 42 — **CHATTOOGA RIVER/SECTION I—THE WEST FORK**

EASTERN BLUE RIDGE

Fig. 42 - Chattooga River/
Section I

(page references in parentheses)

  2 John Teague Gap/Three Forks Hiking Trail
      (198)
  3 Fisherman's Trail (198)
  4 Old Splash Dam remnants (198)
  5 Billingsley Creek Road (198)
  6 trail & log road (198)
  7 Three Forks (199)
  8 Overflow Falls (199)
  9 Lower Big Creek Falls (199)
 10 Big Creek trail (199)
 11 Upper Big Creek Falls (199)
 12 old log road to Big Creek (199)
 13 falls on upper Big Creek (199)
 14 High Falls on upper Big Creek (199)
 15 Old Burrell's Ford Road (199)
 16 Buzzard's Rock Cliffs (199)
 17 Hanging Rock Cliffs (199)
 18 Cedar Cliffs (199)
 19 Rock Shelter (199)
 20 Heddon Creek Falls (199)
 21 Laurel Creek corundum mine (200)
 22 Persimmon Gap trailhead (200)
 23 Dam ruins (200)
 24 river road from Russell Bridge/Adline
      Branch (194, 200)
 25 Russell Bridge (194, 195, 201)
 26 camping, Russell Bridge to Reed Creek
      (195)
 27 Reed Creek Bottoms (195)
 28 Reed Creek (194)
 29 White pine with club moss & pink lady
      slippers (195)
 30 Reed Creek Gorge (195)
 31 Reed Creek Falls (195)
 32 Persimmon Gap (195)

SECTION I - THE WEST FORK

The West Fork of the Chattooga River begins at Three Forks [Fig. 42(7)], the intersection of three creeks—Holcomb, Overflow and Big Creek. From there the West Fork flows seven miles to the southeast to meet with the Chattooga. The entire West Fork, plus one mile upstream along Overflow Creek, is included within the boundaries of the Chattooga National Wild and Scenic River.

The upper portion of the West Fork is one of the most beautiful river sights in Georgia—a river of low falls and deep green pools hemmed in by bluffs and steep forested slopes. From Overflow Creek Road bridge down to the junction with the Chattooga, the river is relatively calm with long, deep pools ideal for lazy floating or swimming. Fine picnic and strolling sites are accessible and reached by road.

This is a country of beautiful but unknown waterfalls. One is on Overflow just above Three Forks. There are three on Big Creek; the middle one is outstanding. It is along the West Fork's headwaters that the last remnants of the old splash dam logging system can be seen. Old Burrell's Ford Road offered the only former access to the Chattooga's East Fork which, in the 1940's was discovered to be Georgia's famed "mystery river." Large brown trout kept turning up but no one would reveal their source until it was found that the inaccessibility of both the east and west forks had protected a remarkable fishing resource. The West Fork is also an area rich in mining lore. The ultrabasic deposits along the lower river below Pine Mountain have yielded asbestos and soapstone and were the site of Georgia's most famous corundum mine at Laurel Creek. Most maps show that Laurel Creek, Reed Creek and Warwoman Valley form one of north Georgia's most remarkable geologic features, a straight line or lineament, the "Warwoman Shear," that continues to control topography as far west as Tray Mountain. After float logging divested the West Fork of much of its hardwood timber, white pine seeded in. Abundant by 1950, it was subsequently harvested, this time via log roads.

DIRECTIONS: *From US 441 in Clayton where US 76 turns west, turn east onto paved Warwoman Road; once on Warwoman, turn right (not hard right) at the stop sign; proceed past the Georgia Power building; follow Warwoman Road for about 14 miles to the intersection with Overflow Creek Road (FS 86). From Highlands, North Carolina, take NC 28 south to the intersection of Warwoman Road; turn right onto Overflow Creek Road (FS 86) [Fig. 42(1)]. Beaver dams can be seen below the road.*

~ACCESS TO RIVER CROSSINGS.

WARWOMAN ROAD BRIDGE. Follow Warwoman Road 14 miles east from Clayton.

OVERFLOW ROAD BRIDGE. Follow Warwoman Road 14 miles from Clayton. Cross the West Fork, then turn left onto FS 86 (Overflow Road) and follow approximately 1.3 miles to a one-lane bridge.

~HIKING TRAILS AND ACCESS POINTS.

JOHN TEAGUE GAP AND THREE FORKS HIKING TRAIL.
[Fig. 42(2)]   While the Three Forks Trail originates on Rabun Bald (see Rabun Bald), it is most often hiked from John Teague Gap. From there it gently descends through a forest typical for the area—oak/hickory slope forest with scattered patches of white pines. At 0.7 mile the path crosses the blue-blazed boundary of the Chattooga National Wild and Scenic River. Three-tenths mile further it dips to a three-way intersection with an old jeep road. Here the Three Forks Trail, occasionally blazed with white diamonds, turns left and heads downhill following the road to a slab of bedrock overlooking a cascade on Holcomb Creek. This is the end of the designated trail. The remainder of the route down this gorge is on the north side of Holcomb Creek (cross the creek) down a ravine with pot-holed rocks and falls that reach all the way to Three Forks (about 0.25 mile). It is not difficult bushwhacking, but one must pick a path through hemlock/rhododendron heath which, along with white pine, forms the bulk of the streamside zone of vegetation.

FISHERMAN'S TRAIL. [Fig. 42(3)] The trail passes rock shelters and cliffs harboring colonies of wood rats.
DIRECTIONS: *Upstream on north side of West Fork from where FS 86 crosses West Fork.*

OLD SPLASH DAM REMNANTS. [Fig. 42(4)] Around the turn of the century, loggers in this area built what were termed "splash dams" across creeks like Holcomb and Overflow. Cut logs were dragged down to the creeks and backed up behind the dam. At a prearranged signal, dams on several creeks were broken at one time, sending water and logs raging down the stream. Called "float logging," this method was used to harvest many of the slope forests, including streamside hemlocks. Logs from the West Fork were destined for Madison, South Carolina.
DIRECTIONS: *About 0.25 mile below where Billingsley Creek Road crosses Holcomb Creek. Cross the bridge and go down the north side of the creek.*

BILLINGSLEY CREEK ROAD. [Fig. 42(5)] Built by the Forest Service so that Overflow Creek watershed could be logged.

TRAIL AND LOG ROAD. [Fig. 42(6)] Joins with Blue Valley and Clear Creek road system.

THREE FORKS. [Fig. 42(7)] The intersection of Holcomb Creek, Overflow Creek and Big Creek divides the forest landscape into four neat quadrants and rewards determined hikers with the light, sound and color of one of the most delightful scenes in Georgia. Other than by the Three Forks Trail route (see above), Three Forks can be reached via NC 28. See directions below.

OVERFLOW FALLS. [Fig. 42(8)] Waterfall about 0.5 mile above Three Forks.

LOWER BIG CREEK FALLS. [Fig. 42(9)] Waterfall on Big Creek [Fig. 42(10)] and Upper Falls on Big Creek [Fig. 42(11)]. old log road [Fig. 42(12)] provides a good hike to Big Creek.

FALLS ON UPPER BIG CREEK. [Fig. 42(13)]

HIGH FALLS ON UPPER BIG CREEK. [Fig. 42(14)]
DIRECTIONS: *Proceed on GA 28 to Satolah, Georgia, at the bridge over Big Creek. Just north of the bridge, turn off and park on the west side of the highway. Find a Forest Service log road which crosses a little branch immediately and follow this easy graded road all the way to Three Forks. The middle and upper Big Creek Falls can be found either by walking the creek or by their roar. The lower Big Creek Falls is a rugged series of cascades that plummets all the way to Three Forks and is only for hardy adventurers.*

BURRELL'S FORD ROADS. In the 1940's reports filtered out of the north Georgia mountains of giant brown trout from a "mystery river." Eventually it was discovered that the mystery river was the Chattooga above Burrell's Ford, reached from Georgia only by Old Burrell's Ford Road (FS 121) [Fig. 41(15), Fig. 42(15)], which turns east off NC 28. The new Burrell's Ford Road [Fig. 42(47)] turns north off GA 28 just before the Russell Bridge

BUZZARD'S ROCK CLIFFS [FIG. 42(16)], HANGING ROCK CLIFFS [FIG. 42(17)] AND CEDAR CLIFFS [FIG. 42(18)]. These are a series of high cliffs reached only by bushwhacking. On Cedar Cliffs is found Georgia's only location for sand myrtle. These cliffs are adorned with a picturesque spike moss, which forms thick, photogenic mats with twisted, hairlike spines. On Cedar Cliff Mountain is a rock shelter [Fig. 42(19)] containing evidence of both goats and the rare wood rat.

HEDDON CREEK FALLS. [Fig. 42(20)] This falls on Heddon Creek Road is accessible only by four-wheel drive. Just beyond the falls is a flat swampy area, the site of a shrub bog.

Wood rat
Neotoma floridana

This large, gentle, hairy-tailed rodent builds bushel-basket-sized caches of sticks, cones and seed pods beneath dry cliff overhangs. It lives in colonies and is quite rare. It has been found along the West Fork of the Chattooga River and in the cliffs atop Blood Mountain.

DIRECTIONS: *Take FS 121 east off GA 28 about two miles south of Big Creek Bridge. About four miles down FS 121 the road fords Heddon Creek. To reach the falls, turn left up the creek.*

LAUREL CREEK CORUNDUM MINE. [Fig. 41(21), Fig. 42(21)] Georgia's most famous corundum mine, unworked since 1894 when a huge block of peridotite fell, closing the tunnels. In addition to corundum, which is the second hardest mineral (only diamond is harder) and is used in the manufacture of abrasives for grinding and smoothing, the mine produced excellent specimens of blue and red corundum, though seldom of ruby and sapphire quality. The peridotite outcrop covers several hundred acres including two rough, barren hills. The private owners of the land at the road terminus have not objected to hikers and parking. The trail can also be reached at the opposite end from Persimmon Gap on New Burrell's Ford Road (FS 646).

DIRECTIONS: *Laurel Creek is the first creek crossed going south from the junction of Warwoman Road and GA 28. After crossing the creek (about one mile), turn east.*

PERSIMMON GAP TRAILHEAD. [Fig. 41(22), Fig. 42(22)]

DAM RUINS. [Fig. 41(23), Fig. 42(23)] Water was dammed to power a turbine which turned machinery for milling asbestos ore. The ore came from a mine just across the river on Dockins' Mountain. A nearby soapstone deposit at Adline Branch [Fig. 41(24), Fig. 42(24)] was cut into blocks with crosscut saws and used to build the blacksmith forge at the Laurel Creek Corundum Mine and to line local fireplaces.

~CANOEING AND BOATING. The lower section of the West Fork, from Overflow Creek Road Bridge to the junction with the Chattooga, is a slow-moving, gentle stream suitable for the novice canoeist. Two Class II rapids, Dam Sluice and Big Slide, provide excitement for the beginner. The take-out is at Long Bottom Ford [Fig. 43(6)].

MAP REFERENCES: *USGS 1:24,000 series: Satolah - Tamassee.*

Mountain camellia
Stewartia ovata

This is one of the rarest of our native trees. It grows on bluffs and in ravines and streamside zones, particularly along the Tallulah River [Fig. 38(9)] and the upper Chattooga River [Fig. 41(38)]. Its large, white flower resembles that of a dogwood or magnolia.

SECTIONS II, III AND IV

These sections of the Chattooga accommodate those who enjoy the thrills of whitewater boating or watching others negotiate dangerous rapids. On the Georgia side of the river, a good hiking trail, the Chattooga River Trail, later joined by the Bartram Trail, parallels the river between the US 76 and SC 28 bridges. Below US 76 there are very limited trails along the river (see page 207) and the gorge is navigable only by floating. At normal water levels, Section III is a good Class III run. At low water, outfitters avoid Section III and run Section IV, which extends from the US 76 bridge downriver to Lake Tugalo.

~ACCESS TO RIVER CROSSINGS.

RUSSELL BRIDGE. [Fig. 41(25), Fig. 42(25)] Follow War-woman Road 14 miles east from Clayton, cross the West Fork of the Chattooga and go to the junction with GA 28. Turn right (south) on GA 28 and go approximately three miles to the bridge.

HIGHWAY 76 BRIDGE. [Fig. 45(23), Fig. 44(23)] Nine miles east of Clayton on US 76. This is the take-out for Section III and put-in for Section IV.

~ACCESS TO RIVER.

RUSSELL BRIDGE, LONG BOTTOM FORD PUT-INS. On SC 28 1.25 miles south of the Russell Bridge is a parking and put-in area [Fig. 43(4)]. One-half mile below here a dirt road turns off south to Long Bottom Ford [Fig. 43(6)], where a low-water bridge and ford were the major river crossings for the early settlers around Pine Mountain on the West Fork. Boaters can put in here. Most cars can travel the road.

SOUTH CAROLINA ACCESS TO EARL'S FORD AND SANDY FORD. Downstream, Earl's Ford is the next point of access. At Mountain Rest about 3.75 miles turn right (south) on FS 196 and go 3.25 miles to a four-way stop at Whetstone; turn right (west) and go off pavement at 1.75 miles on a good gravel road for 1.25 miles. There [Fig. 44(7), Fig. 43(7)] is a camp specially designed to accommodate horses and horse trailers, and from it radiate horse trails that explore the area. If one turns left here on FS 721A, in 1.25 miles the river corridor is reached, and a trail leads 0.25 mile to the river. This is the Sandy Ford access [Fig. 44(9), Fig. 43(9)] from the South Carolina side. Continuing straight on Whetstone Road one mile past the horse camp, one reaches a parking area and trail to Earl's Ford [Fig. 44(8), Fig. 43(8)].

EASTERN BLUE RIDGE

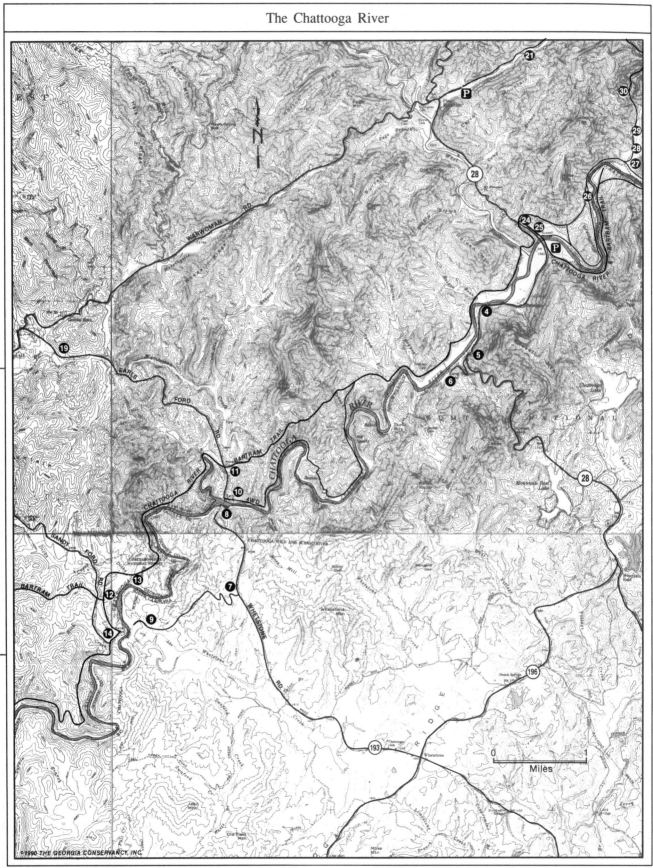

Figure 43 — **CHATTOOGA RIVER/SECTION II**

EASTERN BLUE RIDGE

Fig. 43 - Chattooga River/
Section II

(page references in parentheses)

4 Russell Bridge parking & put-in (201)
6 Long Bottom Ford (200, 201)
7 horse & trailer camp (201)
8 Earl's Ford (201)
9 Sandy Ford access (201)
10 Section II/Earl's Ford Road (203, 209)
11 Warwoman Creek Ford (203)
12 Bartram Trail (203)
13 viewing platform (203)
14 Sandy Ford (203)

GEORGIA ACCESS TO EARL'S FORD AND SANDY FORD. Georgia has access to both Earl's Ford and Sandy Ford, but the roads in are long, sometimes muddy and are not used by the commercial outfitters. The Georgia Earl's Ford Road access [Fig. 44(10), Fig. 43(10)] can be reached by ordinary car, except that in high water Warwoman Creek [Fig. 44(11), Fig. 43(11)] cannot be forded. (It is possible to drive, with care, to Sandy Ford.) In both cases, roads go to the river's edge, unlike those in South Carolina. However, the protective corridor extends 0.25 mile from the river. All vehicle traffic is required to stay well away from the riverbanks.

On the Georgia side above Sandy Ford [Fig. 44(14), Fig. 43(14)] is a beautiful 50-foot-high waterfall on Dick's Creek. Take the Bartram Trail north [Fig. 44(12), Fig. 43(12)] about 0.5 mile past the Dick's Creek Ford to a side trail and viewing platform constructed by the U.S. Forest Service [Fig. 44(13)Fig. 43(13)].

FALLS CREEK ACCESS. The next access is best approached off US 76. Two miles east of the US 76 bridge turn left (north) onto the Chattooga Ridge Road (FS 196), the first paved road to the left. Go two miles, take the gravel road (FS 722) [Fig. 44(15)] left (west). At the second fork (two miles), the right hand fork (FS 723) goes to an access point [Fig. 44(16)] with a very steep trail to the river (0.25 mile). The left fork (FS 769) leads to a less steep but longer trail [Fig. 44(17)]. There are two lovely waterfalls on Falls Creek [Fig. 44(18)] and [Fig. 44(19)].

THRIFT'S FERRY. The next access is at Thrift's Ferry [Fig. 44(20)], reached by a gravel road (P795) which turns north about one mile east of the US 76 bridge.

US 76 SHOULDER ACCESS. Farther downriver, there is a special short access trail (parking is on US 76 shoulder) [Fig. 45(21), Fig. 44(21)] where some outfitters put in for short runs over Bull Sluice [Fig. 45(22), Fig. 44(22)].

BULL SLUICE TRAILS. There are two trails upriver to Bull Sluice, at high water levels a very dangerous, roaring Class V rapid. Some visitors choose to walk up the better trail on the east (South Carolina) bank [Fig. 45(23), Fig. 44(23)] from the US 76 bridge parking area to watch the rafters come through the sluice. Photographers often prefer to walk up the west bank (Georgia) trail [Fig. 45(24), Fig. 44(24)], which is less well maintained but offers better views of the falls from below. (This is not the Chattooga River Trail. One has to walk too far on the CRT to reach Bull Sluice, while this trail is a short hike.)

WOODALL SHOALS. [Fig. 45(25)] This is a beautiful spot for picnicking and for swimming in the pool below the rapids. *Do not*

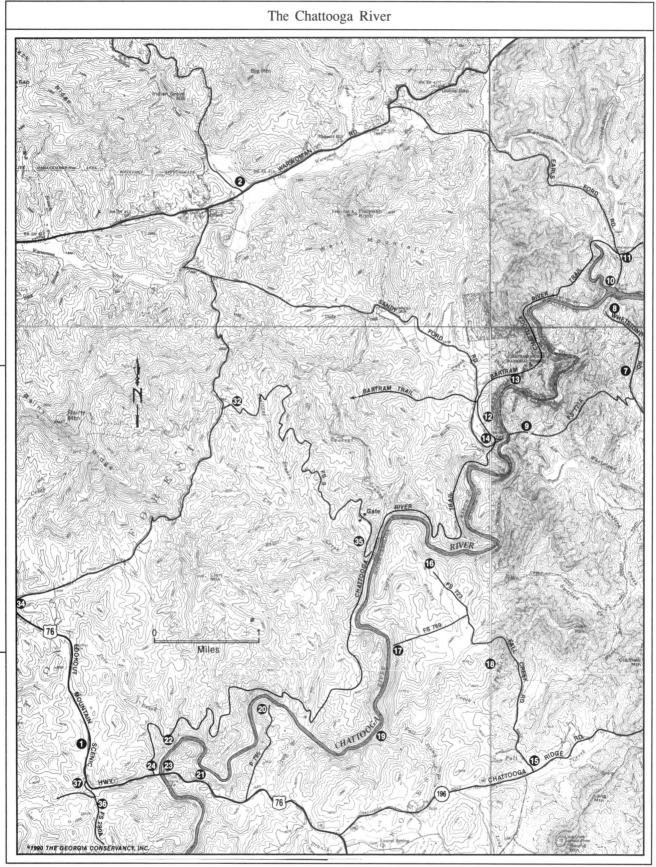

Figure 44 — **CHATTOOGA RIVER/SECTION III**

EASTERN BLUE RIDGE

Fig. 44 - Chattooga River/
Section III

(page references in parentheses)

7   horse & trailer camp (201)
8   Earl's Ford (201)
9   Sandy Ford access (201)
10 Earl's Ford access (203)
11 Warwoman Creek Ford (203)
12 Bartram Trail (203)
13 waterfall on Dick's Creek (203)
14 Sandy Ford (203)
15 FS 722 (203)
16 Falls Creek access (203)
17 trail to Falls Creek (203)
18 waterfall, Falls Creek (203)
19 waterfall, Falls Creek (203)
20 Thrift's Ferry (203)
21 US 76 access trail (203)
22 Bull Sluice (203)
23 US 76 bridge/Bull Sluice trails [SC]
    (201, 203, 209)
24 Bull Sluice trail [GA] (203)
32 Lick Log access road [FS 9] (205, 207)
34 gravel access road (207)
35 access road (207)
36 Sutton Hole Road [290A] (207)
37 gravel road [290] (207)

attempt to swim or body surf Woodall Shoals. Rated a Class VI rapid, it is considered the most dangerous on the river. Given proper water levels it can be run by or with professionals, but normally it should be portaged. Visitors should be content to explore below the rapid. On the east side of Woodall Shoals is one of the best places in north Georgia to see how Blue Ridge Mountain rocks have been metamorphosed by heat and pressure, as compared to the sedimentary or "layer cake" type mountains of the Cumberland Plateau in the northwestern part of the state. In fact, this site is said to be the "Rosetta Stone" for the interpretation of the changes that have taken place in the rocks of the Eastern Blue Ridge. Most of the rock at Woodall Shoals is a gneiss with black mica, but in it are dark bands and lumps of calcium-rich amphibolite, which furnishes good nutrition for nearby plant communities. Fresh rock is exposed here, courtesy of Mr. Woodall who apparently dynamited the west side of the river several decades ago so his logs would not be trapped by the rapids along the east bank. Woodall Shoals is reached by turning right (south) 2.5 miles east of the US 76 bridge, and again right at the first gravel road to the right. It is about two miles to the parking and camping areas. Note that camping is prohibited here within the Wild and Scenic corridor.

LONG CREEK FALLS. [Fig. 45(26)] Below Woodall Shoals there is a beautiful falls on Long Creek, where most rafts stop for a swim and photographs. It can also be reached by a trail [Fig. 45(27)]. Turn south off US 76 4.5 miles east of the US 76 bridge. After turning at Long Creek, go 2.5 miles, turn right (west) on FS 758 and go 1.25 miles; turn left onto a gravel road, which in 1.5 miles becomes a jeep road, and proceed until the trailhead is reached. This is the Long Creek Road.

'POSSUM CREEK FALLS. The 'Possum Creek Falls [Fig. 45(28)] is reached by a 1.5-mile trail which turns south in a bend [Fig. 45(29)] 0.5 mile off the paved road at Battle Creek, the same access to Long Creek Road.

TUGALO LAKE ROAD. The last access road on the South Carolina side is off this same paved road about four miles south of US 76. Turn right (west) onto the gravel Tugalo Lake Road [Fig. 45(30)]. Be cautious in wet weather. This is the road used by buses to pick up rafters who have made the Section IV trip [Fig. 45(31)]. Length is 3.5 miles.

LICK LOG. Coming down the river on the Georgia side below Sandy Ford is the Lick Log access road [Fig. 44(32)]. It is reached by turning south off Warwoman Road at the Antioch Church turn-off to Sandy Ford, bearing left at the first fork (0.5 mile), then bearing right at the second fork (about 0.25 mile). Then take the

EASTERN BLUE RIDGE

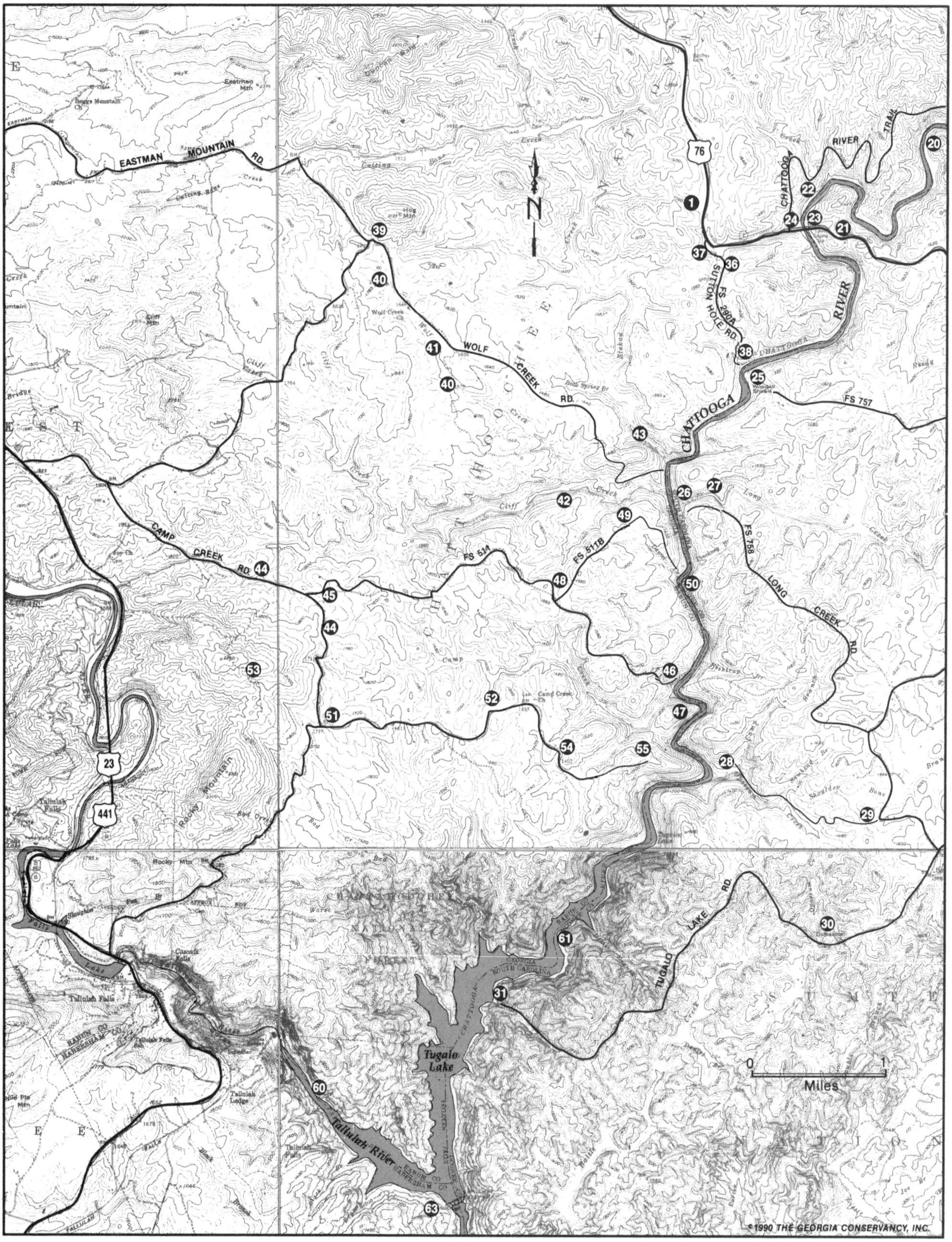

Figure 45 — **CHATTOOGA RIVER/SECTION IV**

206

Fig. 45 - Chattooga River/
Section IV

(page references in parentheses)

21 US 76 access trail (203)
22 Bull Sluice (203)
23 US 76 bridge/Bull Sluice trails
    (201, 203, 209)
24 Bull Sluice trail [GA] (203)
25 Woodall Shoals [Class VI] (203)
26 Long Creek Falls (205)
27 trail to Long Creek Falls (205)
28 'Possum Creek Falls (205)
29 trail to 'Possum Creek Falls (205)
30 Tugalo Lake road (205)
31 Tugalo Lake rafter pick-up (205, 209)
36 Sutton Hole Road [290A] (207)
37 gravel road [290] (207)
38 Sutton Hole (207)
39 Wolf Creek Road (207)
40 wild Japanese paper plant (207)
41 beaver dams (207)
42 Cliff Creek (207)
44 Camp Creek Road (207, 208)
45 gravel road [511] (207)
46 road to river (207)
47 Five Falls (207)
48 jeep road [511B] (208)
49 ridge (208)
50 Raven Rock Pool (208)
51 road [73] (208)
52 rock crystal ridge (208)
53 rock crystal knob (208)
54 Camp Creek Church (208)
55 trail terminus (208)
61 Lake Tugalo (166)

next left-hand road (FS 9). (See Rabun Bald section for road access from Warwoman Road). These are gravel roads suitable for all vehicles.

FS 9 APPROACH. Another Georgia approach is off US 76 east from Clayton, 2.8 miles past the Willows. Turn north (left) on gravel road [Fig. 44(34)], go 3.5 miles, take FS 9 [Fig. 44(32)] east (right) 3.8 miles to a gate. An old road [Fig. 44(35)] goes down a ridge to the river.

SUTTON HOLE ROAD. About 0.75 mile west of the US 76 Bridge a gravel road (FS 290) turns south [Fig. 45(37), Fig. 44(37)]. Within 0.5 mile the short Sutton Hole Road (290A) [Fig. 45(36), Fig. 44(36)] goes down to the river corridor, where the outfitters overnight their two-day-trip customers at Sutton Hole [Fig. 45(38)]. This is a jeep or pick-up truck road, not for ordinary cars.

WOLF CREEK ROAD. [Fig. 45(39)] This route requires about a one-mile walk to the river. To reach it, turn right (east) off US 441, four miles north of Tallulah Falls Bridge, onto the second paved road to the right. Keep straight for about three miles (the road turns to gravel). Turn right (east) at the Wolf Creek Church sign (FS 515). This is an interesting area. From above the church along Wolf Creek, the strange, introduced Japanese paper plant grows wild [Fig. 45(40)]. Botanical groups often visit this site to see it. Farther down Wolf Creek below the church are at least a dozen beaver dams [Fig. 45(41)]. A jeep can go down to within one mile of the Chattooga (stay on the right hand road). This road leads to two potentially exciting areas which have not been much explored nor apparently logged. The gorge of Cliff Creek [Fig. 45(42)] and lower Stekoa Creek (refer to Rainey Mountain quadrangle) are excellent places to explore.

CAMP CREEK ROAD. [Fig. 45(44)] This is one of the most exciting access points to the Chattooga. It is a gravel road 2.9 miles north of the Tallulah Falls Bridge, or 8.25 miles south of US 76, on US 441. Turn right at the first fork, 0.65 miles east of 441 (stay on gravel). About two miles from the highway is a second fork. It is about four miles to the river corridor if the visitor stays on the good gravel road (Rd 511) [Fig. 45(45)]. Drive with care; logging trucks and buses carrying rafters also use the road. There is an old road down to the river's edge [Fig. 45(46)]. Walking downstream along a thickly overgrown trail, one soon comes to the first of a series of Class V rapids [Fig. 45(47)] with names like Corkscrew, Jawbone and Sock'em Dog. In good weather, it is quite a show to watch river runners go through this whitewater. A ford at or near the mouth of Camp Creek was evidently the main old settlers' route to

EASTERN BLUE RIDGE

South Carolina, a wagon road reportedly down which herds of hogs were driven to market.

Back about a mile from the terminus of FS 511, a jeep road (FS 511B) [Fig. 45(48)] turns north, terminating on a ridge [Fig. 45(49)]. A trail drops down 0.75 mile to the Raven Rock Pool [Fig. 45(50)], a grand, scenic place to have lunch, fish and watch the rafters go by.

The trail terminates across the river from Raven Rock Cliffs, a 200-foot escarpment. Just upstream, Raven's Chute, a solid Class IV drop, challenges boaters.

The main Camp Creek Road (FS 511) continues south [Fig. 45(44)] and is paved nearly to a fork; it then turns left (east) [Fig. 45(51)] on FS 73 (FS 74 continues on to come out at Terrora Park on Tallulah Falls Lake). It is about two miles to the Camp Creek Church. Just west of it is a ridge which has yielded rock crystals [Fig. 45(52)] which also occur on a rocky knob several miles to the west [Fig. 45(53)]. On these rocky ridges and southward around Tallulah Gorge the dominant pine is often the rare table mountain pine, with cones so prickly that it can hardly be handled. One can park past the Camp Creek Church [Fig. 45(54)]. A jeep can go only another 0.5 mile; then one takes a trail. In this area, as in the area southward around Tallulah Gorge, the dominant heath is Carolina rhododendron, which has a purple bloom, as well as abundant azalea. At the terminus of the trail [Fig. 45(55)] one will be able to gaze off into the gorge of the Chattooga. This is the fabled "Sinking Mountain," where the visitor who stands long enough in one spot can feel the ground giving way underfoot. Bulldozers left overnight have been known to sink a foot or two. An Indian myth attributes this to a race of spirit people or "little people" who mined beneath the mountain, which is now caving in on their tunnels.

~CANOEING AND BOATING.

The Chattooga River is an outstanding whitewater experience that attracts boaters from all over the U.S. and Canada. While it is one of the finest recreational resources Georgia has to offer, it can be extremely unsafe—even deadly—for those who approach it unaware of its hazards. Many individuals, experienced as well as inexperienced boaters, have lost their lives in the river, particularly on Sections III and IV. A variety of books and maps details the river's boating pleasures and its dangers, and one or more of these resources should be consulted before attempting to navigate any section of the river. Reliable river guidebooks are listed in Appendix D. In addition, a number of outfitters provide canoeing and rafting expeditions on the Chattooga (See Commercial Rafting Trips, below). *No one* should attempt Sections III and IV of the Chattooga without first going with an experienced guide.

The Forest Service requires a minimum of two boats in any boating party and that each party boating on the Chattooga register and provide proof of that registration on the river. *Rangers frequently check for registrations at the take-out points and issue $50.00 fines if the registration is not produced.* Registration booths are located at the Russell Bridge parking and put-in area, the Earl's Ford parking area, the US 76 Bridge parking area and the Woodall Shoals parking area. Boaters entering the river at a put-in location without a registration booth must first register at a site with such a booth.

Section II - GA 28 to Earl's Ford. [Fig. 43(10)] One Class III rapid (Big Shoals) and other shelf-like rapids make Section II an excellent area for novice to intermediate whitewater boaters.

Section III - Earl's Ford to the US 76 Bridge. [Fig. 45(23), Fig. 44(23)] At this point the river becomes much more dangerous, requiring greater expertise in negotiating boulders, gorges and ledges. There are several Class III and IV rapids and one Class V at Bull Sluice, just above the take-out point near the US 76 bridge.

Section IV - From the US 76 bridge to Tugalo Lake. [Fig. 45(31)] The infamous Woodall Shoals, a Class VI rapid which has taken many lives, is located on this section a short distance below the bridge. From here on, the river narrows and concentrates into several Class IV and V rapids before entering Lake Tugalo where a 1.5-mile paddle across the lake to take out is required. Both Sections III and IV are dangerous and should be attempted only by experienced boaters.

~Commercial Rafting Trips. Guided river trips are available from three local rafting companies—Southeastern Expeditions, Wildwater Limited and Nantahala Outdoor Center, all carefully regulated by the federal government. These outfitters conduct canoe clinics and raft trips lasting from a half day to two days, with an overnight camp-out available. Commercial operations usually run from late March through October, depending on stream flow and weather. For a listing of outfitters, see Appendix C.

Map References: *USGS 1:24,000 series: Cashiers - Highlands - Satolah - Tamassee - Rainy Mountain; USFS Chattooga River Corridor map.*

Northern water snake
Nerodia sipedon sipedon

This is probably the only snake you will see along streams in the eastern Blue Ridge. A similar form, the midland water snake (*N. sipedon pleuralis*), occurs in the Piedmont, northwest Georgia and probably the western Blue Ridge. Markings and colors cause it to be confused with the copperhead. The coppery-red head and distinct hour-glass markings of the copperhead are helpful in distinguishing the two snakes.

EASTERN BLUE RIDGE

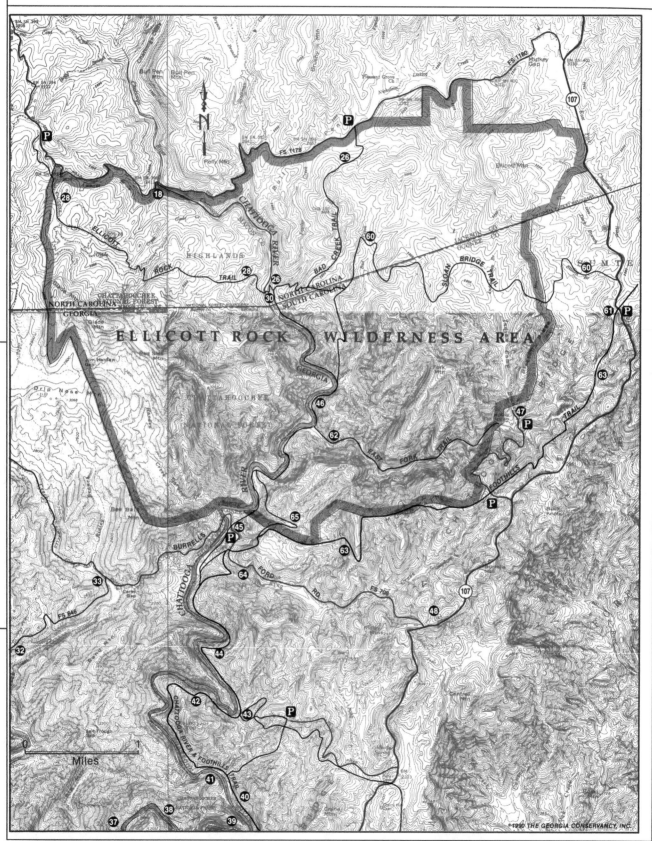

Figure 46 — **ELLICOTT ROCK WILDERNESS**

EASTERN BLUE RIDGE

The Ellicott Rock Wilderness

Fig. 46 - Chattooga River/Ellicott Rock Wilderness

(page references in parentheses)

18 Ammons Branch Campground (193, 220, 223)
26 Bad Creek Trail (211, 212, 220, 221)
28 Ellicott Rock Trail (211, 220, 221)
30 Ellicott Rock (193, 211, 212, 221)
45 Burrell's Ford Campground (193, 194, 212, 213)
46 Chattooga River Trail (211, 213)
47 Walhalla Fish Hatchery (212)
60 Sloan Bridge Trail (212)
61 Sloan Bridge Picnic Area (212)
62 East Fork Trail Picnic Area (212)
63 Foothills Trail (212)
64 King's Creek Falls (213)
65 Spoon Auger Falls (213)

This is a 9,012-acre tract of unspoiled mountain land which surrounds the point at which Georgia, North Carolina and South Carolina come together. The first boundary, a small scenic area, was identified and established in 1966. It and a much larger area were made a part of the National Wilderness System in 1975 and thus became fully protected by guidelines of the 1960 National Wilderness Protection Act.

This primitive land is isolated and well protected, allowing a near-wilderness experience within its rocky, mountainous terrain.

The Wild and Scenic Chattooga River flows through the wilderness, cascading from 2,381 feet to 2,100 feet within its boundaries. Fork Mountain, 3,294 feet above sea level, is the second highest point in South Carolina.

This wilderness has several unique plant communities, a number of rare and endangered plants growing alongside the trails, evergreen forests with dense understory of mountain laurel, streamside rhododendron which defies human penetration, a diverse population of large and small animal life and many fish, including the eastern brook trout.

Hiking is the only method available for exploring the interior of Ellicott Rock Wilderness. The automobile-access roads merely provide a way to get to the trailheads. No horses, bicycles or motorized vehicles are permitted. Camping is allowed within the wilderness, but campsites must be over 0.25 mile from an approach road and 50 feet from a stream or maintained trail.

The Forest Service has recommended a 2,000-acre addition to this wilderness in the Sumter National Forest. The addition would be bounded by SR 107 on the east and the New Burrell's Ford Road on the south.

~TRAILS.

CHATTOOGA RIVER TRAIL. [Fig. 41(46), Fig. 46(46)] This portion of the Chattooga River Trail within the wilderness is over 3.4 miles of old Indian trail. It runs beside the east bank of the Chattooga River from a Burrell's Ford trailhead near the river to an intersection with the East Fork Trail (1.5 miles), then to Ellicott Rock (1.6 miles) [Fig. 46(30), Fig. 48(30)] to join Bad Creek Trail [Fig. 46(26), Fig. 48(26)] and Ellicott Rock Trail [Fig. 46(28), Fig. 48(28)] (0.3 mile). The trail is a moderately easy climb through patches of rhododendron and old-growth stands of hemlock, white pine and mixed hardwood. Bad Creek is easily crossed during low water but may have to be waded when water is high.

DIRECTIONS: *To reach the trailhead from the intersection of US 64 and NC 107 in Cashiers go south on NC 107 to New Burrell's Ford Road, FS 708; turn right (west) and proceed to the trailhead near the river.*

EASTERN BLUE RIDGE

ELLICOTT ROCK TRAIL. [Fig. 46(30), Fig. 48(30)] See trail information in the Highlands section.

BAD CREEK TRAIL. [Fig. 46(26), Fig. 48(26)] See trail information in Highlands section.

SLOAN BRIDGE TRAIL. [Fig. 46(60), Fig. 48(60)] This is a moderately difficult trail in good condition. From Sloan Bridge Picnic Area [Fig. 46(61), Fig. 48(61)], it joins Bad Creek Trail (6.3 miles), then proceeds to Ellicott Rock (1.4 miles). Sloan Bridge Trail is perhaps best used for overnight camping after leaving a shuttle at some other trailhead, such as the Walhalla Fish Hatchery [Fig. 46(47)].

Also called Fork Mountain Trail, it crosses SC 107 and approaches the wilderness from the east. The trail ascends and descends, steeply at times. It climbs to near the top of Fork Mountain and falls to streamside, where it passes opulent woodland flora. Ornithologists find the trail of interest because of the diverse species of bird life related to altitude and flora. Hawks and eagles are often seen in this most remote area of the wilderness.

DIRECTIONS: *To reach the trailhead from the intersection of US 64 and NC 107 in Cashiers, go south on NC 107 to about 0.75 mile south of the North Carolina/South Carolina border. Ample parking is available at Sloan Bridge trailhead north of the picnic area.*

EAST FORK TRAIL. [Fig. 46(62)] Sometimes called the Fish Hatchery Trail, this path immediately enters the wilderness and runs downstream alongside the East Fork of the Chattooga for 2.5 miles until it intersects the Chattooga River Trail. The renowned "Forty Thousand Dollar Bridge" which spans the mouth of the East Fork is located here. To reach Ellicott Rock, follow the river upstream 1.7 miles.

Many water-carved rocks, cascades and deep pools in the Chattooga combine with the streamside hemlock and white pine forest to make this a particularly appealing area. There is a stand of old-growth hemlock preserved near the hatchery. The trail is marked with black blazes, and the round trip of about 8.1 miles is easily covered on a full-day hike.

DIRECTIONS: *To reach the trailhead from the intersection of US 64 and NC 107 in Cashiers, go south on NC 107; turn right on the road to the Walhalla Fish Hatchery [Fig. 46(47)]. The trailhead is at the parking area of the Chattooga Picnic Area, next to the hatchery.*

FOOTHILLS TRAIL. [Fig. 41(63), Fig. 46(63)] 6.6 miles. This is a long, well-marked and well-maintained South Carolina trail. It approaches the Ellicott Rock Wilderness Area across the road from Burrell's Ford Campground parking area [Fig. 41(45), Fig. 46(45)] and skirts the southeastern boundary of the wilderness to leave the area at Sloan Bridge Picnic Area on SC 107. Unlike the other trails in this section, it does not penetrate the interior of the wilderness. After leaving the Burrell's Ford parking area, the trail climbs Medlin Mountain, passes the Fish Hatchery Road (3.3 miles) on the Chattooga Ridge escarpment and proceeds to the Sloan's Bridge Picnic Area (3.3 miles). The Medlin Mountain climb is moderately difficult, but other areas of the trail are traveled with ease. The trail has segments which may be chosen for day hikes, overnight camping or extended visits along the wilderness border and/or into the Chattooga River corridor.

DIRECTIONS: *To reach the Burrell's Ford trailhead from the intersection of US 64 and NC 107 in Cashiers, go south approximately 13.5 miles on 107 and turn right on New Burrell's Ford Road; go to the parking area and trailhead.*

To reach the place where the trail crosses Fish Hatchery Road from the intersection of US 64 and NC 107 in Cashiers, go south on NC 107 approximately 12 miles and turn right on Fish Hatchery Road; go to the trail crossing, which is plainly marked.

To reach the Sloan Bridge trailhead from the intersection of US 64 and NC 107 in Cashiers, go south on NC 107 approximately 10 miles to the Sloan Bridge Picnic Area.

~WATERFALLS.

SPOON AUGER FALLS. [Fig. 41(65), Fig. 46(65)] This picturesque, cascading falls can be visited by taking an easy loop trail starting across from the entrance to Burrell's Ford Campground parking lot [Fig. 41(45), Fig. 46(45)]. The trail climbs gradually through lovely hardwoods and rhododendron for about 0.5 mile to the falls, crosses the creek and continues on about 1.7 miles until it interconnects with the Chattooga River Trail [Fig. 41(46), Fig. 46(46)]. Returning to the parking lot via the Chattooga River Trail and New Burrell's Ford Road is a walk of about 1.5 miles.

KING'S CREEK FALLS. [Fig. 41(64), Fig. 46(64)] Located on a beautiful mountain stream surrounded by dense hardwoods and an undergrowth of hemlock and rhododendron. At the falls, water can be seen freely falling for approximately 80 feet into a picturesque pool. The falls is located about 0.5 mile from the Burrell's Ford Campground parking lot [Fig. 41(45), Fig. 46(45)]. It is easily reached on a loop trail starting at the display board on the east side of the parking lot. The trail crosses King's Creek and follows the creek upstream about 300 yards to the base of the falls. One can then backtrack 0.7 mile to the parking lot, continue downstream 0.5 mile to the campground or go down the loop trail to its intersection with the Chattooga River Trail. The return to the parking lot on the Chattooga River Trail is about two miles.

MAP REFERENCES: *USGS 1:24,000 series: Tamassee - Satolah - Highlands - Cashiers; USFS Chattooga Corridor map.*

Northern dusky salamander
Desmognathus fuscus fuscus

Of the three large, dark-colored salamanders found under rocks along streams in the eastern Blue Ridge, this species is most likely to be confused with the very similar seal salamander (*D. monticola*). Both are sold as expensive live bait for bass and provide income for many mountain youth.

EASTERN BLUE RIDGE

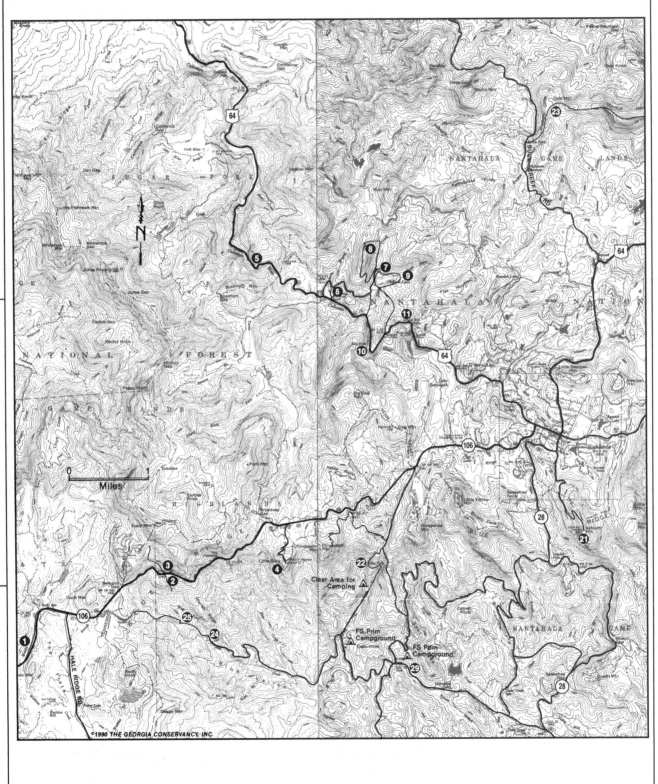

Highlands, North Carolina

EASTERN BLUE RIDGE

©1990 THE GEORGIA CONSERVANCY, INC.

Figure 47 — **SCALY MOUNTAIN AND HIGHLANDS**

214

Fig. 47 - Scaly Mountain/Highlands
(page references in parentheses)

1 NC 106 [views] (215)
2 Osage Mountain overlook (215)
3 "Catstairs" ascent of Scaly Mountain
   by Bartram Trail (215)
4 The Mountain (Little Scaly) (215)
5 Cullasaja River Gorge (220)
6 Vanhook Glade Campground (223)
7 Cliffside Lake Recreation Area (223)
8 Ridgeline loop trail (223)
9 loop trail around Cliffside Lake (223)
10 Dry Falls (220)
11 Bridal Veil Falls (220)
21 Satulah Mountain (217)
22 Glen Falls (Blue Valley) (222)
23 Yellow Mountain Trail (222)
24 Trailhead to Old Tiffany Sapphire Mine
    (222)
25 Trail to Old Tiffany Sapphire Mine
    (222)
29 Blue Valley Primitive Camping Area
    (223)

Highlands, North Carolina

Central to this remarkable and highly scenic area is an unusually high (4,000-foot) plateau on the southern edge of the Blue Ridge. Unique in the Southern Appalachians are numerous mountains in this area with steep granite cliffs which create imposing scenery. These cliffs may be seen from NC 106 [Fig. 47(1)] and US 64 and, indeed, throughout the area; but they are best observed from the tops of two remarkable mountains, Whiteside and Satulah. Both of these summits are reached by short, easy trails.

The cliffs and rock outcrops are botanical treasure houses showcasing the southernmost distribution of numerous rock-loving plants which need a combination of altitude, bare rock and high rainfall to survive. These cliffs are excellent places to see peregrine falcons, ravens and wintering golden eagles.

This region encompasses the headwaters of the famed Chattooga River and is the major northern access to the Ellicott Rock Wilderness. Streams such as the Cullasaja fall off the plateau in steep gorges. Waterfalls are frequent. Vistas of the Rabun Bald country and Blue Valley, now an experimental forest, are visible from NC 106, especially at the Osage Mountain [Fig. 47(2), Fig. 47(3)] and Blue Valley overlooks.

~THE MOUNTAIN (LITTLE SCALY). [Fig. 47(4)] A short but narrow road leads to the summit, which is privately owned and affiliated with the Unitarian Church. It is an excellent example of a rock bald with an unusual forest of ancient, "krummholz" (wind-sheared) white oak, along with evergreen heath. This may be the oldest white oak stand in the world. Many trees have been dated between 400 and 500 years of age. A viewing tower is present. This is one of the very few instances in which one can drive to the summit of a granite dome.
DIRECTIONS: *About midway between Highlands and Scaly Mountain on the south side of US 64, a sign designates The Mountain.*

~WHITESIDE MOUNTAIN. [Fig. 48(19)] Whiteside is an outstanding example of the isolated, cliff-sided mountains characteristic of the Highlands/Cashiers area. Its summit offers fine views from a high ridgetop amidst the beauty and solitude of the forest. To the north the visitor can see Devil's Courthouse [Fig. 48(20)], a huge rock outcropping, and the headwaters of the Chattooga River. To the south are Whiteside Cove and a long view back into Georgia.

Whiteside Mountain is a magnificent and popular spot for eagle hacking, hang gliding and technical rock climbing. The mountain was known by the Indians as "the sitting-down place" because they camped there when traveling through the area. Legend says that Spanish explorers also visited the mountain as they passed through this part of the country.

EASTERN BLUE RIDGE

Satulah Mountain

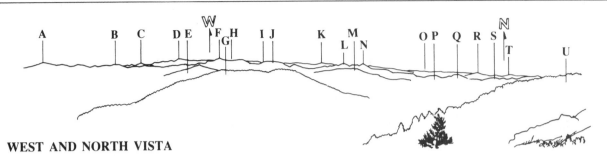

WEST AND NORTH VISTA

A - Rabun Bald
B - Osage Mountain
C - Wolfknob Mountain
D - Ridgepole Mountain
E - Little Scaly (The Mountain)
F - Scaly Mountain
G - Brushy Face Mountain

H - Albert Mountain
I - Wallace Gap
J - Fork Mountain
K - Nantahala Mountains
L - Jones Mountain
M - Dog Mountain
N - Big Fishawk Mountain

O - Great Smoky Mountains
P - Keener Mountain
Q - Rich Mountain
R - Cowee Bald
S - Flat Mountain
T - Plott Balsams
U - Satulah Mountain

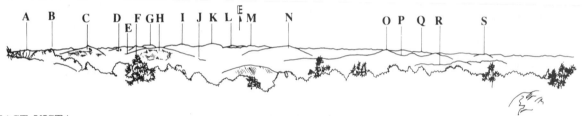

EAST VISTA

A - Richland Balsam
B - Balsam Ridge
C - Whiteside Mountain
D - Rocky Mountain
E - High Hampton Inn
F - Chimney Top Mountain

G - Toxaway Mountain
H - Blackrock Mountain
I - Sassafras Mountain (N.C.)
J - Chattooga Cliffs
K - Terrapin Mountain
L - Sassafras Mountain (S.C.)

M - Pinnacle Knob
N - Ellicott Mountain
O - Glade Mountain
P - Chattooga River Gorge
Q - Blue Ridge Escarpment
R - Buzzard Cliffs
S - Big Stakey Mountain (S.C.)

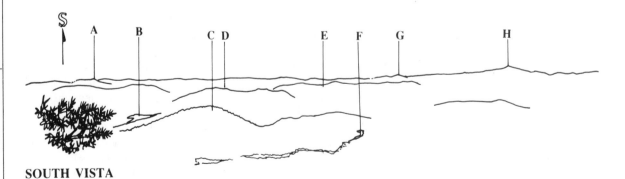

SOUTH VISTA

A - Big Stakey Mountain
B - Big Creek
C - Queen Mountain
D - Three Forks Wilderness

E - Hale Ridge
F - Clear Creek
G - Rainey Mountain
H - Rabun Bald

COMPILED BY CHARLES WHARTON AND NELL JONES
ILLUSTRATED BY MOZELLE FUNDERBURK

The U.S. Forest Service acquired Whiteside in 1974. The old road is now closed to motorized vehicles. The visitor can hike part or all of the two-mile loop trail to the 4,893-foot summit for a view of the valley floor, lying 2,100 feet below the surrounding mountains. The Whiteside Mountain Trail is designated a National Recreation Trail and is a component of the National Trail System.

Both the north and south faces of Whiteside contain sheer cliffs ranging from 400 to 750 feet in height. These cliffs were formed from igneous rock commonly called "whiteside granite" (actually a quartz diorite gneiss). This rock contains a high content of feldspar, quartz and mica, along with such minerals as pyrite and rare monazite. Due to the weathering and drying effects of wind and sunlight, the cliffs on the south side have little vegetation. Their blue-grey hue is the natural rock color. The very noticeable white streaks that decorate this side are veins of feldspar and quartz.

The north face, which receives less sunlight and more moisture, has a darker appearance due to the mosses and lichens that are able to grow in this more favorable environment.

Two distinct plant communities are present on Whiteside. First is the forest where oaks—particularly northern red oak—are dominant. Also commonly found in the forest are Fraser's magnolia, black birch, yellow birch, striped maple and witch hazel. Before the chestnut blight in the early 1900's destroyed all of the large chestnut trees, there was a concentration of chestnut here. There is an abundance of chestnut sprouts in the area, but they seldom reach more than three inches in diameter before dying.

The second community exists in the rock outcrops along the cliffs' edges and along trails. An abundance of flowering and non-flowering plants and shrubs grows here—some rare, all beautiful. The common shrubs include rosebay rhododendron, mountain laurel and flame azalea. Plants include false lily of the valley, several species of trillium, summer bluets, wild strawberry, sand myrtle, mats of spike moss on outcrops, and the rare Carolina hemlock.

FACILITIES: *Parking lot, two primitive toilets.*

DIRECTIONS: *From downtown Highlands, go east on US 64 for 5.5 miles to the Whiteside Mountain Road sign; turn right on paved road NC 1600 and go 0.6 mile; bear left at the Wildcat Ridge Road sign and go 0.35 mile; turn left into a gravel parking lot.*

~SATULAH MOUNTAIN.

[Fig. 47(21)] The summit of Satulah (4,543 feet) is classified as a heath bald. From here the visitor can view the mountains of three states.

Ascending the trail, one first encounters a forest comprised of northern red oak, white oak and chestnut oak. At the first switchback there begins a remarkable stand of mountain pepperbush overhanging the trail. Both chinquapin and witch hazel are common shrubs here. Soon hikers pass into a stunted, virgin oak forest. At the trail fork, go right. As one approaches the summit, the forest becomes heath (rhododendron) with stunted white oak. At the

Mountain pepperbush
Clethra acuminata

This large shrub, or small tree, has attractive flowers. It prefers moist sites with lots of light. It is outstanding along the Satulah Mountain Trail in Highlands. According to mountain lore, the dried fruits have been used as a condiment.

EASTERN BLUE RIDGE

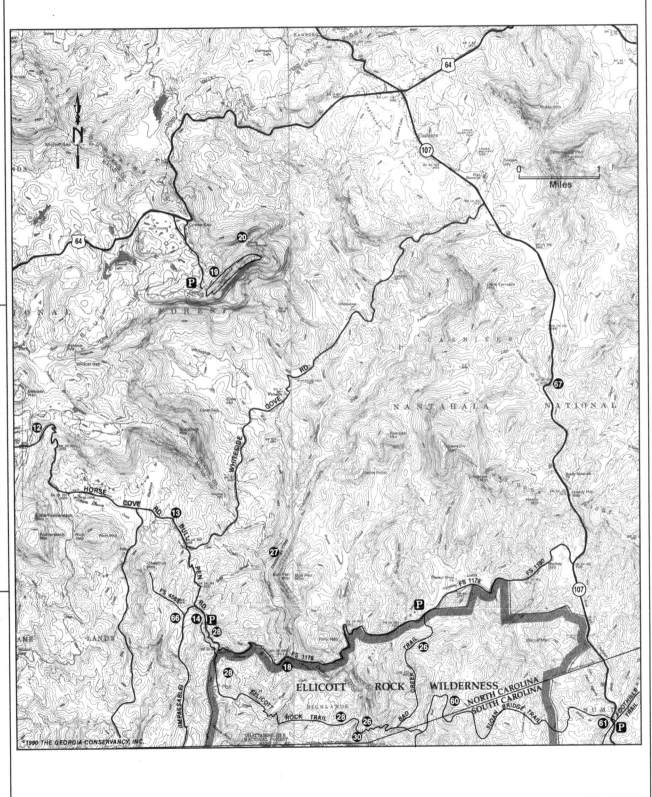

Figure 48 — **HIGHLANDS AND WHITESIDE MOUNTAIN**

EASTERN BLUE RIDGE

Fig. 48 - Highlands/Whiteside
(page references in parentheses)

12 Horse Cove Road (219, 220)
13 Bullpen Road (193, 220)
14 trailhead for Ellicott Rock Trail (221)
18 Bullpen Road Bridge/Ammons Branch
    Campground (193, 220, 223)
19 Whiteside Mountain (215)
20 Devil's Courthouse (215)
26 Bad Creek Trail (211, 212)
27 Chattooga Cliffs (193, 220)
28 Ellicott Rock Trail (211)
30 Ellicott Rock (193, 211, 212)
60 Sloan Bridge Trail (212)
61 Sloan Bridge Picnic Area (212)
66 Gravel Road - FS 121 to Heddon Creek
    Road (220)
67 Silver Run Falls (228)

summit are scattered, dwarfed white oak, some 200 years old. This is a zone with dwarfed pitch pine where a 200-year-old tree may be only 10 inches in diameter. The first purple rhododendron is encountered along with the first pines. Chinquapin is abundant.

The summit provides the best look at unusual plants growing only on the bare granite rock so characteristic of the cliffs of this area and extending into Georgia only on similar cliffs along the Chattooga headwaters. One of the most fascinating, the twisted hair spike moss, forms large, thick mats on the upper cliffs. Another, sand myrtle, grows only at the outer edge of the ground cover extending onto the rocks. A rare juniper forms low-spreading, wind-pruned growth. Exploring the summit, one can find curious potholes, the basement of a former firetower and patches of soil forming in moist depressions in the naked rock. Often on other outcrops, the niche of the pitch pine is filled by the rarer table mountain pine, and hemlocks might include the rare Carolina hemlock. In the spring the evergreen heaths on these balds present unequalled wildflower displays. The mountain summit is protected and offered for public use and education by the Satulah Summit and Ravenel Park, Inc.

DIRECTIONS: *From downtown Highlands, turn south on NC 28 and proceed up Fourth Ave. to Satulah Road, which begins at Calico Cottage Restaurant. Follow the Satulah Summit signs, bearing right at a fork, about 0.5 mile to the end of the pavement and continue 0.3 mile to a small parking area (five-car maximum) at a gated driveway. The trail is the ungated, rocky roadbed to the left.*

~THE HIGHLANDS NATURE CENTER. The center offers daily programs for children and adults, including lectures, nature classes, tours of the botanical gardens and outings. The center offers exhibits on local archeology, geology and biology, including live salamanders, snakes and fish. Fresh wildflower arrangements are available to help visitors identify local plants. Next door is the Appalachian Environmental Art Center, where one may enroll in classes in nature and landscape photography.

DATES/HOURS: *Open Jun.-Labor Day; 10-5 Mon.-Fri., 12-5 Sat.*
DIRECTIONS: *On Horse Cove Road [Fig. 48(12)], an extension of East Main St. in Highlands.*
ADDITIONAL INFORMATION: *The Highlands Nature Center. (704) 526-2623.*

~THE HIGHLANDS BIOLOGICAL STATION. Founded in 1929, the Highlands Biological Station hosts about 20 scientists and students annually for research in the field of biology of the southern Appalachians. On 20 acres, it maintains a rhododendron trail as well as one of the finest wildflower "gardens" in the Appalachians. The garden is a series of loop trails through the forest, with plants labeled along the way.

DIRECTIONS: *Either park at the nature center (above) and walk around back of it, or drive around (Sixth St. off Horse Cove Rd., turn* *right at sign) to where the trails actually start at the parking area of the biological station.*

~HORSE COVE ROAD [FIG. 48(12)] AND BULL PEN ROAD

[FIG. 48(13)]. This very scenic drive is a major entrance to the Ellicott Rock Wilderness from the north.

In Highlands, East Main Street becomes Horse Cove Road shortly before the nature center. Follow this winding paved road into beautiful Horse Cove. As one enters the cove, Wilson Gap Road is on the right. Approximately 200 feet up Wilson Gap Road on the right is the path to a giant poplar, the second largest in North Carolina and one of the three largest in the country. There is a direction sign to the tree. Back to Horse Cove Road, continue east to the fork at the end of the pavement. The right fork is Bull Pen Road, a beautiful one-lane gravel road that is something of a hiking trail for cars. Bull Pen Road crosses the Chattooga on an iron bridge. By the bridge is a good place to stop and view the river. The water has worn basins in the rocks from the size of a thumb print to larger than washtubs.

About 1.25 miles along Bull Pen Road, before reaching Ammons Branch Campground, is an unmarked single-lane gravel road [Fig. 48(66)] that connects FS 121 to Heddon Creek Road. However, it is not recommended as a drive, even with four-wheel-drive vehicles. It closely parallels the western boundary of the Ellicott Rock Wilderness.

From Bull Pen Road there is access to Chattooga River Cliffs Trail [Fig. 48(27)], Chattooga Loop Trail, The Chattooga Wild and Scenic River, Bad Creek Trail [Fig. 46(26)], Ellicott Rock Trail [Fig. 46(28)] and Ammons Branch Campground [Fig. 46(18), Fig. 48(18)]. The road returns to NC 107 south of Cashiers.

The left fork from Horse Cove Road is Whiteside Cove Road. A fine view from the bottom of Whiteside Mountain can be found in Whiteside Cove. This road returns to NC 107 in Cashiers.

~CULLASAJA RIVER GORGE. [Fig. 47(5)] US 64 runs between Highlands and Franklin, North Carolina, following the gorge cut by the Cullasaja River through the granite gneiss mountain and passing a number of waterfalls and scenic areas.

BRIDAL VEIL FALLS. [Fig. 47(11)] This falls cascades from a height of 120 feet over the highway, 1.2 miles west of Highlands. Basswood and yellow birch trees, characteristic of northern hardwood forests, are found in the vicinity.

DRY FALLS. [Fig. 47(10)] 2.1 miles from Highlands. There is plenty of parking, and the short trail down the cliff to the 75-foot falls is well marked. Those who do not mind getting a bit wet can walk under the falls to view the gorge. Mountain laurel is abundant.

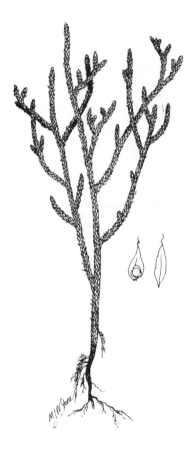

Twisted hair spike moss
Selaginella tortipila

Although not a moss, this unique plant forms dense mats on gentle, acid rock outcrops such as Satulah Mountain [Fig. 47(21), Fig. 42(16,18)] and Cedar Cliffs. Elsewhere, a much more common spike moss, *S. rupestris*, occupies the same niche, as on Tray Mountain [Fig. 26(50)].

In the area around both Bridal Veil and Dry Falls, visitors will see Fraser's magnolia, white pine, eastern hemlock and red maple along with dog-hobble, rosebay rhododendron and wild hydrangea. These falls nurture some extremely rare ferns.

LOWER CULLASAJA FALLS. Eight miles west of Highlands, this falls cascades about 250 feet. It is unmarked, but there is a pull-over area in which to park and view the falls. The trees in this area include tulip poplar, yellow birch, red oak and chestnut oak. Also present are grape, Virginia creeper and wild hydrangea.

~HIKING TRAILS IN THE HIGHLANDS AREA.

The Highlands Ranger District Office of the U.S Forest Service has descriptions and maps of hiking trails and waterfalls in the area, as well as brochures on wildflowers and on Whiteside Mountain. This literature adds to the enjoyment of a visit to the area. The office is on US 64, east of Highlands.

ELLICOTT ROCK TRAIL. [Fig. 46(28)] About 3.75 miles. One of the oldest trails in the area, Ellicott Rock Trail runs from the trailhead [Fig. 48(14)] to the surveyor's rock marking the intersection of Georgia, North Carolina and South Carolina. It follows an old road bed for over two miles, makes a left turn at a fork and descends to the Ellicott Rock Wilderness and the Chattooga River corridor. It then climbs steeply, crosses the Chattooga River and joins the Chattooga River Trail and Bad Creek Trail. Ellicott Rock is downstream on the far bank, inscribed with a simple "NC" [Fig. 46(30)]. The rock which most people find is actually Commissioner's Rock—the true intersection of the three states. It is located 10 feet downstream from Ellicott Rock and inscribed *LAT 35 AD 1813 NC SC*. Both rocks were named for surveyors who marked state boundaries. The return hike is more difficult than going in; the climb requires two hours or more.
DIRECTIONS: *Follow the directions to Bull Pen Road (above). Go on this road past a primitive campground and look for a sign on the right marked FS 441/F, which leads to a parking area. The trail starts on this old roadbed.*

BAD CREEK TRAIL. [Fig. 46(26)] Similar in terrain to the Ellicott Rock Trail (above). This trail follows an old road bed for about 0.75 mile to where an old road, now blocked off, led down to Bad Creek. The main trail continues with gentle ascents and descents for 1.5 miles, where it intersects the Sloan Bridge Trail. It then continues down steeply, with switchbacks for 1.5 miles to the river level. Here it joins the Ellicott Rock Trail and Chattooga River Trail. Ellicott Rock is one-eighth mile down stream.
DIRECTIONS: *The head of the Bad Creek Trail is about three miles east of the Bull Pen Road bridge. The old Forest Service road, 441/F, is closed. Unlimited parking is available about 50 yards away*

EASTERN BLUE RIDGE

across Fowler Creek Bridge. A trailhead marker is to be erected to replace the present Ellicott Rock Wilderness boundary sign.

YELLOW MOUNTAIN TRAIL. [Fig. 47(23)] About 9.4 miles, round-trip. The longest trail in the Highlands area leaves Cole Mountain Gap (4,200 feet) and traverses two peaks—Cole Mountain (4,600 feet) and Shortoff Mountain (5,000 feet)—and ends with a 360-degree panoramic view on Yellow Mountain (5,127 feet). The gneissic, oak ridge forest is dominated by white oak (formerly mixed with chestnut) with unusually abundant serviceberry as a sub-canopy. Offering trailside snacks in late summer and fall are two abundant heaths, deerberry and buckberry. In April to June there are floral displays. Masses of hayscented and New York fern offer pleasing vistas.

DIRECTIONS: *From the junction of US 64 and NC 28 in Highlands, go east on US 64 for 2.6 miles to Cole Mountain Road, also called Buck Creek Road; turn left at the Shortoff Baptist Church sign; go 2.2 miles to Cole Gap and park on the left side of the road. The trail sign is to the right.*

GLEN FALLS (BLUE VALLEY). [Fig. 47(22)] A gravel, one-lane, Forest Service road approximately 1.5 miles southwest of Highlands on the south side of NC 106 leads to Glen Falls. Follow this road about a mile to the parking area and a sign for Glen Falls Scenic Area. It is a short 0.5-mile walk to the falls. Glen Falls is a series of three falls, approximately 60 feet each, on the east fork of Overflow Creek. A steep one-mile trail with steps and places to rest along it goes down to the bottom of the falls, where the view is better. Be cautious, as the trail has washed away in some places. The trail continues down into Blue Valley Campground (primitive). Blueberries and rhododendron grow in the area. Glen Falls offers a magnificent vista over northeastern Georgia and northwestern South Carolina, the Chattooga River valley.

THE OLD TIFFANY SAPPHIRE MINE. In the Highlands/Cashiers area and eastward, corundum deposits have yielded many sapphires of gem quality. One community near US 64 is in fact named Sapphire. Several old mines are quite close to the highway. The trail to this mine is 1.5 miles long and fairly steep.

DIRECTIONS: *Follow the Blue Valley Road (FS 79) six miles west of NC 28 to the trailhead [Fig. 47(24)]. At a broken culvert in the west fork of Overflow Creek, cross the creek and take the right-hand trail [Fig. 47(25)], which was once used to drive livestock up to the grazing grounds in the "flats" between Scaly Mountain and Rabun Bald.*

Carolina hemlock
Tsuga caroliniana

This somewhat rare tree grows only around rocky outcrops. It forms an overstory near Highlands and can be seen around Tallulah Gorge and at Whitewater Falls in the Escarpment Gorge country. The needles are not in neat flat rows but appear scraggly on the twig.

~CAMPGROUNDS AND RECREATION AREAS.

BLUE VALLEY PRIMITIVE CAMPING AREA. [Fig. 47(29)] Go six miles south of Highlands on NC 28, turn right (west) on a gravel road into Blue Valley and then go three miles. The campground is on the right. There is a pit toilet. The water supply is from streams and should be boiled or treated before using. This camp area is recommended for groups.

VANHOOK GLADE CAMPGROUND. [Fig. 47(6)] About 4.3 miles west of Highlands (elevation 3,300 feet). The campground is open from about mid-May until late October, depending on the weather. Each of the 21 quiet, secluded, small campsites has a parking space, grill/fireplace, table and tent pad. A small- to medium-size trailer will fit the parking space; no RV's are allowed. A volunteer host is on site to answer questions. No group larger than family-size is permitted to camp. There are five water spigots and a flush toilet. The area is 1.5 miles from Cliffside Lake by either road or trail.

CLIFFSIDE LAKE RECREATION AREA. [Fig. 47(7)] 4.4 miles west of Highlands and 1.5 miles off US 64, Cliffside is open year-round but no water is available from the end of October until mid-May. There are 11 campsites, picnic tables and shelters, a bathhouse with cold showers and flush toilets and a clifftop vista shelter. There are no facilities for trailers. Cliffside Lake provides good trout fishing and a swimming beach. There are six marked hiking trails in the area ranging from 0.5 mile to 1.5 miles in length, including a loop trail around the lake [Fig. 47(9)] and another longer loop [Fig. 47(8)] which includes the crest of a nearby ridge. White pine and eastern hemlock trees, rhododendron, blackberry and mountain laurel grow in the campground.

AMMONS BRANCH CAMPGROUND. [Fig. 46(18), Fig. 48(18)] Located on the right about 1.5 miles from the fork at the beginning of Bull Pen Road (see above), marked with a Forest Service sign. This little-used, small campground may not be accessible by car after heavy rains. The only water supply is from streams and must be boiled or treated. There are three picnic tables, a grill and a pit toilet. A connector trail leaves from the campground, parallels Bull Pen Road and joins the Ellicott Rock Trail about .2 mile from its head on Bull Pen Road, one mile west of the bridge. There is limited parking at the trailhead.

ADDITIONAL INFORMATION: *Highlands Ranger District, U.S. Forest Service, Rt. 2, Box 385, Highlands, NC 28741. (704) 526-3766.*

MAP REFERENCES: *USGS 1:24,000 series: Highlands - Cashiers - Scaly.*

EASTERN BLUE RIDGE

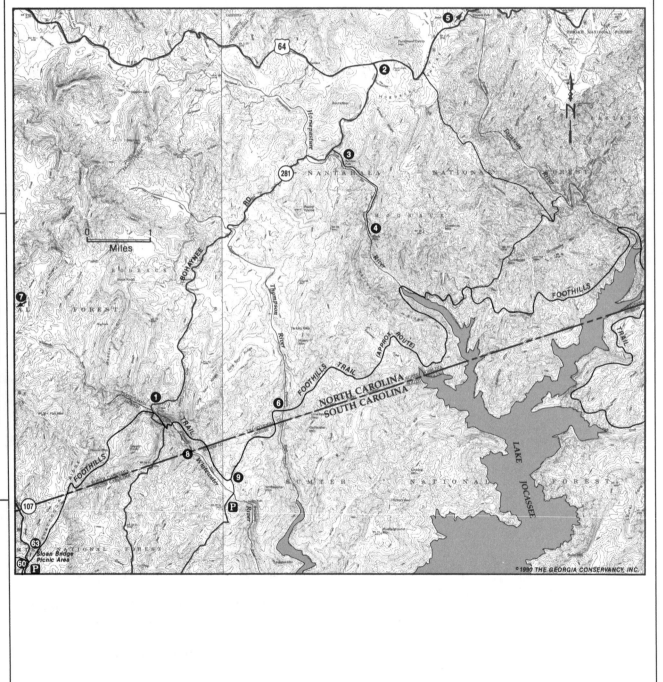

EASTERN BLUE RIDGE

Figure 49 — **ESCARPMENT GORGES**

224

Fig. 49 - Escarpment Gorges
(page references in parentheses)

1   Whitewater Falls (225, 226, 227)
2   Bohaynee Road (225)
3   Horsepasture River (225)
4   Windy Falls (225, 226)
5   Toxaway Dam (226, 227)
6   Thompson River Gorge (227)
7   Silver Run Falls (228)
8   Coon Branch Natural Area (227)
9   Whitewater Falls, lower (227)
61 Sloan Bridge Picnic Area (227)
63 Foothills Trail (227)

The Escarpment Gorges

At the southern edge of the Blue Ridge Mountains the terrain suddenly plunges in a steep escarpment to the Piedmont, over a thousand feet below. In this area rivers form deep gorges and dramatic waterfalls—some near roads and easily seen, others requiring hikes of varying lengths over rugged terrain.

~**WHITEWATER FALLS.** [Fig. 49(1)] At 411 feet, this is one of the highest waterfalls in the eastern United States. A five-minute walk on a paved path takes visitors to an overlook with a dramatic view of the falls.

To the right, about 100 steps down the gorge, is another excellent view. This is also a good place to see the rock-loving Carolina hemlock. Along the trail, just as it descends from the overlook, large colonies of the uncommon faded trillium may be found blooming in early May. The trail descends to Whitewater River in the bottom of the gorge. A spur trail goes north up the Whitewater River to the base of the falls. There Gleason's white trillium occurs. The rare green salamander is known to inhabit crevices below the falls.

To the left of the overlook, the visitor can follow the Foothills Trail (see below), which passes through this point to the head of the falls about a half mile away.

FACILITIES: *Parking area, picnic area, chemical toilet, bulletin board with trail information, paved path to overlook.*

DIRECTIONS: *From the intersection of US 64 and NC 281 (Bohaynee Road [Fig. 49(2)]), go south on NC 281. From I-85 north take SC 11, Cherokee Scenic Highway, north to SC 130/171; turn left and go to the entrance of Whitewater Falls picnic area (SC 130/171 becomes NC 281). Note that NC 281, or Bohaynee Road, crosses Horsepasture, Thompson and Whitewater Rivers on the edge of the escarpment.*

~**HORSEPASTURE RIVER.** [Fig. 49(3)] Includes Drift Falls, Turtleback Falls, Rainbow Falls, Stairstep Falls and Windy Falls [Fig. 49(3-4)]. These are a series of dramatic waterfalls along Horsepasture River, which has been designated a Wild and Scenic River.

DIRECTIONS: *To reach Horsepasture River [Fig. 49(3)] from the intersection of US 64 and NC 107, go east on US 64 and turn right (south) on NC 281, Bohaynee Road; go about 2.2 miles to a small off-road parking area just north of the bridge over Horsepasture River. Several paths and rough roads follow the river downstream and do not consolidate into one identifiable trail until below the first waterfall, Drift Falls. In the summertime this falls becomes a thrilling waterslide for adventurous daredevils. A quarter to a half mile downstream from Drift Falls is Turtleback Falls, where the river turns*

EASTERN BLUE RIDGE

*sharply right. Another quarter mile beyond that is Rainbow Falls,
which drops a stunning 150 feet over darkened, resistant Cashiers
gneiss. A broad spray zone supports interesting bog and seepage
area plants. The white water against the dark rock, and the blast of
spray, make a trip to Rainbow well worth the short hike. Continue
past Rainbow Falls another 0.5 mile to a campsite by a stream.
Cross the stream at the right end of the campsite and follow the trail
up the hill several yards to a path that goes down the ridge
to the river. Take the path to the river, where there is another campsite. To the left of the campsite is a trail following the river downstream. Hike along it to see the aptly named Stairstep Falls. Backtrack to the main trail on the ridge and then turn right and continue
walking old primitive roads. At each possible turn, go to the right.
After about two miles, come to the top of Windy Falls [Fig. 49(4)].
Here the Horsepasture is a roaring, windy, rushing, boulder-strewn
river in a remote gorge. Some boulders at the top of the falls are the
size of small cabins. Only Whitewater Falls [Fig. 49(1)] equals
Windy Falls in scenic beauty. Do not try to reach the bottom of
Windy Falls from the top. It is simply too treacherous. Instead, on a
separate overnight trip, follow the Horsepasture River upstream from
the Foothills Trail to the base of the falls. It is a three-to-four-hour
hike, well worth the time. Windy Falls may also be reached from the
bottom by way of a primitive road from Rosman, using a four-wheel-
drive vehicle.*
Caution: This is extremely rugged and dangerous country. Do not
walk or wade close to the rim of any falls. Rainbow Falls alone has
claimed a number of lives.

~**TOXAWAY DAM.** [Fig. 49(5)] This is the best place in all of
Appalachia to see how vulnerably thin and shallow mountain soil is,
and to witness the fragility of the mountain soils and vegetation. As
recounted in *The Floods of 1916* by the Southern Railway Company,
on July 5-6, 1916, a tropical cyclone came inland from the Gulf of
Mexico, reaching the western Carolinas around the 8th. A second
storm came in from the Atlantic, and there were tremendous rains on
the 15th and 16th in the same area. The French Broad River was
four feet, or flood stage, on the morning of the 15th. It had come
down from 8.8 feet on the 11th. But with the new rains on the
15th, the river rose to 13.5 feet at 8:00 a.m. on the 16th of July. By
9:00 a.m. on the same day, the river rose to 18.6 feet. At 10:00
a.m. the bridge on which the height of the river was measured was
washed away. The crest of the flood was estimated to be 21 feet.
It was this rain that washed away the dam at Lake Toxaway in 1916
and sent waters rushing down 16 miles of the Toxaway River Gorge.
The dam was not rebuilt until 1960. The force of the flood removed
all vegetation from the streamside zone, leaving a remarkable scene
of exposed bedrock clearly evident to the visitor today. The dam

Oconee bells
Shortia galacifolia

One of our rarest plants, *shortia* occurs only in the Escarpment Gorges from Toxaway River west to possibly the Chattooga watershed, where there is at least one possible natural colony. Shortia was found by Michaux in 1788, then "lost" and rediscovered in 1877 north of Lake Jocassee.

creating Lake Toxaway is just on the north side of the US 64 bridge over the Toxaway River [Fig. 49(5)].

~SLOAN BRIDGE HIKING TRAIL. To Whitewater Falls via the Foothills Trail. At the Sloan Bridge Picnic Area [Fig. 46(61), Fig. 48(61), Fig. 49(61)] the Foothills Trail [Fig. 46(63), Fig. 49(63)] goes south towards the Fish Hatchery Road and east to Whitewater Falls, while another trail goes west to Ellicott Rock (see Ellicott Rock section). The Foothills Trail to Whitewater Falls provides an interesting and different approach to the falls. This well-marked trail is only moderately difficult, 4.4 miles each way. Approaching the top of Whitewater Falls from upstream gives the hiker a fine view of the South Carolina Piedmont and the gorge. One could hike another 0.3 mile to the Picnic Area in the parking lot.
FACILITIES: *Picnic tables, a chemical toilet, parking.*
DIRECTIONS: *The beginning point for the hike, the Sloan Bridge Picnic Area, is on NC 107 about 0.2 mile north of SC 413.*

~FOOTHILLS TRAIL. To Thompson River Gorge [Fig. 49(6)]. About five miles one way. From the Whitewater Falls Overlook [Fig. 49(1)] (see directions above), descend into the gorge to the river and walk the Foothills Trail to Thompson River Gorge and the bridge crossing it. The trail follows Whitewater River downstream for about 1.6 miles. It then crosses over ridges and follows old roads for part of the way to Thompson River. Look for wild bergamot and several small falls. There is an especially nice slide just off the trail to the left about 10 yards before the trail makes a sharp right turn from an old road to descend into Thompson River Gorge. The rushing water, huge boulders and steep-sided gorge provide a sense of remoteness from civilization seldom found. Some adventurous hikers may wish to rockhop upriver to Thompson High Falls, one of the most beautiful falls in the Escarpment Gorge region. Allow two or more hours for this trip.

This is also one of the few areas where *shortia* or oconee bells, can be seen. According to Duncan and Foote, *Wildflowers of the Southeastern United States*, this flower is found in only seven counties in Georgia, South Carolina and North Carolina.

On the other side of Whitewater River a nature trail is marked at the point where the Foothills Trail leaves the river at 1.6 miles. Old trail books by Allen de Hart describe a cable bridge which crosses the river to the Coon Branch Natural Area [Fig. 49(8)]. The bridge is not there now, and the river may be too high to ford. The Duke Power folder also describes a road to this area with a parking lot and access to lower Whitewater Falls [Fig. 49(9)]. This access to the lower falls, however, is blocked by the Duke Power Bad Creek Reservoir Project. One can hike to the top of the lower falls, but it is not recommended, as it requires scrambling on unmarked fishermen's paths.

EASTERN BLUE RIDGE

~BACKPACKING ALONG THE FOOTHILLS TRAIL. One of the best ways to understand and learn about the Escarpment Gorges would be to backpack the Foothills Trail from Whitewater Falls to Toxaway River boat access or to US 178 at Laurel Valley. One could set up two cars, one at Whitewater Falls Picnic Area (see directions above) and the other at Laurel Valley. The distance would be 32.7 miles one-way along the Foothills Trail. The hiker would visit the gorges of the Whitewater River, Thompson River, Bear Camp Creek, Horsepasture River and Toxaway River.

DIRECTIONS: *For driving to Whitewater River Picnic Area, see above.*

ADDITIONAL INFORMATION: *For a brochure on the Foothills Trail, contact Duke Power Company Project Recreation, P.O. Box 33189, Charlotte, NC., (704) 373-8032; or the Foothills Trail Conference, P.O. Box 3041, Greenville, SC 29602.*

~SILVER RUN FALLS. [Fig. 48(67), Fig. 49(7)] Silver Run is one of the creeks merging into Whitewater River to create Whitewater Falls. The falls drops 30 feet into a marvelous open pool with its own beach. Sitting on a rock in this pool, one would imagine it to be very far from the road.

DIRECTIONS: *To reach the falls from the junction of US 64 and NC 107, go south four miles on NC 107. There will be a dirt parking area on the left side of the road. There are two such areas along this stretch; the one with the telephone pole is the correct one. The trail to Silver Run Falls starts by the pole and is an easy graded trail for 0.14 mile.*

MAP REFERENCES: *USGS 1:24,000 series: Cashiers - Reid. Duke Power Company Foothills Trail Brochure; Forest Service handout map with falls marked.*

Showy orchis
Orchis spectabilis

The attractive lavender and white flowers of the showy orchis are the crowning glory of spring wildflower displays. This orchid is neither rare, small nor inconspicuous. It spreads its charm on moist and shady slopes and in coves and ravines.

Chestnut-sided warbler
Dendroica pensylvanica

This warbler confines its breeding to high mountain forests—particularly open or brushy areas. Only one other warbler has reddish side markings.

The Cowee Gem Region

During the late 1800's, corundum—a mineral second in hardness only to diamond—was mined extensively in north Georgia and North Carolina. Corundum was valuable in the manufacture of abrasives such as sandpaper. Impurities in the mineral also resulted in gem-quality sapphires and rubies, which were sometimes found during the course of mining corundum ore. In fact, the mineralized zone running northeast and southwest through Georgia and North Carolina was second only to the Mogok region of Burma as a source of high-quality rubies and sapphires. After the discovery that, with plentiful electricity, aluminum oxide could be artificially fused to make corundum, the commercial mining operations quickly closed down, and the economics of gemstone mining never made it a viable industry in the area. Presently, Thailand seems to be the main source of gem-quality rubies and sapphires. In more recent years, serious rock hounds and those just simply curious have discovered that the Cowee gem region and a number of locations around Franklin, North Carolina, still produce valuable gems, primarily for the tourist market.

Most mines in Macon County are placer or gravel deposits. The gems weather out of decomposing bedrock higher in the watershed and are washed down by streams. Most of the gem mines furnish equipment, shovels, screens and running water to wash the gravel. Either there is a flat fee, or one pays for the processed gravel.

~**FRANKLIN GEM AND MINERAL MUSEUM.** [Fig. 50(1)] Located in the 15-year-old brick jail, the museum displays a variety of Macon County minerals, including a 48-pound corundum crystal. This is a good first stop on a visit to the area to become familiar with the appearance of the minerals and gems mined nearby.
DATES/HOURS: *Open May 1-Oct. 31.*
DIRECTIONS: *Located on Phillips St. in Franklin, NC.*

~**MINING OPERATIONS.** [Fig. 50(*)] A number of these mines lie along Caler's Fork [Fig. 50(3)] on Cowee Creek [Fig. 50(2)]. Many of these mines, as well as others in the area, have native gems such as rubies, sapphires and garnets. Some also sell "enriched" gravel by the bucket, meaning that exotic (and inexpensive) stones from all over the world have been added to the raw material.
FACILITIES: *Facilities vary at each mining location, but most have restrooms, picnic and play areas; some have campsites with showers; most provide assistance in learning how to search for gems.*
DATES/HOURS: Most mines are open from 8 or 9 in the morning until 5 or so in the evening, six or seven days a week. Season is generally from Apr. through Oct.
DIRECTIONS: *Go 6 miles north of Franklin on NC 28; turn right at West's Mill [Fig. 50(2)]; take the first road south, then the first road*

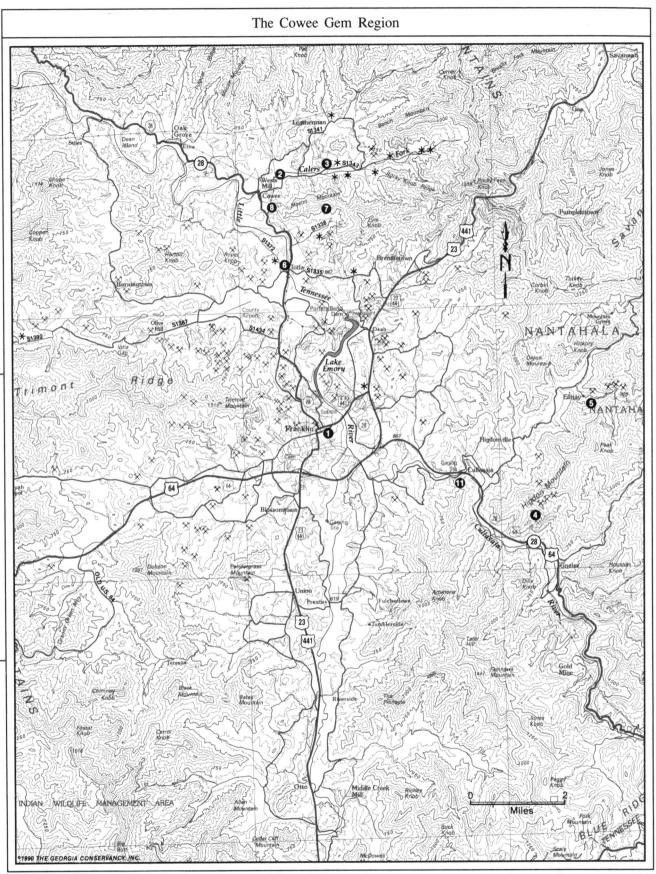

Figure 50 — **COWEE GEM REGION**

Fig. 50 - Cowee Gem Region
(page references in parentheses)

*   Mining Operations (229)
1   Franklin Gem & Mineral Museum/Nikwasi Indian Mound (229, 231)
2   Cowee Creek/West's Mill (229)
3   Cowee Creek/Caler's Fork (229)
4   Corundum Hill (231)
5   Mincey Mine (231)
6   mica open mines (231)
7   Mason Mountain (231)
8   Hwy 28 Marker showing Indian communities (231)
11 US 64 turn-off to Mincey Mine (231)

east (S1340) and follow that as it becomes S1341 and eventually S1343 along Caler Fork. Watch for signs.

~**CORUNDUM HILL.** [Fig. 50(4)] This famous corundum mine has yielded some fine gems, including sapphires in orchid, green, yellow, pink and blue, as well as 587- and 760-carat rubies. This deposit is associated with the ultrabasic rocks serpentine and dunite, as is the corundum at the Buck Creek olivine pine barrens.
DIRECTIONS: *Just north of US 64, about 5.5 miles east of the US 441/64 interchange in Franklin, NC.*

~**MINCEY MINE.** [Fig. 50(5)] This is another well-known deposit of unusual bronze sapphires which "star." No equipment is furnished here.
DIRECTIONS: *Go 2.4 miles east of the US 441/64 interchange on US 64, turning left [Fig. 50(11)] just before the first bridge and proceeding 5.8 miles to Ellijay. Inquire there.*

~**MASON MOUNTAIN.** [Fig. 50(7)] The Franklin area is also noted for the occurrence of a splendid rose-pink variety of pyrope garnet called "rhodolite," first discovered on Mason Mountain. One can visit the Mason Mountain Rhodolite Mine or screen or pan for garnets in the gravels of Mason's Branch, Cowee Creek and Caler Fork. With luck, amateur miners might recover a piece of ruby or sapphire corundum. Mason Mountain is just south of Caler's Fork. Watch for signs.

~**OTHER MINES.** A look at the map will indicate the stunning number of old or active mines in the area around Franklin (mine symbols). All are not gem mines. Some are giant open cuts where mica or other minerals were mined [Fig. 50(6)]. This particular mine has enormous amounts of almost pure-white quartz. Unfortunately there are no good maps to the location of Macon County mines, nor is there information as to what is or was mined at particular sites. A few mines are no longer on revised 7.5-minute topographical maps. Inquiring of local residents seems to be one of the most productive means of finding interesting localities.

~**NIKWASI INDIAN MOUND.** [Fig. 50(1)] The Franklin area is rich in Indian history and pre-history. Practically in the center of Franklin is an Indian mound on the south bank of the Little Tennessee River at the bridge. Near West's Mill there is a marker on NC 28 showing the location of the major Indian communities of Cowee [Fig. 50(8)] on the floodplain of the Little Tennessee River. Explorer and naturalist William Bartram passed through the Franklin area in the late 1700's.

MAP REFERENCES: *USGS 1:24,000 series: Green's Creek - Alarka -Franklin - Corbin Knob (NC).*

EASTERN BLUE RIDGE

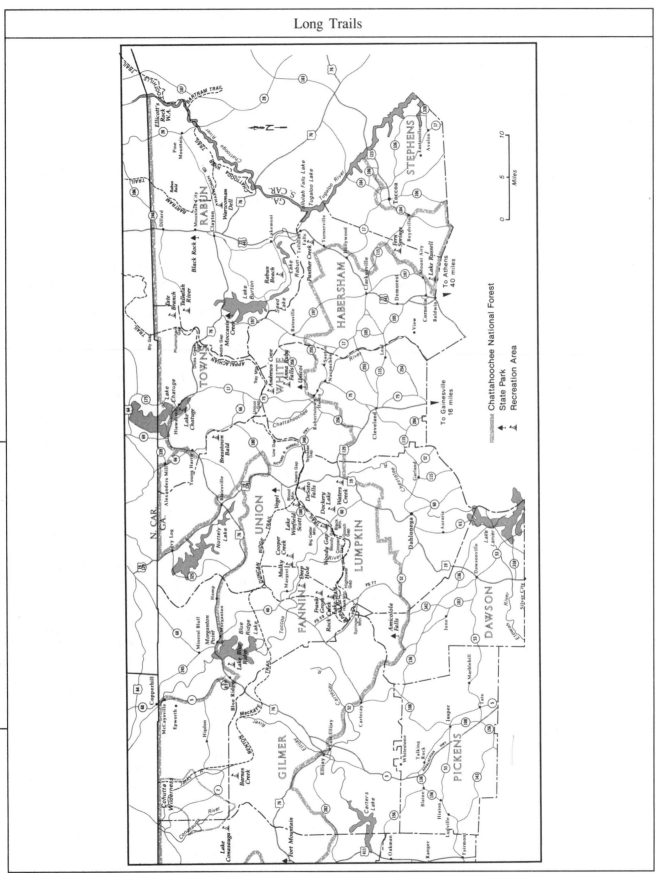

Figure 51 — **LONG TRAILS**

Long Trails

Three long trails—the Appalachian, the Benton MacKaye and the Bartram—provide hikers with an opportunity to cover long distances entirely by foot. In addition, by combining these three trails with the Foothills Trail in South Carolina, the resourceful hiker could travel between 360 to 400 miles across some of the most varied and dramatic scenery in the Southeast.

New England cottontail
Sylvilagus transitionalis

This high-mountain species is reddish in summer and has a dark patch between the ears. This rabbit ranges down the high ridges of the Appalachians and reaches its southern limits in Georgia.

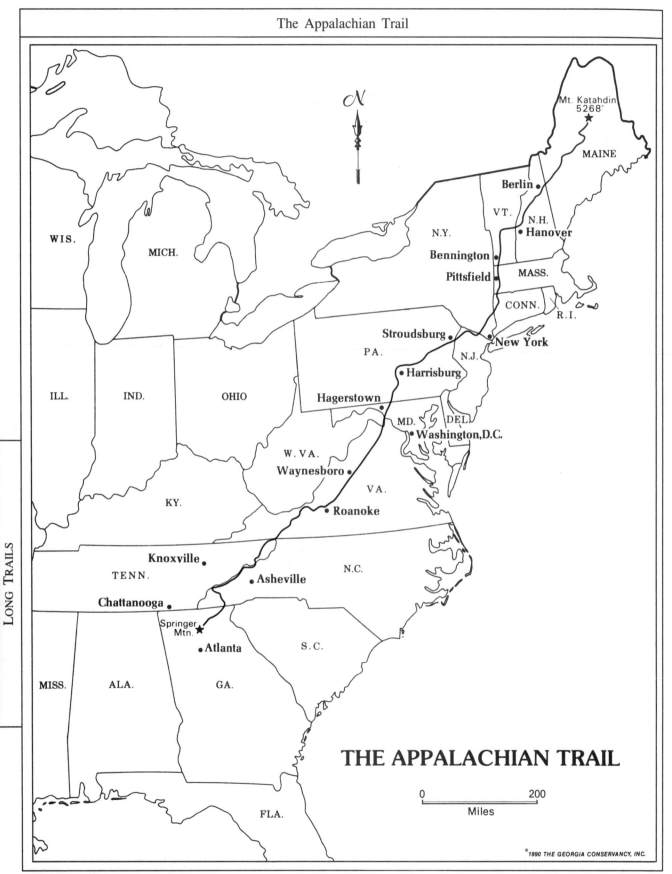

THE APPALACHIAN TRAIL

0   200

Miles

©1990 THE GEORGIA CONSERVANCY, INC.

LONG TRAILS

Figure 52 — **APPALACHIAN TRAIL**

Northern red oak
Quercus rubra

This is a prize timber tree that seldom reaches a density of over 10% of the forest. It is a principal tree on most of the high ridges (3,000-5,000 feet) of the southern Appalachians. Along the Appalachian Trail, red oaks are often dwarfed and deformed by altitude and wind; 200-year-old trees may be only 12 inches in diameter.

The Appalachian Trail

The Appalachian National Scenic Trail is a wilderness footpath that winds over 2,100 miles along the crest of the Appalachian Mountains. It runs through fourteen eastern states, stretching from Springer Mountain in Georgia to Mount Katahdin in Maine. The "A.T.," as it is called, is known throughout the world, each year attracting hikers from many different countries.

The trail began over 60 years ago with a "grand vision" articulated in 1921 by Benton MacKaye—forester, regional planner and conservationist. MacKaye, now known as the "Father of the Appalachian Trail," proposed a "long trail over the full length of the Appalachian skyline, from the highest peak in the North to the highest peak in the South." His proposal, not just a detailed trail plan, envisioned the long trail as an escape for people in the crowded cities of the Eastern Seaboard, a place for regeneration of the human spirit through what he termed "harmony with primeval influences." The work on the trail was to be done primarily by volunteers. Trail enthusiasts, some of whom had also suggested a "grand trunk" trail along the Appalachian ridges, were galvanized into action by Mac-Kaye and his inspiring article. The establishment of the Appalachian Trail was to be the culmination of many years of their hopes and dreams. Early hiking clubs in New England and New York had laid the foundations for this new trail; parts of their existing trails were used to form the first sections of the A.T. In 1925 the Appalachian Trail Conference was formed as a confederation of clubs which was to build and maintain the trail.

In the South little was known of the mountain areas, and a trail route was chosen largely from maps. In 1929 Roy Ozmer, a Georgian and accomplished woodsman, was chosen to scout the entire trail from Virginia through Georgia. Once a route was decided upon, volunteers were recruited, maintenance clubs were formed and, with the help of U.S. Forest Service and Civilian Conservation Corps crews in some places, the trail was built. The last section to be completed was in Maine in 1937.

The trail in Georgia was completed in 1931 through the combined efforts of members of the newly-organized Georgia Appalachian Trail Club and the U.S. Forest Service. The original southern terminus of the trail was Mt. Oglethorpe, near Tate, but development and chicken farming on private land between Amicalola Falls and Mt. Oglethorpe intruded on the wilderness experience of hikers, forcing the terminus to be moved in 1958 to Springer Mountain.

In 1968 Congress authorized the A.T. as the first National Scenic Trail; in 1978 it appropriated funds to acquire lands along the route to protect the trail from encroaching development. Maintenance of the trail rests with the Appalachian Trail Conference (ATC). In 1984, the Secretary of Interior signed a delegation agreement with

LONG TRAILS

ATC assigning to it unprecedented responsibilities for operation, development, monitoring and maintenance of the trail. Volunteers in A.T. clubs carry out these duties.

The Georgia portion of the A.T. extends some 75.6 miles through primitive areas of the Chattahoochee National Forest. Although rising at times to elevations of over 4,400 feet, the trail is mostly along ridges at elevations around 3,000 feet. Ascents and descents are sometimes steep but often rewarded by grand views from rocky outcrops and open summits.

Most of the A.T. goes through deciduous hardwood forest—largely hickory, oak and poplar. Rainfall is heavy and frequent, especially in the spring; ridges are often snow-capped or ice-covered in the winter. Mid-April through mid-May is the peak wildflower season. Flowers found along the trail include trillium, bloodroot, mayapple, bluets, wild azalea and sometimes pink and yellow lady slippers. In June many sections are covered with flowering rhododendron and mountain laurel. The heavy rains ensure lush vegetation during the summer months; ferns are found in abundance all along the trail. The last two weeks of October are usually the best time to find autumn colors at their height. In winter when the leaves are off the trees, the trail offers ever-present scenic vistas of the surrounding countryside and of the mountains of the north and west.

The Georgia portion of the trail is managed and maintained by the Georgia Appalachian Trail Club, through a cooperative agreement with the U.S. Forest Service, Chattahoochee National Forest. Members of the club may be found on the trail almost every weekend cutting weeds, clearing blowdowns, painting blazes, repairing shelters, reconstructing portions of the trail or participating in recreational hikes.

The trail's southern terminus is located atop remote Springer Mountain, near FS 42. Since this area is difficult to reach by automobile, an 8.5-mile approach trail begins at Amicalola Falls State Park on GA 52. Mountains along the trail with outstanding scenic views include Big Cedar Mountain, Blood, Cowrock, Rocky and Tray. One of the many side trails leads from Chattahoochee Gap to the highest point in Georgia, Brasstown Bald. The trail passes through three of Georgia's wilderness areas: Raven Cliffs Wilderness between Neel's Gap and Tesnatee Gap, Tray Mountain Wilderness between Tray Gap and Addis Gap and the Southern Nantahala Wilderness north of Dick's Creek Gap. Bly Gap on the Georgia/North Carolina border is the northern end of the A.T. in Georgia.

The trail is marked throughout its length with rectangular white blazes and is generally easy to follow. Double blazes indicate caution, usually meaning a turn in the trail. Side trails and trails to water are blue-blazed; signs are placed at road crossings, shelters and other important intersections.

Pileated woodpecker
Dryocopus pileatus

With the wetland-inhabiting ivorybill extinct or nearly so, the pileated is our largest and loudest woodpecker. A regal bird, resplendent in black, white and red, it is called "Lord God" by some mountain folk.

LONG TRAILS

There are 11 shelters on the Georgia A.T., placed more or less at intervals permitting easy day hikes. All but one of these shelters are three-sided, open-front types with floors. Springs are reasonably close by. The exception is the stone two-room structure atop Blood Mountain. It has four sides, a fireplace, windows and a sleeping platform. There is no water on top of Blood Mountain.

~**REACHING THE TRAIL.** There is no public transportation to the A.T. in Georgia. The trail can be reached via the six main highways which traverse the mountains; usually the trail crosses at the highway's highest point, where a large hiking trail sign should be visible. Ample parking is available.

~**ROAD CROSSINGS.** Approximate distances from the nearest town and distance by trail to the next paved road crossing:

AMICALOLA FALLS STATE PARK APPROACH TRAIL ON GA 52. Fifteen miles west of Dahlonega, 15 miles northwest of Dawsonville, 20 miles east of Ellijay. 28.8 miles by A.T. to Woody Gap.

WOODY GAP ON GA 60. Fifteen miles north of Dahlonega. 11.3 miles by A.T. to Neel's Gap.

NEEL'S GAP ON US 129/19. Fifteen miles south of Blairsville, 19 miles northwest of Cleveland, 22 miles north of Dahlonega. 5.7 miles by A.T. to Tesnatee Gap, 6.6 miles to Hog Pen Gap.

TESNATEE GAP AND HOG PEN GAP ON GA 348. (Richard Russell Scenic Highway). Twelve miles northwest of Helen, 15 miles southeast of Blairsville. 14.9 miles by A.T. from Tesnatee Gap to Unicoi Gap, 14 miles from Hog Pen Gap to Unicoi Gap.

UNICOI GAP ON GA 75. Ten miles north of Helen, 14 miles south of Hiawassee. 16.6 miles by A.T. to Dick's Creek Gap.

DICK'S CREEK GAP ON US 76. Eleven miles east of Hiawassee, 18 miles west of Clayton. 8.7 miles by A.T. to Bly Gap on North Carolina border (no road access).

NOTE: *The approach to Springer Mountain by automobile involves traveling on rough, unpaved Forest Service roads. One such road, FS 42, which runs from the town of Suches (enter from GA 60 next to Tritt's Store, 1.6 miles north on the highway from Woody Gap) provides access to several points along the trail, passing through Gooch Gap, Cooper Gap, Hightower Gap and Springer Mountain. It*

LONG TRAILS

also connects with FS 58 to Three Forks. An approach from SR 52 is through the Nimblewill community on FS 28/1 and FS 77 across Winding Stair Gap and then on FS 58 down to the A.T. at Three Forks.

~SUGGESTED DAY HIKES.

SPRINGER MOUNTAIN-THREE FORKS AREA. Highlights are views from a rocky outcrop atop Springer Mountain, southern terminus of the A.T.; the magnificent stand of virgin hemlock along Stover Creek; and three beautiful mountain streams which converge at Three Forks. From Springer Mountain both the A.T. and the Benton MacKaye Trail (marked by diamond-shaped white blazes) lead by different routes to Three Forks, intersecting twice to form either two five-mile loop trails or one 10-mile, figure-eight loop trail. Access to Springer Mountain is on unpaved FS 42 and to Three Forks, on unpaved FS 58. Both are moderate climbs.

BIG CEDAR MOUNTAIN. Views from rocky overlook; two-mile round-trip hike north on A.T. from Woody Gap.

BLOOD MOUNTAIN. Grand views from rocky summit and rock outcrops below summit; 4.2-mile round trip to top; south on A.T. from Neel's Gap; 1,300-foot climb.

LAKE WINFIELD SCOTT LOOP. Blue-blazed trail leads from the west side of the camping area one mile to Jarrard Gap on the A.T. and from the east side 2.2 miles to Slaughter Gap on the A.T. By following the A.T. between Jarrard and Slaughter Gaps, one can make a loop hike. An additional 2.2-mile round-trip hike can be made from Slaughter Gap to the summit of Blood Mountain.

NEEL'S GAP TO TESNATEE GAP. 5.7 miles one-way or 11.4 miles round-trip hike along ridge trail, with viewpoints from Levelland, Turkey Pen and Cowrock Mountains. At Neel's Gap the trail passes through the archway between two buildings at Walasi-Yi Inn, a hiking/craft store; moderate climbs.

WILDCAT MOUNTAIN. Viewpoints on summit and on top of ridge out blue-blazed side trail. One-mile round trip to summit plus one-mile round trip on blue-blazed trail; south on A.T. from Hog Pen Gap; easy to moderate climb.

ROCKY MOUNTAIN LOOP. Six-mile loop or three-mile round trip to summit; north on trail from Unicoi Gap. Fine views lie southward along the summit trail. For loop hike, continue along summit on A.T.; descend 1.3 miles to Indian Grave Gap; turn left (north) on forest road following blue blaze for approximately one mile; turn left off road into woods and follow blue blaze back to junction with A.T. (approximately one mile); 1,200-foot climb.

TRAY MOUNTAIN. Views from an open, rocky summit. A 10.8-mile round trip north on the trail from Unicoi Gap; or a one-mile round trip north on the trail from Tray Gap on FS 79 (access from GA 75, two miles north of Helen or two miles north of Unicoi Gap).

~TRAIL DESCRIPTIONS.

APPROACH: AMICALOLA FALLS STATE PARK. From visitor center, trail goes 8.5 miles north to summit of Springer Mountain. Frosty Mountain at mile 4.8 of approach trail; Nimblewill Gap at mile 6.2 of approach trail.

00.0 MILE. Springer Mountain (3,782 feet). Southern terminus of the A.T. Plaque on rock, mailbox with register on nearby tree. Mount Katahdin in Maine is 2,100 miles north via the white-blazed trail.

00.2 MILE. Springer Mountain shelter with seasonal spring. Located down side trail to right of A.T., 2.5 miles. Stover Creek shelter with all-season stream nearby. Located to left of A.T., down old logging road.

05.0 MILES. Long Creek Falls.

07.7 MILES. Hawk Mountain shelter; water from nearby stream.

08.2 MILES. Hightower Gap (gravel FS Rd 42).

16.7 MILES. Gooch Gap shelter to right; good spring 0.2 mile south on A.T.

20.3 MILES. Woody Gap (paved GA 60); parking.

21.3 MILES. Big Cedar Mountain; good rock ledges and views.

29.5 MILES. Blood Mountain (4,461 feet); highest point on the Georgia A.T. Fine views are afforded on clear days. Blood Mountain shelter is located on the summit. Closest water is in Slaughter Gap, one mile and 660-foot descent south on A.T.

LONG TRAILS

31.6 MILES. Neel's Gap (paved US 19); parking at Byron Reese, north on highway.

32.9 MILES. Levelland Mountain; views to right and left.

35.2 MILES. Wolf Laurel Top; views to right in clearing.

36.5 MILES. Cowrock Mountain; views on rocks via side trail to right.

37.3 MILES. Tesnatee Gap on GA 348, Russell Scenic Hwy.; parking.

38.0 MILES. Wildcat Mountain; views. Side trail leads right 1.1 miles to Whitley Gap shelter with dependable spring.

38.2 MILES. Hogpen Gap on GA 348; parking.

42.6 MILES. Low Gap shelter, right via side trail into cove; spring and stream nearby.

47.6 MILES. Chattahoochee Gap with spring, right via side trail, being the headwaters of the Chattahoochee River. 49.4 miles. Site of former Rocky Knob shelter, recently torn down. New shelter 0.5 mile north on trail; spring downhill below old shelter site.

50.0 MILES. Blue Mountain shelter via side trail to left; spring on A.T. just before turnoff to shelter.

52.2 MILES. Unicoi Gap (paved GA 75); parking.

57.6 MILES. Tray Mountain (4,430 feet); outstanding views from summit. On descent going north, obscure trail to right leads out an arm to pinnacle.

58.1 MILES. Tray Mountain shelter left via side trail; good spring behind and down from shelter.

63.4 MILES. Addis Gap shelter to right, 0.3 mile down old fire road; stream in front of shelter.

63.8 MILES. Dick's Creek Gap (paved US 76); picnic tables; seasonal stream.

73.1 MILES. Plum Orchard Gap shelter located to the right of the gap down side trail. Spring near shelter, but better spring down ravine to left of A.T.

77.5 MILES. Bly Gap; the Georgia/North Carolina state line. There is no road access to this gap except by four-wheel-drive vehicles. The gap is often missed by hikers because as one comes from the south, the gap is climbed into instead of descended into. Hikers know they have arrived when there is a gnarled tree to the right and a sweeping vista to the left.

80.7 MILES. Muskrat shelter in North Carolina to right; stream and privy next to shelter.

Lily of the valley
Convallaria montana

This rare plant is found in scattered colonies. The cultivated variety is very similar to the wild one, except the flowers are as tall as the leaves. The plant is poisonous. Like most lilies, it dies down completely in the winter.

LONG TRAILS

The Appalachian Trail in Georgia

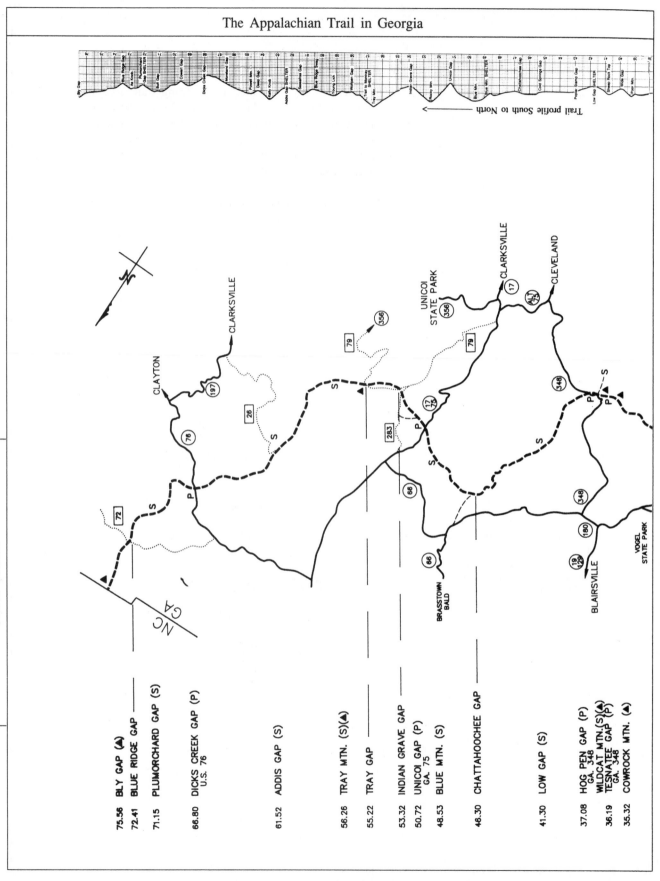

Trail profile South to North

Mileage	Landmark
75.56	BLY GAP (▲)
72.41	BLUE RIDGE GAP
71.15	PLUMORCHARD GAP (S)
68.80	DICKS CREEK GAP (P) U.S. 76
61.52	ADDIS GAP (S)
56.26	TRAY MTN. (S)(▲)
55.22	TRAY GAP
53.32	INDIAN GRAVE GAP
50.72	UNICOI GAP (P) GA. 75
48.53	BLUE MTN. (S)
46.30	CHATTAHOOCHEE GAP
41.30	LOW GAP (S)
37.08	HOG PEN GAP (P) GA. 348
36.19	WILDCAT MTN.(S)(▲) TESNATEE GAP (P) GA. 348
35.32	COWROCK MTN. (▲)

The Appalachian Trail in Georgia

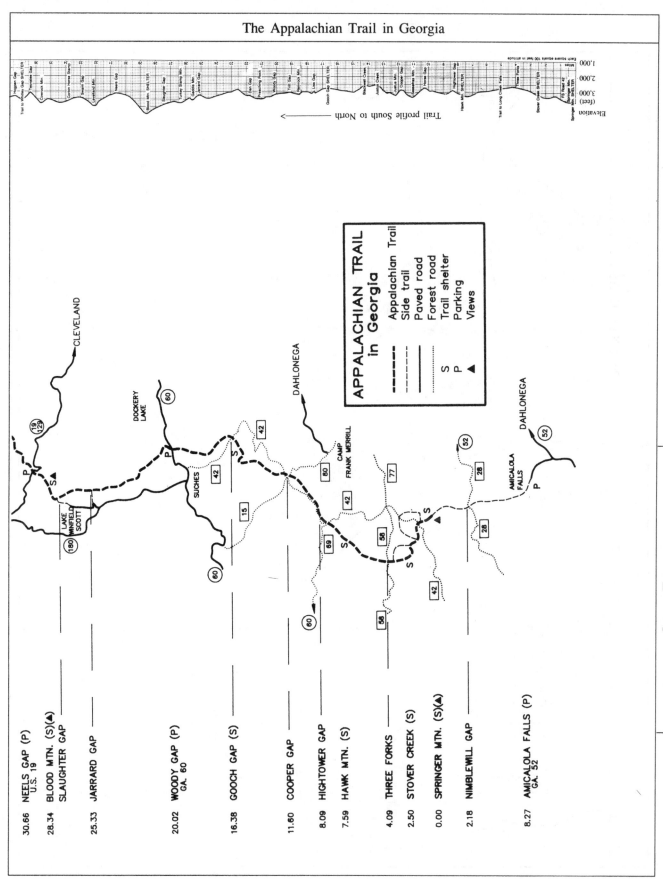

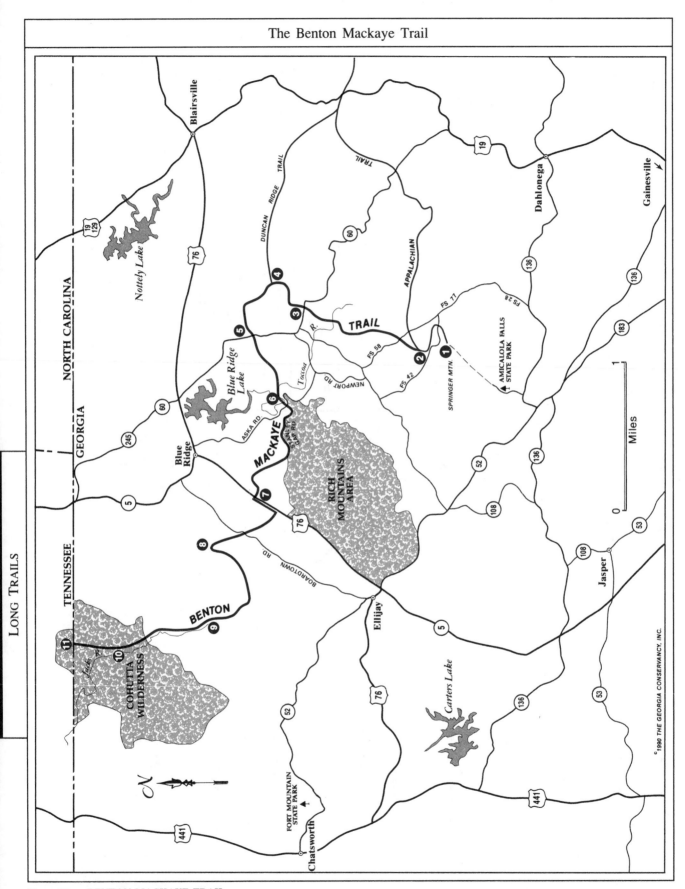

Figure 54 — **BENTON MACKAYE TRAIL**

The Benton MacKaye Trail

Fig. 54 - Benton MacKaye Trail
(page references in parentheses)

1 Springer Mountain (245)
2 Three Forks (245, 246)
3 Georgia Highway 60 (246)
4 Skeenah Gap (246)
5 Wilscot Gap (246)
6 Shallowford Bridge (246)
7 Georgia Highway 5 (246, 247)
8 Bush Head Gap (247)
9 Dyer Gap (247)
10 Watson Gap (247)
11 Double Spring Gap (247)

On October 14, 1989, many volunteers, along with a number of U.S Forest Service employees with whom they had worked jointly on the endeavor, celebrated the opening of the Georgia section of the interesting and diverse Benton MacKaye (pronounced Mac-eye) Trail (BMT). From its beginning at Springer Mountain, the trail's distance covers 78.6 miles to the border of Tennessee in the Cohutta Wilderness. The trail should eventually wind through Tennessee and North Carolina, forming a 250-mile loop with the Appalachian Trail and providing an alternative long-distance footpath in the Southeast.

Named for Benton MacKaye, the "Father of the Appalachian Trail" (see above), this trail grew out of the need to develop an alternative to the popular Appalachian Trail and also to develop a trail that more closely adhered to MacKaye's original trail plan—a plan that envisioned a path reaching to the Cohuttas in the north-central portion of Georgia.

Although the trail is new, volunteers have already documented much of the variety along its path. Two beautiful waterfalls, Long Creek Falls and Fall Branch Falls, are scenic attractions. Atop Rhodes Mountain in the winter, one is afforded a 360-degree view of the surrounding countryside. A striking man-made attraction is the suspension bridge across the beautiful Toccoa River. The terrain varies from laurel-and-rhododendron-covered walks along creeks to timbered land to ridgetop pathways to walks through thick forests. There are areas with quick access to major highways through Georgia, as well as quite remote areas within and south of the Cohutta Wilderness. There is a 26-mile stretch of trail with only two road crossings.

The BMT is blazed with an off-white diamond symbol. The blazes are located at approximate intervals of 200 feet. There may be other blazes present, such as the white, vertical two-by-six-inch stripe of the A.T. or the two-by-six-inch vertical blue blaze of the Duncan Ridge Trail. These blazes are present only along the first 20 miles of the BMT and will not be seen west of Rhodes Mountain. See below for other trail blazes in the Rich Mountain area and in the Cohutta Wilderness area.

ADDITIONAL INFORMATION: *Write the Benton MacKaye Trail Association, P.O. Box 53271, Atlanta, GA 30355-1271.*

~TRAIL DESCRIPTIONS.

SECTION 1: SPRINGER MOUNTAIN [FIG. 54(1)] TO THREE FORKS [FIG. 54(2)]. 5.8 miles, south to north. Easy. This section essentially traverses the pre-1977 corridor of the A.T. It is well-constructed, well-blazed and relatively easy. Access roads are FS 42 and FS 58 (Noontootla Creek Road).

SECTION 2: THREE FORKS [FIG. 54(2)] TO GA HWY 60 [FIG. 54(3)]. 11.4 miles, south to north. Moderate. This section is contiguous in part with the A.T. and entirely with the Duncan Ridge Trail. It is moderate in difficulty and is essentially an overnight hike. Highlights of this section are the dramatic Forest Service suspension bridge over the Toccoa River and the newly created wildlife opening where many animals and plants may be readily seen. Access roads are FS 58 and GA 60.

SECTION 3: GA 60 [FIG. 54(3)] TO SKEENAH GAP [FIG. 54(4)]. 5.7 miles, south to north. Difficult. This section is the most strenuous part of the BMT. The view from the top, however, after the character-building climb up the south face of Wallhalah Mountain, is worth the effort. Note that at Rhodes Mountain the Duncan Ridge Trail turns east-northeast, while the Benton MacKaye Trail regains its own identity and proceeds westward. Access roads are GA 60 and Skeenah Gap Road

SECTION 4: SKEENAH GAP [FIG. 54(4)] TO WILSCOT GAP [FIG. 54(5)]. 5.3 miles, east to west. Moderate. An up-and-down hike through general forest area. This is a very nice day hike, especially in winter, with views of the adjacent ridges and pastoral valleys. Access roads are Skeenah Gap Road and GA 60 at Wilscot Gap.

SECTION 5: WILSCOT GAP [FIG. 54(5)] TO SHALLOWFORD BRIDGE [FIG. 54(6)]. 7.1 miles, east to west. Moderate. The most difficult part of this hike is the initial climb up Tipton Mountain. After this, the trail undulates over Brawley Mountain and Garland Mountain before descending to the beautiful Toccoa River. The climbs will challenge, and the beauty of the forest is rewarding. Access is by GA 60 and adjacent Forest Service road, Dial Road and Aska Road. The number of access points allows for shorter hikes if desired.

SECTION 6: SHALLOWFORD BRIDGE [FIG. 54(6)] TO GA HWY 5 [FIG. 54(7)]. 11.4 miles, east to west. Moderate. This is an obvious overnight trek, but may be shortened to a very pleasant day hike by skipping 3.2 miles of road walk on the eastern end and 1.6 miles of road walk on the western end, taking only the 6.6-mile trail from Fall Branch to Laurel Creek. This section provides many sites atop Rocky and/or Davenport Mountains or Scroggin Knob to stop, rest and enjoy the views. Fall Branch Falls is a highlight right at the start, and the view from Scroggin Knob near the end of the hike is also pleasurable. It is here, climbing Rocky Mountain, that the BMT begins to follow the western arm of the Blue Ridge. White square blazes designating the contiguous Rich Mountain Trail will also be seen here. The BMT will follow this ridge to its current terminus at the Georgia-Tennessee state line at Double Spring Gap. Access to the forested portion is via Stanley Gap Road, 3.2 miles west of where it and Aska Road intersect, and the Weaver Creek Road at its southwest end at the USFS boundary line.

SECTION 7: GA 5 [FIG. 54(7)] TO BUSH HEAD GAP GAP [FIG. 54(8)]. 6.6 miles, east to west. Easy. This is a road walk along the public roads of Gilmer County. The scenery ranges from mobile homes to second-home developments to farm dwellings. Roads include Gilmer County Road 187, Boardtown Road and the Bush Head Gap Road.

SECTION 8: BUSH HEAD GAP [FIG. 54(8)] TO DYER GAP [FIG. 54(9)]. 12.6 miles, north to south and south to north. Moderate. A long day-hike or a very pleasant overnight trip, this part of the BMT is located entirely along the Tennessee Valley Divide. This is general forest land and many activities of the multi-use forest, such as logging, will be seen here. Road access is by the Bush Head Gap Road and FS 64 south of Watson Gap at the northern end.

SECTION 9: DYER GAP [FIG. 54(9)] TO WATSON GAP [FIG. 54(10)]. 4.5 miles, south to north. Easy. A very short segment of the BMT, this footpath traverses riverside forest timber management activity areas, and then climbs a mountain with views of the Cohutta Wilderness before returning to the trailhead. Road access is by FS 64 at Dyer Gap and the old SR 2 at Watsont Watson Gap.

SECTION 10: WATSON GAP [FIG. 54(10)] TO DOUBLE SPRING GAP [FIG. 54(11)]. 8.5 miles, south to north. Moderate. This section along the high ridge is located primarily within the Cohutta Wilderness boundary. It is minimally blazed and semi-primitive in construction. The BMT is contiguous with the Hemptop Trail north of Dally Gap. The blazing changes once again, but the former Forest Service road provides an easily-followed path. Road access is at Watson Gap. Double Spring Gap is at the Georgia-Tennessee state line in the middle of the wilderness. A trail here leads north.

Garter snake
Thamnophis sirtalis

This is the snake most often encountered in terrestrial mountain environments at all elevations. It is fond of frogs and toads.

LONG TRAILS

247

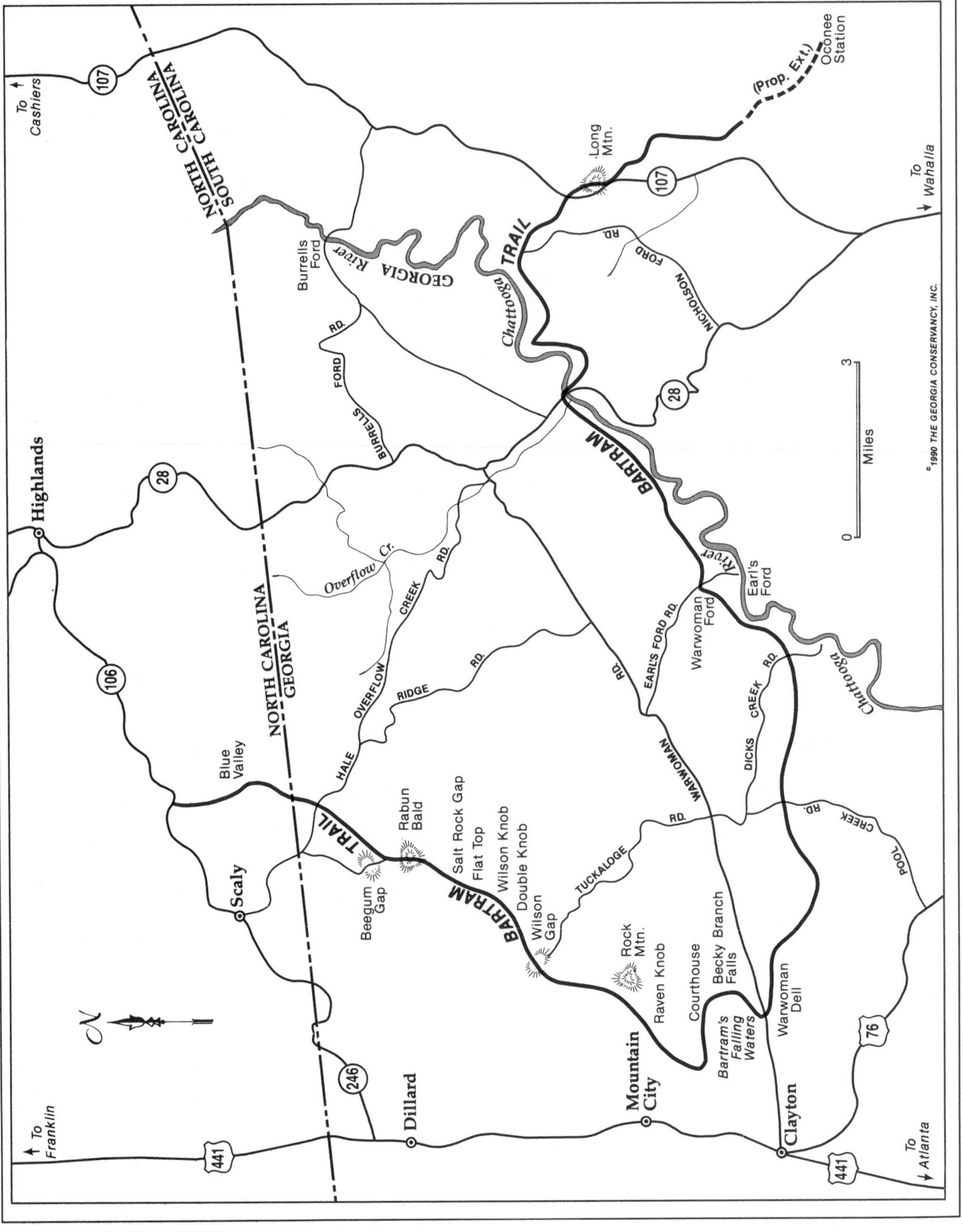

Figure 55 — **BARTRAM TRAIL**

The Bartram Trail

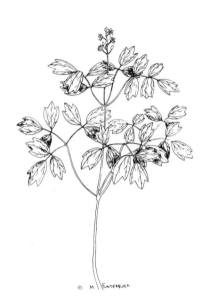

Blue cohosh
Caulophyllum thalictroides

This characteristic plant of the deep mountain coves, unlike some of its cohorts such as baneberry and black cohosh, does not seem to occur in the northern Piedmont. It has blue berries which are poisonous.

William Bartram was a native Philadelphian from a prominent family boasting kinship with Benjamin Franklin. In his early 30's, Bartram first traveled with his father, John Bartram, in Florida and coastal Georgia, becoming enamored with the Southern wilderness—a fascination which was to launch him on a career that would lead to worldwide fame. An instinctive naturalist and explorer, he roamed through Georgia, Florida, South Carolina and Alabama and as far west as Louisiana from 1773 until 1778, studying and drawing the plants and animals of the region and collecting plant specimens for his livelihood. His voluminous illustrated journals of those trips serve as the basis for the Bartram Trail, a portion of which now winds through the north Georgia mountains.

The northern end of the Bartram Trail begins about one mile east of Commissioner's Rock on the Georgia/North Carolina line, where it crosses NC 106 at the Osage Mountain overlook. It heads southwest for approximately three miles across the headwaters of Holcomb Creek. It then joins an old jeep road at Beegum Gap and follows it up a ridge two miles to Rabun Bald—Georgia's second highest mountain at 4,696 feet. At Rabun Bald, an old abandoned Forest Service fire tower was converted by the Youth Conservation Corps into an observation deck utilizing a natural rock base built by the Civilian Conservation Corps in the 1930's. The trail goes southwest for about seven miles, following the Tennessee Valley Divide, and provides several beautiful vistas of the surrounding Blue Ridge Mountains. At Courthouse Gap, the trail turns southeast and follows Finney Creek and Martin Creek for about three miles; a turn back to the west here takes the trail to the crossing of Warwoman Road and into Warwoman Dell Picnic Area. From Warwoman Dell, it winds in a general easterly direction until it reaches Sandy Ford Road where the trail turns north along the Chattooga River for about three miles to its present point of completion on the west bank of Warwoman Creek at Earl's Ford Road. Another section is the portion that continues from Warwoman Creek to the confluence of the West Fork of the Chattooga River with the Chattooga River. In the future, a suspension bridge will carry the trail across the West Fork, where it will continue up the Chattooga to the GA 28 bridge and across into South Carolina.

Although there are extremely large white pines and hemlocks where the trail passes through Warwoman Dell, the vegetation of the Bartram Trail is not spectacular. It does, however, expose hikers to a representative cross-section of north Georgia plant life. Changes in elevation, with a steady drop from Rabun Bald to Warwoman Road, and somewhat abrupt directional changes from shady north-facing slopes to sunny west and south exposures, provide habitat for many distinct plant communities. Sourwood, sugar maple, red maple, sweet birch, hemlock, white pine, pitch pine, Fraser's magnolia (discovered by Bartram) and a variety of oaks and hickories make up the second-growth tree population. Spicebush, sweetshrub, dog hobble and blueberries inhabit the shrub level. The trail cuts through large colonies of galax growing under massive mountain laurel and rosebay rhododendron thickets. Numerous fern species grow on the north-facing slopes and near the small streams and springs that cross the trail, including Christmas, northern maidenhair, royal, cinnamon, interrupted, marginal wood, lady and New York fern. Running ground pine, a club moss, grows in abundance in some areas. Typical wildflowers include Vasey's and Catesby's trilliums, trailing arbutus, partridge-berry, rattlesnake plantain and wild ginger.

MAP REFERENCES: *The Bartram Trail is shown on maps throughout this book.*

Wild turkey
Meleagris gallopavo

This remarkably large ground-dwelling bird, unique to North America, was proposed as a national bird by Benjamin Franklin. It feeds extensively on nuts and berries in the fall. Turkeys roost in trees at night.

Other Long Trails and Cross-Georgia Hike

The Foothills Trail, The Duncan Ridge Trail and the Chattooga River Trail are among the longer trails found throughout the Georgia Mountains. They are descibed throughout this guide.

It has been suggested that one can hike across Georgia on first-class trails from the Cohutta Wilderness to Table Rock State Park in South Carolina. The new Benton MacKaye Trail goes from the Cohuttas to Springer Mountain, where it connects with the Appalachian Trail. The Appalachian Trail can then be hiked to Wayah Bald in North Carolina, at which point it connects with the Bartram Trail. The hiker can then turn east on the Bartram Trail and travel through North Carolina and Georgia (Rabun Bald) to the Chattooga River in South Carolina, where the Bartram Trail intersects with the Foothills Trail. The Foothills Trail can then be hiked to its terminus at Table Rock. It is estimated that the total distance would be 360 to 400 miles, depending on where the Benton MacKaye and Bartram Trails are completed. Spur trails and outstanding features are numerous.

MAP REFERENCES: *Trails are marked on maps throughout this book.*

Fraser's magnolia
Magnolia fraseri

The magnolia is a primitive tree and a southern element that has invaded the mountains. Of the two principal mountain species, Fraser's is easy to identify by the "ear lobes" at the base of the rather large leaves borne in a radial cluster.

A. Map Sources

The enjoyment and usefulness of this guidebook will be greatly enhanced by the employment of maps in conjunction with the text. A vast amount of information is available from the following sources:

~TOPOGRAPHICAL MAPS OF ALL STATES

Powers Elevation Co., Inc., *P.O. Box 440889, Aurora, CO 80044. (800) 824-2550. All USGS topos: $3.75 for 1:24,000, $6 for 1:100,000, plus postage and handling charge from $2 to $10 per order. Visa, Mastercard and American Express accepted. Allow five to ten days.*

Timely Discount Topos, Inc., *9769 West 119th Drive, Suite 9, Broomfield, CO 80020. (800) 821-7609. All USGS topos: $3.50 for 1:24,000, $5.50 for 1:100,000, plus postage and $1 handling charge per order. Checks only. Allow five to ten days.*

The U.S. Geological Survey, *Map sales, Box 25286, Denver, CO 80225. (303) 236-7477. Call 1-800-USA MAPS first for a free index with order form. Cost: $2.50 for 1:24,000, $4 for 1:100,000. Allow six to eight weeks.*

~TOPOGRAPHICAL MAPS OF GEORGIA

Enpro Engineering Reprographics, *1800 Peachtree St., Suite 210, Atlanta, GA 30309. (404) 355-8520. Cost: $3 for 1:24,000, $4.50 for 1:100,000, plus postage and $1.89 if maps are rolled rather than folded. Allow five to eight days.*

The Georgia Geological Survey, *Agriculture Bldg., Room 406A, 19 Martin Luther King Jr. Dr. SW, Atlanta, GA 30334. (404) 656-3214. Cost: $2.50 for 1:24,000; $4 for 1:100,000 plus 5% sales tax and postage. Allow three to five days.*

~TOPOGRAPHICAL MAPS OF WESTERN NORTH CAROLINA AND OF TOWNS COUNTY AND RABUN COUNTY, GEORGIA

Macon County Supply Company, *190 Depot St., Franklin, NC 28734. (704) 524-4428. Cost: $3.75 for 1:24,000. Raised relief maps of GA, NC, SC and TN. $14.95 for 1:125,000.*

Black Rock Mountain State Park, *Mountain City, GA 30562. (404) 746-2141. Raised relief maps of all Central and Southern Appalchian*

APPENDICES

areas (AL through PA). $15.95 for 1:125,000 quads. USA raised relief maps $15.95.

~STATE PARK MAPS

The Georgia Department of Natural Resources, Parks, Recreation and Historic Sites Division, *Floyd Tower East, 205 'Butler Street SE, Suite 1362, Atlanta, GA 30334. (404) 331-5187. To make reservations, call the appropriate park at the number listed in Appendix B.*

~FOREST SERVICE MAPS

The U.S. Department of Agriculture, *Forest Service, Southern Region, Suite 850, 1720 Peachtree Road NW, Atlanta, GA 30367-9102. (404) 347-2384. Or, in limited quantities, from USFS ranger stations throughout Georgia. Cost: free, $2, $5. Maps used for this guidebook included The Cherokee National Forest, The Appalachian Trail, The Chattahoochee National Forest, The Chattooga National Wild and Scenic River, The Cohutta Wilderness, The Nantahala Wilderness, and The Southern Nantahala Wilderness and Standing Indian Basin.*

~TVA MAPS OF LAKES BLUE RIDGE, CHATUGE AND NOTTELY

The Tennessee Valley Authority, Maps and Surveys Dept., *101 Haney Bldg., 311 Broad St., Chattanooga, TN 37402-2801. (615) 751-6277. Cost: $.75 or $1.50 plus a handing/mailing charge of $1, or 10% for orders over $50.*

~ARMY ENGINEERS' LAKE MAPS OF CARTERS LAKE AND LAKE ALLATOONA

The U.S. Army Corps of Engineers, *Public Affairs Office, 30 Pryor Street SW, Atlanta, GA 30303. (404) 331-6715.*

~STATE HIGHWAY MAPS AND COUNTY ROADMAPS

Alabama Highway Department, *1409 Coliseum Blvd., Rm. R-103, Montgomery, AL 36130. (205) 261-6071.*

Georgia Department of Transportation, *Map Sales Division, 2 Capitol Square, Atlanta, GA 30334. (404) 656-5336.*

North Carolina Department of Transportation, *Map Sales Division, Location and Survey Unit, P.O. Box 25201, Raleigh, NC 27611. (919) 733-7600.*

South Carolina Highway Department, *Map Sales Division, P.O. Box 191, Columbia, S.C. 29202. (803) 737-1501.*

Tennessee Department of Transportation, *Map Sales Office, Suite 1000 James K. Polk Building, 505 Deaderick Street, Nashville, TN 37219-5538. (615) 741-2195.*

Note: Information on road conditions in Georgia is available from the Georgia Department of Transportation at (404) 656-5267.

APPENDICES

Chipmunk
Tamias striatus

The chipmunk, or "ground squirrel" as it is known to the mountaineers, also occurs in the Piedmont. It is one of the seven sleepers—mammals that hibernate through the winter. A fellow sleeper is the groundhog, or "whistlepig," seldom found outside the mountain country.

B. State Parks in the Mountains

Georgia's state parks are operated by the Parks, Recreation and Historic Sites Division, Georgia Department of Natural Resources, Floyd Tower East, Suite 1352, 205 Butler St. SE, Atlanta, GA 30334. The following state parks are in the mountain region covered by this guidebook.

Amicalola Falls, *Star Route, Dawsonville, GA 305341. (404) 265-2885.*

Black Rock Mountain, *Mountain City, GA 30562. (404) 746-2141.*

Cloudland Canyon, *Route 2, Box 150, Rising Fawn, GA 30738. (404) 657-4050.*

Fort Mountain, *Route 7, Box 1K, Chatsworth, GA 30705. (404) 695-2621.*

James H. "Sloppy" Floyd, *Route 1, Summerville, GA 30747. (404) 857-5211.*

Moccasin Creek, *Route 1, Lake Burton, GA 30523. (404) 947-3194.*

Red Top Mountain, *Cartersville, Ga 30120. (404) 974-5184.*

Unicoi, *P.O. Box 849, Helen, GA 30545. (404) 878-3366.*

Vogel, *Route 1, Box 1230, Blairsville, GA 30512. (404) 745-2628.*

Georgia's state parks offer excellent opportunities to enjoy a variety of natural environments. There is much to see and do including hiking, swimming, camping, fishing, boating and picnicking.

All state parks in the Georgia mountains offer tent and trailer camping, and all but two ("Sloppy" Floyd and Moccasin Creek) offer cottages for rent. Day use picnicking is not allowed in the camping areas. No fees are charged for fishing in park lakes, rivers and streams, but a valid Georgia fishing license is required of all residents 16 or older. Non-residents must have a valid, non-resident license. Trout stamps are required for fishing in streams. Canoes, fishing boats and boats with motors are available for rent at many state parks.

APPENDICES

~CAMPGROUNDS

Campgrounds are open from 7 am to 10 pm and require registration and payment of a fee before setting up camp. Permits to set up camp should be obtained by 8 pm; checkout deadline is 3 pm. Arrivals at campsite after hours will be asked to pay the following morning.

Camping rigs plus two boat trailers and one pup tent are allowed on each site. Park campgrounds have picnic tables with benches, electrical hook-ups, water faucets, charcoal grills, playground equipment, garbage pick-up and restrooms with hot and cold water, showers and lavatories. Some have sanitary dumping stations, coin-operated laundromats, public telephones and refreshment vending machines. Maximum occupancy of any particular site is 14 days. Campers under 18 must be accompanied by a responsible adult.

Organized groups are expected to use group campsites or pioneer camping areas rather than individual, developed tent and trailer camping areas. No RV's are allowed in these areas.

Group camps, available only to groups with a camp director or official supervising committee, offer sleeping quarters, kitchen, dining/assembly room, craft shops, activity field and swimming area.

Reservations for stays of two days or more can be made up to 30 days in advance by calling the numbers listed below. There is a small non-refundable registration fee. Mastercard and Visa are honored for all camping fees.

~COTTAGES

All cottages in the state parks are fully equipped with stoves and refrigerators, necessary cooking and serving equipment, linens and blankets. All are heated; most are air-conditioned. Maximum period of occupancy is 14 days.

Check-in time for cottages is between 4 and 10 pm; check-out time is 11 am. No pets are allowed in cottages and there are no kennnels available. The cottages are not available to organized groups.

Cottage reservations are accepted no more than 11 months in advance. For June 1 to Labor Day, reservations made more than 30 days in advance must be for a minimum of one week—otherwise, and during the remainder of the year, for two nights. A minimum 72-hour cancellation notice is required for a refund. There is a $10-per-unit cancellation fee.

Mayapple
Podophyllum peltatum

The fruits of mayapple are eaten raw and made into marmalade. Although the vegetative parts are poisonous, both the Indians and early settlers used the plant for medicinal purposes. Sledloads were sold by some mountain families.

C. Outfitters, Guides and Suppliers

The following is a listing of some of the outfitters providing specialized equipment and/or guided expeditions in the Georgia mountains and beyond.

Back Country Adventures. *Sales and rental of backpacking, camping and mountain biking equipment. Guided backpacking and mountain bicycling trips in north Georgia and North Carolina. Rt. 2, Box 2242-A, Persimmon Rd., Clayton, GA 30525. (404) 782-6489.*

Bargain Barn. *Sales of hunting, fishing, archery, camping and backpacking equipment. Hwy. 53, P.O. Box B, Jasper, GA 30143. (404) 735-3340.*

Blue Ridge Mountain Sports. *Sales of backpacking, camping, canoeing and kayaking equipment and rental of backpacking and camping equipment. Lenox Square Mall, 3393 Peachtree Road NE, Atlanta, GA 30326. (404) 266-8372.*

Call Of The Wild. *Sales of backpacking, camping, canoeing, fly fishing and rock climbing equipment and rental of backpacking and camping equipment. 425 Market Place, Roswell, GA 30075. (404) 992-5400.*

Chattooga Whitewater Shop. *Sales and rental of canoeing, kayaking and rafting equipment. Instruction in canoeing, kayaking and rafting. Shuttle service on the Chattooga River. Cost: $10-$30. US 76, Long Creek, SC 29658. (803) 647-9083.*

Georgia Outdoors. *Sales and rental of canoeing, fishing, backpacking and camping equipment. 6518 Roswell Rd., Sandy Springs, GA 30324. (404) 256-4040.*

Go With The Flow. *Sales of canoeing, kayaking and windsurfing equipment and sales and rental of windsurfing equipment. 4 Elizabeth Way, Roswell, GA 30075. (404) 992-3200.*

High Country Outfitters, Inc. *Sales of rock climbing equipment and sales and rental of backpacking, camping, canoeing and kayaking equipment. Location 1: 595 Piedmont Ave., NE, Atlanta, GA 30308. (404) 892-0909. Location 2: 1349 Cumberland Mall, Atlanta, GA 30339. (404) 434-7578. Location 3: 4400 Ashford Dunwoody Rd., 1412 Perimeter Mall, Atlanta, GA 30346. (404) 391-9657. Location 4: The Mall at Green Hills, 2168 Abbott Martin Rd., Nashville, TN 37215. (615) 383-1007.*

APPENDICES

The History Store. *Sales of maps and books on southern Appalachia, official US geological surveys, topography maps, guide books and field guides. 114 North Park St., P.O. Box 358, Dahlonega, GA 30535. (404) 864-7225.*

Mountain Crossing. *Sales of camping and backpacking equipment. Route 1 Box 1240, Blairsville, GA 30512. (404) 745-6095.*

Mountain Crossing at Walasi-Yi Center. *Sales of backpacking and camping gear, specializing in long distance trips. Operation of seasonal hostel (March 1 - May 31) on Appalachian Trail. Advice and information on local trails and campsites. Hwy. 129, Rt. 1, Box 1240, Blairsville, GA 30512. (404) 745-6095.*

Mountaintown Outdoor Expeditions. *Sales and rental of canoeing, kayaking, camping, backpacking and mountain biking equipment. P.O. Box 86, Ellijay, GA 30540. (404) 635-2524.*

Mountain Ventures. *Sales of camping, backpacking, rock climbing, caving and canoeing equipment and rental of camping and backpacking equipment. 3040 N. Decatur Rd., Scottdale (Decatur) GA 30079. (404) 299-5254.*

Nantahala Outdoor Center. *Sales of paddling, bicycling, backpacking, rock climbing and camping equipment and rental of canoeing, kayaking and rafting equipment. Instruction in canoeing, kayaking, backpacking and rock climbing. Guided raft trips on the Chattooga, Nantahala, Ocoee, French Broad and Nolichucky Rivers. Adventure travel expeditions to many destinations within and outside the U.S. U.S. 19 West, Box 41, Bryson City, NC 28713 (704) 488-2175.*

Outback Outfitters & Bikes. *Sales of mountain bikes and accessories, backpacking and camping equipment and apparel. 1125 Euclid Ave. NE, Atlanta, GA 30307. (404) 688-4878.*

REI. *A consumer cooperative offering sales of camping, backpacking, climbing, boating and skiing equipment and mountain bikes. Comprehensive rental department. 1800 NE Expressway, Atlanta, GA 30320 (Intersection of Clairmont and I-85). (404) 633-6508.*

Rock Creek Outfitters. *Sales of rock climbing, camping, backpacking, canoeing and kayaking equipment and rental of backpacks and tents. 4825 Hixson Pike, Chattanooga, TN 37443. (615) 877-6256.*

Smoky Mountain Sports. *Sales and rental of canoeing, kayaking, backpacking and camping equipment. 1226 Clairmont Road, Decatur, GA 30030. (404) 325-5295.*

Southeastern Expeditions. *Guided raft trips on the Chattooga and Ocoee Rivers. 2936H N. Druid Hills Road, Atlanta, GA 30329. (404) 329-0433.*

Wilderness Southeast. *Nonprofit outdoor school offering adventure trips throughout the Southeast and to the Virgin Islands and Costa Rica. 711 Sandtown Road, Savannah, GA 31410. (912) 355-8008.*

The Wildewood Outpost. *Sales and rental of canoeing and rafting equipment. P.O. Box 119, Helen, GA 30545. (404) 865-4451.*

Wildwater Ltd. Outdoor Adventures. *Guided raft trips on the Chattooga and Ocoee Rivers. Long Creek, SC 29658 (803) 647-9587.*

Wolfcreek Wilderness. *Nonprofit outdoor school offering leadership training and instruction in backpacking, canoeing and rock climbing. Rt. 1 Box 1190, Blairsville, GA 30512. (404) 745-5553.*

Turkey vulture
Cathartes aura

Turkey vultures breed on ledges in mountain cliffs. In soaring flight, they may be distinguished by the V-shaped wing profile as seen from front or rear. Hawks and eagles hold their wings in a flat plane.

APPENDICES

Pignut hickory
Carya glabra

Along with the mockernut, the pignut most often occurs in drier ridge and slope forests and in south-facing coves. Gray squirrels are among the few animals that can successfully eat hickory nuts. Hogs are reputed to be able to crack the husks of the pignut. The American Indian crushed hickory nuts with rocks, then mixed them with water so the shells could be easily separated from the meat and oil.

D. Books and References

The following books and booklets will help to illuminate the botany, geology, geography, commerce and culture of the Georgia mountains.

A Directory to North Carolina's Natural Areas *by Charles E. Roe, NC Natural Heritage Foundation, 1987, 1988 (second printing).*

Appalachian Whitewater, Volume 1 The Southern Mountains *by Bob Sehlinger, Don Otey, Bob Benner, William Nealy and Bob Lantz, Menasha Ridge Press, Birmingham, AL 1986.*

The Atlas of Georgia *by Thomas W. Hodler and Howard A. Schretter, The University of Georgia, Athens, GA 1986.*

Atlas of The Vascular Flora of Georgia, A Georgia Botanical Society Project *compiled by Marie B. Mellinger and edited by Harriett L. Whipple, Studio Designs Printing, Milledgeville, GA 1984.*

Brown's Guides series *edited by Alfred W. Brown, Creative Publications and Membership Groups, Inc., Atlanta, GA 1990, 1991.*

Foxfire *series edited by Eliot Wigginton, Anchor Press/Doubleday, Garden City, NY 1975.*

The Chattooga Wild and Scenic River *by Brian Boyd, Ferncreek Press, Conyers, GA 1990.*

The Hiking Trails of North Georgia *by Tim Homan, Peachtree Publishers, Ltd., Atlanta, GA 1987.*

Inns of the Southern Mountains *by Patricia L. Hudson, EPM Publications, McLean, VA 1985.*

More Mountain Spirits *by Joseph Earl Dabney, Bright Mountain Books, Asheville, NC 1980.*

Mountain Getaways *by Rusty Hoffland, On the Road Publishing, Atlanta, GA 1988.*

Mountain Singer, The Life and The Legacy of Byron Herbert Reece *by Raymond A. Cook, Cherokee Publishing Company, Atlanta, GA 1980.*

Mountain Spirits *by Joseph Earl Dabney, Charles Scribner's Sons, New York, NY 1974.*

APPENDICES

The Natural Environments of Georgia *by Charles H. Wharton, Georgia Department of Natural Resources, Atlanta, GA 1978.*

North Carolina Hiking Trails, *Second edition by Allen de Hart, Appalachian Mountain Club Books, Boston, MA 1988.*

Northern Georgia Canoeing *by Bob Sehlinger and Don Otey, Menasha Ridge Press, Birmingham, AL 1980.*

The Travels of William Bartram *edited by Mark Van Doren, Dover Publications, Inc., New York, NY 1955.*

Trees of the Southeastern United States *by Wilbur H. Duncan and Mirion B. Duncan, The University of Georgia Press, Athens, GA 1988.*

Waterfalls of the Southern Appalachians *by Brian Boyd, Ferncreek Press, Conyers, GA 1990.*

Wildflowers of the Southeastern United States *by Wilbur H. Duncan and Leonard E. Foote, The University of Georgia Press, Athens, GA 1975.*

Bird-foot violet
Viola pedata

This plant, often abundant on roadbanks in the mountains, has a large, showy purple flower. Its leaves are divided into a fan-shaped array of lobes resembling a bird's foot.

E. Special Events, Fairs and Festivals

Attendance at a select few annual events in the mountains will give the reader a good insight into mountain history, culture and people. Following are some of the best of these events. Dates are subject to change.

Annual Harvest Sale—*Crafts and antiques show in Blue Ridge in October. (404) 632-5680.*

Clarkesville Fall Festival—*Arts and crafts show, Georgia 115 east of Clarkesville in October. (800) 822-0316.*

Dahlonega Blue Grass Festival—*At Blackburn Park on Old State Rd. 9E, 7 miles west of Dahlonega in June. (404) 864-3721.*

Fall Harvest Festival—*Country music, arts and crafts at fairgrounds in Hiawassee in October. (404) 896-4191.*

Fasching Karnival—*In Helen in December and January. (404) 878-2248.*

Georgia Apple Festival—*Crafts show in Ellijay in October. (404) 635-7400.*

Georgia Mountain Fair—*12 days of crafts exhibits and entertainment at fairgrounds in Hiawassee in August. (404) 896-4191.*

Harvest Festival—*Arts and crafts at farmer's market on U.S. 441 in Dillard. (404) 782-4812.*

Helen to the Atlantic Hot-Air Balloon Race—*May 30-June 1. (404) 878-2521.*

Helen's Oktoberfest—*German food, beverage and entertainment in Helen in October. (404) 878-2521.*

Mountain Maffick—*Arts and crafts festival, Hwy. 441 south of Clayton in May and October. (404) 782-5246.*

New Echota/Cherokee Fall Festival—*Festival of Cherokee Indian culture, on GA 225, 3 miles east of Calhoun in October. (404) 629-8151.*

Prater's Mill Country Fair—*Arts and crafts festival, Ga. Hwy. 2, 10 miles north of Dalton in May and October. (404) 259-5765.*

APPENDICES

The Reach of Song—*An Appalachian drama presenting the Georgia mountains through the life and words of native poet Byron Herbert Reece; in Hiawassee in June and July. (404) 536-3431.*

Sorghum Festival—*in Blairsville in October. (404) 745-5789.*

Spring Country Music Festival—*At fairgrounds in Hiawassee in May. (404) 896-4191.*

F. Conservation and Outdoor Organizations

All of the following are non-profit organizations dedicated to the enjoyment and/or preservation of nature's bounty in the Georgia mountains and beyond.

Atlanta Audubon Society—*Box 29217, Atlanta, GA 30359. (404) 364-9479. Conservation and environmental education, including bird study. Monthly programs on environmental concerns. News hotline concerning programs and bird sightings.*

Atlanta Whitewater Club—*P.O. Box 33, Clarkston, GA 30021. (404). 299-3752. Whitewater canoeing and kayaking. Emphasizes improvement of outdoor skills, safety and appreciation of river sports.*

Benton MacKaye Trail Association—*P.O. Box 53271, Atlanta, GA 30355. Enjoyment and maintenance of the Benton MacKaye Trail. Monthly hikes and trail maintenance along sections of the trail.*

The Dogwood City Grotto—*1865 Ridgewood Dr. NE, Atlanta, GA 30307. Atlanta chapter of the National Speleological Society. Cave protection, conservation and exploration. Monthly outings to explore caves in the Southeast.*

ForestWatch—*1819 Peachtree Road NE, Suite 714, Atlanta, GA 30309. (404) 355-1783. Protection of national forests and the preservation of their biodiversity. Annual workshops and frequent field trips to monitor road building and timbering on national forest land.*

Friends of the Mountains—*Box 368, Clayton, GA 30525. Preservation and enjoyment of the Southern Appalachian Mountain environment. Quarterly business meetings and conservation fair each spring. Monthly outings to natural areas in north Georgia and western North Carolina.*

Georgia Appalachian Trail Club, Inc.—*P.O. Box 654, Atlanta, GA 30301. Maintenance of the Appalachian Trail and approach trails in Georgia. Weekly hikes and outings. Monthly trail maintenance.*

Georgia Botanical Society—*7575 Rico Road, Palmetto, GA 30268. Furthering the appreciation of wildflowers. Monthly or semi-monthly outings throughout Georgia and contiguous states.*

Georgia Canoeing Association—*P.O. Box 7023, Atlanta, GA 30357. River enjoyment and conservation. Training programs and weekly*

Land snail
Anguispira alternata and
Triodopsis albolabris

Land snails and stream-inhabiting salamanders would be the most dependable source of protein food for someone lost in the mountains. Only millipedes are more commonly encountered invertebrates in moist mountain habitats.

APPENDICES

paddling trips in Georgia and contiguous states.

The Georgia Conservancy, Inc.—*781 Marietta Street NW, Suite B100, Atlanta, GA 30318. (404) 876-2900. 711 Sandtown Road, Savannah, GA 31410. (912) 897-6462. Protection of Georgia's environment and the encouragement of responsible stewardship of our vital natural resources. Annual conference, naturalist trips and chapter activities.*

Georgia Ornithological Society—*P.O. Box 1278, Cartersville, GA 30120. Furthering education about and understanding of birds. Semi-annual statewide meetings for field study, fellowship and information exchange.*

Georgia Wildlife Federation—*1936 Iris Drive, Conyers, GA 30207. (404) 929-3350. Conservation of wildlife and its habitat, and state-wide environmental education programs. Sponsors the premier awards program to recognize conservation achievement in Georgia.*

Ens And Outs—*Unitarian Universalist Congregation of Atlanta, 1911 Cliff Valley Way NE, Atlanta, GA 30329. Preservation and enjoyment of nature. Weekly outings to a variety of destinations throughout the state.*

The Nature Conservancy—*1401 Peachtree St. NE, Suite 136, Atlanta, GA 30309. (404) 873-6946. Preservation of rare and endangered species and natural communities through protection of the ecosystems that sustain them. Annual general membership meetings and field trips throughout the year.*

North Carolina Bartram Trail Society—*Route 3, Box 406, Sylva, NC 28779. Development, maintenance and enjoyment of the Bartram Trail.*

The Sierra Club, Georgia Chapter—*P.O. Box 46751, Atlanta, GA 30346. Exploration, enjoyment and preservation of the nation's forests, waters, wildlife and wilderness. Seven chapters throughout Georgia with monthly meetings and frequent outings to locations throughout the Southeast.*

Trout Unlimited, Georgia Council—*5074 Odins Way, Marietta, GA 30067. Protection, preservation and enhancement of cold water fisheries.*

The Wilderness Society—*1819 Peachtree Road NE, Suite 714, Atlanta, GA 30309. (404) 355-1783. Protection of natural areas on our federal lands, including national forests, national parks and national wildlife refuges. Helps coordinate activities of the citizen group, ForestWatch.*

Ringneck snake
Diadophis punctata

Usually only a foot long, this beneficial little black snake with a yellow neck ring eats bugs and worms. It lives under logs and rocks and may, on occasion, enter mountain houses.

G. Safety in the Mountains

~ADVANCE PLANNING — Before setting out on a backpacking or canoeing trip into the mountains, do your homework. Become familiar with the maps of the area and learn to use a compass. Consider taking a short first-aid course to prepare for emergencies. Plan your trip in advance, let others know where you are going and when you expect to return, and travel with a companion.

~EQUIPMENT AND SUPPLIES — Prepare a list of essentials, including the following:

WATER. Carry one or more unbreakable bottles of fresh water. Consider taking also a simple water treatment system for emergency water purification.

FOOD. Carry enough food for the duration of the trip, plus extra for the unexpected. Include quick energy items such as trail mix (*gorp*).

COMPASS AND MAPS. A good map allows exploration of areas which otherwise might not be attempted. If lost without a map of the area, use the compass to walk in a straight line in the direction of a known landmark, such as a road.

FIRST AID SUPPLIES. Carry a basic first aid kit containing bandages, tape, aspirin, moleskin, disinfectant or antiseptic, analgesic tablets, a small mirror and any personal medicines, as well as sunscreen, lip protection, sunglasses and other supplies appropriate to the season and conditions.

FLASHLIGHT. A day outing may last longer than expected. Carry a reliable flashlight and an extra bulb and batteries.

POCKET KNIFE. A multi-purpose knife is essential.

WATERPROOF MATCHES AND/OR LIGHTER. A fire for signaling, warmth or cooking food may become necessary because of injury, delay, isolation or sudden weather change.

SPACE BLANKET. This compact, light-weight material with a reflective side which helps to hold in body heat can be obtained at most sporting goods stores. It also can be used as a lean-to in emergencies.

TWINE OR FISHLINE. Twenty or thirty feet of twine or fishline and several safety pins can be useful for many types of emergencies or for repair to equipment or clothing.

CLOTHING AND RAINWEAR. Always prepare for the possibility of sudden weather change due to rain, snow and wind storms. At a minimum, a lightweight, water repellant windbreaker is recommended. A pair of gloves—wool or pile recommended—and head protection provide additional barriers to heat loss when cold. Dressing in layers of clothing suitable to weather conditions allows you to adjust for temperature changes more easily. Wool will warm even when wet. Select shoes or boots, tents, sleeping bags and other equipment to match your activity and the worst-case conditions you might expect to encounter.

~RESCUE TEAMS — For your security, be advised that many mountain counties have a search and rescue team with a four-wheel drive vehicle. In an emergency, pile up enough wood and light a fire for warmth or for a signal to a plane or helicopter passing overhead. While waiting for help, get under an overhanging rock if possible and if cold use whatever cover is available—even mounds of dry leaves. If possible, send a companion for help. Contact the Sheriff's office or any Forest Service personnel.

~GIARDIA — Years ago, one could safely drink from any stream in the mountains. In the last several decades, however, a protozoan parasite, *giardia*, has spoiled the purity of natural streams worldwide. Not even Alaska, Guam and Colorado are safe. Unfortunately, the disease is difficult and expensive to cure. The parasite, spread by human feces, has been picked up by many mammals, such as beaver and deer, which in turn contaminate surface water. Only spring water is safe. The cysts of *giardia* are destroyed by prolonged boiling of water; by the application of iodine; or by the use of small, light, filtering devices available at outdoor supply stores. Another solution is simply to carry water in unbreakable containers.

~HYPOTHERMIA — Perhaps the greatest real danger in the outdoors is the threat of death by hypothermia, or a prolonged lowering of body temperature. To prevent hypothermia, stay dry. Carry raingear. Wet clothes wick away body heat and lead to rapid chilling. Swimming a few minutes too long in an icy mountain stream may produce hypothermia, even in summer—especially if combined with smoking cigarettes or drinking alcohol. A hiking companion who talks or walks slowly for no apparent reason may be subject to hypothermia. To produce body heat, keep exercising, build a fire, drink hot liquids and use a sleeping bag.

~ROCKS AND MOSS — Probably more people are injured, or even killed, by slipping on wet or moss-covered rocks than by all of the snakes, bears, hornets and other causes combined. Wet rocks, especially if covered with a thin moss, can be the equivalent of stepping on ice. Use a walking stick, wear shoes with gripping soles and exercise extreme care. Stay away from the heads of waterfalls; several people have slipped on them and fallen to their deaths.

~INSECTS — Few places in the world are as free of insects and pests as is north Georgia. Mosquitos and deer flies are nearly absent. In early spring, blackflies may be a temporary annoyance. The most common is the tiny "no-see-um" called "sandfly" on the coast. It can be troublesome in still and moist weather. Carry repellent. Check for and remove any ticks promptly.

~CLOUDBURSTS — Violent rainstorms called "cloudbursts" by mountaineers are frightening. Take shelter under cliffs if possible. Do not stand under isolated or very tall trees, or on ridges or mountain tops, where lightening frequently strikes. Most sudden downpours are over quickly and pose no danger other than getting soaked. If, however, you anticipate fording a mountain river such as the Chattooga or Cooper Creek, keep your eye on water levels. Streams can rise suddenly and cut you off, or force you to swim across and be subject to possible hypothermia.

~BEARS — Bears will always run, unless you stumble closely on a mother with cubs. Don't leave enticing foods around. If ever confronted, stop and slowly back away. Make lots of noise. You will be lucky to glimpse a bear in ten years of hiking in the Georgia mountains.

~HUNTING SEASONS — A far greater danger than bears is to be mistaken for a deer or turkey during the short but intensive hunting seasons. Check to see if there is a hunt in progress in a wildlife refuge where you anticipate hiking. As with bears, whistle and shout at intervals. Wearing bright colors is advisable.

~YELLOW JACKETS — Remarkably, yellow jackets—a ground-dwelling wasp—are probably the only injurious creatures that one will encounter in the mountains. If you hear or see more than one yellow and black "bee" buzzing around your feet, you have probably stumbled upon a nest. Move rapidly away. Usually fifty feet is adequate if you move fast. Do not fear yellow jackets or other species—just be ready to move quickly. Remember that a stung horse can make a sudden leap. Carefully examine the entire area around a tree where any animal is tied. It may be difficult to release an animal in panic state. When bushwhacking away from trails, shorts are not advisable for many reasons, including green-briars.

~**POISONOUS SNAKES** — One can easily hike 10 years in the mountains without seeing a poisonous snake. It is a good idea to talk to local "old timers" if you are exploring trail-less terrain. Our timber rattlesnake is one of the most inoffensive and calm of the world's venomous reptiles. Many do not rattle but lie quietly "hop-ing" they will be passed by unseen (and unmolested). Be cautious and respectful, but not afraid. Simply take care where hands and feet are placed, especially in rocky places and near logs. A walking stick is helpful for getting through thick overgrowth. Never walk at night without a flashlight. In fall and spring, snakes crawl to and from and concentrate around communal dens where they hibernate during the cold months. By the first serious frost, most snakes are underground. Like all animals, an occasional snake will be irritable — possibly due to illiness, being overheated or due to shedding its skin, which obscures its vision — and rattle or appear aggressive.

Timber rattlers come in both yellow and black colorations. Cop-perheads, the only other potentially dangerous snakes in the moun-tains, are more difficult to see in the leaves. Fortunately, they are more rarely encountered in the higher mountains.

If far from transportation, a small kit with suction syringe will lend peace of mind. If done immediately after a snakebite, sucking and spitting out the venom is effective. In serious cases, consider staying put and calling for evacuation by helicopter or by local search and rescue teams. A high-tech solution is a jolt to the bite from a stun gun; but get acquainted with this technique before attempting it. Electricity appears to destroy most venoms.

In summary, plan ahead so that you are well-equipped and pre-pared to deal with the expected, as well as the unexpected. This will not only enhance your enjoyment of the outing by lending peace of mind; it may also save lives.

H. Southeastern Wilderness Areas

Chestnut oak
Quercus prinus

With the largest acorn of our mountain oaks, the chestnut oak is found mostly on rocky ridges with shallow soils. It dominates many lower ridges, while northern red oaks occupy the higher, wetter ridges.

In 1964, Congress passed the Wilderness Act, creating the National Wilderness Preservation System. Wilderness areas designated by Congress either in the original Wilderness Act or in subsequent legislation are areas of federally-owned land preserved in their natural state. People are encouraged to use and enjoy these natural areas, but they are to come as visitors and not as permanent fixtures. Thus, in areas designated as wilderness, certain activities such as road building, timber harvesting, motor vehicle use, mining and dam construction are prohibited. Permitted uses include hiking, fishing, camping, nature study, canoeing, horseback riding and, in Forest Service wilderness areas, hunting. Wilderness not only provides backcountry recreation opportunities but also protects high quality watersheds and fisheries, old-growth wildlife habitat and visual beauty.

The only two areas from the Southeast included in the Wilderness Act of 1964 were Shining Rock and Linville Gorge in western North Carolina's Pisgah National Forest. For a decade, these two areas were the Southeast's only national forest wildernesses. Other areas for possible wilderness designation were not considered by the Forest Service sufficiently primeval. In response to broad grassroots support, Congress passed the Eastern Wilderness Act of 1975, which established the principle that areas that regain their natural, primitive character can and do qualify as wilderness. This Act also established the Cohutta and Ellicott Rock Wildernesses in Georgia.

During a process called "RARE II" in the late 1970's, the Forest Service identified over 200,000 acres of additional eligible wilderness in the Chattahoochee National Forest. In 1984 and 1986, Congress established the Rich Mountain, Raven Cliffs, Tray Mountain, Southern Nantahala and Brasstown Wildernesses and expanded the Cohutta and Ellicott Rock Wildernesses.

Many other outstanding areas need wilderness designation, especially since the Forest Service projects that demand for wilderness recreation will soon outstrip available opportunities in the southern Appalachians. Over the past decade in Georgia, conservationists have identified for wilderness designation other areas such as Blood Mountain, Chattahoochee headwaters, Mountaintown, Overflow Creek and additions to Tray Mountain. As noted in the following appendix on Forest Planning, however, forest management plans call for opening up most of these potential wildernesses to planned development that may degrade their wildland values.

North Georgia has seven wilderness areas totalling 95,647 acres. One, the Cohutta, overlaps into Tennessee; its "sister" wilderness, Big Frog, has 83 acres in Georgia. The Southern Nantahala Wilderness is almost equally divided between North Carolina and Georgia.

APPENDICES

Check with the local Ranger for regulations regarding the use of horses, normally permitted except on the Appalachian Trail. Problems of management such as signs, parking, trail maintenance and emergency evacuation procedures are being addressed by local Forest Service Rangers for each wilderness area.

WILDERNESS AREA	TOTAL ACRES	ACRES IN GEORGIA
Cohutta	37,042	35,247
Rich Mountain	9,649	9,649
Big Frog	8,055	83
Raven Cliffs	9,649	9,649
Tray Mountain	9,702	9,702
Brasstown	11,405	11,405
Southern Nantahala	23,339	10,900
Ellicott Rock	9,012	9,012
		95,647

I. Forest Planning

In the National Forest Management Act of 1976, Congress specifically directed the U.S. Forest Service to reduce clearcutting, provide for biological diversity, protect streams and water quality, limit uneconomic timbering and provide for public input. Responding to these mandates, the Forest Service in 1985 issued a final management plan for the Chattahoochee-Oconee National Forests. Dissatisfied with the management plan, a coalition consisting of The Georgia Conservancy, The Wilderness Society, the Sierra Club, Friends of the Mountains, Georgia Botanical Society, Atlanta Audubon Society and the Georgia Council of Trout Unlimited filed an appeal, or administrative lawsuit, of the plan with the Chief of the Forest Service in Washington, D.C. In return for changes in the plan regarding preservation of special areas and the use of herbicides, the conservation groups withdrew their appeal. They also set up a process for continued review of Forest Service projects by a new citizen group called ForestWatch.*

The Chattahoochee-Oconee management plan provides for 10 to 15 years of specific management direction and in fact will affect the future of the forests for decades to come. It sets high goals for increasing timber harvest over the levels sold prior to the plan and, as a result, opens almost eighty percent of the forest to logging. Conservationists are greatly concerned that this will threaten popular recreation areas, sensitive ecological sites and potential wilderness.

To accomplish the plan's goals, the Forest Service zones the entire forest into different management areas (M.A.) with varying emphasis on timber harvest, recreation, wildlife and visual beauty. Most of the forest is put into category M.A. 16, which allows full timbering, including clearcuts up to forty acres in size, and construction of permanent logging roads.

M.A. 15, another common category, offers opportunities for semi-primitive, non-motorized recreation but allows road construction and some clearcutting.

Some 10 tracts of rugged high elevation terrain either adjacent to wilderness or in areas of potential wilderness are designated M.A. 4 areas, equivalent to backcountry status. These areas will have no logging nor road construction and provide additional semi-primitive recreation. Other management areas are provided for special categories such as the Appalachian Trail, streamside zones and scenic areas.

* For information on how to participate in ForestWatch, contact The Wilderness Society, listed in Appendix F.

American chestnut
Castanea dentata

Although it ranged into the upper Piedmont, this tree reached remarkable densities and large size in rich mountain coves and on slopes and rounded ridges with deep, black soil. Its untimely demise in the 1930's (of an Asiatic fungus) deprived many animals of a major autumn fattening food that enabled them to survive the winter. Our forests are still adapting to this loss, and tulip poplar now grows on many of the sites once occupied by chestnut.

APPENDICES

In recent years, national forest management of the Chattahoochee Forest and elsewhere has become increasingly controversial, due to Forest Service practices of building logging roads into the few remaining remote areas, of selling timber at prices that fail to recover cost, and of failing to give needed attention to recreation and other non-timber multiple uses. Senator Wyche Fowler (D-GA), Chairman of the Agriculture Committee's Forestry Subcommittee, has conducted hearings and taken Congressional action in an attempt to reduce Forest Service road construction and shift emphasis to values other than timber production.

J. Glossary of Plants

Umbrella leaf
Diphylleia cymosa

This plant bears some of the largest leaves of any mountain plant. Resembling a giant mayapple, it grows only in very moist locations along tiny streams and seeps at higher elevations, rarely below 3,000 feet, in north-facing coves. As with many other native plants and animals, its closest relatives are in temperate eastern Asia.

Alabama snow-wreath	*Neviusia alabamensis*
Alum root	*Heuchera sp.*
Arbutus, trailing	*Epigaea repens*
Ash, blue	*Fraxinus quadrangulata*
Ash, mountain	*Sorbus americana*
Azalea, flame	*Rhododendron calendulaceum*
Azalea, pinxterflower	*Rhododendron nudiflorum*
Basswood	*Tilia heterophylla*
Beech	*Fagus grandifolia*
Bent Trillium	*Trillium flexipes*
Biltmore Sedge	*Carex biltmoreana*
Birch, black	*Betula lenta*
Birch, sweet	*Betula lenta*
Birch, yellow	*Betula lutea*
Black locust	*Robinia pseudo-acacia*
Black walnut	*Juglans nigra*
Bloodroot	*Sanguinaria canadensis*
Blue cohosh	*Caulophyllum thalictroides*
Blue Ridge St. John's wort	*Hypericum buckleyi*
Bluebell, Virginia	*Mertensia virginica*
Blueberries, hi-bush and low-bush	*Vaccinium sp.*
Bluestem grass	*Andropogon sp.*
Bluets	*Houstonia sp.*
Buckberry	*Gaylussacia ursinus*
Buckeye	*Aesculus octandra*
Buttercups, mountain	*Ranunculus sp.*
Camellia, mountain	*Stewartia ovata*
Carolina bells	*Halesia carolina*
Cedar, red	*Juniperus virginiana*
Cherry, black	*Prunus serotina*
Chestnut, American	*Castanea dentata*
Chinquapin	*Castanea pumila*
Chokeberry	*Sorbus melanocarpa*
Chokecherry	*Prunus virginiana*
Cinquefoil, three-leaved	*Potentilla tridentata*
Columbo	*Swertia caroliniensis*
Cotton-grass	*Eriophorum virginicum*
Cucumber tree	*Magnolia acuminata*
Deerberry	*Vaccinium stamineum*
Dog-hobble	*Leucothoe axillaris*
Dogwood	*Cornus florida*
Dogwood, alternate-leaf	*Cornus alternifolia*
Dropseed, prairie	*Sporobolus sp.*
Dutchman's breeches	*Dicentra cucullaria*

Elderberry, red	*Sambucus pubens*
False lily of the valley	*Maianthemum canadense*
Fern, bracken	*Pteridium aquilinum*
Fern, Christmas	*Polystichum acrostichoides*
Fern, cinnamon	*Osmunda cinnamomea*
Fern, hayscented	*Dennstaedtia punctilobula*
Fern, log	*Dryopteris celsa*
Fern, marginal wood	*Dryopteris marginalis*
Fern, New York	*Thelypteris noveboracensis*
Fern, rock cap	*Polypodium virginianum*
Fern, walking	*Asplenium rhizophyllum*
Fir, Fraser's	*Abies fraseri*
Fleabane	*Erigeron philadelphicus*
Galax	*Galax aphylla*
Gay-wings	*Polygala paucifolia*
Gentian, fringed	*Gentiana crinita*
Ginger, wild	*Hexastylis sp.*
Ginseng	*Panax quinquefolius*
Goldenrod	*Solidago sp.*
Gooseberry	*Ribes sp.*
Grass of parnassus	*Parnassia asarifolia*
Harbinger of spring	*Erigenia bulbosa*
Hawthorn	*Crataegus sp.*
Hazelnut, beaked	*Corylus cornuta*
Hellebore	*Veratrum viride*
Hemlock, Carolina	*Tsuga caroliniana*
Hemlock, Eastern	*Tsuga canadensis*
Hickory	*Carya sp.*
Holly	*Ilex opaca*
Hop hornbeam	*Ostrya virginiana*
Horse sugar	*Symplocos tinctoria*
Horsetail	*Equisetum sp.*
Hyacinth, wild	*Camassia scilloides*
Hydrangea, wild	*Hydrangea arborescens*
Iris	*Iris cristata* and *Iris verna*
Jack-in-the-Pulpit	*Arisaematriphyllum*
Japanese knotweed	*Polygonum sp.*
Japanese paper plant	*Edgeworthia papyrifera*
Kudzu	*Pueraria lobata*
Lady slipper, pink	*Cypripedium acaule*
Lady slipper, yellow	*Cypripedium calceolus*
Laurel, bog	*Kalmia angustifolia*
Laurel, mountain	*Kalmia latifolia*
Lily, turk's cap	*Lillium superbum*
Lily of the valley	*Convallaria montana*

Locust	*Robinia sp.*
Lovegrass, weeping	*Eragrostis sp.*
Magnolia	*Magnolia sp.*
Magnolia, Fraser's	*Magnolia fraseri*
Maple	*Acer sp.*
Maple, mountain	*Acer spicatum*
Maple, red	*Acer rubrum*
Maple, striped	*Acer pensylvanicum*
Maple, sugar	*Acer saccharum*
Mayapple	*Podophyllum peltatum*
Minniebush	*Menziesia pilosa*
Mock-orange, hairy	*Philadelphus pubescens*
Monkshood	*Aconitum sp.*
Mountain laurel	*Kalmia latifolia*
Moss, primitive club	*Lycopodium sp.*
Moss, reindeer	*Cladonia sp.*
Moss, sphagnum	*Sphagnum sp.*
Moss, twisted hair spike	*Selaginella tortipila*
Nettle, hedge	*Stachys nuttallii*
Oak, chestnut	*Quercus prinus*
Oak, chinquapin	*Quercus muehlenbergii*
Oak, Northern red	*Quercus rubra*
Oak, scarlet	*Quercus coccinea*
Oak, white	*Quercus alba*
Oconee bells	*Shortia galacifolia*
Orchid, purple fringed	*Habenaria psycodes*
Orchis, showy	*Orchis spectabilis*
Oxalis	*Oxalis acetosella*
Pepperbush, mountain	*Clethra acuminata*
Pine, Eastern white	*Pinus strobus*
Pine, loblolly	*Pinus taeda*
Pine, pitch	*Pinus rigida*
Pine, short leaf	*Pinus echinata*
Pine, table mountain	*Pinus pungens*
Pine, Virginia	*Pinus virginiana*
Pine, white	*Pinus strobus*
Polygala, fringed	*Polygala paucifolia*
Poplar, tulip or yellow	*Liriodendron tulipifera*
Poppy, celandine	*Stylophorum diphyllum*
Pussy-toes	*Antennaria sp.*
Ramp (wild mountain onion)	*Allium tricoccum*
Raspberry, flowering	*Rubus odoratus*
Rhododendron, Carolina	*Rhododendron minus*
Rhododendron, catawba	*Rhododendron catawbiense*
Rhododendron, rosebay	*Rhododendron maximum*
Rosy twisted stalk	*Streptopus roseus*

Sand myrtle	*Leiophyllum buxifolium*
Saxifrage	*Saxifraga sp.*
Serviceberry	*Amelanchier arborea*
Silverbell	*Halesia carolina*
Smoketree	*Cotinus obovatus*
Solomon's plume	*Smilacina racemosa*
Solomon's seal	*Polygonatum biflorum*
Sourwood	*Oxydendron arboreum*
Spike moss, rock	*Selaginella rupestris*
Spike moss, twisted-hair	*Selaginella tortipila*
Spikenard	*Aralia racemosa*
Spurge, nodding	*Euphorbia mercurialina*
Squirrel corn	*Dicentra canadensis*
Strawberry bush	*Euonymus atropurpureus*
Strawberry, wild	*Potentilla sp.*
Sweetfern	*Comptonia peregrina*
Swamp pink	*Helonias bullata*
Toothwort	*Dentaria diphylla*
Trillium, faded	*Trillium sp.*
Trillium, Gleason's white	*Trillium sp.*
Trillium, lanceleaf	*Trillium lancifolium*
Trillium, large-flowered	*Trillium grandiflorum*
Trillium, painted	*Trillium undulatum*
Trillium, persistent	*Trillium persistens*
Trillium, Vasey's	*Trillium vaseyi*
Twinleaf	*Jeffersonia diphylla*
Umbrella leaf	*Diphylleia cymosa*
Viburnum	*Viburnum sp.*
Violet, bird-foot	*Viola pedata*
Violet, common blue	*Viola papilionacea*
Virginia creeper	*Parthenocissus quinquefolia*
Watercress	*Nasturtium officinale*
Waterleaf	*Hyrophyllum canadense*
Wild bergamot	*Monarda fistulosa*
Willow, dwarf	*Salix humilis*
Witch hazel	*Hamamelis virginiana*
Wolfsmilk	*Euphorbia purpurea*
Yellowwood	*Cladrastis lutea*
Yellowroot	*Xanthorhiza simplicissima*

NOTE: *sp.* = species, either not known specifically or several different ones represented.

INDEX

Aaron Mountain 75
Ada-Hi Falls 180
Adams Bald 107
Addis Gap 123
Alabama snow-wreath 16
Alex Mountain 188
Alum root 135, 138, 180
American toad 13
Amethyst 153
Amicalola Creek and Dawson Forest Wildlife Management Area 86
Amicalola Falls State Park 85, 86, 239
Andrews Cove Recreation Area 126
Anna Ruby Falls Scenic Area 125
Appalachian Trail, The 79, 86, 97, 99, 102, 103, 108, 109, 121, 122, 126, 131 136, 138, 139, 141, 143, 148-151, 153, 155, 176, 177, 235-241, 245
Arbutus, trailing vi, 172, 250
Archeological Site, Track Rock 132
Armuchee Creek 33
Ash, blue 17
Azalea, flame 139, 148, 149, 179, 181, 217
Bartram Trail, The 185, 188, 193, 201, 203, 249-251
Bat, big brown 8
Basswood 73, 180, 220
Beech 32, 33, 132, 135, 139, 148-151, 154-156
Benton MacKaye Trail, The 75, 82, 102, 238, 245-248
Berry College 39
Betty Creek Valley 175
Big brown bat 8
Biltmore sedge 135, 194
Birch
    black 56, 94, 169, 180, 217
    sweet 107, 250
    yellow 101, 124, 129, 135, 139, 154, 217, 220, 221
Bird-foot violet E-1
Black locust 22, 133
Black Rock Mountain State Park 179-181
Black walnut 103
Blood Mountain 91, 97-99, 102-104, 237-239
Blood Mountain Falls 104
Bloodroot 103, 179, 236
Blue cohosh 180, 249
Blue Ridge Mountain Marina Resort 61, 63
Blue Ridge St. John's wort 135, 177
Blue violet, common -iv
Blueberries 132, 149, 185, 222, 250
Bluestem grass 144
Bluets 81, 132, 217, 236
Bobcat 50

Bogs 139, 145, 147, 18
Bog turtle 139
Boulderfields 59, 75, 97, 101, 121, 123-125, 133, 139, 149, 155, 156, 180 185
Brasstown Bald Visitor Center 129
Bridal Veil Falls 220
Brow Park 19
Buck Creek 139, 143
Buck Creek Pine Barrens 144
Buckberry 222
Buckeye 17, 93, 95, 119, 124, 139
Buttercups, mountain 132
Camellia, mountain 153, 195, 201
Campgrounds 8, 23, 24, 55, 59, 77, 81-83, 93, 96, 97, 99, 102, 117, 126 145, 149, 150, 153, 155, 156, 161-163, 177, 193, 211-213, 219-223
Canadian hemlock viii
Canoeing
    Amicalola Creek 86
    Armuchee Creek 33
    Cartecay River 77
    Chattahoochee, Upper 115
    Chattooga River 200, 208
    Conasauga River 57
    Cooper Creek 95
    Coosawattee River 63
    Etowah River 79
    Lake Burton 163
    Lake Conasauga 55
    Lake Rabun 165
    Lake Seed 165
    Lake Tallulah 165
    Lake Tugalo 166
    Little River, East Fork 23
    Little River 22
    Lookout Creek 11
    Talking Rock Creek 64
    Tallulah Gorge 166
    Tallulah River 157, 163, 165
    Toccoa River 79
Cartecay River 77
Cave Spring 38
Caves
    Lookout Mountain 7
    Pigeon Mountain 15
Cedar, red 17, 124
Chattahoochee River Upper 113, 115
Cherokee 25, 35, 39-41, 55, 71, 85, 87, 97, 115, 118, 129, 143, 148, 158 166, 171, 177, 180, 225
                cave 177
Cherokee Scenic Highway 225
Cherry, black 73
Chestatee Overlook 103
Chestnut, American I-1
Chickadee, black-capped 64

Chieftain's Museum 35
Chipmunk B-1
Chinquapin 17, 136, 172, 217, 219
Chokecherry 139
Chunky Gal Mountain 139, 143
Cinquefoil, Three-leaved 148, 149, 15
Civilian Conservation Corps 32, 47, 55, 65, 72, 99, 131, 187, 235, 249
Cliffside Lake Recreation Area 223
Cloudland Canyon State Park 10-12
Coal Seam, Lookout Mountain 13
Cohutta Wilderness 49, 50, 57, 65, 245
Coleman River Road 157
Columbo 73
Common blue violet -iv
Conasauga River 57
Cooper Creek 91
Cooper Creek Recreation Area 93
Copper Basin 45, 71, 72
Copperhead, northern 2
Corundum 143, 144, 153, 154, 197, 200, 222, 229, 231
Corundum Hill 231
Cottontail, New England 233
Cove forests 102, 105, 143
Covenant College 9
Cowee Gem Region 229, 231
Coweeta Creek Valley 175
Coweeta Hydrologic Laboratory 176
Cucumber tree 93
Cullasaja Falls, Lower 221
Cullasaja River Gorge 220
Dahlonega Gold Museum 87
Deer, white-tail 104
Deerberry 222
DeSoto Falls, Alabama 19, 22, 23
DeSoto Falls, Blood Mountain 97, 99, 126
DeSoto Falls Campground 97
DeSoto Falls Scenic Recreation Area 97
DeSoto Scout Trail 19
Dockery Lake Recreation Area 103
Dodd's Creek 105
Dog-hobble 221
Dogwood 26, 31-33, 81, 85, 103, 172
Driving tours
    Aska Road to Newport Road, Rich Mountains 77
    Bald Creek/Pickens' Nose, Coweeta—Betty Creek 177
    Berry College 39
    Betty Creek Valley 175
    Bull Pen Road 220
    Chickamauga Military Park 26
    Copper Basin 71
    Coweeta Hydrologic Laboratory 176
    Cullasaja River Gorge 220
    Darnell Creek Road, Rabun Bald 187
    Earl's Ford Road, Rabun Bald 18
    Elijay to Blue Ridge—Boardtown Road 77

    Fanny Gap, Cooper Creek 95
    Helton Creek Falls 101
    Horse Cove Road 220
    Little River Canyon Parkway 21
    Lookout Mountain Parkway 5, 9, 23, 27
    McLemore Cove, Chickamauga Valley 25
    Mulky Gap, Cooper Creek 94
    Nantahala Basin 145
    Overflow Creek Road, Rabun Bald 187
    Patterson Gap Drive 176
    Reflection Riding and Nature Center 7
    Rich Mountains 77
    Richard Russell Scenic Highway 109
    Sandy Ford Road, Rabun Bald 187
    Sarah's Creek Road, Rabun Bald 185
    Tallulah River Basin 163
    The Loop, Cooper Creek 95
    Tukalugee Creek Road, Rabun Bald 185
    Upper Tallulah Basin 153
    Warwoman Road, Rabun Bald 185
Dropseed, prairie 144
Dry Falls 220
Duke's Creek Falls 105
Duke's Creek gold mining 115
Duncan Ridge 91
Duncan Ridge Trail 102, 245, 246
Dunite 129, 143, 144, 231
Dutchman's breeches 97, 101
Dwarf willow 129, 135
Eagle, golden
Earl's Ford 201, 203, 209
Echota, New 40
Escarpment Gorges 225-228
Etowah Mounds 42
Etowah River 79
Fern
    bracken 94
    Christmas 109
    cinnamon 139
    log 17
    marginal wood 135
    New York xvi, 222, 250
    rock cap 135
    walking 187, 189
Fir, Fraser's 154
Fleabane 103
Flint Knob Trail 188
Forest
    cove 102, 105, 143
    hemlock 180
    northern hardwood 59, 76, 91, 97, 101, 129, 132-134, 135, 139, 149 154, 156, 185, 220
    ridge 124, 143, 148, 149, 155, 177, 222
    slope 122, 135, 154, 179, 180, 198
    white pine xiii, 212

Index

Fort Mountain State Park 45, 65-67
Fossil sites 9, 29, 33-34
Fossils 34
Franklin Gem and Mineral Museum 229
Fraser's magnolia 169, 217, 221, 250, A-1
Freshwater drum 35
Fringed polygala 158
Galax 67, 81, 87, 180, 250
Garter snake 247
Gay-wings 172, 173
Gentian, fringed 144
Ginger, wild 67, 250
Glen Falls (Blue Valley) 222
Gold mining, Duke's Creek 115
Golden eagle 194
Goldenrod 179
Gooseberry 177
Gorges
    Amicalola Creek 87
    Bear Camp Creek 228
    Beech Creek 154
    Chattooga River 166, 191-208
    Chattooga River 191-209
    Cliff Creek 207
    Cloudland Canyon 11
    Coleman River 153, 157
    Conosauga River 57
    Coosawattee River 63
    Cullasaja River 220
    Escarpment Gorges 225-228
    Horsepasture River 226
    Kenner Creek 176
    Little River Canyon 20-23
    Ocoee River 60
    Panther Creek 171
    Reed Creek 195
    Rock Gorge 194, 195
    Rock Mountain 153, 157
    Shoal Branch 138
    Tallulah Gorge 157-162
    Thompson River 227
    Toxaway River, Escarpment Gorges 226
    Whitewater River 225
Grass of parnassus 144
Grassy Ridge Trail 176
Great Valley 1, 35, 45, 61, 63
Green salamander 16
Grosbeak, rose-breasted 51
Grouse, ruffed 86
Hall Creek 133, 137
Hambidge Center, The 175
Hang gliding, McCarty Bluff 9
Hawk, red-tail 55
Hawthorn 135

Hazelnut, beaked 135, 136
Helen 113, 115
Hellbender 53
Hellebore 71, 139
Helton Creek Falls Drive 101
Hemlock
    Canadian viii
    Carolina 158, 219, 223, 225
    eastern 56, 95, 221, 223
Hemlock/heath forests 18
Hickory 31, 33, 85, 93, 95, 103, 109, 122, 126, 135,
    172, 198, 236, D-1
Hidden Creek Recreation Area 33
High Shoals Scenic Area and Trail 125
Highlands Biological Station   219
Highlands Nature Center   219
Hightower Bald 133, 136
Hiking trails
    Ada-Hi Falls Trail, Black Rock Mountain 180
    Addis Gap, Tray Mountain 123
    Amicalola Falls State Park 85
    Amicalola Falls Trail 85
    Appalachian Trail 235-241
    Angel Falls Trail, Lake Rabun 169
    Arkaquah Trail, Brasstown Bald 131
    Bad Creek Trail, Ellicott Rock 212
    Bad Creek Trail, Highlands, NC 221
    Bartram Trail, Rabun Bald 189, 249-251
    Bear Hair Trail, Vogel State Park 101
    Beech Bottom Trail, Cohuttas 52
    Beech Creek/Chimney Rock Loop, Tallulah 154
    Beech Flats to Rattlesnake Knob, Hightower Bald 136
    Benton MacKaye Trail, 245-246
    Big Acorn Nature Trail, Carters Lake 63
    Big Creek, Big Frog 59
    Big Frog 59
    Big Rock Nature Trail, Fort Mountain 67
    Black Rock Mountain State Park 179-181
    Blue Ridge, Lake 76
    Blue Valley, Highlands, NC 222
    Bottoms Loop Trail, Unicoi State Park 117
    Braille Trail, Marshall Forest Nature Preserve 37
    Brasstown Bald 131
    Buck Creek access trail, White Oak Stamp 139
    Bull Sluice Trails, Chattooga River 203
    Buzzard's Rock Cliffs, Chattooga River 199
    Cable Tower Trail, Tallulah Gorge 160
    Camp Creek Trail, Chattooga River 207
    Chattooga River Trail 193, 211
    Cherokee Cave Trail, Coweeta—Betty Creek 177
    Chestnut Mountain, Big Frog 60
    Chickamauga Creek Trail, Armuchee Ridges 31
    Cliffside Lake, Highlands, NC 223
    Cloudland Backcountry Trails, Cloudland Canyon 12
    Cloudland Canyon 12

Hiking trails (continued)
    Cohutta Wilderness 50
    Conasauga River Trail, Cohuttas 51
    Coosa Backcountry Trail, Vogel State Park 101
    Coweeta Hydrologic Lab, Coweeta—Betty Creek 177
    Deep Gap, Nantahala 148
    DeSoto Falls Trail, Blood Mountain 97
    DeSoto State Park, Alabama 19
    Dockery Lake Trail, Blood Mountain 103
    Duke's Creek Falls Trail, Raven Cliffs 105
    Duncan Ridge Trail, Blood Mountain 102, 245, 246
    Eagle Mountain access, Hightower Bald 137
    East Cowpen Trail, Cohuttas 51
    East Fork Trail, Ellicott Rock 212
    Ellicott Rock Trail, Highlands, NC 221
    Falls Creek access trails, Chattooga River 203
    Fires Creek Basin, Buck Creek 144
    Fish Hatchery Trail, Ellicott Rock 212
    Fishermen's Trail, Chattooga River 198
    Foothills Trail, Ellicott Rock 212
    Foothills Trail, Escarpment Gorges 227
    Fort Mountain Trails 67
    Gahuti Trail, Fort Mountain 67
    Glen Falls Trail, Highlands, NC 222
    Gorge Park Trail, Tallulah Gorge 161
    Grassy Mountain Tower Trail, Lake Conasauga 56
    Grassy Ridge Trail, Coweeta—Betty Creek 176
    Hall Creek access, Hightower Bald 137
    Hemlock & white pine stands, Cooper Creek 93
    Hemp Top Trail, Cohuttas 52
    Hickory Creek Trail, Cohuttas 51
    Hickory Ridge Trail, Cohuttas 52
    Hidden Pond Trail, Carters Lake 61
    High Shoals Trail, Tray Mountain 125
    Holden Cove Trail, Upper Tallulah 157
    Horsepasture River Trail, Escarpment Gorges 225
    Horseshoe Bend Trail, Cohuttas 52
    Jack's Knob Trail, Brasstown Bald 131
    Jack's River Trail, Cohuttas 51
    James Edmonds Backcountry Trail, Black Rock 180
    John's Mountain Trail, Armuchee Ridges 32
    Keener Creek Trail, Coweeta—Betty Creek 176
    Keown Falls Loop Trail, Armuchee Ridges 31
    Kimsey Creek Trail, Nantahala 149, 150
    Lake Conasauga Trail, Lake Conasauga 56
    Lake Loop Trail, Fort Mountain 67
    Lakeshore Trail, Blood Mountain 103
    Licklog Ridge Trail, Big Frog 59
    Little River Canyon Trail, Alabama 21
    Logan Turnpike Trail, Raven Cliffs 108
    Loggy Branch access, Hightower Bald 133
    Long Creek Falls Trail, Chattooga River 205
    Lower Big Creek Falls Trail, Chattooga River 199
    Mill Shoals Trail, Cooper Creek 94
    Minnehaha Trail, Lake Rabun 169

Moccasin Creek Trail, Tallulah Basin 169
Nantahala Basin 150
Neel's Gap to Blood Mountain Trail 99
Non-Game Wildlife Trail, Tallulah Basin 169
North Rim Trail, Tallulah Gorge 161
Old Fort Trail, Fort Mountain 67
Old Skut Gap Trail, Hightower Bald 136
Old Tiffany Sapphire Mine, Highlands, NC 222
Overflow Falls Trail, Chattooga River 199
Panther Creek Nature Trail, Tallulah Basin 171
Panther Creek Trail, Cohuttas 51
Park Creek/Ridge Trails, Nantahala 150
Park's Gap to Dick's Creek Rd, Tray Mountain 123
Penitentiary Branch Trail, Cohuttas 52
Perry Gap, Buck Creek 143
Pickens' Nose Trail, Coweeta—Betty Creek 177
Pocket Trail, The, Armuchee Ridges 32
Pocket Trail, The, Pigeon Mountain 17
'Possum Creek Falls Trail, Chattooga River 205
Rabun Beach Hiking Trail, Lake Rabun 169
Raven Cliffs Falls Trail 105
Rice Camp Trail, Cohuttas 52
Rich Mountain Trail 75
Rocktown Trail, Pigeon Mountain 16
Rough Ridge Trail, Cohuttas 52
Satulah Mountain, Highlands, NC 217
Scataway Creek access, Hightower Bald 137
Shoal Branch Access, Hightower Bald 138
Shooting Creek Bald, Buck Creek 143
Sloan Bridge Trail, Escarpment Gorges 227
Sloan Bridge Trail, Ellicott Rock 212, 227
Smith Creek Trail, Unicoi State Park 126
Songbird Trail, Lake Conasauga 56
Sosebee Cove, Blood Mountain 101
South Rim Trail, Tallulah Gorge 160-162
Spring Cove, Tray Mountain 124
Standing Indian 149, 150
Sugar Cove Trail, Cohuttas 52
Swallow Creek, Tray Mountain 121, 122
Taylor Ridge Trail, Armuchee Ridges 29, 31, 34
Tearbritches Trail, Cohuttas 51
Tennessee Rock Trail 179
Three Day Walk, Nantahala 150
Three Forks, Rabun Bald 188
Three Forks Trail, Chattooga River 198
Thrift's Ferry, Chattooga River 203
Tumbling Waters Nature Trail, Carters Lake 63
Unicoi Lake Trail 117
Upper Big Creek, Chattooga River 199
Virgin old-growth hike, Cooper Creek 93
Vogel State Park 99, 101
Wagon Train Trail, Brasstown Bald 132
Waterfall Trail, Cloudland Canyon 12
West Ridge Loop, Amicalola Falls 86
West Rim Loop Trail, Cloudland Canyon 12

Hiking trails *(continued)*
    Whiteside Mountain, Highlands, NC 215
    Whitewater Falls Trail, Escarpment Gorges 225
    Whitly Gap Trail, Wildcat Mountain 107
    Wolf Ridge, Big Frog 59
    Woodall Shoals access, Chattooga River 203
    Woody Gap, Appalachian Trail 102, 237
    Yellow Mountain Trail, Cooper Creek 94
    Yellow Mountain Trail, Highlands, NC 222
Holden Cove Trail 157
Holly 81, 121, 169
Hop hornbeam 154
Horse sugar 172
Horse trails
    Nantahala Basin 151
    Big Indian Loop 149
Horsepasture River 225, 226, 228
Horsetail 148
Houston Valley ORV Area 31
Hyacinth, wild 16, 17
Hydrangea, wild 221
Hydrologic Laboratory, Coweeta 176
Iris
    wild 103
    dwarf 172
Indian Stomp Ground 154
Jack-in-the-pulpit 54
James Edmonds Backcountry Trail 180
James H. "Sloppy" Floyd State Park 34
Japanese knotweed 72
Japanese paper plant 207
Johnson's Crook 3, 13
Keener Creek Hiking Trail 176
Keown Falls Scenic Area 31
Kilby Creek 148
Kudzu 72
Lake Blue Ridge 75, 76, 79
Lake Burton 112, 157, 163, 165, 167
Lake Conasauga Recreation Area 55, 56
Lake Rabun 165, 166, 169
Lake Seed 165
Lake Tallulah 165
Lake Tugalo 166, 167, 191, 201, 209
Lake Winfield Scott 102
Lake Yonah 167, 171, 172
Lake Yonah Park 171
Laurel, bog 188
Laurel, mountain 13, 31, 32, 67, 79, 85, 93, 95, 105,
  107, 126, 129, 139 148, 150, 172, 177, 179, 180, 194,
  211, 217, 223, 236, 250
Lily of the valley 121, 241
Lily of the valley, false 217
Limesinks 27
Little River Canyon 20-23
Little River, Alabama 19

Little Scaly Mountain 215
Lock and Dam Park 37
Locust 22, 72, 103, 133
Logan Turnpike Trail 108
Loggy Branch 133
Long Bottom Ford 200, 201
Long Trails 231-251
Lookout Creek 5, 11
Lookout Mountain 2-13, 15, 17, 19, 21-23, 25-29, 31
Lookout Mountain Parkway 5, 9, 23, 27
Lost House Branch Falls 127
Lovegrass, weeping 72
Lower Cullasaja Falls 221
Magnolia 103, 169, 250
Magnolia, cucumber 88
Maple
    red 133, 136, 139, 172, 221, 249
    striped 61, 217
    sugar 131, 135, 249
Marshall Forest Nature Preserve 35
Mason Mountain 231
Mayapple 135, 236, C-1
McCarty Bluff 9
McLemore Cove 13, 15, 17, 18, 25, 26
Mincey Mine 231
Mining Operations 71, 229, 231
Minniebush 177
Mock-orange, hairy 16, 17
Monkshood 135, 143
Moss
    primitive club 109
    reindeer 132
    sphagnum 124
    twisted hair spike 219, 220
Mountain laurel 13, 31, 32, 67, 79, 85, 93, 95, 105, 107,
  126, 129, 139 148, 150, 172, 177, 179, 180, 194, 211,
  217, 223, 236, 250
Mulky Campground 93
Museums
    Chickamauga Battlefield Museum 26
    Chieftain's Museum 35
    Dahlonega Gold Museum 87
    Ducktown Basin Museum 72
    Etowah Mounds Museum 42
    Franklin Gem and Mineral Museum 229
    Ochs Museum, Point Park 27
    Tallulah Gorge Park Museum 162
    William Weinman Mineral Museum 41
Muskellunge 76
Nacoochee Valley 115
Nantahala Basin 145-151
Nature centers
    Highlands 219
    Reflection Riding And Chattanooga 5, 7
    Marshall Forest 35

Neel's Gap to Blood Mountain Hike 99
Nettle, hedge 16, 17
New Echota 40
Nikwasi Indian Mound 231
Noccalula Falls Park And Campground 23, 24
Nodding spurge 16, 17
Northern copperhead 2
Northern hardwood 76, 59, 91, 97, 129, 132-134, 135
  139, 149, 154, 156 185, 220
Northern water snake 209
Oak
  chestnut 37, 217, 221, H-1
  chinquapin 17, 172
  northern red 37, 94, 135, 139, 148, 149, 154, 177,
    217, 235
  scarlet 67, 124, 185
  white 67, 122-125, 129, 135, 139-144,
    148-151, 154, 215, 217, 219, 222
Oconee bells 227
Old Tiffany Sapphire Mine 222
Olivine 129, 143, 144, 231
Orchis, showy 228
Overlook, The (Tallulah Gorge) 162
Oxalis clover 135
Panther Creek Recreation Area and Hiking Trail 171
Patterson Gap 176
Pepperbush, mountain 217
Peregrine falcon 78
Pigeon Mountain 3, 14-17, 25, 32
Pilot black snake 163
Pine
  eastern white 56, 95
  loblolly 195
  pitch 124, 144, 169, 176, 219, 250
  short leaf 94
  table mountain 158, 208, 219
  Virginia 67, 86, 109
  white 91, 93-95, 103, 105, 109, 169, 172, 180, 195,
    197, 198, 211, 212 221, 223, 250
Pink lady slipper 85, 167
Pocket Recreation Area, The 32
Polygala, fringed 158
Poplar
  tulip 94, 97, 105, 176, 221
  yellow 32, 33, 93, 101, 147
Poppy, celandine 16, 17
Pygmy shrew 155
Rafting trips, commercial 209
Ramp (wild mountain onion) 121, 122, 139, 166-168
Rattlesnake, timber 29
Raven 105
Raven Cliffs 105-107, 109
Raven Cliffs Falls 105
Recreation areas
  Andrews Cove 126

Blue Ridge 76
Cliffside Lake 223
Cooper Creek 93
Deep Hole 83
DeSoto Falls 97
Dockery Lake 103
Dry Branch (Blue Ridge) 76
Green Creek (Blue Ridge) 76
Hidden Creek 33
Keown Falls 31
Lake Conasauga 55, 56
Lake Winfield Scott 96
Morganton Point 77
Panther Creek
Pocket, The 32
Rabun Beach 165, 169
Tallulah River 163
Warwoman Dell 187
Waters Creek 104
Red elderberry 127
Red squirrel 162
Red-tail hawk 55
Rhododendron
  Carolina 158, 161, 208
  Catawba 97, 122, 150
  rosebay 129, 139, 180, 217, 221, 250
Rich Mountain Trail 75
Rich Mountains 45, 47, 73, 75
Richard Russell Scenic Highway 109
Ridge forests 122, 124, 143, 148, 149, 154, 177, 222
Ringneck snake G-1
Rock spike moss 135
Rose-breasted grosbeak 51
Rosy twisted stalk 122, 124
Russell (GA 28) Bridge 191, 193, 194, 199, 201, 209
Sagponds 16, 27
Salamander
  green 16
  northern dusky 213
  northern red 82
  slimy 19
  two-lined 95
Sand myrtle 199, 219
Sandy Ford 201, 203
Satulah Mountain 217
Saxifrage 124, 132
Scaly Mountain, Little 215
Scenic areas
  Anna Ruby Falls 125
  Coleman River 153, 157
  Cooper Creek 91
  DeSoto Falls, Blood Mountain 97
  Ellicott Rock 211
  Glen Falls 222
  High Shoals Falls 112, 125

Scenic areas *(continued)*
    Keown Falls   31
    Sosebee Cove   101
Scenic drives - see Driving tours
Scenic overlooks
    Blue Bluff, Chunky Top Mountain   132
    Brow Park, Little River   9
    Chatsworth Overlook   67
    Chestatee Overlook   103
    Chunky Gal Mountain   143
    Cloudland Canyon   12
    Cool Springs Overlook   67
    John's Mountain   31
    Lookout Mountain   13
    McLemore Cove   13
    Overlook, The--Tallulah Gorge   162
    Reflection Riding and Chattanooga Nature Center   7
    Richard Russell Scenic Highway   109
    Tallulah Gorge   160
    Tray Mountain   119, 121
    White Oak Stamp   139
    Woody Gap   102
Seeps, spring   177
Serviceberry   172, 222
Shoal Branch   133, 138
Silver Run Falls   228
Silverbell   73, 76, 132, 172
Sloan Bridge Hiking Trail   227
Slope forests   122, 135, 154, 179, 180, 198
Smith Creek Trail   126
Smoketree   17
Snail, land   F-1
Solomon's plume   132
Solomon's seal   132
Sosebee Cove Scenic Area and Hiking Trail   101
Sourwood   32, 33, 103, 179, 249
Southern Nantahala Wilderness   133
Spoil Cane Creek Falls   127
Spring Cove   124
Spurge, nodding   16, 17
Squirrel corn   97, 101
St. John's wort   135, 177
Standing Indian   148, 149, 151
State Parks
    Amicalola Falls   85, 86, 239
    Black Rock Mountain   178-181
    Cloudland Canyon   10-12
    DeSoto (Alabama)   19, 22, 23
    Fort Mountain   45, 65-67
    James H. "Sloppy" Floyd   34
    Moccasin Creek   123, 167
    Table Rock (South Carolina)   251
    Unicoi   117, 125-127
    Vogel   99, 101
Strawberry bush   177

Strawberry, wild   217
Swallow Creek   121
Swamp pink   188
Sweetfern   176
TAG   7
Tallulah Basin   145, 149, 153-173
Tallulah Gorge   63, 157-164, 166, 167, 208
Tallulah Gorge Park   161-163
Tallulah River   145, 150, 153, 156-161, 164-167
Tanager, scarlet   44
Taylor Ridge   29, 31, 34
Tennessee Rock Trail   179
Terrora Park and Visitor Center   162
Timber rattlesnake   29
Titmouse, tufted   56
Toad, American   13
Toccoa River   79
Toothwort $_s$132
Toxaway Dam   89, 226
Track Rock Archeological Site   132
Tray Mountain   99, 109, 112, 120-124, 125, 169, 197, 236, 240
Treefrog, grey   118
Trillium
    bent   17
    Gleason's white   225
    lanceleaf   17
    large-flowered   43
    painted   151
    persistent   158
    Vasey's   3
Trout
    rainbow   83
    brook   145
    brown   191
Tufted titmouse   56
Turkey vulture   C-3
Turtle, bog   139
Twinleaf   16
Umbrella leaf   179, J-1
Unicoi State Park   117
Vanhook Glade Campground   223
Vann House   39, 40
Viburnum   135
Violet
    bird-foot   E-1
    common blue   -iv
Virginia creeper   221
Vogel State Park   99, 101
Vole, red-back   xi
Vulture, turkey   C-3
Walasi-Yi Interpretive Center   99
Warbler, chestnut-sided   229
Wasilik, John, Memorial Tree   147
Water snake, northern   209

Watercress 32
Waterfalls
   Ada-Hi Falls 180
   Amicalola Falls 85
   Ammons Creek Falls 188
   Anna Ruby Falls 125
   Armuchee Ridges area 29
   Becky Branch 188
   Big Creek Falls 197, 199
   Blood Mountain Falls 104
   Bridal Veil Falls 220
   Chattooga River, S.C. trail 195
   Cochran's Falls 85
   Cooper Creek 96
   Daniel's Creek 12
   DeSoto Falls, Alabama 19, 22, 23
   DeSoto Falls, Blood Mountain 97, 99
   Dick's Creek 203
   Drift Falls 225
   Dry Falls 220
   Duke's Creek Falls 105
   Estatoah Falls 188
   Etowah Falls 79
   Fall Branch Falls 82, 245
   Falls Creek 203
   Glen Falls 222
   Grace High Falls 21
   Hall Branch Falls, 138
   Helton Creek Falls 101
   High Falls on Upper Big Creek 199
   Holden Cove Trail 157
   Jack's River Falls 52
   Keown Falls 31
   Kerner Creek 176
   King's Creek Falls 213
   Little Rock Creek Falls 82
   Loggy Branch 133
   Long Creek Falls 81, 245
   Lost House Branch Falls 127
   Lower Big Creek Falls 199
   Lower Cullasaja Falls 221
   Mill Creek 123
   Noccalula Falls 23
   Overflow Creek 197

   Panther Creek 51
   Patterson Creek Falls 176
   Pocket Trail, The 17
   Rainbow Falls 225
   Raven Cliffs Falls 105
   Ruby Falls (cave) 8
   Sea Creek Falls 82
   Silver Run Falls 228
   Spoil Cane Creek Falls 127
   Spoon Auger Falls 213
   Stairstep Falls 225
   Sweet Sixteen Falls 158
   Turtleback Falls 225
   Waterfall Branch 16
   Whitewater Falls 225, 228
   Windy Falls 225
Waterleaf 101
Waters Creek Recreation Area 104
Weeping lovegrass 72
West End 115, 126
White Oak Stamp 122-124, 140-142, 143, 150, 157
White pine forests 212
Whiteside Mountain 215, 221
Whitewater Falls 225, 228
Whitley Gap 107
Wild bergamot 227
Wild boar 185
Wild strawberry 217
Wild turkey 250
Wildcat Mountain 107
Willow, dwarf 129, 135
Witch hazel 176, 217
Wolfsmilk 143
Wood frog 60
Wood rat 199
Woodland Indians 65
Woodpecker, pileated 236
Woody Gap 102, 237
Yellow lady slipper 85
Yellowroot 169
Yellowwood 101, 122, 133, 135, 147
Yonah Mountain 109, 118, 119
Zahnd Tract 3, 13

THE GEORGIA CONSERVANCY

The Georgia Conservancy is an independent, nonprofit organization of citizens, community groups and businesses dedicated to protecting Georgia's environment and encouraging responsible stewardship of vital natural resources. In pursuing this mission, The Georgia Conservancy works to ensure a balance between environmental concerns and the demands of social and economic progress.

Since its founding in 1967, The Georgia Conservancy has built a solid reputation for its reasoned, pragmatic approach to environmental problem-solving and its well-practiced ability to build consensus on difficult and complex issues. Through education and advocacy, The Georgia Conservancy plays a key role in developing public policy and enhancing environmental quality. Achievements include the designation of Cumberland Island as a National Seashore, protection of the Cohutta Mountains and Okefenokee Swamp as Wilderness Areas, creation of the Chattahoochee River National Recreation Area, initiation of state growth management policies, development of a national forest management plan, and protection of coastal marshes, sand dunes and freshwater wetlands.

As Georgia continues its unprecedented growth, the pressures on our environment increase. The Georgia Conservancy is committed to its leadership role as the state's primary resource for environmental information and advocacy. The *Guide to the North Georgia Mountains*, like its companion book, *A Guide to the Georgia Coast*, celebrates our magnificent natural heritage and is a testament to the compelling need to protect it for present and future generations.

Georgia Conservancy Membership Benefits

When you join The Georgia Conservancy, you join thousands of citizens who have decided to act positively for environmental quality. Basic membership benefits include:

* *Subscription to bimonthly newsletter, "Panorama"*
* *Action alerts about important environmental issues*
* *Georgia Conservancy decal*
* *Opportunities to identify, research and address environmental issues*
* *Weekend adventures and monthly naturalist day trips*
* *Annual environmental conference*
* *Chapter activities where available*
* *Representation with local and national environmental decision makers*
* *Personal satisfaction in making a positive difference for Georgia's natural environment.*

Special membership benefits are available to members at Sustaining, Donor and Cambium levels.

Make the Natural Decision.
Join The Georgia Conservancy.

Yes, I/we would like to join The Georgia Conservancy and safeguard Georgia's natural beauty. Enclosed is a tax deductible contribution of:

$1,000 Gold Cambium $40 Family/Dual
$ 500 Silver Cambium $40 Nonprofit organization
$ 250 Bronze Cambium $25 Individual
$ 100 Donor $15 Retiree
$ 70 Sustaining $15 Student

I/We would like to give a gift membership at the level marked above to the following. The acknowledgement should read:

From _____

Name _____

Address _____

City _____

Telephone (work) _____ (home) _____

Please make your check payable to The Georgia Conservancy. Mail to 781 Marietta St., Atlanta, GA 30318.